125

The City
in American Life

The City
in American Life

A HISTORICAL ANTHOLOGY

Edited by Paul Kramer
and
Frederick L. Holborn

G. P. PUTNAM'S SONS NEW YORK

Acknowledgments

Grateful acknowledgment is made to the following publishers and individuals for permission to reprint material which is in copyright or of which they are the authorized publishers:

The Bobbs-Merrill Company, Inc.: From *The Church and the City,* edited by Robert D. Cross, copyright © 1967, by The Bobbs-Merrill Company, Inc.; reprinted by permission of the publishers.

Columbia University Press: James Sterling Young, *The Washington Community, 1800–1828,* Prologue and Chapter Two, "The National Bantling."

Harper and Row, Publishers, Inc.: Gilbert Osofsky, *Harlem: The Making of a Ghetto,* Chapter 9, exclusive of all illustrations.

Harvard University Press: Robert M. Fogelson, *The Fragmented Metropolis, 1850–1930,* Chapter 7, "The Urban Landscape," Sam Bass Warner, Jr., *Streetcar Suburbs,* Chapter 7, "The Consequences" and Table 1 of Appendix B. Morton and Lucia White, *The Intellectual Versus the City,* Chapter XIV, "The Outlines of a Tradition."

The Journal of American History: Arthur M. Schlesinger, "The City in American History," *Mississippi Valley Historical Review,* XXVII (June, 1940).

Oxford University Press: Richard C. Wade, *Slavery in the Cities: The South 1820–1860,* copyright © 1964 by Oxford University Press, Inc.; reprinted by permission.

Pacific Northwest Quarterly: Waldo O. Kliewer, "The Foundations of Billings, Montana," July, 1940, *Pacific Northwest Quarterly.*

Princeton University Press: Constance McLaughlin Green, *The Secret City: A History of Race Relations in the Nation's Capitol,* Chapter VII, "The Withering of Hope, 1879–1901"; reprinted by permission of the Princeton University Press.

The Public Interest: James Q. Wilson, "The Urban Unease," Summer 1968.

The University of Pennsylvania Press: Samuel Bass Warner, Jr., *The Private City: Philadelphia in Three Periods of Its Growth,* copyright © 1968; reprinted with the permission of the Trustees of the University of Pennsylvania Press.

Contents

Preface

The object of this book is to trace, through a selective collection of individual essays, the story of the urbanization of the United States from the colonial period to the present. It is the hope of the editors that the reader can derive from these readings both a chronological sense of the evolution of the American city and an appreciation of the diverse forms cities have taken—from the early Eastern Seaboard cities to the river cities to the railroad cities to the metropolitan centers we have today.

The growth of our cities has not had its Bancroft, Parkman, or Prescott. The transformation of this country from a rural to an urban one lacked penetrating treatment until well after the turn of this century, when it became one of the themes in the magistral history of Edward Channing and, somewhat later, a main focus of the research of Arthur M. Schlesinger, Sr., and of his students. Indeed, other disciplines, especially sociology, probed our urban setting before it became an accepted field of historical research. Only recently have the cities been seen as the primary seat of creativity and social change.

Events have forced the historian to shift his preoccupations. Our urbanization is so sovereign a fact that the American historian can no longer be betrayed by either his preferences or his aversions. The degree of our urbanization compels a reexamination of its development. In no other way can we accept the Actonian view that "history made and history making are scientifically inseparable and separately unmeaning." If we know our urban past, we better understand the urban environment in which we live today.

It is not easy to convey in a brief space the full richness and complexity of either the past or the present. In making our selections we have tried to illustrate the nature and consistency of our urban tradition from colonial times to the present, while at the same time giving recognition to the various stages of our urban development. We have not tried to force a rigid interpretative pattern on our subject. Rather we have sought to find selections that can stand alone as pivots for discussion and controversy even while illuminating some episode or strand in our urban experience. We have tried to avoid a book which is but a medley of extracts and fleeting *aperçus* in favor of essays that permit the reader to encounter a fully developed thesis or a well-textured piece of research that moves beyond the normal grooves of textbook or survey. Where the choices have been generous, we have generally made a selection which also conveys the work of leading and influential writers and teachers—such as Schlesinger, Handlin, Wade, Mrs. Green, Moynihan and Glazer, and Warner.

Inevitably we have had to exclude much good material. We have also included some which a decade or two hence will have been superseded by the new research whose intensity is now evident in history, as in other disciplines. We have also had to exclude some important types of material which bear the American urban tradition, such as the literature of city planning and the perspectives of men such as Lewis Mumford. To embrace all approaches would have made this too diffuse a collection, and we have chosen instead to make this a book the core of which is history. We hope that the book will stir the reader to explore further the many unchartered areas of urban history and our urban condition today.

The City
in American Life

1

A Panoramic View: The City in American History

by ARTHUR M. SCHLESINGER

When the city encroaches sufficiently on the country and the country on the city, there will come an opportunity for the development of a type of civilization such as the world has never known.

"Only very recently . . . has the urban historian been accorded a limited degree of recognition in the establishments of American history," writes Charles Glaab:

Formerly, anyone who labeled himself as such [urban historian] was usually considered an antiquarian in disguise, who might have proper academic credentials but who debased the craft by searching for ancestors in a favorite city. Lately, he has been regarded more as an enemy agent from the camp of the social sciences who comes to history armed with secret weapons of precise definition and statistics, seeking to undermine the authority of a tried and true humanistic discipline. The urban historian himself has never been sure if either of these views is accurate, nor has he been sure of what role he ought to be playing in the community of scholarship.*

No figure in American historical scholarship did more during his life to bring coherence and relevance to the study and writing of American history than Arthur M. Schlesinger, Sr. Frederick Jackson Turner, on whose frontier thesis of American history Schlesinger cast doubt, once

---

* Charles N. Glaab, "The Historian and the American City," reprinted from *Wisconsin Magazine of History* in A. S. Eisenstadt, ed., *The Craft of American History*, Vol. II (New York, Harper Torchbook, 1966), p. 36.

13

said that his aim had been not to produce disciples but to propagate inquiry. This is precisely what Schlesinger accomplished. His own body of writing was not copious—several carefully wrought books and a moderate output of articles and lectures. But all he published had high specific gravity and influence. Moreover, the students he trained have carried forward what he began, as is seen in the selections by Professors Handlin and Wade in this volume.

No scholarly assignment more fully engaged Schlesinger's attention and energies than his co-editorship with Dixon Ryan Fox of the twelve-volume *A History of American Life* over a full decade. To this he contributed the most notable volume, *The Rise of the City,* published in 1933, in which he sought to make the urban movement the unifying theme of the events between 1878 and 1898. He made a further effort to provide a wider focus and a more generalized formulation in the article reprinted here.

As the Whites make clear in Chapter 11, the city has not been one of the intellectual ganglions in our history. Most thinkers and writers have viewed the city with hostility or at best mixed pride. What A. Whitney Griswold in his book *Farming and Democracy†* called the "moral ascendancy of agriculture" and themes of small-town pastoralism and frontier growth were dominant until Schlesinger and others opened new channels of research in the 1930's and 1940's.

"The City in American History" gives a view of what the historical craft had contributed to the study of the American city in 1940. Some of the material in this essay seems today somewhat shallow, and some of the complexities in defining both the role of the city and the mission of the urban historian are elided; it is nonetheless an admirable point of departure and remains a landmark in the study of the city.**

Professor Schlesinger, born in Xenia, Ohio, for a time a teacher of history at the University of Iowa, spent most of his career as a professor of American history at Harvard, where at the time of his retirement in 1955 he held the Francis Lee Higginson chair. Among his other important books are *The Colonial Merchants and the American Revolution, New Viewpoints in American History, The American as Reformer.* He had a lifelong interest in civil liberties and in promoting higher standards of

† New York, Harcourt, Brace and Co., 1948.
** More recent articles worthy of attention both for thematic and historiographical guidance include Charles Glaab, *supra;* W. Stull Holt, "Some Consequences of the Urban Movement in American History," *Pacific Historical Review,* LVII:919–29 (1952); and Eric E. Lampard, "American Historians and the Study of Urbanization," *American Historical Review,* LXVII:49–61 (1961). Broader surveys of special merit include Blake McKelway, *The Urbanization of America, 1860–1915* (New Brunswick, N.J., Rutgers University Press, 1963); and Charles N. Glaab and A. Theodore Brown, *A History of Urban America* (New York, Macmillan, 1967).

press freedom and performance. He was long associated with the program of Nieman Fellowships for journalists at Harvard. In 1942 he was elected president of the American Historical Association. He died in 1965.

This article is reprinted from Volume XXVII (1940) of the *Mississippi Valley Historical Review* with the permission of the Organization of American Historians.

"The true point of view in the history of this nation is not the Atlantic Coast," declared Frederick Jackson Turner in his famous paper of 1893, "it is the Great West." Professor Turner had formed his ideas in an atmosphere of profound agrarian unrest; and an announcement of the superintendent of the census in 1890 that the frontier line could no longer be traced impelled him to the conclusion that "the first period of American history" had closed.[1] His brilliant essay necessitated a fundamental reappraisal of the springs of national development. Today, however, it seems clear that in his zeal to correct older views he overlooked the antithetical form of social organization which, coeval with the earliest frontier, has played a significant and ever-enlarging part in American life. Turner himself wrote in a private letter in 1925, though with evident misgiving, "There seems likely to be an urban reinterpretation of our history."[2]

A reconsideration of American history from the urban point of view need not lead to the distortion which Professor Turner feared. It should direct attention to a much neglected influence and, by so doing, help to illumine the historian's central problem: the persistent interplay of town and country in the evolution of American civilization. Recent historical writings reveal an increasing interest of scholars in the role of the city. It seems desirable, if only in broad outline, to develop certain of the larger implications of these studies and to indicate some of the further possibilities of the general subject for scholarly investigation.

Though agriculture occupied the vast bulk of the colonists, many of them, through personal liking or for economic reasons, preferred town life.[3] Usually the first object upon reaching the Atlantic shore

[1] Frederick J. Turner, *The Frontier in American History* (New York, 1920), 3, 38.

[2] Letter to A. M. Schlesinger, dated Madison, Wisconsin, May 5, 1925.

[3] Recent works concerned with urban aspects of American colonial history include Carl Bridenbaugh, *Cities in the Wilderness, The First Century of Urban Life in America, 1625–1742* (New York, 1938); Ernest S. Griffith,

was to found an urban community which might serve as a means of companionship and mutual protection and as a base from which to colonize the neighboring country. In time these towns did duty as business centers, assembling the agricultural products of the adjacent regions for export and paying for them with imported wares. Without access to English-made goods—hardware, tools, firearms, house furnishings, medicines, books, and the like—life in the colonies might easily have approached that of the savages.

Small as these places seem by modern standards, they compared favorably in size and wealth with English provincial cities before the Industrial Revolution began to pile up their populations. As the larger American towns gained in corporate consciousness, they reached out for dependent territories and engaged in contests with one another for economic dominion. Much of colonial history might be rewritten in terms of these activities. Boston, the first to enter the race, possessed special trading advantages which enabled her for nearly a century to maintain a position of primacy, with New York, Philadelphia, and lesser centers hardly more than commercial satellites. These other towns, however, strove for their share of ocean-borne traffic and briskly cultivated their own local trading areas. Thus, the New Yorkers bitterly fought the proposal of the East New Jersey proprietors to erect a rival port at Perth Amboy, and for a time prevailed upon the provincial legislature to tax and otherwise shackle the commerce of Boston with eastern Long Island.[4] Incidentally, the intense application of New York, Philadelphia, and Charleston to the fur trade acted as a powerful stimulant to westward exploration.

As the eighteenth century progressed, Boston's rivals, helped by the occupation of their back-country districts, securely established their independent right to existence. New York completed her sway over western Connecticut and eastern New Jersey as well as over her own hinterland, while Philadelphia held in thrall western New Jersey, Pennsylvania, Delaware, and northern Maryland. It is evidence of the energy and enterprise of urban business that the chambers of com-

History of American City Government. The Colonial Period (New York, 1938); Virginia D. Harrington, *The New York Merchant on the Eve of the Revolution* (New York, 1935); Michael Kraus, *Intercolonial Aspects of American Culture on the Eve of the Revolution with Special Reference to the Northern Towns* (New York, 1928); and Leila Sellers, *Charleston Business on the Eve of the Revolution* (Chapel Hill, 1934).

[4] Curtis P. Nettels, *The Money Supply of the American Colonies Before 1720* (Madison, 1934), 108–109, 117–118.

merce of New York and Charleston, formed respectively in 1768 and 1774, antedated all others in English-speaking lands. Beneficial as were the relations of these towns to their dependent areas, urban dominance bred jealousies and resentments which were to reach critical intensity in the later history of the nation. The ascendant city of a given district became a symbol of deception and greed. "A Connecticut Farmer," venting his spleen against New York in the *New-London Gazette*, August 17, 1770, expressed the fervent hope that "the plumes of that domineering city may yet feather the nests of those whom they have long plucked."

From the outset the inhabitants of the towns were confronted with what would today be called "urban problems." The conditions of living in a circumscribed community forced attention to matters of common concern which could not be ignored even by a people individualistically inclined. Lighting, fire protection, the care of streets, crime prevention, sewage disposal, water, community health, marketing facilities—such needs as these evoked remedial efforts which, if primitive in modern eyes, matched those of English cities of comparable size. In some places public-spirited citizens for a time maintained night watches out of their own purses, or else the towns required persons to serve their turns on penalty of fines. Sooner or later, however, policing after dark was accepted as a regular charge on the taxpayers. The removal of garbage generally devolved on roving swine and goats, while drainage remained pretty much an unsolved problem, though in a few communities householders laid private sewers. The fire hazard early stirred the municipal authorities to impose regulations as to the construction of chimneys and the keeping of water buckets. Civic spirit in the eighteenth century supplemented official efforts with the formation of volunteer fire companies which, long after the colonial period, continued to be the principal agency of fire fighting. The pressure of urban needs also fostered American inventiveness, producing Franklin's lightning rod and the fireplace stove.

As these illustrations suggest, the people of the cities evolved a pattern of life increasingly unlike that of the countryside or the frontier. The necessary concern with the general welfare contravened the doctrine of individualism and nourished a sense of social responsibility. This training in collective action, constantly reenforced by the everyday contact of the citizens in less formal undertakings, assumed a commanding importance as the Revolution approached. Happily for the future independence of America, the new policy of the British government, begun in 1763–1764, struck deeply at the roots of urban prosperity. The business classes rallied promptly to the defense of their interests and, heedless of the possible political consequences, enlisted the support of the artisan and mechanic groups. Throughout the decade of controversy the seaport towns set the pace of colonial resistance, furnishing most of the high-pressure leaders, staging turbulent demonstrations at every crisis, and laboring to mobilize rural support for the cause. Even in agricultural commonwealths like Maryland and Virginia, the most effective steps of opposition were taken when the colonists assembled at the provincial capitals for legislative purposes. Boston's preeminence in such exertions may well have been due to the fact that, having recently fallen behind Philadelphia and New York as an emporium, she was resolved at any cost to stay the throttling hand of the British government. With the assembling of the first Continental Congress the direction of the patriot movement shifted to Philadelphia, where presently the first capital of the new republic was established.

It would be a misconception, however, to consider the colonial town merely as an expression of political or economic energies. The city, then as now, was a place where men found a variety of outlets for their special talents, an opportunity to cultivate the art as well as the business of living. Ports of entry for European settlers and goods, the larger places were also ports of entry for European ideas and standards of taste. In nearly every respect city life had a transforming effect on all who came within its orbit. A knowledge of the "three R's" was more widely diffused there than among rural inhabitants. The urban monopoly of the printing presses, newspapers, and bookstores insured both the preservation and the extension of knowledge at many levels. In such an atmosphere men took time for thought while stirred to mental activity. The resulting spirit of innovation expressed itself in intellectual as well as commercial undertakings. It was city folk who took the lead in founding schools and colleges. The protracted battle to establish inoculation as a preventive against smallpox was fought out in the towns. The first great victory for freedom of the press greeted the efforts of a Philadelphia lawyer defending a New York editor.

The man whom a recent biographer has called "the first civilized American" was a product of not one but many cities. Boston, Philadelphia, London, and Paris, each contributed to Franklin's intellectual growth and social understanding. Few elements of modern American culture but are indebted to his fostering care: printing, publishing, *belles-lettres*, journalism, education, the postal service, applied science. All these achievements rested, in final analysis, on that interest, encouragement, and financial support which a populous community alone could provide. How sedulously Franklin utilized these advantages appears in his autobiography, which reveals the care with which he educated his fellow Philadelphians to the need of such projects as a lending library, a hospital, and the formation of the American Philosophical Society. Yet Franklin with all his many-sidedness was less "civilized" than urban society as a whole. His range of interests did not include the theater, concerts, the improvement of architecture, or an active concern with art. In all these lines the pre-Revolutionary city, with the increase of wealth and leisure, showed a growing maturity.

It would be folly to deny that the city, both in its internal life and its external relations, played a role of critical importance in colonial society. Just as the biologist learns about complex organisms from studying the simpler forms, so the historical student may enrich his understanding of the later implications of urbanism by a better knowledge of colonial conditions. Though only Philadelphia contained as many as 30,000 people on the eve of Independence, and though less than one out of every twenty-five Americans lived in places of eight thousand or more, these towns revealed in embryo the shape of things to come.

If it be true that the percentage of townsfolk temporarily declined during the troubled years of the war and the Confederation,[5] this fact merely accentuates the pivotal influence of urban leadership in the movement for a stronger federal government. As Professor Beard has shown, the adoption of the Constitution signalized the triumph of the business and creditor classes, largely domiciled in the cities, over the debtors and small farmers of the back country. The initial Congress under the Constitution was promptly greeted with petitions for tariff protection from Philadelphia, New York, Boston, and Baltimore. This event foreshadowed a conflict of interest in the new government between city and country, which led directly to the formation of the first national parties. Hamilton's so-called financial plan was designed to implement the purposes of the urban capitalists. Jefferson, imbued with physiocratic notions and himself an agricul-

[5] *A Century of Population Growth* (Washington, 1909), 15.

turist, disapproved the trend of Federalist policy. "For the general operations of manufacture," he declared, "let our workshops remain in Europe." He perceived good even in the yellow-fever epidemic as a means of discouraging the growth of great cities.[6] The contrasting social ideas and economic motives reflected in this early alignment of parties engendered divergent views as to constitutional interpretation and produced recurrent clashes over specific measures. From that day to this the chief business of American politics has been to reconcile these interests in the service of the national welfare.

The spectacular size of the westward movement beginning shortly after the Revolution has obscured the fact that the city not only soon regained its relative position in the total population, but after 1820 grew very much faster than the rural regions. In 1790 one out of every thirty Americans lived in places of eight thousand or more; in 1820 one out of twenty; in 1840 one out of twelve; and in 1860 nearly one in every six.[7] The explanation of this apparent paradox is to be found in a number of factors, not the least of which is the success of the trans-Appalachian country in breeding its own urban communities. These raw western towns at first served as distributing points for commodities between the seaboard and the interior; but they soon became marts where the local manufacturer and the country dweller plied a trade to mutual advantage. Pittsburgh early began to branch out into manufactures; already by 1807 her atmosphere was described as choked with soot. Two years later Cincinnati possessed two cotton mills. Up and down the Ohio Valley many a rude settlement sought to emulate their example; the ambition to become a city dazzled nearly every cluster of log huts. The Indiana

[6] Paul L. Ford, ed., *The Works of Thomas Jefferson* (New York, 1904–1905), IV, 86, IX, 147.

[7] W. S. Thompson and P. K. Whelpton, *Population Trends in the United States* (New York, 1933), 20. Secondary works helpful for an understanding of urban history from 1783 to 1860 include Robert G. Albion, *The Rise of New York Port, 1815–1860* (New York, 1939); Lewis E. Atherton, *The Pioneer Merchant in Mid-America* (Columbia, 1939); Charles A. Beard, *An Economic Interpretation of the Constitution* (New York, 1913); Beverley W. Bond, Jr., *The Civilization of the Old Northwest, 1788–1812* (New York, 1934), chaps xii–xv; E. Douglas Branch, *The Sentimental Years, 1836–1860* (New York, 1934); R. A. East, *Business Enterprise in the American Revolutionary Era* (New York, 1938); James Ford *et al.*, *Slums and Housing with Special Reference to New York City* (Cambridge, Mass., 1936), I, 54–149; Bessie L. Pierce, *A History of Chicago* (New York, 1937–), I (to 1848); Sidney I. Pomerantz, *New York: An American City, 1783–1803* (New York, 1939); and Robert R. Russel, *Economic Aspects of Southern Sectionalism, 1840–1861* (Urbana, 1924).

pioneers, for instance, hopefully named their tiny hamlets Columbia City, Fountain City, Saline City, Oakland City, and Union City or, flaunting their ambitions more daringly, called them New Philadelphia, New Paris, and even New Pekin.[8]

Meanwhile, in the East, scores of new cities sprang into being, generally at the fall line of the rivers, where water power was available for utilizing the industrial secrets which sharp-witted Americans had recently filched from Britain. It has often been remarked of the early days of New England manufacturing that the farmers' daughters went to the mill towns while their brothers sought the fertile West. But it is clear that, in this section as well as in the Middle Atlantic states, many a farm lad also joined the urban procession; for, long before the great foreign immigration of the forties, the leading cities began to increase rapidly in size. To such places went young men gregarious in temperament, or of a mechanical bent, or ambitious of early movement from country to town and to the related subject of gain, or fond of book learning. Much study remains to be given this early movement from country to town and to the related subject of the migration from city to city. As Professor Albion has shown, new-comers from New England dominated the business activities of New York City from about 1820 to the Civil War. "It is a singular fact," wrote a New Yorker in 1863, "that a foreign-born boy, or one from the New England States, will succeed in this city, and become a partner in our largest firms, much oftener than a born New York boy." [9]

With the settlement of the trans-Appalachian hinterland, New York, Philadelphia, and Baltimore engaged in a mighty struggle with one

---

[8] Note also Burns City, Cambridge City, Clay City, Coal City, Lincoln City, Hartford City, Michigan City, Monroe City, Rome City, Shirley City, and Switz City, not to mention numerous place names ending in "town," "burg," "port," and "ville," and the designation of the capital of the state as Indianapolis. Few of these "cities" ever attained the minimum census definition of a city (2500 inhabitants). In J. K. Paulding's novel, *Westward Ho!* (New York, 1832), II, 179, Zeno Paddock, coming upon one of these aspiring midwestern settlements, found "on the very spot where the court-house stood on the map, a flock of wild turkeys gobbling like so many lawyers . . . but the founder of New Pekin swore it was destined to be the great mart of the West, to cut out St. Louis, Cincinnati, and New Orleans, and to realize the most glorious speculation that was ever conceived by the sagacity or believed by the faith of man."

[9] J. A. Scoville (Walter Barrett, *pseud.*), *The Old Merchants of New York City* (New York, 1863), I, 194, cited with other evidence in Albion, *Rise of New York Port*, 241–252.

another for the conquest of western trade. Content no longer with near-by tributary districts, they sought to carve out economic dependencies and spheres of influence in the more distant country. This conflict of urban imperialisms was most strikingly evidenced in the rivalry for transportation routes connecting with the West. It is unnecessary here to do more than recall the main weapons with which this prolonged contest was waged—first with turnpikes, then with canals and, finally, with the all-conquering steam railroad. Meanwhile middle-western cities, inspired by the eastern example, entered upon a somewhat similar struggle for power, each seeking to enlarge its orbit of trading operations at the expense of rivals and to benefit from the new ties with the seaboard. With a view to the commercial possibilities of the farther West, Chicago, St. Louis, Memphis, and New Orleans pushed competing plans for the construction of a Pacific railroad, a maneuvering for position which had important national political repercussions, notably in the Kansas-Nebraska Act.

This protracted strife for transportation facilities in the pre-Civil-War era determined the trend of future urban growth in all parts of the North. The Erie Canal, reenforced by the later railroad construction, established conclusively the preeminence of New York on the seaboard and in the nation. As the new lines of communication penetrated Middle America, they expedited settlement and energized cities into being; oftentimes the railroad ran through the main street.[10] The rise of populous centers increased the market for foodstuffs, accelerated the invention of labor-saving implements such as the steel plow and the reaper, and thus furthered commercial agriculture, which in turn contributed to city growth. Chicago, though still far behind New Orleans, St. Louis, and Cincinnati in size and wealth, had by 1860 already acquired the economic sinews which would make her New York's chief rival before the century closed.

If the urban advance be measured in terms of the size of cities abroad, it is instructive to recall that in 1800 London, the largest European city, possessed around 800,000 people, Paris somewhat more than a half million. Philadelphia, then America's chief center, had less than 70,000, New York only 60,000. Though both London and Paris trebled in size by 1860, New York with 800,000 inhabitants (not counting Brooklyn) ranked as the third city of the Occidental

---

[10] "With the exception of such cities as Chicago, St. Louis and Cincinnati, settlers can hardly be said to have chosen their own localities," wrote Anthony Trollope, *North America* (New York, 1862), 441.

world, while Philadelphia with nearly 565,000 surpassed Berlin. Six other American cities contained more than 100,000, four of them west of the Appalachians.

To master the new intricacies of metropolitan living called for something more than the easy-going ways of colonial times. Yet the municipal authorities, loath to increase taxes, usually shouldered new responsibilities only at the prod of grim necessity. It required the lethal yellow-fever epidemics of the 1790's to induce Philadelphia to set the example of installing a public water system. But with the speeding up of urban concentration after 1820 improvements came thick and fast. Over a hundred municipal water works were introduced before the Civil War, though in every case ignorance of the germ theory of disease necessarily centered attention on clear water rather than pure water. In 1822 Boston inaugurated gas lighting, and the following year she installed the first public-owned sewerage system. About the same time, regular stagecoach service was begun on the streets of New York, to be followed in the next decade by the introduction of horse-car lines. The primitive system of fire fighting by volunteer companies, however, continued everywhere until Boston in 1837 established a paid municipal department.

These civic advances were, of course, unevenly distributed. The smaller cities felt less keenly the pressure for change, while even the larger ones tended to subordinate community need to ulterior considerations. Thus, New York and Philadelphia, daunted by the political power of the volunteer companies, delayed the creation of fire departments until 1865 and 1870. Nor did any city try to combat the evil of slums which began to flourish along the seaboard in the 1840's as a result of the enlarging influx of immigrants. Recruiting their strength from the slum dwellers, the criminal classes, and the fire companies, political machines came into being, trafficking in franchises for the new municipal services and preparing the way for the notorious misrule of cities after the Civil War. The use of municipal offices for partisan purposes long antedated the introduction of the spoils system into state and national politics.

Despite such deterrent influences, it was from the cities that issued most of the humanitarian impulses of the pre-Civil-War period. The compactness of living dramatized all inequalities of condition, facilitated the banding together of the tender-hearted, and sometimes enlisted the support of wealthy philanthropists. The Tappan brothers of New York City spread their largess over a wide variety of reform causes. From the cities came the effective energies behind the establishment of free public education, the more humane treatment of the insane, penal reform, the beginning of free public libraries, and the woman rights' movement. Such places also exerted an important influence on the struggle for manhood suffrage, the effort to abolish war, and the antislavery cause.

In the cities, too, were felt the first stirrings of the labor movement. For the increasing numbers of urban wage-earners the so-called safety valve of the frontier failed to work. "The wilderness has receded," declared an eastern observer in 1840, "and already the new lands are beyond the reach of the mere laborer, and the employer has him at his mercy." [11] In self-protection the workingmen early in the 1830's organized trade unions, first along the seaboard and then in such inland cities as Buffalo, Pittsburgh, Cincinnati, and St. Louis; and for a time the principal centers combined in a national federation of labor. Though the depression beginning in 1837 shattered most of the unions, the hard times turned men's thoughts to other schemes for curing the "diversities of extreme poverty and extreme wealth" [12] which city life rendered so glaring. Some fared forth into experimental communities where, by grace of Fourier, they hoped to demonstrate the practicability of just and humane living conditions.[13] Others like George H. Evans and his group proposed to drain off the excess urban inhabitants by means of free homesteads. This thought figured prominently in the early discussions of the subject in Congress.[14] Evans' suggestion of providing free transportation for settlers failed to gain support, however, and soon the whole homestead question became enmeshed in the slavery controversy.

The determined purpose of the city reformers to employ the power of government to remove social inequalities heightened the contrast between urban and frontier conceptions of democracy; the lag of the rural sections in cultural achievements marked an even wider gap between the two ways of life. The enlargement and multiplication of urban centers not only insured a greater appreciation and patronage of arts and letters, but immensely broadened the field for the recruit-

[11] Orestes A. Brownson, "The Laboring Classes," *Boston Quarterly Review,* III, 1840, p. 372.

[12] E. H. Chapin, *Humanity in the City* (New York, 1854), 20.

[13] For a vigorous indictment of urban "incoherence and waste," see Albert Brisbane, *The Social Destiny of Man* (Philadelphia, 1840), chap. vii.

[14] Fred A. Shannon, "The Homestead Act and the Labor Surplus," *American Historical Review* (New York), XLI, 1935–1936, pp. 641–643.

ment of talent. To such communities were drawn many of the best minds of the countryside, for, as Dr. Holmes remarked, every considerable town had its "intellectual basin, or *suction-range*," as well as its economic gravitation field.[15] The people in the cities, too, were the first to feel the stimulating impact of new currents of European thought.

A varied and vital intellectual life resulted, of which any nation might be proud. Magazines proliferated until every taste and interest was regaled; newspapers became legion; publishing houses sprang up to supply the unprecedented demand for books. The story of this richly creative period in American letters can be told almost wholly in terms of Boston and its environs and of New York. Imaginative literature, however, also had its devotees in Cincinnati, St. Louis, and other inland cities. In the related arts the urban record showed less distinction; yet, apart from architecture, American civilization made fresh advances. Architecture suffered because the mushroom growth of cities required new construction at a rate that caused utility and pretentiousness to overshadow aesthetic considerations. Progress in music consisted chiefly in the broadening of musical appreciation, though in Stephen C. Foster Pittsburgh supplied a composer of genius. The theater became firmly established as an urban institution, and players like Charlotte Cushman and Edwin Booth won a repute in England as well as at home. Painters no longer felt the urgent need of seeking inspiration and support abroad. Their prestige was high, the products of their brush found a ready market, and, with the formation of the National Academy of Design in 1826, New York became the nation's art center.

Whatever the benefits accruing to the higher life, the waxing importance of the city occasioned increasing fear and resentment among country dwellers. This was especially true of the years from 1820 to 1860, which saw the urban population grow elevenfold. Country ministers denounced big cities, "cursed with immense accumulations of ignorance and error, vice and crime"; farm journals exhorted young men not to sacrifice their independence in order to "cringe and flatter, and . . . attend upon the wishes of every painted and padded form of humanity." [16] The printing press poured forth books, such as Clement

15 Oliver Wendell Holmes, *The Autocrat of the Breakfast Table* (Boston, 1892), *The Works of Oliver W. Holmes,* I, 127.

16 Quoted in Harold F. Wilson, *The Hill Country of Northern New England* (New York, 1936), 70–72.

Robbins' *Vampires of New York* and the anonymous paper-back series published by C. H. Brainard on the *Tricks and Traps* of New York, New Orleans, St. Louis, and Chicago. Writers of popular fiction, sensing the sales possibilities, eagerly embroidered upon the theme. George Lippard's melodramatic novel, *The Quaker City . . . . A Romance of Philadelphia Life, Mystery and Crime* (1844), ran through twenty-seven editions in five years.[17] Whether the net effect was to lessen or enhance urban fascination would be difficult to say. Byron, it will be recalled, wrote of "Saint Augustine in his fine Confessions, which make the reader envy his transgressions."

Politics also reflected the deepening rural distrust of city domination. The western opposition to the second United States Bank sprang largely from alarm at the control of credit facilities by the branch banks at Boston, New York, Philadelphia, and Baltimore. Likewise, the widening breach between South and North rested in considerable part on differences between rural and urban ways of life. The South, possessing few sizable towns and believing itself yoked to agriculture by slavery, became increasingly isolated from the currents of civilization flowing through the northern cities. It did not join in establishing free public schools; it feared and misunderstood the social experimentation rampant in the urban North; and, lacking the necessary nerve centers for creative cultural achievement, it fell far behind in arts, science, and letters. Moreover, southern economic life lay under constant tribute to northern urban enterprise. "It is a hopeless task," affirmed William Gregg, "to undertake to even approximate to the vast sums of wealth which have been transferred from the South to the North by allowing the Northern cities to import and export for us." [18] For twenty years before the war southern commercial conventions sought ways and means to escape this subordination, but their hope of building their own trading centers had no chance for success so long as lands and Negroes held a superior attraction for capital.

Historians might well give greater attention to the question of the extent to which southern secession was a revolt against the urban imperialism of Yankeedom. The grievance of the planting elements seems clear; and the bitter comment of the *Charleston Mercury*, May 20, 1858, that "Norfolk, Charleston, Savannah, Mobile, are only

---

[17] George A. Dunlap, *The City in the American Novel, 1789–1900* (Philadelphia, 1934), 67.

[18] William Gregg, "Southern Patronage to Southern Imports and Domestic Industry," *De Bow's Review* (New Orleans), XXIX, 1860, p. 82.

suburbs of New York," suggests the rankling resentment of the population centers.[19] As Professor Russel's researches show, the southern towns and cities gave their powerful support to the movement for separation. Even New Orleans, despite its large admixture of northerners and foreign born, chose twenty secessionists and only four unionists to the state convention. According to the Missourian, John B. Henderson, the business class of Charleston believed that, once outside the Union, "Charleston in the course of ten years will become a New York. The merchants of Savannah . . . the merchants of Mobile and the merchants of New Orleans have the same opinion." [20] It is significant that one of the early acts of the Confederate and state authorities was to outlaw the accumulated indebtedness of many millions owing to northern merchants, bankers, and manufacturers.[21]

The years following the Civil War ushered in the modern era of cities.[22] In the East and the Middle West urbanization proceeded apace. By 1890 New York-Brooklyn with nearly two and a half million people rivaled Paris, and Chicago and Philadelphia with more than a million each ranked as the sixth and seventh cities of the Occident. Hardly less significant was the rise of cities in the Far West and the New South. If most of them seemed small by the new yardsticks of urban magnitude, their rate of growth was spectacular, and even their size would earlier have gained them respect. Thus, Los Angeles jumped from less than 5000 in 1860 to more than 100,000 in 1900, and Denver from nothing at all to 134,000, while Memphis with 23,000 in the earlier year exceeded 100,000 in the later. In the nation as a whole, the proportion of people living in towns of eight thousand or more grew from one out of every six persons in 1860 to about one out of four in 1880 and by 1900 to one in every three. Moreover, of this increasing horde of urban dwellers, considerably more than half resided in places of twenty-five thousand or more.

The city had at last become a national rather than a sectional insti-

19 For the means employed by New York in "enslaving the cotton ports," see R. G. Albion, *Square-Riggers on Schedule* (Princeton, 1938), chap. iii.

20 Russel, *Economic Aspects of Southern Sectionalism*, 184, 239–243, 251, 284–286.

21 Contemporary estimates of the amount varied from forty to four hundred million dollars. John C. Schwab, *The Confederate States of America, 1861–1865* (New York, 1901), 110–123.

22 Allan Nevins, *The Emergence of Modern America, 1865–1878* (New York, 1927), and Arthur M. Schlesinger, *The Rise of the City, 1878–1898* (New York, 1933), Arthur M. Schlesinger and Dixon R. Fox, eds., *A History of American Life*, VIII, X, explore many aspects of the new role of the city.

tution. This development rested on the occupation of the Great West and the economic rehabilitation of the post-war South and, in all sections, on an application of business enterprise to the exploitation of natural resources such as the world had never known. To recount this material transformation at length would be to recite an oft-told tale. The urban dynamic, grotesquely magnified, was the governing force. Railroads, industrial combinations, financial power, legislative favors, formed the instruments of conquest. A complex of city imperialisms arose, each scheming for dominion, each battling with its rivals for advantage, and each perforce yielding eventual tribute to the lord of them all. "Every produce market, every share market," declared James Bryce, "vibrates in response to the Produce Exchange and Stock Exchange of New York." [23]

As urban centers grew in size and wealth, they cast an ever-stronger enchantment over the mind of the nation. Walt Whitman, returning after a short absence to New York and Brooklyn in September, 1870, hymned the "splendor, picturesqueness, and oceanic amplitude and rush of these great cities." Nature's triumph lay in her mountains, forests, and seas, but he observed, "The work of man too is equally great . . . in these ingenuities, streets, goods, houses, ships—these hurrying, feverish, electric crowds of men." [24] Little wonder that young men and women yielded to the potent allure. "We cannot all live in cities," wrote Horace Greeley in the *New York Tribune*, February 5, 1867, "yet nearly all seem determined to do so. Millions of acres . . . solicit cultivation . . .; yet hundreds of thousands reject this and rush into the cities."

Historians in their preoccupation with the dispersion of settlers over the wide expanse of the public domain have given little attention to this countermovement which even more profoundly altered the tissue of American life. In many parts the pull of the city depopulated the countryside. Over two-fifths of the townships of Pennsylvania, three-fifths of those of New England, and more than two-thirds of New York's suffered depletion between 1880 and 1890,[25] while the cities in these states grew by leaps and bounds. Similar rural losses

[23] James Bryce, *The American Commonwealth* (2 vols., London, 1888), II, 692.
[24] Walt Whitman, *Democratic Vistas* (London, 1888), 13–14. Dr. Holmes, weary of hearing sentimentalists quote Cowper's line, "God made the country, and man made the town," retorted, "God made the *cavern* and man made the *house!* What then? " Holmes, *Works*, V, 303.
[25] Josiah Strong, *The New Era* (New York, 1893), 167.

occurred in the Middle West, though there the attraction of free homesteads doubtless played a larger part. The rapid dwindling of the open frontier during this decade came with little shock to a people who for many years had shown an increasing preference for city life and an eagerness to avail themselves of its social amenities and expanding economic opportunities. From 1790 to 1890 the whole population of the republic had grown 16-fold, the urban population 139-fold. The historic announcement of the superintendent of the census in 1890 was significant less as marking the end of an old America than as a long-overdue admission of the arrival of a new one.

If, as Walt Whitman thought, the city was the most comprehensive of the works of man, its lusty growth created problems which tried to the utmost the resourcefulness of the inhabitants. In some measure European experience furnished a guide, but to an increasing extent, notably in rapid transit, lighting, and communication, America pointed the way for the Old World. The record is extraordinary. Hardly had New York undertaken the first elevated railway in 1868 than San Francisco contrived the cable car, and hardly had this new means of conveyance begun to spread than Richmond demonstrated the superiority of the electric trolley system, and presently Boston added the subway. The need for better lighting led to the invention of Brush's outdoor arc-light and of Edison's incandescent bulb for indoors. Still another application of electric power, the telephone, laced the urban population into the texture of a neighborhood. By means of the multicelled department store, cities simplified the problem of shopping; and by means of the steel-framed skyscraper, they economized ground space by building their business districts upward.

This civic advance, however, entailed a shocking degradation of political standards. Americans had gained their experience in self-government under rural conditions; they had yet to learn how to govern concentrated populations. Preyed upon by self-interested men eager to exploit the expanding public utilities, municipal politics became a saturnalia of corruption. As Francis Parkman wrote, "Where the carcass is, the vultures gather together." [26] The Tweed Ring in New York was the symptom of a disease that afflicted Chicago, St. Louis, Minneapolis, San Francisco, and other communities as well. In Andrew D. White's measured opinion of the conditions, "With very few exceptions, the city governments of the United States are

[26] Francis Parkman, "The Failure of Universal Suffrage," *North American Review* (Boston), CXXVII, 1878, p. 20.

the worst in Christendom—the most expensive, the most inefficient, and the most corrupt." [27]

Against the entrenched forces of greed and graft the reformers fought undismayed. Defeated at many points, they at least awakened the nation to the growing problems of social maladjustment and human misery which the teeming cities exhibited. Through a concerted attack on the slum evil they induced the New York legislature to adopt a series of laws for better housing, though the results proved disappointing. They replaced the indiscriminate alms-giving of early times with scientific principles of charity, and established social settlements and playgrounds. Organized religion, harking to the need, responded with slum missions, institutional churches, and the preaching of the social gospel. In the cities, too, the modern labor movement was born, wresting concessions from the employing class through sheer bulk of numbers, joining with the humanitarians in securing factory legislation, and organizing labor's strength on an intercity, nationwide basis. Occasional voices speaking with a foreign accent cried up the advantages of socialism or anarchism, while Edward Bellamy, appalled by the ever-greater contrast between wealth and want in urban life, produced an American version of communism in his fanciful description of Boston as it would be in the year 2000.

The increasing tension of city life was reflected in a variety of ways. Hordes of people habituated to a rural environment had suddenly to adapt themselves to the frantic pace of urban communities. To this circumstance is to be attributed the startling growth of nervousness or neurasthenia, designated by one contemporary as "the national disease of America." [28] A New York medical authority, writing in 1881, descanted learnedly on the effects on the human organism of the heightened speed of movement, the constant struggle for survival, the discordant sounds of the streets, and the ceaseless mental excitements and endless distractions.[29] It was from this swelling number of nerve-racked urban folk that Mary Baker Eddy secured most of her converts to the new religion of Christian Science. It was partly due to the same reason that city dwellers for the first time turned to the systematic development of organized sports. If flabby muscles kept most of them from direct participation, each year saw

[27] Andrew D. White, "The Government of American Cities," *Forum* (New York), X, 1890–1891, p. 357.

[28] Edward Wakefield, "Nervousness: the National Disease of America," *McClure's Magazine* (New York), II, 1894, pp. 302–307.

[29] G. M. Beard, *American Nervousness* (New York, 1881).

greater throngs seeking an anodyne for their cares while watching professional contests.

Urban communities, however, made their greatest contribution as a cultural force. The larger cities now rounded out their cultural equipment. The establishment of art museums, the multiplication of public libraries, the increase of publishing houses, the founding of art schools, conservatories of music, and new universities—these were signs of urban maturity which deeply affected all who came in contact with them. Statistical studies, concerned in considerable part with men who won note during these years, merely confirm what has already been evident as to the relation of urban birth to leadership in fields of achievement. Based on analyses of *Who's Who in America, American Men of Science,* and similar compilations, these investigations show conclusively the advantages resulting from concentrated wealth, superior educational and cultural opportunities, the friction of mind on mind, and the encouragement given to arts and letters. One student found that towns of eight thousand or more produced nearly twice as many persons of distinction as their proportionate share.[30] In particular fields, such as science, literature, art, and engineering, the urban differential was far greater. Such findings, however, understate the significance of the city, for they leave out of consideration the countless gifted individuals who, born in rural districts or in other nations, found in the urban world their Promised Land.

Statistical generalizations suggest the broad base of the city's cultural pyramid rather than its height. Only a full historical survey could disclose the emergence of towering figures in nearly every field of science, learning, arts, and letters during these years. Suffice it to say that the present generation gladly attests its indebtedness to the creative efforts of such men as Simon Newcomb in astronomy, J. Willard Gibbs in physical chemistry, Lester F. Ward in sociology, Charles W. Eliot in education, Augustus Saint-Gaudens in sculpture, H. H. Richardson in architecture, Edward A. MacDowell in music, and William Dean Howells in literature.

[30] F. A. Woods, "City Boys versus Country Boys," *Science* (Cambridge, Mass.), N. S., XXIX, 1909, pp. 577–579. S. S. Visher, *Geography of American Notables* (Bloomington, 1928), *Indiana University Studies,* XV, no. 79, an illuminating analysis, lists other important studies in the footnotes to pages 7–8. Frederick J. Turner's discussion of "The Children of the Pioneers" in *The Significance of Sections in American History* (New York, 1932), chap. x, fails to distinguish between midwestern notables of rural birth and those born in the towns and cities.

As the city forged ahead, imposing its economic fiat on the rest of the nation, developing ever more sharply its special way of life and opening new vistas of civilization, the rift between town and country reached threatening proportions. This antagonism has generally been conceived by historians in broad geographic terms. An accredited scholar, writing in the 1890's, saw the issue with clearer eyes. The "new sectionalism," he affirmed, is geographic only "in so far as the East is the section of the cities, while the South and West are the sections containing the bulk of the farmers." The decisive difference everywhere, he asserted, lay between urban and rural communities. "The people on the farms and in the villages in the East have shared no more in the advancing wealth of the past quarter of a century than the people on the farms and in the villages of the South and West." He estimated the average wealth of urban families at nearly three times that of rural families.[31]

If the typical country dweller had little conception of these larger economic factors, the passage of years brought him a growing sense of deprivation in his daily round of living. Contrasted with the rewards of urban life, he felt cheated of his due share of opportunities, comforts, and pleasures. Herbert Quick, looking back on his childhood days in Iowa, spoke particularly of the farm women, "pining for neighbors, for domestic help, for pretty clothes, for schools, music, art, and the things tasted when the magazines came in." [32] Though many of the younger generation escaped to the cities, this rendered life all the more irksome for those who, unable to leave or preferring the land, believed themselves saddled with unfair handicaps. Undoubtedly the farmer accepted too readily the urban estimate of his calling. That opinion had changed with the increasing dominance of cities. In the words of a contemporary, "The tiller of the soil, who in the days of our fathers was the embodiment of economic independence," is now the "stock figure . . . only of the humorist. . . . The 'sturdy yeoman' has become the 'hayseed.' " [33]

To this rural feeling of inferiority, this deepening sense of frustration, the historian must look for the basic explanation of the recur-

31 Charles B. Spahr, *An Essay on the Present Distribution of Wealth in the United States* (New York, 1896), 44–49. He drew the line between country and city at towns of 4000 inhabitants.

32 Herbert Quick, "Women on the Farms," *Good Housekeeping* (New York), LVII, 1913, pp. 426–436, esp. 427.

33 Anon., "The Political Menace of the Discontented," *Atlantic Monthly* (Boston), LXXVIII, 1896, p. 449.

rent agrarian uprisings. Tangible economic grievances, particularly in times of agricultural depression, merely stirred the smoldering embers into blaze. Such grievances assumed a variety of forms, but all of them represented extensions of urban imperialism at the cost of rural welfare. Farm leaders likened the big cities to giant cuttlefish running out their suckers into the blood stream of the countryside. It was left to the greatest of the agrarian champions, addressing the Democratic convention of 1896, to hurl the ultimate challenge to urban pretensions. "Burn down your cities and leave our farms," he cried, "and your cities will spring up again as if by magic; but destroy our farms and the grass will grow in the streets of every city in the country." [34] In the election that followed, the great cities of the North and West responded by casting decisive majorities against Bryan and free silver.[35]

Few persons in 1900 could have foreseen the trends of urban development which the twentieth century has brought forth. These attest the vast recuperative powers of American society. One of the most notable advances has been the concerted effort to bridle the predatory forces which, in James Bryce's phrase, had made municipal government "the one conspicuous failure of the United States." [36] To this end, four hundred and fifty cities have adopted the commission-manager plan. A radical departure from the clumsy nineteenth-century form which had been based on the analogy of state governments, the new system seeks to apply to complex urban communities the principles of expert management rendered familiar by business corporations. Along with this change have occurred the first systematic and sustained attempts to substitute forethought for drift in the development of cities. Dating from 1905, the movement has spread in every direction, yielding rich dividends for community welfare and civic sightliness. In its wider consequences city planning has

[34] William J. Bryan, *The First Battle, A Story of the Campaign of 1896* (Chicago, 1896), 205.

[35] *Nation* (New York), LXIII, November 12, 1896, p. 358.

[36] Bryce, *American Commonwealth*, I, 608. Recent works shedding light on the twentieth-century city include Harlan P. Douglass, *The Suburban Trend* (New York, 1925); Murray H. Leiffer, *City and Church in Transition* (Chicago, 1938); William F. Ogburn, *Social Characteristics of Cities* (Chicago, 1937); Roderick D. McKenzie, *The Metropolitan Community* (New York, 1933); Thompson and Whelpton, *Population Trends in the United States;* and Urbanism Committee of National Resources Committee, *Our Cities, Their Role in the National Economy* (Washington, 1937).

stimulated interest in county planning and state planning, and helps to account for the recent emphasis on regional and national planning.

The new municipal ideals, operating with varying intensity in different parts of the nation, made progress in face of the continued headlong rush into the cities both from the countryside and from foreign lands. With a third of the people living in places of eight thousand and upward in 1900, approximately half did so by 1930.[37] In the latter year nearly a third of the population resided in centers of one hundred thousand or more. During the three decades the country population gained less than eleven and a half million while the city population leaped more than thirty-five million. In reality, urban preponderance was bigger than these figures indicate, thanks to the rise of great metropolitan districts in all parts of the nation. These supercommunities had begun to form in the nineteenth century as swifter means of transportation and communication flung the population outward into the suburbs. But it was the coming of the automobile and the motor truck that raised them to their paramount position in the national economy. The census of 1930 disclosed ninety-six metropolitan districts, composed of one or more central cities with peripheral towns and rural communities, each district comprising a territory united by common social, industrial, and financial interests. The metropolitan areas of New York City lay in three states, embracing a region twice the size of Rhode Island and containing 272 incorporated communities. Greater Chicago in 1930 included 115 incorporated places, and greater San Francisco, 38.

These urban provinces, new to the American scene, possess greater economic, social, and cultural unity than most of the states. Yet, subdivided into separate municipalities and often lying in more than one state, they face grave difficulties in meeting the essential needs of the aggregate population. Some students of local government, despairing of any other solution, have proposed separate statehood for the largest metropolitan districts without regard to existing state lines.[38] It is clear that new and unanticipated strains are being placed

[37] By using the census definition of a city as a place of 2500 or more, 51.4 per cent of the people instead of 43.8 may be regarded as urban dwellers in 1920, and 56.2 per cent instead of 49.1 in 1930. The back-to-the-land movement, which affected perhaps a million persons during the years 1930–1933, seems to have been only a temporary effect of the Great Depression.

[38] Howard W. Odum and Harry E. Moore, *American Regionalism* (New York, 1938), 127.

on the federal system framed by the Fathers for a simple agricultural economy.

Of all the new trends in urban development, however, none has had such profound effects on American civilization as the altered relationship between country and city. Historians usually ascribe the subsidence of the agrarian revolt of the nineties to the discovery of fresh sources of gold supply. But perhaps a more fundamental explanation lies in the amelioration of many of the social and psychological drawbacks of farm life. The last decade of the century beheld an ampler provision of rural educational facilities, a rapid extension of the good-roads movement due to the bicycle craze, the penetration of the countryside by an increasing network of interurban trolley lines, the introduction of rural free delivery, and the spread of farm telephones following the expiration of the basic Bell patents. All these events helped to break down the ancient isolation and loneliness, and lent a new attraction to country existence.

Yet these mitigations seem small, compared with the marvels which the present century has wrought. The automobile has shortened all distances, while the radio and the movie have brought urbanizing influences to nearly every rural home. At the same time the tractor and other labor-saving devices have lightened the drudgery of the day's task.[39] Between 1900 and 1935 the mechanical power used in agriculture grew nearly eight-fold. Moreover, both the state and national governments have increasingly employed their powers to improve the economic and social status of the farmer. Some of the farthest reaching New Deal policies, such as the Tennessee Valley development, the triple-A effort, and the rural-electrification program, have had this as a major purpose. Though many inequalities remain, the country dweller has achieved a position in American society of which his Populist forebears could not have dreamed.

While the farmers have shared more richly in advantages once confined to townsfolk, urban life in turn has become increasingly ruralized. Parks, playgrounds, and tree-lined boulevards have multiplied far out of proportion to the growth of population, while enlarging numbers of city workers have used the new means of transit to go farther and farther into the rustic suburbs. Retail trade has also felt the centrifugal pull, and even factories have shown a tendency to move outward into villages where taxes are low, and food and rent

39 E. G. McKibben and R. A. Griffin, *Changes in Farm Power and Equipment: Tractors, Trucks, and Automobiles* (Philadelphia, 1938).

cheap. The extension of giant power will doubtless accelerate this diffusion and afford an increasing number of wage-earners a chance to work and live in semi-rural surroundings.

When the city encroaches sufficiently on the country and the country on the city, there will come an opportunity for the development of a type of civilization such as the world has never known. The old hard-and-fast distinction between urban and rural will tend to disappear, and a form of society take its place which, if America is to realize her promise, will blend the best features of the two traditional modes of life.

From humble beginnings in the early days of settlement the city has thus traced a varied course. In Europe the urban community emerged by imperceptible stages out of the town economy and culture of the Middle Ages; by comparison the American city leaped into being with breath-taking suddenness. At first servant to an agricultural economy, then a jealous contestant, then an oppressor, it now gives evidence of becoming a comrade and cooperator in a new national synthesis. Its economic function has been hardly more important than its cultural mission or its transforming influence on frontier conceptions of democracy. A force both for weal and woe, the city challenges the attention of scholars who will find in its ramifying history innumerable opportunities for rewarding research.

2

The Private City: The Environment of Private Opportunity

by SAMUEL BASS WARNER, Jr.

*Within the town three conditions confirmed its privatism—
its individualized structure of work, its general prosperity, and
its open society and economy.*

Two unique aspects of the American urban experience are its depth
and its early liberation from many of the medieval restrictions pertaining
to Western European urban life.

The 150 years of American colonial history ended with the emergence
of five colonial cities—Boston, Newport, New York, Philadelphia, and
Charleston—all highly important urban centers by the standards of those
times. Indeed, Philadelphia was then one of the largest cities in the
British Empire. This urban experience* was such, by 1776, as to be a vital
factor in the War of Independence and the formation of the Union.
Although the majority of the inhabitants of the Thirteen Colonies were
rural, it was this urban society, for example, that produced such Revolutionary War leaders as John Hancock, Alexander Hamilton, and Benjamin
Franklin.

Highly important to the subsequent urbanization of America was the
freedom of these early cities from the restrictions that pertained to
Western European life during the same period. Laissez-faire prevailed in
America before it became an espoused European philosophy. Guild
concepts never took firm root in America, and, according to Samuel Bass
Warner, Jr., "no invidious distinctions between land and trade favored
some occupations over others." Privatism flourished.

In 1968 Mr. Warner published *The Private City: Philadelphia in Three*

---

* Carl Bridenbaugh's *Cities in the Wilderness* and *Cities in Revolt* remain
the authoritative works on this period.

Periods of Its Growth. This scholarly and detailed study examined three periods of Philadelphia's history: 1770–80, when it was an eighteenth-century town; 1830–60, when it was a big city; and 1920–30, when it became an industrial metropolis. It is Mr. Warner's view that "Philadelphia's history has been repeated, with minor variations, again and again, across the nation, in Cincinnati, in St. Louis, in Chicago, in Detroit, in Los Angeles, in Houston." Certainly Mr. Warner's first chapter, reproduced here with the permission of the Trustees of the University of Pennsylvania Press, provides the reader with vital material on the fundamentals of early American urban life, as well as significant suggestions on how traditions and commonplace events have interacted in the past to build the present.

Mr. Warner, a former student of Professor Oscar Handlin at Harvard, has in a few years become one of the most prolific of our historians of the city. Once editor of the weekly Watertown (Mass.) *Sun*, he has been associated with the Joint Center for Urban Studies at Harvard and MIT and with the Washington University Institute for Urban and Regional Studies in St. Louis. He has also taught at Harvard and Washington University and is now a professor of history at the University of Michigan. In 1962 the publication of *Streetcar Suburbs*, a selection from which is reproduced as Chapter 13 in this anthology, established Mr. Warner as one of the nation's leading historians of the city.

American cities have grown with the general culture of the nation, not apart from it. Late eighteenth-century Philadelphia was no exception. Its citizens, formerly the first wave of a Holy Experiment, had been swept up in the tides of secularization and borne on by steady prosperity to a modern view of the world. Like the Puritans of Massachusetts and Connecticut, the Quakers of Pennsylvania had proved unable to sustain the primacy of religion against the solvents of cheap land and private opportunity. Quaker, Anglican, Presbyterian, Methodist, Pietist—each label had its social and political implications—but all congregations shared in the general American secular culture of privatism.[1]

Already by the time of the Revolution privatism had become the American tradition. Its essence lay in its concentration upon the indi-

[1] Quaker historians agree that the Holy Experiment died from materialism and secularization during the eighteenth century, Frederick B. Tolles, *Meeting House and Counting House* (Chapel Hill, 1948), 240–243; Sydney V. James, *A People Among Peoples* (Cambridge, 1963), 37–43, 211–215; and see the charges against his contemporaries in John Woolman, *The Journal of John Woolman* (F. B. Tolles, Introduction, New York, 1961).

vidual and the individual's search for wealth. Psychologically, privatism meant that the individual should seek happiness in personal independence and in the search for wealth; socially, privatism meant that the individual should see his first loyalty as his immediate family, and that a community should be a union of such money-making, accumulating families; politically, privatism meant that the community should keep the peace among individual money-makers, and, if possible, help to create an open and thriving setting where each citizen would have some substantial opportunity to prosper.

To describe the American tradition of privatism is not to summarize the entire American cultural tradition. Privatism lies at the core of many modern cultures; privatism alone will not distinguish the experience of America from that of other nations. The tradition of privatism is, however, the most important element of our culture for understanding the development of cities. The tradition of privatism has always meant that the cities of the United States depended for their wages, employment, and general prosperity upon the aggregate successes and failures of thousands of individual enterprises, not upon community action. It has also meant that the physical forms of American cities, their lots, houses, factories, and streets have been the outcome of a real estate market of profit-seeking builders, land speculators, and large investors. Finally, the tradition of privatism has meant that the local politics of American cities have depended for their actors, and for a good deal of their subject matter, on the changing focus of men's private economic activities.[2]

In the eighteenth century the tradition of privatism and the social and economic environment of colonial towns nicely complemented each other. Later as towns grew to big cities, and big cities grew to metropolises, the tradition became more and more ill-suited to the realities of urban life. The tradition assumed that there would be no major conflict between private interest, honestly and liberally viewed, and the public welfare. The modes of eighteenth-century town life encouraged this expectation that if each man would look to his own prosperity the entire town would prosper. And so it had.

Founded in 1682 under William Penn's liberal instructions, and settled first with Quaker artisans and a few Quaker merchants, the town had since prospered as the capital of a thriving colony.[3] By

---

[2] Howard Mumford Jones, *O Strange New World* (New York, 1964), 194–272, treats with this tradition as a blend of Christian and classical ideas.

[3] Tolles, *Meeting House,* 41.

1720 Philadelphia was said to have 10,000 inhabitants; by 1775 it had more than doubled to 23,700.[4] The townsite bordered the Delaware and Schuylkill rivers, both of which tapped rich forests and excellent farm lands. The line of north-south trade ran nearby, and Philadelphia also lay within reach of the Susquehanna and Potomac rivers openings to the west. Philadelphia, thus, soon excelled in most of the staples of colonial trade, exporting furs, lumber, staves, iron, wheat, and flour, and importing rum, sugar, wine, and English manufactures.

Conditions outside the colony encouraged a heavy immigration of new settlers. Because Pennsylvania had been founded late, by comparison to other Atlantic colonies, west-bound space abounded on ships sailing from Great Britain and the Low Countries. Quakers, of course, fleeing persecution in England came to the colony in large numbers, but by the early eighteenth century their group came to be rivaled by Scotch-Irish and German immigrants. The Act of Union joining Scotland to England opened up the entire British Empire to poor Scots, while Irish wars and famines, and rack-renting landlords drove their fellow Presbyterians from Ulster. On the continent west German peasants fled the destruction of Louis XIV's repeated wars. Finally, in America the Indian control of upstate New York deflected the flow of westward settlers south to Pennsylvania. The result of all these outside events was a boom in the colony and the town; Pennsylvania and Philadelphia had everything, settlers, natural resources, capital, religious freedom, and comparatively little government.[5]

Within the town three conditions confirmed its privatism—its individualized structure of work, its general prosperity, and its open society and economy. When eighteenth-century Philadelphians spoke of the individual and his search for wealth as the goal of government they were simply basing their political arguments on the commonplace fact of town life. The core element of the town economy was the one-man shop. Most Philadelphians labored alone, some with a helper or two. A storekeeper tended his shop by himself or with the aid of his

---

[4] Carl Bridenbaugh, *Cities in the Wilderness* (New York, 1938), 303; and see notes to Table I. Also, James T. Lemon "Urbanization of the Development of Eighteenth Century Southeastern Pennsylvania," *William and Mary Quarterly* XXIV (October, 1967), 502–542; Hannah B. Roach, "The Planning of Philadelphia," *Pennsylvania Magazine*, XCII (January and April, 1968).

[5] Marcus L. Hansen, *Atlantic Migration* (Cambridge, 1940), Ch. II.

family or a servant. Craftsmen often worked with an apprentice, or more rarely with another skilled man.[6]

More than at later times, this Philadelphia was a town of entrepreneurs. Artisans sewed shoes, made wagons, boiled soap, or laid bricks for customers who had already placed an order. Workers did not labor under the close price and time disciplines of manufacture for large-scale inventories or big speculative wholesale markets. Most Philadelphians were either independent contractors hiring out on a job-by-job basis, or they were artisan shopkeepers retailing the products of their work. Even the establishment of a large merchant more resembled a small store than a modern wholesale house. Such a merchant frequently had a partner and the two partners carried on the business with the aid of a full-time clerk and an apprentice or servant to help with errands.[7] When a cargo arrived at the pier the partners would hire some laborers to unload the goods and move them to the storehouse. Thus, a very large proportion of the town's men—artisans, shopkeepers, and merchants—shared the common experience of the individual entrepreneur.

In later years the work groups of factories, offices, stores, and construction crews would have enormous significance for the discipline, acculturation, and education of Philadelphia's residents. Such groups were almost entirely absent from the eighteenth-century town. Shipyard, ropewalk, and distillery workers labored in groups of five and even ten, but theirs were exceptionally large urban production units. In the colonial era the plantation, whether for agriculture or manufacture, was the characteristic place of large work gangs.[8] In 1775, associated with Philadelphia's general run of family enterprises were only about 900 indentured servants, 600 slaves, and perhaps 200 hired servants who lived with their employers.[9] These helpers shared the discipline of family life and work; they did not live by the modes of

[6] Comments suggesting an individualized or family work structure, Carl Bridenbaugh, *The Colonial Craftsman* (New York, 1950), 126–129, 136–139, 141–143.

[7] Harry D. Berg, "The Organization of Business in Colonial Philadelphia," *Pennsylvania History*, X (July, 1943), 157–177; Arthur H. Cole, "The Tempo of Mercantile Life in Colonial America," *Business History Review*, XXXIII (Autumn, 1959), 277–299.

[8] Richard B. Morris, *Government and Labor in Early America* (New York, 1946), 38–40.

[9] Indentured servants and slaves, Table I. The reconstruction of the Middle Ward as of April 8, 1773 showed seventeen hired servants in residence there. On this basis two hundred such servants were guessed for the city, see notes to Table III.

the work gang. Taken all together the eighteenth-century exceptions to the entrepreneurial role had but little significance for the functioning of the town's society.

A German visitor of 1750 wrote: "Pennsylvania is heaven for farmers, paradise for artisans, and hell for officials and preachers." [10] By the same token, Philadelphia on the eve of the Revolution was a town of freedom and abundance for the common man. For young persons there was a great demand for apprentices in all lines of work. An unskilled laborer without connections could find work with board and wages to begin accumulating a little money for tools. An artisan who wanted to carry a few shopkeeping goods in his shop, or a storekeeper with a good reputation, could get his stock from the merchant and settle for his advance a year later.

The ordinary artisan or shopkeeper, if his health was good, could be assured of a comfortable, if frugal, living. To be sure, houses were small and rents high, and furnishings were spare compared to later levels of living: no carpets, no upholstered furniture, a sandscrubbed floor, and whitewashed walls. Stoves and fireplaces only partially heated drafty rooms, and in severe winters the cost of firewood or imported coal was a major item of family expense. Nevertheless, at the city's markets food was cheap and plentiful. The earnings of the ordinary artisan and shopkeeper could support a wife and children without their having to take outside employment. The rapid growth of the town and its trade meant regular work and good earnings for artisans and easy business, if not wealth, for shopkeepers.[11]

Although the customary hours of work were long, sunrise to sunset, the pace of work was often easy and varied with the season. Those who worked outside their homes, like men in the building trades, took an hour for breakfast, a break in the middle of the day, and an hour for dinner in the afternoon. Coopers, shoemakers, smiths, and men who practiced their craft in their own houses and yards must have stopped work as customers and friends came in, and a trip or two to the local tavern must also have been usual. Although there were no formal vacations, the traditional English holidays and frequent *ad hoc* town celebrations provided about twenty days off each year.

[10] Gottlieb Mittelberger, *Journey to Pennsylvania* (Oscar Handlin and John Clive, eds., Cambridge, 1960), 48.

[11] Jackson Turner Main, *The Social Structure of Revolutionary America* (Princeton, 1965), 74–83, 115–163; Chapter IV; Mittelberger, *Journey*, 48–51, 74–75.

Franklin's *Autobiography* abounds with injunctions for regular habits, and the reputation for diligence he established by staying at his bench for the entire formal working day suggests that his was an extraordinary pace. For most workers rush seasons of hard work and long hours alternated with slack times. These variations meant days for fishing or spare moments for gossip on the streets and visits to the tavern.

Such a commonplace prosperity, generous at least by eighteenth-century standards, confirmed the privatism of the town and its age. As important a confirmation came from the openness of its economy and society. The failure of the craft guilds to control the trades of the town gave newcomers and resident artisans alike an occupational freedom unknown in Europe. Shopkeepers and artisans—and often one man was both—could take up any craft or open any line of business they wished. Although Philadelphia had inherited English regulations favoring the "freemen" of the town, established artisans could not maintain their control of the town's businesses against newcomers. The carpenters and cordwainers managed to form associations to set prices for their work, but failed when they attempted to close the membership of their trades. In Philadelphia men added trades and lines of goods as they thought demand justified. Although this freedom undoubtedly produced a great deal of incompetent craftsmanship, the importance to the individual artisan or shopkeeper of open trades and plentiful work cannot be overestimated. It meant for the common man that there was always a chance for a fresh start. This chance for a new beginning was the urban equivalent of the contemporary farmer's chance to pick up and try again in the West.[12]

Already in these years the American pattern of social mobility by property obtained. No invidious distinction between land and trade favored some occupations over others. As eighteenth-century Philadelphians grew rich they kept their original occupations, whether they were carpenters, distillers, printers, or lawyers. Whatever a man's occupation, there were only a few channels for investment open to the rising man. Since there were no banks, private money lending was the most important investment opportunity in the town. Houses and land were also a favorite way of using savings both among the rich and those with a little capital. Only 19 percent of the families of

---

12 Morris, *Government and Labor in Early America,* 2–3, 141–143; the American jack-of-all-trades tradition, Mittelberger, *Journey,* 42–43; artisans' associations, Bridenbaugh, *Colonial Craftsman,* 141–143.

Philadelphia owned their houses and therefore home rentals offered a safe investment. Other opportunities were shares in voyages, marine insurance, and, of course, land and farms outside the town.[13]

The prosperity and abundant opportunity of the town should not be confused with an even distribution of wealth. According to the published tax list for 1774 the upper tenth of the taxpaying households owned 89 percent of the taxable property. In this respect late eighteenth-century Philadelphia resembled the later Philadelphias— it was a pyramid of wealth in which about five hundred men guided the town's economic life. Its unique quality lay in the general prosperity of the common artisan and shopkeeper and the widely shared entrepreneurial experience and goals of the artisan, shopkeeper, and merchant.[14]

The wealthy presided over a municipal regime of little government. Both in form and function the town's government advertised the lack of concern for public management of the community. The municipal corporation of Philadelphia, copied from the forms of an old English borough, counted for little. Its only important functions in the late eighteenth-century were the management of the markets and the holding of the Recorder's Court. A closed corporation, choosing its members by co-option, it had become a club of wealthy merchants, without much purse, power, or popularity.

By modern standards the town was hardly governed at all. The

[13] Wilbur C. Plummer, "Consumer Credit in Colonial Philadelphia," *Pennsylvania Magazine,* LXVI (October, 1942), 385–409. The homeownership percentage was calculated from the number of homeowners and renters listed in the manuscript version of the Seventeenth Eighteen Penny Provincial Tax of April 8, 1774 (in possession of the Pennsylvania Historical and Museum Commission, Harrisburg). A reconstruction of the Middle Ward as of April 8, 1774 shows holdings of land and houses in small lots, and pairs of structures, not big tracts. Rich men, like Israel Pemeberton, and men of few investments, both participated in the housing market (see notes to Table III).

[14] The published version of the Seventeenth Eighteen Penny Provincial Tax, *Pennsylvania Archives, 3rd Series,* XIV (Harrisburg, 1897), 223–445, was used for a quick calculation of the distribution of taxable wealth. The taxpayers on this published list were arranged in order of the size of their published "assessment." The top ten percent, or 498 names, accounted for 89 percent of the 86,100 pounds of assessment given for Philadelphia, the Northern Liberties, and Southwark. This published list is not a sufficient guide to the distribution of wealth since the tax was largely a real property tax to which a head tax and a few personality items were added. The very important property of stock-in-trade and money-on-loan went untaxed and hence unlisted. Also, the compilers of the published list mixed in many cases the taxes-paid entries with the assessment entries thereby distorting even the assessment distribution.

constable in each ward and a few watchmen provided an ineffective police, the safety of the house and shop being secured by citizens' helping each other to drive away intruders or pursue thieves.[15] Most streets went unpaved, the public wharves little repaired. There were no public schools, no public water, and at best thin charity.

The enduring contribution of the colonial era to Philadelphia government lay in its inauguration of the committee system of municipal government. This system, if system it may be called in the eighteenth century, consisted of placing the administration of specific tasks in the hands of independent committees, or commissions. The Pennsylvania Provincial Assembly, lacking faith in the municipal corporation, created a number of commissions. First came the Board of Assessors established to raise money to pay the debts of the corporation and to require that wharves and streets be repaired and a workhouse erected. Then came separate street commissioners, next the City Wardens to manage the night watch and the lighting of the streets, and, still later, a Board of Overseers of the Poor. None of these commissions' performance would satisfy modern municipal standards. The commissioners were elected officials, chosen under the colonial fifty-pound, freehold qualification by the voters of Philadelphia. Like the town's fire companies, lending libraries, and tavern clubs these commissions helped train Philadelphians to the habits of committee government, a form of management they would have to call upon when creating a new independent government during the Revolution. Like many of the laws and forms of the colonial era which passed into the usage of the subsequent Commonwealth of Pennsylvania, the committee system of government was the legacy of colonial municipal life to later Philadelphias.[16]

The real secret of the peace and order of the eighteenth-century town lay not in its government but in the informal structure of its community. Unlike later and larger Philadelphias, the eighteenth-

---

[15] There are charming accounts of private policing in Henry D. Biddle, ed., *Extracts from the Journal of Elizabeth Drinker* (Philadelphia, 1889), robbery in her alley, Dec. 15, 1777; insane soldier wanders into the house, June 30, 1778; "saucy Ann" and her soldier, Nov. 25, 26, Dec. 2, 1777, Jan. 4, 1778. A call for more considerate treatment of the town watchmen, Advertisement, *Pennsylvania Gazette,* Jan. 20, 1779.

[16] For a description of the colonial government of Philadelphia, Judith M. Diamondstone, "Philadelphia's Municipal Corporation, 1701–1776," *Pennsylvania Magazine,* XC (April, 1966), 183–201; Edward P. Allinson & Boise Penrose, "The City Government of Philadelphia," *Johns Hopkins Studies in Historical and Political Science,* V (Baltimore, 1887), 14–33.

century town was a community. Graded by wealth and divided by distinctions of class though it was, it functioned as a single community. The community had been created out of a remarkably inclusive network of business and economic relationships and it was maintained by the daily interactions of trade and sociability. Because it was small and because every rank and occupation lived jumbled together in a narrow compass the town suffered none of the communications problems of later Philadelphia.

At most, 23,700 people lived in Philadelphia on the eve of the Revolution, 16,500 in the city proper, 7,000 in the adjacent districts of Northern Liberties and Southwark (Table I). The town crowded next to its shore. Its wharves and warehouses stretched a mile and a half along the Delaware River, but the built-up blocks of houses at their deepest point, along Market Street, reached back from the river at most half a mile to about Seventh Street.[17]

The settlement pattern of the town combined two opposing social tendencies. The clustering of marine trades and merchants next to the Delaware suggested the beginnings of the specialized industrial quarters then characteristic of European cities. On the other hand, the rummage of classes and occupations found in many Philadelphia blocks continued the old tradition of mixed work and residence characteristic of American and English country towns.

Ship carpenters, ship joiners, ship smiths, and sail makers lived and worked along the Delaware River shore. Sailors and stevedores dwelt among the yards and wharves along the entire shore, but they gathered especially on the south side of town (Dock Ward and Southwark). Mixed among them were many of the houses and shops of the merchants which were concentrated one block back from the riverfront. Together the shipbuilders, the marine trades, and the merchants pre-empted the narrow strip of frontage between the river and Second Street.[18]

The crowding of marine trades and commerce next to the port also influenced the location of other Philadelphians. Tailors, hatters, tin-

[17] The tax records and constables' returns of 1774 and 1775 show dense settlement to Seventh Street with but a few families living on scattered farms west from this point to the Schuylkill River (see notes to Middle Ward, Table III). A map made by John Reed of the City and Liberties of Philadelphia, supposed to have been made in 1774 (now in the possession of the American Philosophical Society) was shaded to show dense settlement to Tenth Street.

[18] Evidence of these concentrations was gathered from the tabulations made to construct Table II, Index of Dissimilarity.

TABLE I

POPULATION OF URBAN PHILADELPHIA 1775

Ward	Maximum Population			Indentured Servants			Slaves			Free	
	Adults	Children	Total	Adults	Children	Total	Adults	Children	Total	Adults	Children
Dock	2,064	1,985	4,049	90	179	269	63	105	168	1,911	1,701
Walnut	268	218	486	16	6	22	30	7	37	222	205
South	432	315	747	18	27	45	19	15	34	395	273
Middle	945	740	1,685	41	61	102	49	22	71	855	657
Chestnut	337	248	585	10	32	42	23	7	30	304	209
Lower Delaware	312	304	616	17	33	50	35	19	54	260	252
High Street	391	391	782	12	29	41	22	14	36	357	348
North	947	829	1,776	37	63	100	60	16	76	850	750
Mulberry	2,699	2,087	4,786	81	101	182	44	32	76	2,574	1,954
Upper Delaware	574	474	1,048	20	33	53	18	12	30	536	429
Sub Total, City of Philadelphia	8,969	7,591	16,560	342	564	906	363	249	612	8,264	6,778
East Northern Liberties			2,340								
West Northern Liberties			1,758								
Southwark			3,081								
Total Urban Philadelphia			23,739								

smiths, and silversmiths clustered in the central wards of town (Walnut, Lower Delaware, and Middle Wards) to be near, if not in, the portside concentration of customers. Conversely, those who needed large lots, or those who could not afford expensive land, drifted toward the edge of town. Here on the fringes the building trades, weavers, dyers, tanners, distillers, and laborers dwelt in more than normal proportions.

TABLE II

INDEX OF DISSIMILARITY

INDUSTRIAL GROUPINGS AND SOME ADDITIONAL CATEGORIES
PHILADELPHIA, NORTHERN LIBERTIES, AND SOUTHWARK,
1774; PHILADELPHIA COUNTY, 1860

1774	*Index*	*1860*	*Index*
Laborers	37.2	Negro, free, native born	47.3
Metalworking, ex. iron, steel	32.5	Miscellaneous textiles	40.3
Iron, steel, shipbuilding	29.4	Germany, foreign born	34.1
Paper & printing	29.4	Bakeries	30.7
Transport, ex. rail, transit	24.7	Iron, steel, shipbuilding	29.0
Misc. textiles	24.3	Hotels, laundries, domestic	25.9
Clothing	22.3	Metalworking, ex. iron, steel	25.6
Building trades	21.2	Professional, ex. entertainment	25.4
Wholesale & retail	20.5	Laborers	21.9
German surnames	19.7	Clothing	21.8
Professional, ex. entertainment	19.7	Ireland, N S, for. born	19.8
Bakeries	16.7	Transport, ex. rail, transit	19.6
Hotels, laundries, domestic	15.1	Paper & printing	19.0
Homeowners	6.1	Britain, ex Ireland, for. born	17.5
		Building trades	16.4
		Pennsylvania, native born	10.1
		Wholesale & retail	9.6

The differential pricing of land seems to have affected the laborers more than any other occupational group in the colonial town (Table II). Surprisingly enough, they were more segregated in this period than in the mid-nineteenth century, when the immigrant laborer was such a prominent element of the city. In 1774 the special locations of the laborers were the northern and southern edges of town—the Northern Liberties and adjacent parts of the Mulberry Ward, and Southwark.

A slight ethnic clustering also existed in eighteenth-century Philadelphia, but by no means of the same intensity as later twentieth-century ethnic and racial ghettos. German immigrants and their descendants had concentrated north of Market Street, over half of them living in the North, High, and Mulberry wards of Philadelphia and in the adjacent Northern Liberties Districts. This was also the Quaker side of town. Such ethnic and religious clusters, however, did not seem to have important effects upon the functioning of the town.

One can get some idea of the quality of urban life imposed by this settlement pattern by looking at one ward in a little detail. The Constable in making his enumeration of the residents of the Middle Ward left notes on his list showing when he turned the corner of a street. This record, plus some material from tax ledgers, make it possible to reconstruct the settlement pattern of this ward in 1774.

As its name suggests, the Middle Ward lay in the center of town, bounded on the north by Market Street, then the highway connecting Philadelphia to Chester and the south and to Lancaster and the west. The ward also was next to the market traffic. The sheds of the farmers' market in these years stretched up Market Street from the Delaware River only as far as Fourth Street. The Middle Ward was not a crowded dockside ward, but began just behind the dockside wards at Second Street. Its well-filled section covered five blocks to Seventh Street, Market to Chestnut. Beyond these blocks of houses the farms of the ward extended all the way west to the Schuylkill River.

Many famous Philadelphians lived within the ward. The old-fashioned Quaker radical, Anthony Benezet, the Proprietors John and Richard Penn, two opponents of the British who later turned Tory, Joseph Galloway, and James Allen, and the steadfast revolutionaries Benjamin Franklin and Daniel Clymer all lived in the center of the ward. The State House Yard (now Independence Square) stood across Chestnut Street between Fifth and Sixth streets. Such distinction, however, did not create the solid blocks of *haut bourgeois* fashion that they would today; rather it embroidered the commonplace fabric which was the revolutionary town. In 1774 the Middle Ward was the home of at least 1,401 men, women, and children of every degree and condition from Proprietor to slave (Table III).

The physical arrangements of the ward reflected the high cost of eighteenth-century housing and the crowding of Philadelphians near their port. Each of the Middle Ward's five settled blocks contained slightly less than five acres of land. On the first block of the ward (between Second and Third streets, the area nearest the Delaware

River) there stood 137 dwellings, on the next 65, on the next 67, on the next 29, and on westernmost 39. To accommodate so many

---

TABLE III

THE MIDDLE WARD OF PHILADELPHIA, APRIL 8, 1774

Free Adults (346 households x 2 for wives)	692
Children	469
Negro Slaves	78
Bound Servants in Residence	65
Hired Servants in Residence	17
Inmates (other free adults living in households)	80
Population	1,401
Homeowners	80
Houserenters	266
Taxpayers living with other families	102
Total Taxpayers	448

---

families in so little space some of the blocks of the ward had been cut by alleys so that little houses might be crowded onto the back lots of the houses facing the main streets. Strawberry Alley and Elbow Lane cut through the first block, Petty's Alley divided the third block, and Benjamin Franklin had begun the alley process with his house lot off Market Street in the second block of the ward. He had built a row of three houses on Market Street, thereby turning his home yard into an interior lot. His son-in-law Richard Bache, a merchant, rented one of the new row houses, Eden Haydock, a plumber, rented another, and Frederick Stonemetz, a cooper, took the third. In the early nineteenth century Franklin's home parcel became Franklin Court, an alley lot which opened up the interior of the block.[19]

Such density of housing and such methods of land division had by 1774 destroyed the hopes of Penn and his surveyor for a "Green Town." [20] The practice of subdividing blocks with alleys and jamming tiny houses on vacant rear yards continued strongly for the next ninety years. By 1860 the density of population in Philadelphia's

[19] Edward M. Riley, "Franklin's Home," *Historic Philadelphia* (American Philosophical Society, *Transactions,* XLIII, 1953), 148–160.

[20] Anthony N. B. Garvan, "Proprietary Philadelphia as Artifact," *The Historian and the City* (Oscar Handlin and John Burchard, ed., Cambridge, 1964), 177–201.

inner wards reached its all-time peak.[21] Then, in the second half of the nineteenth century the street railway opened up vast tracts of cheap suburban land and thereby destroyed the market for new alley construction. The old alleys with their dark and cramped houses, however, did not disappear at once. Rather they remained standing for years, giving discomfort to Philadelphia's poor for many generations, and the history of some alleys is not yet closed.

Already in the 1770's the crowding of the land exceeded the sanitary capabilities of the town. The streets and alleys reeked of garbage, manure, and night soil, and some private and public wells must have been dangerously polluted. Every few years an epidemic swept through the town. In the 1790's the city would pay a terrible price in deaths from recurring yellow fever.[22]

Though dangerous to health the eighteenth-century pattern of settlement guaranteed every citizen a knowledge of town life. At such density and small scale no generation could be raised ignorant of the other side of town, of the ways of life of the working class, or of the manners of the *haut bourgeois*. Within the Middle Ward at least 346 families with 469 children, 17 hired servants, 65 indentured servants, 78 Negro slaves, and 80 tenants share the settled 25 acres (Table III). Those who left a record carried on seventy different occupations (Table IV).[23]

Although merchants and shopkeepers, hatters, innkeepers, and tavernkeepers concentrated more heavily in this ward than in most others, variety best characterizes the occupational structure of the

21 Philadelphia City Planning Commission Map, "Year of Population Peak, Philadelphia, by Wards," dated August, 1949.

22 Bad conditions in alley "huts" of the poor, presumably one-story houses with a sleeping attic reached by a ladder as in the typical rural one-room cabin, Benjamin Rush, *Autobiography of Benjamin Rush* (American Philosophical Society, *Memoirs*, XXV, 1948), 83–84; cellar of a drunken, perhaps insane woman oyster seller, *Journal of Elizabeth Drinker,* Sept. 2, 1793; eighteenth-century epidemics, small pox, yellow fever, dysentery or typhoid, John Duffy, *Epidemics in Colonial America* (Baton Rouge, 1953), 78–100, 142–161, 220–230, and Struthers Burt, *Philadelphia Holy Experiment* (New York, 1946), 159.

23 No authority tells to what extent eighteenth-century artisans worked at home as opposed to working outside. With the exception of the building and marine trades most artisans are supposed to have worked at home. This supposition gets some indirect confirmation from the general agreement that most men labored alone and that most businesses in the city were family businesses. Neither Bridenbaugh in his *Colonial Craftsman* nor Morris in his *Government and Labor* tell of many urban establishments which might have employed many workers outside of their own homes.

ward as it did all the other wards of the first Philadelphia. The Proprietors, the merchants, and the doctors shared the narrow compass of the Middle Ward with such ungenteel occupations as laborer, porter, carter, skinner, watchman, crier, paver, grazier, and even goatkeeper. The outer three blocks of the ward also housed several breweries and a distillery, and every one of the five blocks contained one or more of those notorious enemies of sweet residential air— the stable.[24]

One cannot, at this late date, reconstruct in detail the communications patterns of eighteenth-century Philadelphia, but the crowded living of the age encouraged a street and tavern life which more resembled the social habits of the later nineteenth and early twentieth-century immigrant ghettos than the isolated private family life of today's working class and middle class.

The high cost of building kept houses small, cramped, and in short supply. The common artisan's or shopkeeper's house was a narrow structure, about seventeen feet wide and twenty-five feet deep. A story-and-a-half high, it offered about eight hundred square feet of floor space on its ground floor and attic. Most often the owner plied his trade in the largest front room. The Middle Ward records show that although some families had five to seven children, most had few. The average number of children per household was 1.3, and counting servants and slaves the average household was four persons. The small houses, thus, were cramped but not severely crowded. If the artisan or shopkeeper prospered he would add a kitchen ell or more likely move to a house of similar proportion with a kitchen ell at the rear. The house of an ordinary merchant, or even a craftsman who had grown rich, would be like the artisan's house with the ell, but would be two and one-half stories instead of one and one-half. Such houses of the prosperous also possessed deep lots for gardens, a shed for a cow and some chickens, and perhaps a horse.[25]

A town of small houses, where most houses also served as stores,

[24] A good sense of what the mixed settlement pattern of the city meant is given by Alexander Graydon, *Memoirs of a Life, Chiefly Passed in Pennsylvania* (Harrisburg, 1811), 34–35.

[25] The tax records of 1774 give evidence of a colonial housing shortage, for the ratio of occupied to unoccupied dwellings did not exceed two percent that year. Artisans' houses, Grant M. Simon, "Houses and Early Life in Philadelphia," *Historic Philadelphia*, 282–3; typical house for the prosperous, Advertisement, *Pennsylvania Gazette*, March 17, 1779.

TABLE IV

275 PERSONS WHOSE OCCUPATIONS CAN BE IDENTIFIED

MIDDLE WARD, APRIL 8, 1774

23	Shopkeepers	2	Druggists
19	Merchants	2	Livery stables
17	Laborers	2	Silversmiths
15	Cordwainers	2	Stablekeepers
13	Hatters	2	Staymakers
13	Tailors	2	Stockingweavers
13	Tavernkeepers	2	Tobacconists
11	Innkeepers	1	Boatbuilder
10	Bakers	1	Breechesmaker
10	Carpenters	1	Cheesemonger
7	Joiners	1	Crier
7	Saddlemakers	1	Distiller
6	Coopers	1	Engraver
5	Colonial Officers	1	Ferryman
5	Schoolmasters	1	Goatkeeper
4	Brewers	1	Grazier
4	Hucksters	1	Grocer
4	Porters	1	Harnessmaker
4	Skinners	1	Heelmaker
3	Barbers	1	Lawyer
3	Blacksmiths	1	Minister
3	Carvers	1	Painter
3	Coppersmiths	1	Paver
3	Curriers	1	Plumber
3	Mariners	1	Printer
3	Potters	1	Reedmaker
3	Smiths	1	Ropemaker
3	Tinkers	1	Scrivener
3	Watchmen	1	Sheriff
2	Bookbinders	1	Snuffmaker
2	Brushmakers	1	Threadmaker
2	Butchers	1	Upholder
2	Carters	1	Watchmaker
2	Chaisemakers	1	Wheelwright
2	Cutters	1	Workhouse keeper
2	Doctors		

offices and workshops, encouraged people to live out upon the streets. Moreover, the pace of work, most of it governed by the seasons or advance orders from customers, was irregular, what one would call today a rural pace. Both the physical structure of the town and the pace of its work thus encouraged a more public, gossipy style of life than could later be sustained when a steady pace of work and larger interiors drove people into sharply defined spaces for work and residence.

The ordinary housewife shopped daily, going to the baker's for her bread, and taking her meat and pies to the baker's oven to be cooked. Street peddlers called her out for fish, eggs, and produce, and twice a week the farmers of Philadelphia County held a full market at the public stalls. As in the nineteenth century with its dark tenements and crowded row houses, sunlight must have been a great source of pleasure for women sewing and spinning and many must have worked at these and other household chores out on their doorsteps, as their tenement sisters did years later.

For the husband the eighteenth-century custom of men's gossip at the tavern provided the first Philadelphia's basic cells of community life. Every ward in the city had its inns and taverns. The 1774 tax list recorded 93 tavernkeepers and 72 innkeepers in the city of Philadelphia, Southwark, and the Northern Liberties, approximately one neighborhood drinking place for every 140 persons in the city (23,000/165). The Middle Ward, alone, held 18 inns and taverns. Some must have served purely a neighborhood custom; others, like the London Coffee House or the City Tavern served as central communications nodes for the entire city.

Then, as now, each one had its own crowd of regulars and thus each constituted an informal community cell of the city. Out of the meetings of the regulars at the neighborhood tavern or inn came much of the commonplace community development which preceded the Revolution and proved later to be essential to the governance of the city and the management of the ward. Regular meetings of friends, or men of common occupations, led to clubs of all kinds and of every degree of formality from regular billiard sessions to fire companies and political juntos. Benjamin Franklin and the many community innovations of his junto showed the potential of these informal tavern groups. They provided the underlying social fabric of the town and when the Revolution began made it possible to quickly gather militia companies, to form effective committees of correspondence and of inspection, and to organize and to manage mass town meetings.

At the center of the town's communications system stood the merchants' coffee houses. On the eve of the Revolution Philadelphia had two such major meeting places—the old London Coffee House (established 1754), run by William Bradford, the newspaper publisher, and the new City Tavern (established 1773), just founded by a syndicate of merchants. The London Coffee House, located at Front and Market streets, adjacent to the town's principal market stalls and overlooking the Delaware, had been for many years the place where merchants gathered every noon to read incoming newspapers, to discuss prices, and to arrange for cargoes and marine insurance. These noon meetings in time ripened into the specialized institutions of exchanges, banks, and insurance companies. As yet, Philadelphia had but one insurance company and its merchants' business depended on the variety of functions of these daily tavern gatherings. For many years ship captains and travelers first stopped at the London Coffee House when they arrived in town, messages were left, auction notices posted and auctions held. Frequently on market days, after a parade through the streets, horses were auctioned in front of the tavern doors. Slaves and indentured servants stood before the same block.

As the town grew the importing merchants no longer had a need to be near the market dealers. The merchant community split into at least two parts. The new City Tavern surpassed the old London Coffee House as a place of fashion with the importing merchants, though its function remained that of its competitor. On May 19, 1774, Paul Revere brought his news of the closing of the Port of Boston to the City Tavern, and here numerous Revolutionary committees gathered. The still extant Philadelphia Assemblies were held at this new tavern, as was the endless series of banquets and balls which served the town with high entertainment.[26]

Because the merchants' tavern was a public place in a small town it escaped the limitations of later Philadelphia merchant centers—the exchanges, the Chamber of Commerce, and the gentlemen's clubs. These later gatherings were either meeting places of specialists and thereby encouraged only the brokers' or downtown merchants' view of the city, or they were closed organizations which directed their members' attention inward toward the sociability of the group. The eighteenth-century tavern, however, opened out to all the life of the street and it did not shield the leaders of the town from contact with the life that surrounded them.[27]

[26] The name "coffee house," which had been imported from England, merely designated a genteel tavern. Coffee, tea, lemonade, and beer were served, but the customers favored wines and liquors, Robert E. Graham, "The Taverns of Colonial Philadelphia," *Historic Philadelphia,* 318–323.

[27] Graydon tells an amusing story of the confrontation of Benjamin Chew, lawyer for the Penns and then Recorder of the town and an alderman with two drunken British officers, *Memoirs,* 43–44; an excellent review of travelers'

It was the unity of everyday life, from tavern, to street, to workplace, to housing, which held the town and its leaders together in the eighteenth century. This unity made it possible for the minority of Revolutionary merchants, artisans, and shopkeepers to hold together, run the town, and manage a share of the war against England, even in the face of Quaker neutrality and Tory opposition.

and visitors' accounts mentions the importance to the social structure of the town of immigrant societies like St. David's and St. Tammany, Whitfield J. Bell, Jr., "Some Aspects of the Social History of Pennsylvania, 1760–1790," *Pennsylvania Magazine,* LXII (July, 1938), 301.

3

The Washington Community, 1800-28

by JAMES STERLING YOUNG

With extraordinary faithfulness, the community plan for Washington repeats the organizing principles, even the ambiguities, of the constitutional plan for government.

The capital city of the United States has a character and inner structure unlike those in any Western nation. Only Bonn, being the seat of government, yet generating few of the nation's heartbeats in finance, commerce, education, or cultural ferment, has some of its characteristics. Washington is a city without important private industry, without a genuine national university, without a stock exchange, without a real harbor, without being a vital nexus of transportation. It is both more planned and more contrived than other large cities in America. If government were lifted from it, Washington would be sapped of its energies. As James Young says of the early city, "Washington was more than a capital. It was a company town of the national government—owned by the government, occupied by the government, conceived and created by the government to serve exclusively the purposes of government, and good for nothing else but government." The city long baffled foreign visitors and even more recent residents such as John F. Kennedy, who described it as "a city of Northern charm and Southern efficiency."

When President Washington chose the location and laid out the boundaries for the capital city within a semiwilderness, there was a definite purpose to escape the pressures and rivalries within an existing state or city. But it took several decades before Washington was much more than a town or cluster of villages. Its growth was slow; the size of government remained small and its demands on the city seasonal. It was a city of solitude and isolation. The master designer of the city, Major Pierre L'Enfant, and Thomas Jefferson foresaw a community soon expanding in size to at least 100,000, yet when Jefferson died in 1826,

57

the population still hovered close to 10,000 ; at that time there is a report of a seine cast near what is now Pennsylvania Avenue and Tenth Street netting several barrels of herring. Settlement was patchy with a few cellular centers on Capitol Hill, in the White House vicinity, and in Georgetown.

Despite the little cosmopolitan patina and the lack of enterprise other than government, the city held tenaciously to the ambitious vision and design of L'Enfant. After the Civil War, there was a real estate takeoff, a surge of public and private building, and a new concern with landscaping. L'Enfant's garments finally began to fit the city. His patterns found approbation in the administration of Theodore Roosevelt, when the McMillan Plan adapted L'Enfant's to contemporary needs. This plan under sponsorship of a Senate committee was largely the work of a galaxy of advisers that included the architects Charles F. McKim and Daniel Burnham, the landscape architect Frederick Law Olmsted, Jr., the sculptor Augustus St. Gaudens, and the critic Charles Moore.

Professor Young has written a graceful and penetrating account of both the ambience and governing establishment in the capital's first three decades. It is a book drawing on historical, sociological, and political science materials. This blend finely supplements the two-volume history of Washington by Constance McLaughlin Green.* Young's book was selected for both the Bancroft Award of Columbia University and for the Bancroft Prize in history in 1967. He teaches American government and politics at Columbia University, from which he received his Ph.D. This selection, which encompasses the Prologue and Chapter 2 of *The Washington Community,* is reprinted here with permission of the Columbia University Press © 1966.

THE COMMUNITY PLAN

Though they seem to be always with man, communities and governments are seldom the creatures of man's inspired intellect. Human needs and discontents will endlessly reshape them and impart to them a variety of design; but most are, in their form, the products of cultural convention and, in their purpose, the creatures of necessity. Rare indeed is it to encounter communities or governments which have originated in a truly creative impulse: unprecedented in form, conceived out of nothing save men's visions, and planned into exist-

---

* *Washington: Village and Capital, 1800–1878* (Princeton, Princeton University Press, 1962) and *Washington: Capital City, 1878–1950* (Princeton, Princeton University Press, 1963).

ence. History is not so lavish with the opportunity to create, and men more often imitate than innovate institutions so intricate as these.

The world's first successful rebellion against colonialism presented such an opportunity to the people of the United States, and politicians were at hand to make creative use of it. From their effort, itself unique in human history, there issued a government that was unique in history. Not so widely appreciated is the fact that this extraordinary creative effort was soon followed by another, equally bold. Its issue was a new community, also unique in human history. This was the community of rulers which the world today knows as "Washington."

Washington was created specifically for the national government, a new community for a new sovereign. As fully as any can be, it was a planned community: planned as the occupant government itself had been planned, and in no less detail; planned but four years after the governmental plan itself had been completed; planned for the same larger purpose of securing the institutions of power against the influence of historical fortuities; the product of that same revolutionary urge—masquerading, illogically, as a love of order and form where power was concerned—which had inspired the Constitution of 1787.

Customarily, understanding of the legal entity that is American national government begins with scrutiny of the governmental plan, the Constitution. To understand the human entity that emerged as the government of the new nation, the community plan, conceived for the site at which the governors were to live and work, may usefully serve as the point of departure. For the community plan, no less than the Constitution, is a blueprint for the governing establishment. No less than the Constitution, the community plan lays down principles of organization to be followed by the rulers of the nation. Both plans prescribe frameworks for action, place the actors, set the stage for the drama of power.

Equally important, the community plan of 1791 projects—as the constitutional plan of 1787 does not—an image of the new government as seen by the men who actually ran it. The community plan for Washington is not only the first unambiguous evidence on record but also, in its way, the most eloquent statement on record about the kind of government that was envisaged and desired by the pioneer politicians whose job it was to rule the new nation. While authorship of the plan technically belongs to Major Pierre Charles L'Enfant, there is a certain hard justice in the relative obscurity to which history has consigned this unusual figure.[1] For the real authors of the plan for Washington, in all but the narrow and technical sense, were the rulers themselves. It was they who commissioned a plan from L'Enfant. It was they who altered his plan, though in minor ways only, to render it conformable to their desires: some of the ornamental features called for in the plan were discarded for reasons of economy; and the governing politicians greeted with profound disinterest L'Enfant's provisions for a national church to be placed near the heart of the governmental community. It was they who approved the plan, thus amended, with their "universal applause," [2] as being eminently suited for a community of republican rulers. It was they who implemented the plan, even though they saw fit to dismiss L'Enfant himself. It was the governing politicians of the new republic and the generations of politicians following them at Washington who chose to preserve the L'Enfant plan and to make it, still today, the ground plan of the governmental community. For all practical purposes the plan is thus not L'Enfant's at all. In the broader and more meaningful sense, it is the plan of men who were not artists or engineers, as Major L'Enfant was, but politicians and rulers.

What kind of government was it, then, that these ruling politicians envisaged, desired, and intended when they made the plan for the governmental community on the Potomac?

Picture, thrown down upon a rural landscape like a piece of jigsaw puzzle not yet fitted into place, an odd-shaped mosaic of unconventional design, dotted over with open spaces having the appearance of focal points which are laced together by a busy web of streets— avenues of communication radiating outward to every point of the compass: the blueprint for the governmental community. . . . The plan at once suggests two dominating objectives on the part of the planners: first, to create a community divided into separate and discrete units; second, to create an accessible community, dependent upon some distinctive kind of interaction with the outlying society.

There is no single center in the ground plan of the governmental community, no one focus of activity, no central place for the assembly of all its members. What catches the eye instead is a system of larger and lesser centers widely dispersed over the terrain, "seemingly

[1] See Elizabeth S. Kite, *L'Enfant and Washington,* Johns Hopkins Press, 1929, for a documentary record of L'Enfant's involvement in the planning and building of the capital.

[2] The phrase is George Washington's, quoted *ibid.,* p. 159.

connected," as L'Enfant put it,[3] by shared routes of communication. It is clear that the planners intended a community whose members were to work or live not together but apart from each other, segregated into distinct units. Among these units, three major centers vie for dominance. They are separated by a considerable distance, and situated so as to command different aspects, avoiding mutual confrontation. One is assigned to the Congress; one to the President; and one to the Court. President Washington had approved this arrangement as being necessary "to obtain the primary object—i.e., the ground and means" for each governmental function.[4] Major L'Enfant offered this percipient explanation: "The main establishment . . . should be begun at various points equidistant as possible from the center; not merely because [separated] settlements . . . are likely to diffuse an equality of advantages over the whole territory allotted . . . but because each of these settlements by a natural jealousy will most tend to stimulate establishments on each of the opposed extremes." [5]

On the highest elevation in the terrain the plan places the Congress. Only one large structure being planned to accommodate its members and component units, this segment of the community appears to have been conceived as a collective entity, to be engaged in collective work.

A mile and a half away, with a different outlook on the landscape, is the center for the executive branch. Unlike Congress the executive has not been treated as a collective entity. The dominating structure here is to be created not by bringing together component units under one roof but by building a palace, a combined office and residence for the President which is oversized for its solitary occupant. This segment of the community was intended, then, to have a ranking personage, suggesting organization along hierarchical or status lines.

As to the subordinate units of the executive branch, their place in the plan had been the subject of controversy. John Adams, presiding officer of the Senate, felt they should all be located near Congress. President Washington, on the other hand, urged a location adjacent

---

[3] Quoted *ibid.*, p. 53.

[4] Quoted in Joseph B. Varnum, *Seat of Government*, 2d ed., Washington, D.C. 1854.

[5] Quoted in Kite, *L'Enfant and Washington*, p. 78. Although a few congressmen complained that the President's house was not made adjunct and subordinate to the halls of Congress, L'Enfant's scheme was readily preferred over other modes of organizing the community. Jefferson's idea for the capital, though it differed in other respects, coincided with L'Enfant's plan in separating the presidential and the congressional centers. See District of Columbia Sesquicentennial (exhibition catalogue), plate no. 57.

to the executive mansion. His reason for insisting, Washington explained, was that "the daily intercourse which the secretaries of the departments must have with the President, would render a distant situation extremely inconvenient to them, and not much less so would one . . . close to the Capitol; for it was the universal complaint of them all, that, while the legislature was in session [during the government's residence at Philadelphia], they could do little or no business, so much were they interrupted by the individual visits of members, (in office hours), and by calls for papers." [6] While the plan allows space for some executive departments next to the presidential mansion, it fails clearly to define any place for them in the over-all pattern of the community, leaving the determination in large measure to be worked out by the participants themselves.

Wide promenades or avenues radiate in many directions from each of these two major centers of the community, extending outward to its perimeter and opening directly on to the hinterlands beyond. For the Congress and the President the planners thus prescribed independent and coequal systems of communication with the outlying society. Noteworthy is the fact that this objective has taken priority over any effort to interconnect the two: communication between them is provided by a single route which extends beyond both to the edge of the future city. Not only distance but formality and visibility were apparently considered appropriate for the relations between Congress and the President, access being provided by a broad avenue suitable for communication of a ceremonial nature. "No message to nor from the President is to be made," L'Enfant explained, "without a sort of decorum." [7]

The third element of the triad, the Court, is made distinctive in the plan by its exclusion from these lines of communication. Placed roughly equidistant from the presidential and congressional centers, the site for the Court is provided no avenues to render it accessible to either of its coordinate centers within the community or to the outlying society. In a community in which outside communication is planned to figure so prominently it would seem that this segment is an anomaly.

The plan sets aside no space for the productive use of natural resources, and the dispersion of focal centers over the entire expanse of terrain, with the remaining space taken up by elaborate networks

[6] Quoted in Varnum, *Seat of Government*, p. 38.

[7] Quoted in Kite, *L'Enfant and Washington*, p. 57.

of streets, leaves little room for facilities of production on a scale commensurate with the planned size of the community and the needs of its prospective population. While "laid out on a dimension proportioned to . . . greatness," [8] the community is not, therefore, to be a self-supporting economic unit.

Is its greatness, then, to derive from arms? Clearly not. The sole provision for military protection is to be a naval yard occupying less land area than the grounds of the President's mansion. The plan calls for no battlements, no earthworks, no moats, no enclosing walls, no protecting barriers of any sort. Armed boundaries would be wholly incongruous, indeed incompatible, with the basic design of the community, its perimeter pierced on all sides by the open termini of wide avenues facilitating access directly to the centers of the community. Defensibility has not, therefore, merely been ignored in the plan. The plan specifies an open community, intentionally and peculiarly vulnerable to penetration; its accessibility has been preferred over its defensibility, and at the cost of defensibility. The possession of military strength by this community was evidently a prospect feared more by its planners than its survival was valued—its survival by military might, at least. Military considerations having no importance in the ground plan of the community, it may be assumed also that military personages were not intended to occupy dominant positions among its membership. Furthermore, from its accessibility—indiscriminately to friend and foe—this community was meant to be limited to those activities favorably received and supported by its environing society.

Militarily indefensible and economically unproductive, the community was intended, in short, to be a dependent community, not self-directing, without the means to control its own destiny. The wide-ranging avenues which sweep outward from the interior foci of the community plan thus assume importance as the community's intended lifelines, and suggest that the very survival of the occupant institution was meant to be conditioned upon open and free interaction with the outlying society. They reflect, too, an extraordinary effort to inculcate in the community members a sense of this dependence—to instill in them, as L'Enfant expressed it, "grand and far-distant points of view." [9]

But while the community was intended to be in regular, or at least periodic, communication with the outlying society, the routes of

[8] *Ibid.,* p. 47.
[9] *Ibid.,* p. 37.

communication provided for the plan have not been integrated into any preexisting system of communication in the society. They stop short at the community's frontier, there unjoined to any incoming routes of passage. The pattern of accessibility that is so distinctive of the community plan thus appears to have been dictated by the intrinsic requirements of the institutional design, and not to have been created in response to the pressures of traffic thrusting toward the community from the exterior. While access was invited, one suspects that it was not widely sought. Could a community so planned survive in isolation? In the extension and in the vitalizing of these lines of communication with the outside society appear to lie a major unplanned area of development for the community, and its own greatest need.

Many of the above precepts of the L'Enfant plan require little translation to become familiar. They are renderings, in a different language, of the constitutional prescriptions for the structure and functions of the national government. The plan for government, like the plan for the governmental community, intends a tripartite segmentation of governing personnel, with legislative, executive, and judicial functions assigned to differently composed and differently organized groups within the government. The failure of the community plan clearly to define a place for the administrative units of the executive branch finds its parallel in the ambiguity of the Constitution itself regarding the place of these units in the scheme of "separation of powers." Constitutional and community plan alike specify a subordinate role for the military. The accessibility to the hinterland society of the presidential and congressional centers in the community plan, each independently, has its obvious analogue in the representative character of the constitutional government, and in the establishment of a chief executive elected independently from the legislature. The reclusive situation assigned to the Court in the community plan accords with the situation prescribed for it in the Constitution, its members being nonelective, intentionally sheltered from popular influence outside the government and from presidential and congressional influence inside the government. The dependence of the community on sustaining responses of support and approbation from its environing society that is intended by the community plan reflects the constitutional principle of government by the consent of the governed.

With extraordinary faithfulness, the community plan for Washington repeats the organizing principles, even the ambiguities, of the constitutional plan for government. The similarities between these two plans suggest, therefore, that the principles and values of the practicing politicians who approved the L'Enfant plan coincided, to a most extraordinary degree, with the principles and values of those who had framed the Constitution.

So far, indeed, did constitutional values pervade the thinking of the power-holders themselves—at least in 1791—that they proposed, by their plan for Washington, to make a legal structure originally devised for the limited purpose of policy-making into a pattern for their own community living at the seat of power. The highly contrived, unconventional compartmentations of personnel called for by the Constitution were to be carried over to the whole community structure of the ruling group. The same roles and relationships, the same institutional checks upon power which the Constitution imposed upon their official activities, the governing group elected to impose upon their extraofficial activities as well, in their corporate existence as a community. Here was more than mere token allegiance to the Constitution. Here was an intention to carry the organizing principles of the Constitution far beyond the purposes for which it had been conceived.

Suggestive though it is, however, the plan for the Washington community, like the constitutional plan for government, remains in essence little more than a statement of the kind of governmental establishment the politicians *intended* to create. The two plans, converging in their implicit values and in their organizing principles, may reveal much, or they may reveal little, about the kind of establishment that actually emerged in early Washington. To what extent did the new ruling establishment conform to the paper establishment planned in 1787 and in 1791? Once settled in their new community beside the Potomac, did the ruling politicians actually have the sustaining responses of citizen interest which the community plan suggests they so vitally needed? Once settled on the terrain, how did the ruling politicians actually organize themselves? To what extent did they share the attitudes of the constitutional framers, share their mistrust of power, carry into their extraofficial relationships the constitutional separations of personnel designed to check power? With what implications for the performance of government, the stability of the governing group, the future course of governmental and political development?

What place, in a ruling establishment so planned, was left for the political party?

These are the questions of political significance which arise when the plan for the governmental community is brought under scrutiny.

"THE NATIONAL BANTLING"

Almost no one, it seemed, could find anything flattering to say about the capital in the Jeffersonian years. To travelers and diplomats from abroad, the showcase of the new nation was a gigantic monument to pretension, the confirming evidence that the Americans had attempted something beyond their capacities. "Voilà un Capitol sans Ciceron; voici le Tibre sans Rome," said one visitor, and recited Thomas Moore's famous gibe about "This embryo capital, where Fancy sees/Squares in morasses, obelisks in trees." [1] Among Americans, also, the capital became a butt for jokes, and poking fun at Washington became something of a national pastime. "The national bantling" it was dubbed, the benighted and ungainly offspring of the nation. "The Federal city is in reality neither town nor village," crowed a Philadelphia editor; "it may be compared to a country seat where state sportsmen may run horses and fight cocks; kill time under cover and shoot Public Service flying. . . . There sits the President . . . like a pelican in the wilderness, or a sparrow upon the housetop." [2]

And to those whom ambition and desire for service brought to Washington, it became "this city which so many are willing to come to and all [are] so anxious to leave." [3] For the utter desolation that public disinterest had made of their environment was not the least of those "splendid torments" that Jefferson called the political vocation: Washington was an ever-present reminder to the men in power of the low esteem in which power was held.

The stage for the national drama was a vast construction site "bearing the marks of partial labour and general desertion." [4] Two unfinished stark white citadels towered above the terrain from hilltops on opposite shores of a dismal swamp, more like ruins amid the fallen

[1] Alfred J. Morrison, ed., *The District in the XVIIIth Century*, Section V, p. 45; Beckles Wilson, *Friendly Relations*, Boston, 1934.

[2] Samuel C. Busey, *Pictures of Washington*, Washington, D.C., 1898, pp. 56–57.

[3] Constance McLaughlin Green, *Washington: Village and Capital, 1800–1878*, Princeton, 1962, pp. 66.

[4] E. Howitt, *Letters*, J. Dunn, (1820?), p. 78.

fragments of their own stone than new and rising edifices. Where monuments had been planned, brush piles moldered and rubbish heaps accumulated. Where majestic avenues were to sweep, swaths of tree stumps stood, rough quarried stones marking the intersections. Where houses were to be, barren hillocks, stripped of vegetation, rose like desert islands amid a sea of bogs and marshes.

Cows grazed on future plazas and bullfrogs chorused on the mall. Wildlife overran the premises. "Antoine killed a brownish snake, two feet long, in the house, at the foot of the staircase," reads the diary of the Secretary of State; "the heat of the weather almost unremitted, with myriads of flies, bugs, and vermin of all filths, adds to the discomforts, if not to the anxieties of this occupation." [5] Hogs rooted in the refuse that was discarded in the roadways and it was not until 1820 that scavengers were hired to clean it away.[6] Epidemics of fever were chronic, abetted by "several immense excavations of brick yards always full of green stagnant water . . . and numerous dead carcasses left to putrify," and by the sluggish Tiber which fed mosquito-infested marshes.[7]

Except for poverty's children, subsisting in windowless shacks in the copses and in the heatless chambers of an unfinished hotel, population was not much in evidence. "One might take a ride of several hours within the precincts without meeting with a single individual to disturb one's meditation." [8] "There was a stillness and vacuity over the whole place." [9] "In the very heart of the city . . . not a sound is to be heard" by day,[10] and, by night, only the sounds of idleness emanated from the little house-rows dotting the woods around: baying dogs, squalling cats, parlor music, and domestic feuds—"yelling of savages in the wilderness would be as much if not more entertaining," a Treasury auditor wrote of summer evenings along executives' row.[11] "Every thing here seems in a dead calm," observed a newly arrived congressman; "an absolute supineness overwhelms all." [12]

[5] John Quincy Adams, *Memoirs,* IV, Philadelphia, 1874–5, p. 409.

[6] Green, *Washington,* p. 94.

[7] *Ibid.*; Henry Adams, *The Life of Albert Gallatin,* New York, Peter Smith, 1943, p. 253.

[8] Augustus J. Foster, *Jeffersonian America,* San Marino, 1954, p. 17.

[9] Howitt, *Letters,* p. 80.

[10] Una Pope-Hennessy, ed., *The Aristorcratic Journey,* New York, 1931, p. 165.

[11] Mary Lee Mann, ed., *A Yankee Jeffersonian,* Cambridge, 1958, p. 202.

[12] William W. Story, ed., *Life and Letters of Joseph Story,* Vol. I, Boston, 1851, pp. 160, 162.

To this Rome, with its Tiber and its Capitoline, few roads led. The bridge across the Potomac that was the capital's main link to the west was fired during the British occupation in 1814, simultaneously by the enemy on the Washington side and a zealous American corporal on the Virginia side.[13] To the east communication was restricted largely to the Bladensburg Road, which had its terminus in Georgetown. Members sometimes had difficulty finding their way to the capital. The President's wife once got lost in the woods en route from Baltimore, "wandered two hours without finding . . . the path," and at last came upon a vagabond whom she engaged as a guide "to extricate us out of our difficulty." [14]

It was almost as difficult to find one's way inside the capital as into it. There were no sidewalks or lamps to guide one by night, no signs as guides by day, and roads meandered into cow trails. A group of congressmen returning from a dinner party near what is now called Haines Point got lost and spent until daybreak in their carriage weaving through bogs and gullies in search of Capitol Hill, only a mile away.[15] Houses were so far between and so few of the streets had been laid out that the inhabitants found it necessary to identify their place of residence in directories not by house number nor street but by the public building nearest them—"a few paces from the Capitol," "near the President's house," "west of the War Office," "opposite the Treasury." As late as 1817 a cabinet officer gave for his address in the *Congressional Directory* the "high ground north of Pennsylvania Avenue." And even in 1832 this intended thoroughfare was yet so undeveloped that the new Treasury building then erected was later discovered to have been placed athwart it, preempting the President's vista eastward to Capitol Hill and necessitating a permanent detour of traffic between the Capitol and the White House.[16] When Anthony Trollope spoofed Washington in 1862 he was realistically describing the city in the Jeffersonian era,

> where a man may lose himself . . . not as one loses oneself in London between Shoreditch and Russell Square, but as one does so in the deserts of the Holy Land, between Emmaus

[13] Wilhemus Bogart Bryan, *A History of the National Capital*, New York, 1914, Vol. I, pp. 626–27.

[14] Abigail Adams, *Letters of Mrs. Adams*, Vol. II, Boston, 1841, p. 240.

[15] Margaret Bayard Smith, *The First Forty Years of Washington Society*, New York, 1906, p. 10.

[16] Helen Nicolay, *Our Capital on the Potomac*, New York, 1924, pp. 272–73.

and Arimathea. In the first place no one knows where the places are, or is unsure of their existence, and then between their presumed localities the country is wild, trackless, unbridged, uninhabited and desolate. . . . Tucking your trousers up to your knees, you will wade through bogs, you will lose yourself among rude hillocks, you will be out of the reach of humanity.[17]

Paved streets were unknown and roads were few, dust bowls in dry weather and morasses when it rained. To venture forth upon them was to risk life, limb, and vehicle. Diplomats in full regalia, paying state visits, would find themselves marooned outside the executive mansion in their magnificent equipages, mired in the red mud of Pennsylvania Avenue "to the axletree. . . . It was necessary to leave the carriage, which had to be dragged out and scraped to remove the mud and slush which stuck to it like glue." [18] "It was a mercy that we all got home with whole bones," wrote a cabinet officer upon returning from an evening visit; "our carriage . . . was overset, the harness broken . . . and at the Treasury Office corner we were obliged to get out of the carriage in the mud. I called out the guard of the Treasury Office and borrowed a lantern." [19] Made dangerous by the condition of the roads and arduous by the unprecedented "distances to be traversed in the ordinary intercourse of society," [20] the communication that is necessary for even a rudimentary social life was no mean logistical problem for the members of the early governmental community. "The house Mr. G.[allatin] has taken is next door to the Madisons' and three miles distant from us. I regret this circumstance, as it will prevent that intimate intercourse which I wished to enjoy." [21]

Against this desolate landscape the halls of government stood as Henry Adams was to see them decades later, "unfinished, . . . white Greek temples in the abandoned gravel-pits of a deserted Syrian city." [22] To the men who occupied them they brought no reassurance

[17] Allen C. Clark, *The Trollopes*, Columbia Historical Society *Records*, XXXVII–XXXVIII, 91, Washington, 1937.

[18] Quoted in Anne Hollingsworth Wharton, *Social Life in the Early Republic*, Philadelphia, 1902, p. 60.

[19] John Quincy Adams, *Memoirs*, IV, 74.

[20] Thomas Hamilton, *Men and Manners in America*, Vol. II, London, 1833, p. 30.

[21] Margaret B. Smith, *First Forty Years*, pp. 27–28.

[22] Henry Adams, *The Education of Henry Adams*, Modern Library Edition, New York, 1931, pp. 44, 99.

of dignity and little comfort. Those most charitably inclined likened them to "the splendid ruins of Roman grandeur." [23]

Commanding the terrain from the tallest hill, the Capitol was built to be seen. But failure to erect the central portion, connecting the Senate and House wings, made it an architectural monstrosity—twin boxes of white stone on a shrubless heath of hard-packed stone dust, the void between them bridged by a covered boardwalk resembling the construction sheds that dotted the grounds. The Senate wing boasted an elegant semicircular auditorium furnished with chairs of red morocco leather to serve for debates and, on its periphery, a lounge with couches arranged about two massive fireplaces where Senators could escape from chilling drafts while remaining within earshot of the floor proceedings. But behind the showy façade shoddy workmanship and poor design soon became apparent. Part of the ceiling fell in 1803, narrowly missing the Vice President's chair and necessitating an adjournment.[24] Columns supporting the gallery split open and were wrapped with white muslin to conceal the defects.[25] Printed notices warned spectators in the balcony "not to place their feet on the board in the front of the gallery, *as the dirt from them falls upon Senators' heads.*" [26] The House chamber had a glass-domed ceiling which leaked so badly that pools of water were left on the floor after heavy rains.[27] Hot-air furnaces installed beneath the floor emanated heat to a degree that was "noxious and insupportable, and it has affected me to fainting," a Representative complained; "I have at length prevailed on the Speaker to forbid our subterranean fires. The effect produced by them is that upon an oyster baked in a Dutch oven." [28] The acoustics were, as Woodrow Wilson found them half a century later,[29] abominable. Whispered confidences resounded in the far corners of the chamber while shouts to a person ten feet distant were absorbed in a well of silence: "It must have been long since perceived, by every gentleman in the House," declared a Representative from the floor, "that the splendid hall in which they were as-

[23] Bryan, *History,* I, 618.
[24] *Ibid.,* p. 610.
[25] *Ibid.,* p. 610.
[26] John H. B. Latrobe, *The Capitol and Washington at the Beginning of the Present Century,* Baltimore, 1881, pp. 25 ff.
[27] Charles Burr Todd, *The Story of Washington,* New York, 1889, p. 63.
[28] Edmund Quincy, *Life of Josiah Quincy,* Boston, 1868, p. 137.
[29] Woodrow Wilson, *Congressional Government,* 13th ed., New York, 1898, pp. 86–87.

sembled was perfectly unfit for the purpose of legislation, and that it was impossible in its present state, either to hear or be heard; they were consequently under the necessity of voting on questions which they could not understand, much less the reasons offered for or against them." [30]

Too cavernous for a home, too shabby for a palace, the executive mansion made its occupant "an object of ridicule with some and of pity with others." [31] Abigail Adams found only six of its thirty rooms plastered and "not a single apartment finished . . . the principal stairs . . . not up . . . not the least fence, yard, or other convenience without, and the great unfinished audience-room I make a drying-room of, to hang the clothes in." [32] Eight years elapsed before the staircase to the second floor was built. The ceiling in the audience chamber collapsed before the room was sufficiently finished to be used, and when the room was first opened for entertaining in the administration of John Quincy Adams it was still partially unplastered.[33] Not even the exterior of the building had been finished when the British burned it in 1814. The roof "leaked in such a manner as materially to injure the ceilings and furniture," reads an official report from 1809, and the timbers of the building, less than twenty years old, "are in a state of considerable decay." [34]

For years the grounds remained cluttered with workmen's shanties, privies, stagnant pools of water in basins once used for mixing mortar, "ruins of old brick-kilns, and the remains of brick yards and stone-cutters' sheds," "so that, in a dark night [according to a visitor in 1806] instead of finding your way to the house, you may, perchance, fall into a pit, or stumble over a heap of rubbish." Guests, after negotiating hazards in the yard, had to ascend to the mansion by rough board steps almost a full story aboveground.[35] "When I per-

---

[30] *Annals of Congress,* XVII (10th Congress, 1st sess.), 1061.

[31] George Gibbs, *Memoirs of the Administrations of Washington and John Adams,* Vol. II, New York, 1846, p. 377.

[32] Abigail Adams, *Letters,* p. 241.

[33] Bryan, *History,* II, 236; Esther Singleton, *The Story of the White House,* Vol. I, New York, 1907, p. 16; Margaret B. Smith, *First Forty Years,* p. 246.

[34] "The cause of decay, both in this house and in the Capitol is to be found . . . in the green state of the timber when first used, in its original bad quality, and its long exposure to the weather, before the buildings could be roofed." Quoted in Singleton, *White House,* I, 16.

[35] *Ibid.,* pp. XXIII, 16; Nicolay, *Our Capital,* pp. 67–68; Bryan, *History,* I, 377; Charles William Janson, *The Stranger in America, 1793–1806,* New York, 1935, p. 213.

ceive the President's circumvallation unfinished, his garden in gullies and the room[s] of his house unplastered," a resident wrote in 1810, "I ask—can these disgusting scenes to strangers be pleasing to the citizens? " [36] "This parsimony destroys every sentiment of pleasure that arises in the mind, in viewing the residence of the president of a nation," commented a foreign visitor, "and is a disgrace to the country." [37]

To the worse than Spartan comfortlessness of the surroundings was added the unnerving monotony of politics unrelieved by diversion. "Il nous ne manque ici," wrote a Senator to a European acquaintance, "que maisons, caves, cuisines, hommes instruits, femmes aimables et autres petites bagatelles de cette espèce, pour que notre ville soit parfaite . . . c'est la ville du monde où on peut le mieux vivre—dans l'avenir." [38] There were only two places of public amusement in the capital, one of them a racetrack where "persons of all descriptions . . . collected together . . . shouting, betting, drinking, quarrelling and fighting";[39] the other a theater "most astonishingly dirty and void of decoration," [40] where boys of the town gained admittance by lifting loose boards and crawling through the floor.[41] "One must love the drama very much," commented a Treasury official, "to consent to pass three hours amidst tobacco smoke, whiskey breaths, and other stenches, mixed up with the effluvia of stables, and miasmas of the canal, which the theatre is exactly placed and constructed to receive." [42]

With only such escape as these facilities afforded, and having little other society except shopkeepers and laborers, the members of government were necessarily thrown upon each other in leisure hours as well as at work. Thus their social life, rather than affording them relief from politics, became itself another arena of politics. Who was and who was not invited to a tea, a dinner, or a reception, who accepted

36 Irving Brant, *James Madison, the President, 1809–1812*, Indianapolis, 1956, p. 32.

37 Janson, *The Stranger*, p. 213.

38 Anne Carey Morris, ed., *The Diary and Letters of Gouverneur Morris*, Vol. II, New York, 1888, pp. 394–95. "All we lack here are good houses, wine cellars, decent food, learned men, attractive women and other such trifles to make our city perfect . . . it is the best city in the world to live in—in the future."

39 Quoted in Green, *Washington*, p. 45.

40 Frances M. Trollope, *Domestic Manners of the Americans*, Vol. I, London, 1832, p. 333.

41 Christian Hines, *Early Recollections of Washington City*, Washington, 1866, p. 75.

42 Mary Lee Mann, ed., *A Yankee Jeffersonian*, Cambridge, 1958, p. 207.

and who declined, who was and who was not calling upon whom, became matters pregnant with political significance. "General Jackson has not visited Mr. Crawford," President Adams noted of his successor, but their "ladies have interchanged visits . . . [and it appears that they] will effectually knit the coalition." [43] Like it or not, party-going and party-giving tended to become obligatory, essential to the maintenance of one's political position. "Washington . . . is the only place in the Union where people consider it necessary to be agreeable, —where pleasing . . . becomes a sort of business";[44] one was "obliged to go to other peoples parties, sick or well, for fear of giving offence." [45] The social round, so far from providing relaxation for the members, became itself a chore: "Such a party could give me no pleasure," commented a hostess, "but I hope it did others." [46]

Unable to get away from each other except by solitary walks into the woods or along the Potomac's banks to hunt, fish, or swim, "brutalized and stupefied . . . from hearing nothing but politics from morning to night and from continual confinement," [47] the members staged an eager retreat from the capital as soon as the public business could be disposed of each year. Thus, as the public structures dominated the landscape and as politics dominated society, so even the rhythm of Washington life became the rhythm of governmental activity itself. Once, in the autumn, with the arrival of the public persons from the hinterlands, the community came alive, and reverted to dormancy as they returned to their homes and constituencies in the springtime, leaving a ghost town behind: houses boarded up, the halls of Congress silent and empty, the White House deserted, the foreign legations closed. "The winter campaign is over—the tents are struck and the different parties are leaving the field—Congress has adjourned. . . . A universal dullness pervades." [48]

Such was power's home in a nation wedded to the doctrine of the sovereignty of the people: a pleasureless outpost in the wilds and wastes, manned for only part of the year, abandoned for the rest.

[43] John Quincy Adams, *Memoirs*, VI, 478.
[44] Hamilton, *Men and Manners*, II, 35.
[45] Margaret B. Smith, *First Forty Years*, p. 213.
[46] *Ibid.*, p. 137.
[47] Foster, *Jeffersonian America*, p. 9.
[48] Margaret B. Smith, *First Forty Years*, p. 273.

4

Boston's Immigrants:
The Economic Adjustment

by OSCAR HANDLIN

---

*From the day they landed, the immigrants competed for jobs
that were fewer than men.*

In 1840, 3,936 immigrants landed in Boston. By 1849, 28,917 landed.
These newcomers were overwhelmingly Irish. Similar mass migrations
of people were occurring elsewhere along the Atlantic seaboard during
the period to the extent of changing the character of the federal cities.
Many of these new immigrants had entered an urban way of life both
foreign and unfavorable to their peasant backgrounds so that "for a long
time they were fated to remain a massive lump in the community, un-
digested, undigestible." There thus developed a new American urban
problem, variations of which remain to this day—namely, the economic
adjustment to urban life of large numbers of migrants from the rural
countryside without previous training or capital to prepare them for urban
society. And for this reason Oscar Handlin's study *Boston's Immigrants*
is of importance to the urban historian. "The Economic Adjustment" is
Chapter III of this book, which was originally published in 1941 as
Volume L of the Harvard Historical Studies. A revised edition was published in 1959. This selection has beeen reprinted with the permission of
the publishers, The Belknap Press of the Harvard University Press, copyright 1941, 1959, by the President and Fellows of Harvard College.

Oscar Handlin was born in Brooklyn, New York, in 1915 and educated
at Brooklyn College and at Harvard. He joined the faculty of Harvard
in 1939, became a professor of history there in 1954, and is now director
of the Charles Warren Center for the Study of American History. While
Dr. Handlin was a graduate student at Harvard, Professor Arthur Meier
Schlesinger suggested the subject of his doctoral dissertation, and this

formed the basis of the book *Boston's Immigrants*. Among Dr. Handlin's other works are *This Was America, The Uprooted, Race and Nationality in American Life, Al Smith and His America, Immigration as a Factor in American History,* and *Children of the Uprooted.*

The elements conditioning the emigration of the foreigners, together with the social structure of Boston as they found it, determined their position in the community. These factors limited the whole orbit of the immigrants' lives in their new homes. Their work, their health and longevity, their housing, their relations with the government, with their neighbors, and with one another, all were implicit in these two forces. What drove the Europeans to Boston and what they found there together produced a new society, far different from its antecedents, yet unmistakably their heir.*

The course of adjustment created a fundamental difference between two categories of immigrants. Those who quickly resumed familiar routines easily merged in interests and activities with native Americans. But those whose memories held no trace of recognition for any feature of the new land, made room for themselves, if at all, only with the utmost difficulty. Many faltered, hesitated, were overwhelmed and lost, because in the whole span of their previous existence they found no parallel to guide them in their new life.

The most pressing concern of all newcomers on landing was to obtain employment. Those whose background had equipped them with an industrial skill or mercantile trade had little difficulty in adjusting to the economic conditions of their new world. Most, however, had escaped into a way of life completely foreign and completely unfavorable to them. Thousands of poverty-stricken peasants, rudely transposed to an urban commercial center, could not readily become merchants or clerks; they had neither the training nor the capital to set up as shopkeepers or artisans. The absence of other opportunities forced the vast majority into the ranks of an unemployed resourceless proletariat, whose cheap labor and abundant numbers ultimately created a new industrialism in Boston. But for a long time

---

* The original footnotes of this essay are here omitted. Most of them refer to Dr. Handlin's doctoral dissertation and other sources not readily available to the average reader. They can be found in the 1959 edition of *Boston's Immigrants,* (Cambridge, Mass., The Belknap Press), pp. 316–26.

they were fated to remain a massive lump in the community, un-digested, undigestible.

Since at the beginning, at least, the immigrants did not form an integral part of Boston's economy, it is difficult to know precisely how they managed to exist. They played no role in the usual accounts of her commercial and industrial life. Their contemporaries were aware that Europeans were there, of course, but completely neglected them in describing the business of the city. Save for occasional cursory notices of the number of arrivals, trade papers and journals through-out the forties and fifties consistently ignored the newcomers, and travelers' accounts which did mention them frequently misled, as they often do, by emphasizing the curious rather than the commonplace.

For an accurate analysis of what happened to the immigrant in the maze of Boston's business life one must turn to the cold statistics of DeBow's federal census of 1850, the first to enumerate both nativity and occupations. In Boston it revealed a total of 136,881 inhabitants, of whom 37,465 were adult males; and it listed the vocations of 43,567 persons. . . .

The 43,567 persons for whom material was available were engaged in over 992 distinct pursuits—an average of no more than forty-four persons per occupation in the entire city. This widespread diversity emanated directly from Boston's complete orientation towards small-scale skilled enterprises and away from large-scale unskilled ones. As the nucleus of an important economic area, the town contained a multitude of retail trades. The center of a prosperous urban life, it encouraged the growth of highly skilled handicrafts to satisfy the demands for consumers' goods. Commercial rather than industrial in character, it possessed no large-scale establishments and therefore no great accumulations of labor in any industry or trade. Broad occupational diversification was normal and inevitable in this society.

Viewed according to the nativity of those employed, this hetero-geneity was particularly significant, for it reflected the economic health of any group within the city. A high degree of dispersion denoted the presence of considerable numbers of trained workmen, retailers, and merchants who conformed closely to the city's economic pattern. A low degree indicated a deficiency of such elements and presaged a period of difficulty in adjustment. . . .

. . . While the 13,553 persons of Massachusetts birth worked at over 660 different occupations and New England's 7,986 at 564, Ireland's 14,595 were confined to only 362.

The unusual degree of Irish concentration in an economic organization where dispersion was the rule arose from their convergence in two unskilled employments. A single occupation accounted for 48 per cent of the total Irish laboring force, another for almost 15 per cent more, and a third for 7 per cent. . . .

The concentration of nearly 65 per cent of the Irish working population in two occupations was an anomaly forced upon them by the conditions of their arrival. The vast majority left their ships in East Boston without the slightest conception of how they would earn a livelihood and with only enough money to keep them fed and sheltered for a week or two. "Unable to find employment or transportation elsewhere, . . . without one penny in store, the question, how they should live, was more easily put than solved." Some had the way partly cleared by relatives or friends who assisted them; others managed to go west or to more prosperous eastern cities; and not a few, immediately discouraged by the "overstocked labor market," turned back to Ireland. But most were completely immobilized; the circumstances that brought them to Boston compelled them to remain there, to struggle on as best they could.

They faced exhausting difficulties in making a place for themselves in the city's economic life. There was no one to help them; the hard-pressed Catholic priest and the overburdened benevolent and immigrant-aid societies could assist only a few. Many fell into the clutches of the "Intelligence Bureaus" and the "Swindling Shops," traders in human misery which fleeced the guileless strangers. More generally, the Irish relied upon their own simple ingenuity in finding employment. Tramping the crooked streets from shop to shop, they might, if they were fortunate, find someone to use their heavy labor. Frequenting the docks, watching the arrival of ships from across the water, they sometimes met a short-handed stevedore boss or wharfinger. They procured casual employment on the streets or in the public works that were transforming the physical aspects of the city. But every element of selectivity was denied them. The pressing need for immediate earnings destroyed the possibility of choosing a job or preparing for a trade. Want swept them into the ranks of those 7,007 unskilled, insecure day laborers who informed the census takers that they were just laborers—a classification descriptive not of their function, but of their lack of function. Well might the good Irish priest, Dr. Cahill, lament that "the emigrants from Ireland . . . to escape the horrors . . . of the emaciating poorhouse fly to this country with barely the passage money; and they have often landed . . . [without] a single penny! . . . It is a clear case that these poor friendless strangers, having no money, must have recourse to their only means of subsistence—namely, street or yard laborers or house servants."

No other nationality depended so heavily upon unskilled work. There were 1,545 laborers in the city other than Irish, but in no group did they form a significant proportion. Among the natives no more than 5 per cent were so employed, and only the Negroes and the Germans had as much as 10 per cent. But even in these cases the actual number was small: 115 Negroes and 107 Germans.

An employed laborer could not earn enough to maintain a family of four. And as long as the head of the Irish household obtained nothing but sporadic employment, his dependents lived in jeopardy of exchanging poverty for starvation. Supplementary earnings—no matter how small—became crucial for subsistence. The sons were first pressed into service, though youngsters had to compete with adults willing to work for boys' wages. To keep the family fed, clothed, and sheltered the women also were recruited. In Ireland they had occupied a clearly defined and important position in the cottiers' economy. That place being gone, they went off to serve at the table of strangers and bring home the bitter bread of banishment.

There was room in the comfortable households of Boston's middle classes for the Irish daughter or sister who wished to lighten her family's load by supporting herself and perhaps contributing a little something besides. There had long been an acute shortage of domestics in New England. Generation after generation of housewives had either done their own work or paid relatively high wages to natives who insisted on being "help," not servants. The supply of such labor had been extremely unsatisfactory and transitory in character. Most Americans "would rather want bread than *serve* to gain it," and farm girls in service for a few years while waiting to be married usually lacked the essential attributes of servility and loyalty. Under these circumstances the "Irish help" were triply welcome for their good spirits, their loyalty, and their cheap wages. In all hotels and in thousands of native homes Bridget became a familiar, indispensable figure. By 1850, at a conservative estimate, 2,227 Irish girls worked as domestic servants in Boston.

For all other groups, the percentage in service was uniformly low. None numbered more than 10 per cent, and of these, many were governesses and housekeepers rather than menial servants. To some extent this preponderance of Irish domestics sprang from the greater percentage of females among the immigrants from Ireland; but above all, it derived from the pressing need to send women out to help support the family.

The tenuous character of their status drove the Irish into a constant search for better jobs and more secure employment. All aspired to skilled positions that would enable them to support their families alone. But the reluctance to employ Irishmen in any but the lowest capacities, added to their lack of capital and of training—itself an insuperable obstacle—rigorously excluded them from such occupations. Early attempts to ban foreigners from certain professions by law had failed, but by 1845 the caption "None need apply but Americans" was familiar in Boston newspaper advertisements. Prejudice became more intense as competition for jobs grew keener, though it proved no formidable barrier to those who had a trade to ply or a skill to offer. But while other groups filtered into the city and were accepted, the Irish remained unneeded and unabsorbed. The few who arrived with professions, or rose from the ranks of the unskilled by a gradual process of recruitment, did not leaven the mass.

The degree of their penetration into any trade varied inversely with its desirability. Employments involving an element of personal service, and therefore repugnant and degrading to Americans, quickly fell to the lot of the Irish. Many found work in the care and service of horses, the city's chief transport agent. As these trades called for menial labor of a rather low sort, few competed with the Irish for them. By 1850, more than 300 of the 877 smiths, more than those of any other nativity group, were Irish. The hostlers and stablers were also predominantly Irish, although the stablekeepers, who needed capital, were not.

The same divergence prevailed in services to men as well as to beasts. Everywhere the waiters were Irish, while the skilled cooks were not. Barbers, also skilled workers, were traditionally Negroes, and the elegant and fashionable hairdressers and *coiffeurs* were Frenchmen or Italians. With these exceptions the Irish had the service occupations almost entirely to themselves.

In the truly skilled employments, however, their percentage was low indeed. Only in the building trades did they have any opportunity at all, and that because Boston, like most American cities, was passing through a construction boom. The wealthy merchants were building grand residences down Beacon Hill and on toward the newer

Back Bay. The middle classes, moving out to East and South Boston, were erecting hundreds of new dwellings. By their very presence even the Irish created a demand for more housing. They preëmpted the slums and the low rental sections of the city, pushing out the former inhabitants and stimulating the demand for new abodes. In 1843, more than 1,118 new structures were reared, and the annual number grew thereafter. As a result labor was in demand. The various building trades embraced some 5 per cent (775) of the total Irish working population. This compared unfavorably with the 11 per cent (1,594) of Massachusetts birth and with that of the other nativities. But it represented skilled employment for a significant section of the Irish community by which some actually acquired enough influence and capital to become contractors and construction bosses.

In the other skilled occupations and handicrafts, most of which had been well developed before 1845 and did not expand thereafter, the Irish were, in the main, unimportant. They numbered only twenty-eight of the total of 450 employees in the maritime industries, and made no headway in furniture building or cabinet making, where highly trained workmen were needed. Nor did they progress very far in the crafts dealing with precious metals or with the manufacture of musical instruments. Among the ordinary mechanics and machinists their proportion was smaller than any other group's, and relatively few became transport workers, truckmen, coachmen, or even sailors.

They were more poorly represented in the commercial occupations than in the handicrafts. Though many fancied the dignity and independence of the traders' status, few attained it. Among the Irish immigrants were some shopkeepers and merchants who had followed their customers to the New World. A handful of others had accumulated a modicum of capital and longed to join the large and prosperous group of retail distributors of all sorts who supplied the necessities of life to Boston and its hinterland. In most branches of retailing, however, they competed directly against the superior skill and resources of other groups and were doomed to failure from the start.

In some spheres immigrants had an advantage over their native competitors. Where they relied on the patronage of their compatriots they prospered. Food dealers—butchers, fruiterers, and, above all, grocers—dealt directly and intimately with immigrant women who preferred to purchase from those who spoke their own language, carried familiar foodstuffs, and served them as a friend, confidant, and adviser. Each national group, therefore, supported a comparatively large number of grocers and food dealers. With the exception of the Irish and Negroes, newcomers did not suffer by comparison with the native whites. Among the Irish, as among the Negroes, deficiencies of capital and skill weighed more heavily in the balance, and their percentage of such retailers was lower than in any other group.

For the humble immigrant the easiest ingress to commerce was through its least elegant form, peddling. Peddlers needed no permanent place of business. They required only a small capital investment and but passing acquaintance with trading methods. With their stock upon their backs they could move among their countrymen, deal with them on terms of confident familiarity, and earn a respectable livelihood. These inducements were attractive enough to draw approximately 2 per cent of the Irish, and even larger contingents from other groups into itinerant trading.

In other forms of minor retailing involving close personal contacts, each nativity group created a demand for the services of its own members. Inevitably, a circle of saloons, restaurants, boarding houses, and a few hotels catered to foreigners. Germans would never think of residing or dining where they might have difficulty in securing their lager. It comforted the Irish to hear the old country brogue and feel the security of being with their own kind. Like the McGinnis in Mrs. Dorsey's novel, most immigrants added to their income by keeping a few lodgers of their own nationality. To meet the needs of the unmarried, of sailors, and of those who had either not yet settled down in the city or were on their way west, every group—particularly the Irish and Germans—provided a large number of boarding houses. There were also German lunchrooms, restaurants, and *lagerbier* saloons, Irish bars and dance halls, and even some English coffee houses. From these enterprises many foreign-born saloonkeepers and bartenders earned their livings.

The abundance of boarding houses and saloons was encouraged by, and in turn caused, a paucity of hotels. Hotelkeeping was a substantial business managed and owned by Americans, and none of the foreign establishments in Boston ever gained as high a reputation as the Revere or Tremont House. There were, no doubt, a few Frenchmen and Italians who became prominent as purveyors of food in the genteel tradition of Continental cookery. Although a place always remained for the puddings and *bombes* of the *confiseurs,* even the high esteem in which that tradition was held and memories of the great Julien did not sustain Nicholas Ouvre, Gallieni, and the other *pensionaires* and *restaurateurs* very long. Only those supported by an adequate foreign clientele survived. By the forties the French and Italian places declined visibly. In 1846 Antoine Vigne gave up the Perkins House, a "tremendous establishment" in Pearl Street, and moved to New York where he opened the *Hotel de Paris* on Broadway. No Irish hotel existed in the city until Henry Dooley, a jovial host from the British American Provinces, took over the Merchants Exchange on State Street. Prospering from the favor of the Irish societies which met there, it remained the only important foreign public house in the city.

If the Irish progressed only slowly in the handicraft and retail trades, they made no impression at all on the financial occupations central to the city's commercial life. Merchants and bankers constituted the keystone of Boston's prosperity. Linked with them were the salesmen and agents, and at a yet lower level, the store clerks and bookkeepers, indispensable cogs in the functioning of the business machine. These classes, despite the differences among them, were all high in respectability and economic position. Theirs was the most favored place in Boston life. The foreigners such as the Frenchman, P. P. F. Degrand, and the Spanish Jew, Abraham Touro, who entered into these ranks, were conspicuous chiefly for their singularity.

Generally, the only opportunity for aliens to figure in commerce or finance grew out of the patronage of their own communities. Foreign ship agents frequently saved enough from the profitable business of remitting funds to Ireland to engage in banking operations for their compatriots. The Tri-Mountain Insurance Company was directed by and at the Irish, and the Germania Life and Germania Fire Insurance Companies, by and at the Germans. The New England Land Company united the prominent Irishman, Patrick Donahoe, with several well-known Bostonians (among them the Know-Nothing mayor, J. V. C. Smith), in a scheme to move the Irish to the west, and a number of other immigrant-controlled real estate agencies prospered. But the commercial community was overwhelmingly American. Almost 90 per cent of all the merchants—3.4 per cent of the total native working population—were native born. In no foreign group were the merchants proportionately or numerically significant. They ranged from .5 per cent of the group in the case of the Germans to 1.4 per cent in the case of the English. The Irish, as usual, lagged far behind, with only .1 per cent. In the lower categories the non-

American groups played as small a role. More than 86 per cent of the agents and 88.2 per cent of the clerks were Americans, while only 4.2 per cent and 3.6 per cent, respectively, were Irish.

The fact that Americans had somewhat recently entered the professions complicated the same basic pattern in that field. At one time Europeans had played a fairly prominent part in the city's professional life. In 1794 the number of qualified Americans was so limited that the builders of the Middlesex Canal advertised for a supervising engineer in French. By 1850, however, the native professionals outnumbered the foreign born in every field, though in all but the government services, where Americans always predominated, the non-Irish immigrants were proportionately as important. These classes amounted to between 3 and 5 per cent of the total of each nativity group, except the Irish, which had only .2 per cent.

In some spheres foreigners usually retained an advantage. They dominated the plastic arts and monopolized the dance, both as performers and teachers. Boston ladies insisted upon taking lessons from Mr. Williams of London, M. Duruissel of Paris or, most of all, from the glamorous Lorenzo Papanti of Leghorn. They liked to study foreign languages either with Frenchmen or Italians, particularly when combined with "tuition on the Piano Forte." There were many prominent foreign musicians. The Englishman Hayter and the German Zeuner, the Frenchman Du Lang and the redoubtable Irishman, Patrick Gilmore, established firm reputations. But the rank and file of professional musicians and music teachers were American-born, as were instructors in most other branches of education.

A small number of professionals served their own co-nationals. A few taught in evening and commercial schools, catering to the special needs of immigrants. All groups demanded priests familiar with their ways and using their own language. Likewise, they preferred lawyers of their own kind, friends they could understand and trust when it was necessary to cope with the law or the government. It comforted the Germans to learn that their doctor was a relative of the oculist to the King of Saxony, and the Irish to believe that their apothecary or physician had practiced for twenty-seven years in County Kerry.

The exceptional Irishman who found satisfactory employment failed to mitigate the abject circumstances of the group as a whole. With no adequate outlets in the handicrafts, in commerce, or in the professions, the rank and file remained totally or partially unemployed. In this respect they differed from every other element. Unabsorbed laborers in other groups were more than counterbalanced by their skilled co-nationals already integrated in the scheme of Boston life. Even the Negroes, who stood closest to the Irish in occupational experience, fared better than they. Emancipation before 1790 did not wipe away the stigmata and disabilities of slave status. It was always difficult to acquire education, skill, or capital, and the prejudices of the classes immediately above confined the Negroes to unpopular tasks. Yet, though their employments were not particularly desirable or well paid, they had specific functions. Negroes were acquainted with the by-ways of Boston's economic organization, and, as time went on, adapted themselves to it. They did not remain simple unskilled laborers to the same extent as the Irish. Despite the risk of being sold as slaves on long voyages, many became seamen; others were barbers, chimney sweeps, and traders. Some, like Robert Morris, a prominent lawyer, even rose to the professional ranks. By the time Walt Whitman visited Boston in 1860 the Negroes were better off there than elsewhere in the United States. While their position shone chiefly by comparison with less fortunate members of their race, it was clearly closer to that of the natives than the Irish. The latter unquestionably were lowest in the occupational hierarchy.

But unless it contained a reliable and constant productive element, no group could continue to subsist by employment in the service trades and by dealing with one another. As it was, the large body of casual, unskilled Irish labor created tremendous social problems and called for more adaptations than either the individual or his family could make for long. Though only a temporary escape was possible, the temptation to try it was great.

Paradoxically, the same immobility that rooted the Irish immigrants in Boston also drove them out to work in all parts of the United States. Surplus labor was an unthinkable anachronism in the body of American economic life. In so many places cheap labor was essential, yet lacking, that it was inevitable the Irish should be used for more productive purposes. In the west, in the south, and in Canada vitally important projects awaited the application of their brawn. From every part of the United States construction bosses in embankments and water projects, tunnels, canals, and railroads called on Boston for the cheap man-power they knew was always available there. Thus the city's role as labor reservoir assumed national proportions; often the Boston Irish newspapers, in single issues, printed advertisements for more than 2,000 men wanted in widely scattered places.

Sooner or later the immigrant in search of employment discovered the labor contractor in search of men. In the columns of their weekly newspapers they saw, or heard read to them, the incredible, tempting advertisements detailing the blandishments of good wages, fine food, and excellent lodgings. The attractions of steady employment were hard to resist. True, railroading meant living a riotous camp life and the absence for a year from women, family and friends, and from the ministrations of the priest. But these partings were not novel to Irish life, for many sons and daughters had already left the family to earn a living. Moreover, before coming to America, the men had been accustomed to this type of migration; each fall the spalpeens had left their plots on the "ould sod" and crossed the Irish Sea to work for English landlords. In Boston as in Ireland, the wives and children remained behind to shift as best they could, sometimes assisted with occasional remittances, often becoming a burden upon the community. In any case, within a year the laborers were back, usually no better off than before.

Unscrupulous exploitation was the theme of the construction camp; and dirt, disorder, and unremitting toil were its invariable accompaniments. Wages ranged from $1.00 to $1.25 a day, though skilled stone-layers and masons often got from $2.00 to $2.50. The more prudent contracted for board as part of their pay, or for their upkeep at a flat weekly rate. But most were victimized by rapacious sub-contractors who monopolized supplies in isolated construction camps and took back in exorbitant prices what they paid out in wages. The railroads themselves frequently resorted to equally dishonest practices. The Irish, after traveling several hundred miles, had no recourse when the company decided to pay less than it had advertised. Many roads, by deliberately asking for more men than they needed, built up large labor reserves with which to bludgeon down the wages of those already working for them. With reason enough, the *Boston Pilot* advised "all laborers who can get employment elsewhere to avoid the railroads . . . to . . . do anything . . . in preference to 'railroading.' " But the Irish were the guano of the American communications system. "Ferried over the Atlantic, and carted over America," despised and robbed, downtrodden and poor, they made the railroads grow.

Back in Boston, the quondam railroaders, like those who stayed behind, still faced the problem of securing permanent employment.

Some found openings of a sort as sweepers and janitors in the textile factories of neighboring cities. These were the most wearisome jobs in the mills, the least skilled and the lowest paid—the ones the native operatives would not take. Mill owners soon perceived the potentialities of this docile labor supply. The New England girls who had been working in the factories were independent, militant, and impermanent. "Amateur" rather than "professional" proletarians, they left abruptly when marriage set them free for their true careers. Their insistence upon decent working conditions proved burdensome and led to increasing costs, particularly after Sarah Bagley started the Lowell Female Labor Reform Association in 1845. With men available at rates lower than those paid to women, the manufacturers turned to the Irish to run their machines, raising them from the meaner chores to higher ranks, and eventually using them for all tasks. And, as immigrants invaded the textile field, it lost status; native girls became more reluctant to enter it. By 1865, male employees outnumbered females in woolens and were gaining on them in cottons. Foreign labor, for which Boston served as a convenient recruiting ground, manned both.

Almost as important as textiles was the shoe industry. Before 1850 it had been loosely organized on a handicraft household basis as a supplement to fishing and farming. When the first practical shoe machinery was invented, cheap labor in nearby Boston facilitated the transition to the factory system in towns like Quincy and Lynn. "Green hands," anxious to be exploited, replaced skilled artisans, enabling the "garret bosses" to reap tremendous profits and become large-scale manufacturers. Throughout the fifties and the Civil War the presence of a labor surplus in Boston stimulated infant industries and accelerated the process of industrialization in New England.

This transformation of New England followed the general shift from craftsmanship towards mechanization in all phases of American economy. Emphasizing cheapness and mass production rather than skill, it required an abundant supply of labor. Wherever this essential condition existed, the trend left its impact; without it the change could not be effected. The process was particularly significant in Boston where a consistent deficiency of labor had seriously hampered the growth of industry until the forties. Between 1837, when the first business census was taken, and 1845, the total number of employees in the city's major industries (all those which at any time between 1837 and 1865 employed 100 persons) probably did not increase at all. Few grew significantly, and many actually declined. The prospective manufacturer desiring a site for a new establishment, or the capitalist with an "abundance of money seeking an outlet," found little encouragement. And even those already established who wished to expand were inhibited by the apparently inflexible labor supply.

But in the two decades after 1845 the Irish energized all aspects of industrial development in Boston by holding out to investors magnificent opportunities for profits from cheap labor costs. The total of industrial employees doubled between 1845 and 1855, and again between 1855 and 1865. Between 1837 and 1865, the number of workers in the older industries rose from 9,930 to 33,011, and, in addition, 6,272 appeared in new ones. Meanwhile the stream of immigration through the early fifties replenished the supply of workers already drawn off into factories, and their presence guaranteed a continuance of low prices. Because it possessed this labor reserve after 1845 Boston could take advantage of every opportunity. Within little more than two decades it became the nation's fourth manufacturing city.

There was the ready-made clothing industry, for instance, which had grown appreciably in Boston since its inception by John Simmons in the early thirties. At first an adjunct to the trade in secondhand apparel, then a part of the ship store business which supplied "slops" to sailors on shore leave, it eventually turned to producing cheap garments for southern slaves, for western frontiersmen, and for California miners to whom considerations of style and fit meant little. Until the mid-century, however, Boston was at a disadvantage with New York. Her rival on the Hudson was as accessible to supplies and, as a greater seaport, catered to more sailors and enjoyed more intimate connections with both the south and the west. Wages were also lower in New York, at least to 1845, and the cost of labor was the most important as well as the most variable factor in production, since the industry always "tended to concentrate at the points of cheapest labor." As a result Boston remained behind, unable to compete on equal terms with New York.

Yet it was an exceedingly tempting industry promising high profits if only a way could be found of producing clothes good enough to command a wide market at a price lower than those made in New York. But cheap clothes depended upon cheap wages; and until 1845 the labor force consisted entirely of the ordinary journeyman tailors who worked primarily on custom clothes. The "ready-made" clothiers, unable to pay the same wages as the custom tailors, were compelled to produce only during the twenty-eight weeks or less each year when the journeymen were not busy at their usual work. On this basis the industry could never develop to significant proportions. No matter what degree of standardization the technical process of manufacturing reached, the absence of a cheap labor supply precluded conversion to factory methods. Machines alone could not create a factory system in Boston when only the 473 tailors employed in 1845 were available to man them.

The situation changed, however, with the influx after 1845 of thousands of Irishmen ready to work for any wages. The manufacturers fully realized how important these immigrants were; and on the occasion of a journeymen's strike in 1849 they pointed out to Mayor John P. Bigelow that they had no need of his services as arbitrator, for an abundance of other labor sources was available to them. Henceforth they expanded their business, firm in the assurance that profits would not be menaced by labor costs or strikes. Erstwhile peasants were unskilled, of course, and knew nothing of tailoring. But the simpler parts of the trade were not difficult to learn and it was profitable to press the raw immigrant into service at wages which no true tailor would consider. The invention of Howe's sewing machine in 1846 in Cambridge came just in time to facilitate the training of the Irish by mechanizing and simplifying the sewing operations. By 1850 the 473 tailors of 1845 had grown to 1,547, of whom more than a thousand were Irish. The Civil War brought rush orders for thousands of uniforms and capped the process of expansion. By 1865, these circumstances had produced a distinctive method of factory production known in the trade as the "Boston System." Achieving an ultimate exploitation of cheap hands, it combined machinery with an infinite division of labor "which completely eliminated the skilled tailor."

The factory failed to emerge during this period in New York primarily because of the absence of the labor surplus that made it possible in Boston. Instead, the pressure for cheaper costs led to the growth of the outside shop where the efforts of the entire family were utilized. As a result Boston manufacturers gained an advantage, for the factory system permitted them to reduce wages while producing more *per capita*. The average value of the goods turned out there by a single worker in 1860 was $1,137 as compared with $788 in New York. Moreover the New York employers paid from $8.00 to $10.00 a week for labor, and the Bostonians only from $4.50 to $5.50. These differentials more than offset New York's other advantages. On this basis George Simmons' "Oak Hall," employing 3,000 tailors, became a national institution by 1860, and the whole industry in Boston quadrupled the value of its products between that year and 1870. By then the city had become the center of the factory manufacture of ready-made clothing in the United States, a position it retained as long as cheap labor was available.

Precisely the same development revolutionized other industries. Because of the relative importance of transportation costs, Boston, like New York and Philadelphia, had early become a sugar refining center. In the first four decades of the nineteenth century sugar boiling was a highly skilled but small occupation, carried on in Boston largely by German artisans. Before 1845 the industry employed only about a hundred persons. In the forties, however, a series of mechanical inventions necessitated a complete change in plant and process. All over the country refineries, unable to make the adjustments, closed their doors. In Boston, those surviving put more money into expanded factories, and hired additional hands. The number of employees, many of them Irish, tripled between 1845 and 1855; and the industry grew rapidly after 1858 when the Adams Sugar Refinery built the country's second largest plant in the city. The manufacture of paper hangings experienced a similar transformation. When J. R. Bigelow entered the business in 1841, it was organized on an individual handicraft basis. By 1853 it became completely mechanized and Bigelow's factory itself employed 200 workers.

Many old industries forced out of business by high costs before 1850 resumed on the basis of cheap immigrant labor, and many which suffered no radical change expanded because the surplus of wage-earners was available. In 1848, Jonas Chickering boasted that he employed one hundred men in his piano manufactory; when his sons opened a new plant in 1853 they required 400. Meanwhile the Mason & Hamlin Organ Company opened a mammoth factory in the West End and the total number of workers in the industry rose from 368 in 1845 to 1,248 in 1855. A shortage of hands would have thwarted growth indefinitely.

The creation of new industries most clearly exemplified the importance of cheap labor. The expansion of Boston after 1845 was truly remarkable, particularly in the heavy industries where strong muscles counted most. Scores of new factories, drawing upon the services of hundreds of Irishmen, sprang up in East and South Boston. In 1837 only 776 persons were employed in casting furnaces, in copper and brass foundries, and in making machinery; by 1845 this number had grown to only 859. But in the next decade it almost tripled. By 1855, 2,412 persons worked in these industries and an additional 1,097 in new rolling mills, forges, and rail factories. In this decade, at least seven important iron works began operations in Boston. The Hinckley and Drury Locomotive Works, one of the earliest, expanded steadily after 1848 until it employed four hundred men regularly. Between 1846 and 1848, John Souther launched the Globe iron works, manufacturing locomotives, the first steam shovels, and dredging and sugar mill machinery, an enterprise which alone eventually employed four hundred laborers. In 1847, Harrison Loring built the City Point Iron Works to make engines, machinery, and iron ships. During the same year the Bay State Iron Company was founded in South Boston, and within the next few years, Hawes and Hersey, the Gray and Woods Machine Company, and Chubbuck and Sons established plants in Boston. Meanwhile the older Alger works broadened its own activities rapidly.

In 1845 Donald McKay moved his shipyards to East Boston where he started the most active works in the country. This marked the beginning of a resurgence of shipbuilding in the city. Only eighty-six persons worked in shipyards in 1837, and but fifty-five in 1845. But ten years later the number had increased to 922 and the business flourished thereafter. And this growth characterized all types of industry. Felton and Sons developed their distilleries in South Boston; and James J. Walworth brought his steam fitting and foundry shops from New York, setting up plants in Boston and Cambridge. In these years, too, the Boston Rubber Shoe Company, Robert Bishop and Company, and the Shales and May Furniture Company opened important factories in the city. Upon the discovery of oil and the development of kerosene, the Downer Kerosene Oil Company and the Jenney Manufacturing Company established prominent refineries in Boston. The invention of the sewing machine created an industry which employed 168 persons in 1855 and 245 in 1865. The manufacture of glass found a place in the city in the fifties when machinery made possible the employment of unskilled labor, while the shoe industry and the cognate tanning business drifted in from suburban regions in response to cheap labor costs founded on the presence of the Irish.

In the development of the new Boston the Irish woman was almost as important as the Irish man. When other forms of employment failed her, she turned to the ultimate expedient of women who needed money, sewing at home. The labor of women was used in the domestic manufacture of men's shirts, of women's dresses, and of millinery, where the "making" operations were simple enough to be carried on without supervision. Wages were abysmally low; by constant toil a good seamstress might earn as much as $3.00 a week, but most received as little as $1.50—just enough for a single woman to pay her rent. For this pittance hundreds of women toiled under miserable conditions through all hours of the day.

> Sewing at once with a double thread
> A shroud as well as a shirt.

Home sewing had always existed, but after 1845 an increasing number of women found it their only support. By 1856 more were seeking such work than could find it, though a single large firm such as Whiting Kehoe and Galouppe sent material out to more than 8,000 women in the city and through all parts of New England. Many German, English, and native women participated, but most were Irish.

To find employment outside the home was a refreshing release from such conditions. After 1846 occurred a gradual but emphatic shift by Irish women to the factory manufacture of women's garments. By 1860 there were at least ten large establishments in Boston, some of which employed as many as one hundred girls to produce cloaks, mantuas, and dresses. After 1850 the number of immigrant women in all types of industry increased steadily until by the time the war broke out they were prepared to step into whatever places men left vacant. In 1865 fully 24,101 women of native and foreign birth were employed in Boston as compared with 19,025 men. Apart from the 19,268 women workers in the clothing trade, there was a significant number in other occupations, many even in heavy industry. The majority of the workers were Irish who, like their men, were contributing an element of fluidity to Boston's economy.

Therein lay the significance of the Irish in the city's economic life. Before their arrival the rigid labor supply had made industrialization impossible. It was the vital function of the Irish to thaw out the rigidity of the system. Their labor achieved the transition from the earlier commercial to the later industrial organization of the city. Without it "the new and larger establishments could not have been operated." Capitalists readily admitted that they could not "obtain good interest for their money, were they deprived of this constant influx of foreign labour."

Those who benefited most from the transition were native Americans. Very few foreigners were manufacturers. English merchants, like Boott and Lodge, did invest in industrial enterprises, and some Irish and Germans figured prominently in fields where they could readily exploit the labor of their own countrymen. Thus, the Irish firms of Carney and Sleeper and of Mahony and Kenna, and the German, Leopold Morse, were among the leading clothing makers. Contrary to the rule, a few other businesses remained in the hands of the immigrants who founded them: John Donnelly, "city bill poster," who helped establish modern out-door advertising, William S. Pendleton, an Englishman who introduced lithography into the United States, and two highly skilled German silversmiths maintained their positions. But generally Americans gained control even of the piano industry, the manufacture of glass, brewing, and other industries established in Boston by alien newcomers.

Immigration advanced other classes in the community as well as the manufacturers. Since the Irish could not satisfy their own needs, others had to. Irishmen needed doctors and teachers; they consumed dry goods and food, thereby quickening the city's commercial life. The demand for professional and commercial services directly aided the merchants and clerks, the traders and artisans,—the bulk of the American population of the city. A rise in the prevailing occupational level of the native Bostonians resulted from the general decline in labor costs and the increased value of their own services.

The only Americans who suffered permanently from the Irish invasion were the unskilled laborers and domestics, few in number, who competed directly with the newcomers. More important, although they eventually adjusted to the new conditions on favorable terms, was the injury to the artisans displaced by the combination of machinery and cheap labor. They were a large group, eminently respectable, hitherto prosperous, and always influential in the community. Their protest against the use of green hands was one of the significant factors complicating the social orientation of the Irish in Boston.

But though the industrial workers as a class lost ground throughout the period, and though most of the individuals within that class suffered immediately by the transition, in the end they gained. The flexibility of the economic organization of the United States enabled the displaced artisans to set up as manufacturers, to enter other trades, or to move west. Edward Everett Hale pointed out:

> We are here, well organized, and well trained, masters of the soil. . . . It must be, that when they come in among us, they come to lift us up. As sure as water and oil each finds its level they will find theirs. So far as they are mere hand-workers they must sustain the head-workers, or those who have any element of intellectual ability. Their inferiority . . . compels them to go to the bottom ; and the consequence is that we are, all of us, the higher lifted because they are here. . . . If into the civilized community made up of hand-workers, and workers in higher grades, you pour in an infusion of a population competent at first only to the simplest hand-work, they take the lowest place, and lift the others into higher places. . . . Factory . . . and farm work comes into the hands of Irishmen. . . . Natives . . . are simply pushed up, into foremen . . . , superintendents . . . ,railway agents, machinists, inventors, teachers, artists, &c. . . .

And the experience of all other groups, even of the Negroes, was similar to that of the native whites. With the minor exceptions occasionally noted above, there was little to distinguish them occupationally. Only the Irish stood apart.

The lads who left Skibbereen and Mallow and Macroom where daily wages ranged from sixpence for common laborers to one shilling sixpence for carpenters, the spalpeens who fled from Cork and the west where cash was scarce, received higher pay in Boston. Of that there was no doubt. They came expecting better wages and got them. Those who once measured their income in terms of potatoes found dollars, no matter how few, a fair return indeed. But mercilessly linked to these fine dollars was the price system, a ruthless monster which devoured the fruits of Irishmen's labor before they could gather them. The "pratties" and milk were gone from their garden; the garden itself was gone; and there was no room for the pig in Dock Square. Faced for the first time with the necessity of purchasing their own food and clothing, the peasants found costs high beyond anything they could have conceived, and rising rapidly throughout this period. By contrast, the much more leisurely increase in wages counted for little. The British consul noted that in spite of the rise in wages "it may be doubted if more food and raiment can be purchased by the workman than previously." As a result, the Irish found the value of their labor low, often too low to support them and their families.

The conditions of work were as bad as its price was low. The laborers and their employers spoke a different language. Their work week in Ireland had not included Sundays, but in Boston they must toil the full seven days. Their day at home had not excluded time off to chat, to smoke, or just to rest; now they had to accept the rigid discipline of the factory or the contract boss. The leisurely independent peasant life was ended—replaced in a fifteen-hour working day by a feverish struggle for bread under the commands of an alien master.

But no matter—if only that struggle were consistently successful. It never was. From the day they landed, the immigrants competed for jobs that were fewer than men. Through all these years unemployment was endemic to the economic system. Even the Civil War brought no surcease; the condition of labor deteriorated steadily. The depression of the first year threw great masses of men out of work, particularly in industrial South Boston, where they starved in their hideous slums. Not until the war had drawn thousands of men into the army and stimulated new manufacturing developments did the demand for labor approximate the supply. By that time employers were making hurried efforts to attract new immigrants—new workers to restore the labor surplus.

Tossed in the swell of impersonal economic currents, the Irish remained but shabbily equipped to meet the multifarious problem imposed upon them by urban life. Rising prices, ruthless factory exploitation, and unemployment caused "the wreck and ruin that came upon the Irish race in the foreign land!" In the new society "one in a hundred may live and prosper, and stand to be looked at as a living monument of . . . prosperity, but ninety-nine in a hundred are lost, never to be heard of."

5

The River Cities: 1800-50

by PAUL KRAMER

*The sudden and rapid growth of cities in the Mississippi-Ohio
Valley from 1800 to 1850 is one of the milestones in the history
of the urbanization of the modern world.*

A phenomenon of American history is that parallel with the opening
of our frontier and the clearing of the wilderness, there grew up large
and prosperous cities never far removed either in time or place from the
Indian and the primeval forest.

The Treaty of Greenville of 1796 lifted the Indian menace from the
Ohio Valley. Thirty-five years later Cincinnati had 25,000 people and forty-
five years later 45,000. At the same time, New Orleans was twice as big,
and Pittsburgh and St. Louis were not far behind Cincinnati. These river
cities, in but a few years not only acquired size and evolved a history
of their own, but also attained a deep and rewarding urban experience,
which, when combined with the earlier American urban experience on
the Eastern Seaboard, afforded the country a depth of knowledge of
the urban man and his problems that was the equal of anything else in
the world. Admittedly Paris and London were bigger, but insofar as the
problems of provincial cities were concerned—and most cities were and
are provincial—there was little to be gained by looking toward Europe.
For this reason the early history of the American river cities, the story
of their times during their periods of greatest growth and relative importance, is significant. For what happened became part of the total
fabric of urban America and served as a guide and inspiration for the
railroad cities and the big cities that were yet to come.

Paul Kramer, the author of this essay, was born in Cincinnati, Ohio,
in 1914. Mr. Kramer received his AB degree from Princeton University
in 1935 and an MLitt degree from Cambridge University, England, in
1938 for his work in history under the late H. W. V. Temperley and
G. P. Gooch. He was one of the first to join Nelson Rockefeller's staff
when Rockefeller was appointed coordinator of commercial and cultural

relations between the American republics in 1940. In 1943 he joined the U.S. Navy as an intelligence officer and later worked for the newly formed Central Intelligence Agency, which he left in 1951 to become a partner in a New York Stock Exchange firm. He has also been an officer and director of a number of industrial corporations in Latin America, where he lived for several years.

His contributions to scholarly journals include the essay "Lord Acton and Latin America" published in the *Inter American Quarterly* in January, 1963, and "The International Geophysical Year" published in *Science and the Social Studies* in 1957. In 1967 G. P. Putnam's published Kramer's *The Last Manchu*. This book has also been published in Great Britain, France, and Spain. In 1968 Putnam's published his *Latin American Panorama,* an anthology of key writings by the major social and historical interpreters of Latin American culture which he edited with Robert E. McNicoll.

All the colonial cities of the United States were seaports. They were essentially commercial communities seeking wealth by foreign trade. All of them had a maritime orientation which was a genuine expression of their colonial careers. Across their wharves and up their streets moved the immigrants and goods necessary to populate the wilderness and sustain life in the new lands. Down their streets, into their warehouses, and across their wharves moved the agricultural surplus of the new lands to the consumer in Western Europe and the West Indies. It was the profits from these pursuits, plus the profits derived from the increase in land values and from local expenditures by government, that permitted their growth and embellishment.[1]

Curiously it was essentially this same process that was to be repeated by the river cities from 1800 to 1850, the difference being that the entire process was vastly speeded up so that, for example, whereas it took Philadelphia more than ninety years to grow from 0 to 50,000, it required Cincinnati only forty years to reach the same size.

But like the colonial cities, the six river cities—Pittsburgh, Cincinnati, Louisville, Memphis, St. Louis, and New Orleans—all were maritime in orientation, the distinction being that they had landings rather than piers and were freshwater rather than saltwater ports. The rivers on which they were located were economically only a sweetwater extension of an ocean-borne commerce. Their original trade was not with the nation to the East but, via New Orleans, with Europe and, to a lesser extent, Mexico. Later, of course, they acted

[1] Carl Bridenbaugh's *Cities in the Wilderness* and *Cities in Revolt* deal in detail with American urban life from 1625 to 1776.

POPULATION OF THE RIVER CITIES

	Cincinnati	Pittsburgh	Louisville	Memphis	St. Louis	New Orleans
1800	750	1,565	600		1,000	9,650
1810	2,540	4,768	1,350		1,400	17,141
1820	9,602	7,243	4,012	53	4,123	27,176
1830	24,831	21,412	10,306	663	6,694	46,310
1840	46,338	36,478	21,214	1,799	16,649	102,296
1850	115,438	67,871	43,277	8,841	74,439	120,951

as wholesalers and suppliers to the immediate hinterland from which they derived the agricultural surpluses which sustained them, just as the colonial cities had done.

It was the Treaty of Paris of 1763 that defined the terms from which the river cities were to have their origin. By eliminating the French, the Indian—and the Indian alone—became the sole enemy if the new lands to the West were to be colonized. As a first step, forts at strategic points were required for the red man's subjugation.

The military importance of the land at the confluence of the Monongahela and the Allegheny rivers had been fixed, of course, long before the Treaty of Paris. Pittsburgh began as a military base. Louisville, too, began as a military base. Although the founding of Cincinnati had its origins in a real estate venture, in its earliest years it served chiefly as Fort Washington, headquarters for armies fighting against the Indians. It was not until 1802 that it was incorporated and the soldiers were moved across the river to Newport. Although Memphis was originally created by land jobbers, one of whom, Andrew Jackson, was subsequently to become a U.S. President, its location on a bluff overlooking the Mississippi endowed it with a geostrategic location that was its original appeal. St. Louis and New Orleans were, of course, special cases, but St. Louis in the beginning, too, had essentially a strategic paramilitary orientation. After the Treaty of Paris the New Orleans fur traders—and New Orleans at the time was essentially a fur-trading community—needed a new post on the west bank of the Mississippi; all French claims on the east bank had been surrendered to the British, from which to administer and supply their fur trading. Several miles below the point where the Missouri River enters the Mississippi, a party of men sent out by the New Orleans traders found a limestone bluff which offered excellent possibilities, a place which, as the chief of the party said, "might become, hereafter, one of the finest cities in America." The following year, 1764, the construction of St. Louis began. The settlement did not grow rapidly until a much later date. Nevertheless, here in the middle of an almost unpopulated continent there were by 1800 about 1,000 people. St. Louis was an administrative headquarters for the governing authorities, as well as a key point in the widespread fur-trading business.[2]

[2] See Constance McLaughlin Green, *American Cities in the Growth of the Nation* (New York, Harper and Row, Harper Colophon Edition, 1965) for a historical summary of both St. Louis and New Orleans.

New Orleans from the beginning was both civil and military in outlook. Founded by the French in 1718, and a Spanish colony from 1763 to 1800, it was for almost eighty years the capital of the Louisiana Territory, and by the imperial design of its colonial administrators in Paris and Madrid, the city had in its midst impressive reminders of its civil as well as its military ties to Catholic and Latin Europe. A cathedral, an archiepiscopal palace, and a convent were built to remind its inhabitants that they were Catholic, and resident French and Spanish colonial governors maintained as much pomp as its climate and surrounding swamps would permit. Its Gallic population obtained a large share of its living from the fur trade and was as much guided in its social behavior by taboo as by law and convention. Slavery was highly institutionalized, but there was less hostility between the races than in the United States. The semi-savage white Anglo-Saxon Protestant frontiersmen who began to drift down the river into the city in the late 1700's were frowned upon and subject to rigorous supervision. "New Orleans had probably more of the flotsam and jetsam of two continents than any other city in North America." [3] It was also very unhealthy.

The economic key to the growth of the river cities during the period was derived from their terms of trade; later it was their terms in combination with their volume. In the earlier decades volume was never high. But by 1835 it had become appreciable so that New Orleans was then the leading export city of the nation; 1,372 steamboats were docking along its levee annually, carrying 401,500 tons of freight. Furthermore, these figures do not include the 4,000 flatboats on the Ohio, Mississippi, and Missouri rivers that were also floating freight downstream to New Orleans. By 1845 the value placed on Western produce was $220,000,000. Of this, one-third was exported, and New Orleans handled twice as much of this export as all the other seaports put together. In this way New Orleans became the third largest city in the nation. It became the funnel through which the river cities and river lands to the North poured their commerce.

And it must not be forgotten how profitable this commerce was.[4] In those days it was news of the big profits, rather than the volume, that attracted the settlers, who in turn created the booming land prices,

<hr/>

[3] *Ibid,* p. 67.
[4] Flatboat trips were profitable for the owners—often $2,000 a voyage. See Harriet Connor Brown, *Grandmother Brown's Hundred Years* (New York, Blue Ribbon Books, 1929).

news of which attracted more settlers. Land value appreciation was no less than fantastic. In 1802 a lot on Vine and Fourth Streets in Cincinnati, for example, was sold for $220. In 1839 the original owner repurchased a small portion of the lot for $150 per front foot. Lot 77 along the Cincinnati public landing cost originally $2 in the late 1790's. In 1841 it was valued at $237,500.[5] And these were not isolated instances of real estate appreciation. The truth is that there were countless examples of land appreciation that far exceed the increase in value of highly regarded growth stocks today.

In the great days of the river cities some commodities sold for much more than they do today, others for less, but the profit potential was higher. In 1840, wheat, for example, sold for well over $2 a bushel; it sells for about $1.20 today. Cotton was roughly 11 cents a pound; it is worth about 22 cents today. But the 11-cent cotton was grown and processed by slave labor. When wages were paid to people to produce and ship these goods, they were appreciably lower than today. Andrew Carnegie, for example, wrote that in Pittsburgh as a young man in 1850 he was paid $2 a week for his first job. Later his salary became $2.50 a week as a telegraph delivery boy, and he regarded this as magnificent.[6] George H. Devol, the famous Mississippi gambler, was paid $4 a month as a cabin boy aboard the *Wacoousta* in 1849; later this was raised to $7 aboard the *Walnut Hills*. Skilled labor was highly paid. Steamboat caulkers received $4 a day.[7] It is true, of course, that in those days it required many more men to produce a bushel of wheat or a bale of cotton or 100 pigs than it does today. Nevertheless, costs of production were apparently far lower than they are now. Furthermore, the soil from which the river cities then drew their produce was often virgin. Yields per acre were high, and blight was rare.

During the period 1800 to 1850 the Allegheny Mountains remained a major obstacle to the commercial junction of the river cities with the populous cities of the East.

As late as 1830, Mrs. Trollope,[8] for example, spent eight days

[5] Charles Cist, *Cincinnati in 1841: Early Annals* (Published for the author in Cincinnati, 1841), pp. 263–66.

[6] Andrew Carnegie, *Autobiography* (New York, Doubleday & Co., 1933), pp. 35–36.

[7] George H. Devol, *40 Years a Gambler on the Mississippi* (New York, Henry Holt & Co., 1926); p. 5.

[8] Frances Trollope, *Domestic Manners of the Americans*. This book, first published in England in 1832, became a best seller and made its author a celebrity. It remains even today one of the best travel books ever written,

reaching Baltimore from Cincinnati, and in 1850 it still took three days to travel from Pittsburgh to Philadelphia. Passengers went by canal to the foot of the Allegheny Mountains, then traveled 30 miles by rail to Hollidaysburg. They then took a canalboat again to Columbia, where they could transfer to a railroad for the final 81-mile leg of the journey.[9]

Pittsburgh remained essentially a river city until the Civil War. According to Andrew Carnegie, "the great event of the day" in 1850 "was the arrival and departure of the steam packet to and from Cincinnati [which] for daily communication had been established." [10]

The importance of the railroads during the period was recognized by the river cities, just as canals were, not primarily as devices for linking the Midwest and South with the East Coast but rather as a means of extending the viable economic surroundings of the cities into broader environs so that they could gather more local goods for processing and packing and shipping downriver to New Orleans and ultimately to Europe. An exception to this attitude was St. Louis, which from the beginning of the railroad era tended to think more in transcontinental terms, perhaps because it was from its earlier days a staging area for exploration of the West.

Many of the river cities actively engaged in railroad construction, and this took a form that reflected their local power structure. Before the Civil War a great problem in the economic development of the nation was lack of capital. Railroads, even local ones, were expensive to build, and their need for capital exceeded the ability of the local entrepreneur to raise on his own. But since most of the river cities were Whig-dominated and the Whig power structure was entrepreneurially inclined, solutions were found within this political combination.

All the river cities, with the exception of Pittsburgh and Memphis in its earlier days, because of their size and relative wealth vis-à-vis the states in which they were located, were far more powerful politically in relation to their state governments than they are today. It was not difficult in those times for the rich and powerful citizens to obtain from the state governments charters that permitted municipal investment in one form or other in privately owned railroads and

and was reprinted in 1949 by Alfred Knopf with a history of Mrs. Trollope's adventures in America by Donald Smalley.

  [9] Frank C. Harper, "Pittsburgh of Today," American Historical Society, 1931, Vol. II, pp. 667–668.

  [10] Andrew Carnegie, *op. cit.*, p. 39.

banks. And since the same group that obtained the charters also tended to control the city governments, it was not difficult to obtain municipal consent to these plans. 1800 to 1850, insofar as the river cities were concerned, was a time when what we now call the private sector combined its municipal power with its entrepreneurial power to use the borrowing and taxing power of the municipalities to promote its own investments.

Thus, for example, Memphis' municipal debt from 1847 to 1860 rose from $80,000 to more than $1,000,000. At the same time, this smallest of the river cities invested $500,000 in the Memphis and Charleston Railroad, $100,000 in the Memphis and Ohio, $250,000 in the Mississippi and Tennessee, and $350,000 in the Memphis and Little Rock. The city suffered a loss of $582,000 on these investments as a result of railroad insolvency, but nevertheless, Memphis' shipments of cotton rose from 75,000 bales in 1845 to 360,653 in 1860, and it was the local railroads, by making the steamer landing accessible to the fields where the cotton was grown, that made such a rise possible. The planked roads that were first built to permit Memphis to encompass economically the hinterland were never the success that the feeder railroads became. This was also a period when the Whigs achieved and retained power in Tennessee.[11]

In St. Louis it is a similar story. Here in 1848 the city won permission from the state legislature to invest in the Ohio and Mississippi Railroad even though its tracks were to be laid not in the state of Missouri but across the river in Illinois. Having achieved this, the city government then formed vigilance committees to win municipal approval for the investment in each of its wards. The issue was decided in favor of the loan. Subsequently a loan was made to what was to become the Missouri Pacific Railroad. St. Louis was always the most transportation-conscious of the river cities.

In the other river cities in the period this combination of the municipal sector with the private sector was also followed and was an expression of government activity that then enjoyed special favor among conservatives, rather than liberals.

The public health of the river cities was never good. In fact, it was appallingly bad and became progressively worse as one proceeded south to New Orleans. The period 1800 to 1850 was a time when

[11] Gerald Capers, *Biography of a River Town* (Chapel Hill, University of North Carolina Press, 1939), p. 113.

the mosquito's connection with yellow fever, dengue, and malaria was unknown.[12] Pittsburgh, being the farthest north of the river cities, with an abundance then of freshwater and with few mosquitoes, was the healthiest. But writers at the time did not really understand why this was the case and attributed its comparative good health to the fact that the city was "farthest removed from baneful exhalations of the swampy borders of the Mississippi" and because the "combustion annually of ten million bushels of bituminous coal fills the atmosphere with . . . impalpable dust of carbon . . . it is anti-miasmatic." [13] Many people believed alcohol was an efficacious safeguard against the "miasma," so that it was not infrequent for even substantial citizens of the river cities to ingest a tumbler of whiskey on arising in the morning to "ward off the ague."

The most common preventative from illness and death during epidemics, however, was flight either to the countryside, which was thought to be healthier than the city, or, if one could afford it, north by river packet.

Among the more prosperous citizens of the river cities this periodic flight north forged another unifying link. It was not an uncommon thing in those times for families in Louisville and Cincinnati and St. Louis to have a houseful of guests from Memphis and New Orleans, usually the wives and children of business associates and relatives from farther south. Friendships and romance flourished. A certain amount of intermarriage resulted which had the effect of linking even more the commerce and society of the river cities.

Within the framework of their ignorance, the river cities took a few positive steps on behalf of public health. These were primarily limited to the development of waterworks and the piping of freshwater along the principal streets. Essentially, however, this was done as a fire prevention measure, rather than for reasons of public health. Also, since there was no garbage collection in those days, hogs were used as scavengers, and residents were required to place their garbage in the middle of the streets, where it was more readily accessible for collection. Since most of the river cities copied Philadelphia in their general layout and were thus laid out in squares bisected by alleys, these too required sanitary measures, yet there is little evidence

[12] "Yellow Fever in Memphis in the 1870's," by Gerald C. Capers, reprinted in this anthology as Chapter 8, includes an accurate summary of health conditions in a river city.

[13] Quoted in Neville B. Craig, *The History of Pittsburgh* (Pittsburgh, J. R. Weldin Company, 1917), pp. 296–97.

that they received them. Mrs. Trollope in 1828 sneered at the filth that accumulated in Cincinnati's alleys.

The river cities built orphan asylums, usually with libraries and schools operated in connection with them and with provision for housing infants. There were also public hospitals, usually run in conjunction with the poorhouse and containing separate apartments for the insane. It is interesting to note that in the new river cities, despite the flood of German immigrants, the British Elizabethan concept of poor laws prevailed. There was, from the beginning and in face of the almost complete commercial orientation of the communities, an acceptance of the philosophy that the care of the poor was an obligation of government, at least insofar as whites were concerned.

But all this was only a beginning. What was accomplished was not enough to impair the basic belief that if one wished to raise a family to maturity, it was best to have many children since half of them would perish before reaching maturity. Nor was the condition of public health sufficiently good to destroy a sense of the impermanence of life. This, coupled with the enormously rapid growth of the river cities, impelled people toward the conviction that if one wished to "get ahead," acquire some land, and some money, it was best not to spend too much time on education and training, or the race would be over before it could be won. Besides, there was not nearly so much to learn as there is today. Periods of apprenticeship were short, and the professions did not require college degrees. One could graduate from Dr. Drake's medical school in Cincinnati in seven months after finishing high school, and a bricklayer or butcher or baker could acquire professional status in a few weeks. A successful baker on Main Street in Cincinnati in 1845 learned his trade a few years earlier from his wife while floating down the Ohio River on a flatboat from Pittsburgh. This, more than anything else, accounted for the lack of quality of workmanship about which Mrs. Trollope also complained so bitterly.

There was an enormous diversity in the religious life of the river cities, just as there was in the nation as a whole. The consequence of this was that although almost all the inhabitants of the river cities were Christian (out of a total population of 115,438 in Cincinnati in 1850, there were 3,346 Jews), Christianity itself did not serve as a unifying force. On the contrary, it was a divisive force politically, socially, and culturally.

It was never the case with the river cities, as it had been with many of the old New England villages and as was also the case with many rural villages in Ohio, Kentucky, Indiana, Illinois, and Tennessee, that the church was identified with the community and its congregation with all the people, regardless of class or race or national origin. Admittedly, of course, New Orleans and St. Louis, so long as they were French, had an established church that encompassed all classes, but during the period under discussion, 1800–50, the religious life of these communities was extraordinarily diverse and in no way theocratic. Even the Catholic Church was divided as to the national origin of its communicants upon the arrival of the German Catholic immigrants in the river cities.

Take Memphis, for example. Society in Memphis was divided into four readily identifiable parts by 1850. There was the top bourgeoisie, who for the most part were native American, largely of Southern origin; the Germans; the Irish; and the Negroes. In 1852 the German Catholics left the largely Irish St. Peter's Church to organize the Society of St. Bonifice, which in turn became St. Mary's German Catholic Church. Meanwhile, German Protestants organized the Evangelical Lutheran Trinity Church.[14]

Much the same thing was true of Cincinnati. Cincinnati, in the beginning, had an active Catholic Church, and the cathedral, which is still used, was completed in 1845. Architecturally it was an eighteenth-century British structure of striking beauty. By 1850 there were seventeen Catholic churches besides the cathedral in Cincinnati, six of which were described as "German congregations."

The Protestant sects were also divided, not only on lines of national origin but also on lines of race. Thus in Cincinnati, for example, there were seven Baptist churches, two of which were colored; fourteen Methodist churches, three of which were German. The Welsh Calvinistic Methodists had their own church. There were fourteen Methodist Episcopal churches, three of which were German, and four Disciples churches, one of which was German. There were also, of course, a variety of Presbyterian and Congregational churches.[15] The churches were also divided along class lines if only because much of the residential area of the city was class-oriented.

---

14 See Capers, *Biography of a River Town*, p. 111.
15 Charles Cist, *Cincinnati in 1851* (Cincinnati, Wm. H. Moore & Company, 1851), pp. 77–83.

The rich Whig bourgeoisie—bankers, steamboat, canal and railroad people, landholders, and entrepreneurs—tended to live along Fourth Street. Thus the Fourth Street churches were upper-class. The Germans settled on the far side of the canal so that the churches in that area were German, and since originally, the Germans were almost without exception artisans and laborers, their churches were oriented to class as well as to national origin. The Irish settled near the river, and there the churches were Catholic. The Jews were divided. Those who arrived in Cincinnati before 1848 and who, for the most part, had lived elsewhere in the United States before coming to Cincinnati tended to live in the eastern part of the city. They had their own synagogue. Those Jews who came in 1848 and 1849 settled on the west side of town and had their synagogue. They did, however, share a common burying ground.

As a result of the Northwest Ordinance of 1787, public education in Cincinnati flourished. By 1851, according to Cist,[16] there were nineteen public schools with 138 teachers supported roughly half by a grant from the State of Ohio from the proceeds of the sale of state lands and half by city tax. These schools had about 40 children to a classroom. The first free schools were established in 1830 and 1831. An interesting feature of them was that they held night classes for working people who had not previously been educated. There were 12,240 white children in the public school system and 1,069 colored children in the segregated colored schools. In all schools the Bible was read daily without note or comment. Even by 1850 there was a highly developed system of thirteen parochial schools with 4,944 children in attendance. To complete the educational picture, Cincinnati had fifty private schools, three colleges, one law school, four medical colleges, five mercantile colleges, and five theological schools.

The distinction, however, between high school and college was not as clearly defined in those days as it is today. Most of the so-called colleges were in fact high schools, and Woodward College was later to become a public high school. Endowed at an early date, it held free night classes for employed men in mathematics, the skilled trades, bookkeeping, etc.

Cincinnati was the leader among the river cities culturally, and many Cincinnati-trained preachers, doctors, etc. moved on to other

16 *Ibid.*, p. 57.

river communities to pursue their careers. Despite the common belief that developed in the 1880's and 1890's that this was due to the German influence, the facts indicate otherwise, since the city's cultural orientation, with the exception of the field of music, preceded the arrival of the Germans and had a distinct nativist American characteristic. Culture seemed to survive in the community despite the overriding mercantile preoccupation of its inhabitants.

The upper classes of the river cities read Voltaire and especially appreciated the lives of Franklin and Washington. Later, of course, Dickens and Scott enjoyed enormous popularity. Hastily written biographies of Presidential candidates were widely read. Since the politics—not the economy—of the time was the only real organized binding force that held the river cities to the East, there was a passionate interest in the details of the lives of national politicians. An "immense exhalation of periodical trash" was also widely read, according to Mrs. Trollope. Bryant ranked high as a poet, and both William Ellery Channing and the posthumous works of Jefferson were widely read.

From the standpoint of the philosophical development of the river cities—Pittsburgh, Cincinnati, Louisville, and St. Louis—Alexander von Humboldt is perhaps most important. All educated people knew of his travels and his meeting with Jefferson and Madison. Humboldt's passion for collecting flora and rocks served as an impetus for similar conduct in the river cities. There was a passion in those days for classifying plants and rocks and not only displaying natural curiosities but also walking about and examining them in their natural surroundings. But more important was Humboldt's argument that nature determined the patterns of development of society and his claim that the peoples of the world would move along an isothermal zone where yearly temperatures were most favorable for civilization.

As Glaab and Brown have pointed out, these theories were popularized in nineteenth-century America by William Gilpin (1813–94) and Jesop Scott (1799–1873) [17] who interpreted Humboldt's geographical determinism to mean that "the great Basin of the Mississippi" would become "the ampitheatre of the world." But there is much evidence to support the view that the bourgeois elite of the river cities knew their Humboldt even before Gilpin and Scott popularized him. We know from diaries and secondhand bookstores that copies of

[17] Charles N. Glaab and A. Theodore Brown, *A History of Urban America* (New York, The Macmillan Co., 1967), pp. 75–81.

[18] Helmut de Terra, *Humboldt* (New York, Alfred A. Knopf, 1955), p. 377.

Humboldt's works were on library shelves. Between 1804 and 1856 Humboldt was granted honorary membership in nine United States learned societies; three counties, seven towns, one mountain, and one bay were named after him.[18] Also, both Dr. Drake and Cist of Cincinnati, in their books designed to boost Cincinnati, reflect the determinism of Humboldt by including data on climate and geography to prove that a great city had to grow up on the Ohio river opposite the mouth of the Licking River. Other writers did the same for Louisville with respect to the Falls of the Ohio, and Pittsburgh's location at the junction of the Monongahela and Allegheny rivers, and St. Louis vis-à-vis the confluence of the Missouri and the Mississippi.

In the Presidential election of 1824 there were five candidates—John Quincy Adams, Clay, Calhoun, Crawford, and Jackson. None received a majority of the electoral vote, and the choice went to the House of Representatives, which finally selected Adams. The confusion over this election and other factors stimulated the development of highly organized national political parties. The followers of Adams and Clay organized the National Republicans, later called Whigs, and the followers of Jackson gave a new character to the Democratic Party. Very broadly speaking, the Whigs were conservative and the Democrats liberal, and these two conflicting political philosophies of government, as a result of the development of the two parties on a national basis, reached down through the river cities into their wards to divide opinion and create class consciousness. In addition, there were residents of the river cities who eschewed allegiance to the two national parties and preferred negativist political groups. The period 1800 to 1850 saw the rise of the Know-Nothing or Native American Party, which was based on hostility to the Irish and German immigrants who were pouring into the river cities in such great numbers. The Know-Nothings became strong enough to elect mayors in various of the river cities. Also Free-Soil feeling toward the end of the period became strong enough to become a political factor on the local level.

But despite the passions and the violence generated by the prevailing political philosophies of the time, the intense commercial preoccupation of the river city man, the commitment to personal enrichment, and the acceptance of geographic determinism acted as a brake on the divisive aspect of river city politics. There was a prevailing feeling in the river cities that political passions, if they should become

too intense, were bad for business and could well delay the time when
the cities were to become the center of America, if not the world.
There was the feeling that the thing to do was forget the Irish, the
German, the Negro, the rich, the poor, the Mexican War, etc. and
get on with the production and distribution of goods and the development and embellishment of the river cities. If despite this attitude,
issues became too obtrusive, there was always the ultimate solution—
compromise.

Although the humanitarian enlightenment of the eighteenth century
had done much for the welfare of the urbanites of the American
Eastern Seaboard cities, the same cannot be said of the urban Negro
of the river cities of the first half of the nineteenth century. In four
of the six river cities he was, of course, enslaved,[19] and the nature of
this slavery was such that there was no real body of laws or legal
code that endowed the Negro slave with rights and duties of his own.
In the South, both urban and rural, the Negro was chattel with the
historical consequence that no real recorded history evolved to the
extent that would have been the case had the law courts played an
active role in the administration of the institution.

In Cincinnati, however, this was not the case. The Cincinnati Negro
did evolve a history of his own which, to some extent has been recorded. Here there are records and archives with which to work,
and this is of great importance to the urban historian. For the Cincinnati black man was never a slave, and Cincinnati soon became,
in the period under discussion, the largest inland city in America.
Patterns of living and occupation and family relationships, as well as
a relationship to a white society, were being established. It was thus
in Cincinnati, if only because it occurred first insofar as the history
of the nonslave American West is concerned, that a fabric of urbanization in a free society of blacks and whites not only was established,
but has persisted to this day. The urbanization of the American
Negro that occurred later in the railroad cities and subsequently in
the big cities seems to have followed the "norms" first established in
Cincinnati.[20]

[19] Slavery in the Southern river cities is described by Richard C. Wade in
his book *Slavery in the Cities* (New York, Oxford University Press, 1964).
A chapter from this authoritative work is included in this anthology, and
hence this subject is not treated here.

[20] The story of the urbanization of the Cincinnati black man is of importance historically, and it is a comment on the shallowness of our national

Negro students of the black scene in Cincinnati have divided its early black history into three distinct periods: 1800 to 1826, which was a period of toleration; 1826 to 1841, a period of persecution; and 1841 to 1861, a period of amelioration.[21]

Through 1850 there were never many Negroes in Cincinnati. In 1819 there were 410 when the total population was 9,602. In 1826 there were 690 when the total population was roughly 18,000. In 1840 there were 2,255 out of a total population of 46,338, and in 1850, 3,237 out of a total of 115,538. In other words the black population ran roughly 3 to 5 percent of the total.

The basic circumstances of Negro residence in Cincinnati were derived from the State of Ohio's black laws of 1804 and 1807, the first of which provided that all Negro residents of the state be able to prove their freedom and the second of which provided that no Negro could settle in Ohio unless he could give a $500 bond to guarantee his good behavior and his ability to support himself.

Although these two laws were never really enforced, their existence on the statute books of the state gave Cincinnati's Negro population an insecure basis for functioning in a capitalist society. Furthermore, they also provided the anti-Negro with a legal channel and framework within which to operate. Always the cry of the anti-Negro during periods of rioting was "enforce the black laws."

But regardless, Negroes slowly gathered in Cincinnati, became urbanized, earned a living there, and reared families. From the beginning segregation developed in living quarters, and a distinct Negro section of the city, called Bucktown, developed, east of Sixth and Broadway. This section was visited by Lafcadio Hearn in 1874. But the pattern of segregated life evolved long before Hearn's visits in regard to both Bucktown itself and the area where the more prosperous Negroes lived on the top of the hill west of Bucktown.

Bucktown was a collection of shacks on a hillside that also served as a fill. Thus, as the years passed, the shacks and shanties in which its inhabitants lived tended to descend below the surface so that by the time of Hearn's visits from 1874 to 1877 he speaks of descending

historiography (white as well as black) that our knowledge of this process in Cincinnati is so limited. Here is indeed a subject for genuine and original historical research in depth from which many might profit.

[21] See by Wendell P. Dabney *Cincinnati Colored Citizens* (Dabney Publishing Company, 1926).

down into its front doors.[22] But even in the 1850's it was still on the surface. The better Negro quarter on top of the hill enjoyed good living conditions, apparently infinitely superior to the tenements housing the German immigrants after 1848 who were considered to be the worst housed of any urban people in the United States at the time. There were Negro churches, Negro schools, Negro entrepreneurs.

A curious feature of Negro life in Cincinnati at the time was The Dumas, which was a sort of colored hotel consisting of two large eighteenth-century-type substantial row houses run together and well known in all the river cities at the time. The Dumas had both a large dining room and a ballroom. Big poker and faro games were held there, and essentially the establishment seems to have been a center of expensive vice for whites operated and staffed by blacks. It was, for example, at The Dumas that white travelers housed their black traveling companions while visiting the city, rather than at the Burnet House, built in 1849 and regarded by many as the finest hotel in America at the time.

This catering to the vices of the white man by the blacks of the period seems to have been one of the characteristics of the time and transcended both class and economic considerations, and it was a genuine source of income for both the black man and the black woman and persisted both in Bucktown and in the better Negro quarter. Certainly by 1840 in Cincinnati, the white man in search of drugs, illicit sex, and gambling turned to the Negro, and furthermore, this was not accomplished on a completely segregated basis. All observers of the time noted the fact that white women were to be found living with Negro men in the Negro sections of Cincinnati.

To some extent the history of the Negro in Cincinnati in the period is one of his class evolution. In the beginning, during what is known as the period of toleration, there was the greatest difficulty finding employment except at the most humble occupations, and since wages for all unskilled labor, as distinguished from skilled labor, were so low at the time, capital accumulation was out of the question.

In 1829 there were severe race riots in Cincinnati. For three days Negroes were insulted, attacked in their houses, and even killed. Afterward some 1,200 are said to have left. Existing research does not make it wholly clear who instigated the riots either directly or indirectly. However, the Irish citizens of the city seem to have parti-

---

[22] Lafcadio Hearn, *Children of the Levee*, O. W. Frost and John Ball, ed. (Lexington, University of Kentucky Press, 1957), pp. 32–48.

cipated in great numbers, and the excuse for the riots was, of course, that the black laws were not being enforced so that through this argument the mob acquired an "extra legal" status.

Two things happened after these disturbances that ameliorated the condition of the black community. Certain whites came forward as defenders of the Negro and his position in the community. Some of the wealthy older landholding families found the hostility of the white Irish lower classes and the newer middle classes wholly repugnant and sought to identify anti-Negro hostility with lower and middle-class ignorance and depravity as distinguished from upper-class tolerance.

The development of steamboat passenger travel also contributed to the amelioration of the condition of the blacks. For the steamboat gave employment to the Negro as a servant to the traveling public at wages that were sufficiently high (if tips were included) so that for the first time a Negro interested in capital accumulation could save money with which to go into business, invest in land, or provide children with an education. And this led to Negro class stratification, for the Negro who worked as a roustabout on the levee or the lower decks of the steamboat formed the lower class of Negro society. Illiterate and of great physical strength because of the nature of his work, he lived in Bucktown or near the waterfront. The better educated Negro whose real wages were far higher served the traveling public on the upper decks. He lived on the top of the hill, contributed to the churches, sent his children to school, had middle-class aspirations and in some cases achieved a genuine middle-class status. By the 1850's there were several prosperous Negro business establishments in Cincinnati. Knight and Bell were contractors, A. V. Thompson became a well-known tailor, Henry Boyd patented a corded bed and had eighteen to twenty-five white and Negro employees, and Samuel T. Wilcox became a successful grocer worth $59,000 in 1859.

All this was accomplished despite a second race riot in August, 1841. A feature of this riot was that the Negroes fought back to defend their homes. It started with a quarrel between some Irishmen and Negroes and lasted at least three days. Martial law was declared, and an undetermined number of Negroes were killed and at least twenty to thirty wounded. The mayor of the city personally intervened in an effort to stop the rioting; he persuaded several hundred Negroes voluntarily to go to jail as a means of quieting the white rioters and guaranteed protection of their property during their absence. The blacks consented, but many of their homes were looted and burned anyway.

Again some of the aristocratic white families sought to set an example of toleration and, by doing so, also sought to make public demonstrations of their contempt for the lower- and middle-class whites who they regarded as perpetrators of the disturbances. Nicholas Longworth, following the riots, for example, came forward and established a Negro orphan asylum. Other prominent wealthy white families did similar things. Theodore Weld, the radical Lane Seminary student leader, carried on with his welfare work and poverty and self-help programs and "resurrection" ideals. In some ways he was the country's first radical student integrationist leader. From this time on to the Civil War there appears to have been a steady amelioration in the condition of the black man in Cincinnati. There developed a genuine awareness on the part of the whites of the absurdity of the black laws, and the Negro himself, having found for the first time an economic occupation that could contribute toward capital accumulation, developed realizable goals within the framework of the existing capitalistic society.[23]

By 1850 none of the river cities had homogenous populations. There were whites and there were blacks; and there were native-born American Protestants and native-born American Catholics. There were also foreign-born Irish and foreign-born Germans. In all this fusing of nationalities, religions, and races, New Orleans and St. Louis formed a special variant. Here the original settlers and landholders were not Anglo-Saxon Protestants but French Catholic, so that the early part of the period is to some extent the story of the subversion of French Catholic political and economic power by white Anglo-Saxon Protestant power.

By 1818 the population of St. Louis was estimated as two-thirds French and one-third American, although the principal language of the town was still French. By 1829 the first Presbyterian Church had been built, and in the city's first election, in 1823, William Carr Lane, the American candidate, defeated Auguste Chouteau, the

---

[23] The black laws were repealed by the government of Ohio in 1849. Some historians claim that this was a result of a tie in the Ohio legislature between the Whigs and the Democrats, with a handful of Free-Soilers holding the balance of power. The Free-Soilers agreed to vote with the Democrats and permit them to organize the legislature and receive the state jobs in exchange for a repeal of the black laws, the establishment of free schools for black children, and the election of Salmon P. Chase to the U.S. Senate.

French candidate. American-French rivalry continued until 1827 and took the form of a commercial struggle between the Astor fur interests (American) and the French fur interests, which the Chouteaus represented. This, too, was resolved in favor of the Americans in 1827, when Pierre Chouteau, Jr., joined his fur interests with the American Fur Company (Astor), so that one may conveniently take this date, 1827, as the year when the original French Catholic majority clearly became a minority in a white Anglo-Saxon Protestant oriented community.

The story of New Orleans is a similar one, although, of course, on a far larger scale. Here the American "immigrants" had great difficulty buying land and, because of this, were forced to develop their own separate "city" above Canal Street from the French Quarter. But even after this, French-American rivalry continued over city improvements. The Americans claimed that the French spent all the municipal revenues on their part of the city. In 1835 the state gave the city a new charter that divided it into three separate municipalities. This permitted the Americans to develop their part of the city without French obstructionism. Soon thereafter the Americans were almost entirely out of the French Quarter which became a commercial backwater.[24]

But all this is only one aspect of the ever-changing fabric of the river cities. Irish minorities and later German minorities also appeared, the Germans before 1848, not after, as is commonly supposed. The first German immigrants to arrive in St. Louis, for example, appeared in 1834 in the form of 500 members of the Giessen Society. Part of the group came via New Orleans, the other part via Baltimore. Cist's census figures on Cincinnati indicate that as early as 1840 the German minority there was 28 percent of the total population.

Minority problems even in those days were to some extent the warp and woof of municipal politics. Some leaders emerged who hated foreigners; others befriended them. And the Know-Nothing Party (Native American), as we know, was active in the period from 1846 to 1860. Thus, in St. Louis, no sooner was the political and economic struggle between the French and the native Americans won by the latter than a new struggle developed between the Know-Nothings and the anti-Know-Nothings. In 1874 St. Louis had a Know-Nothing mayor, Peter G. Camden, who was defeated for reelection in a three-

[24] Rita Katherine Carey, "Samuel Jarvis Peters," *Louisiana Historical Quarterly*, Vol. 30, No. 2 (April, 1947), pp. 455–68.

cornered race by Bryan Mullanphy, an independent, who soon
emerged as a public figure deeply committed to and personally involved in the problems of the immigrant, whose cause he publicly
espoused. Rich, well educated in France and England, charitable, Mullanphy was mayor at a time of heavy Irish immigration. The immigrant came to St. Louis upriver by boat from New Orleans. These
packets were charnel houses of disease, primarily typhus. Mayor
Mullanphy had hospitals built to receive the immigrants on an island
in the river and personally saw that they were fed and cared for and
that priests were present to deliver last rites.

On August 6, 1855, the Know-Nothings precipitated a bloody riot
in Louisville which had the effect of curtailing immigration there.[25]

We have noted how in Cincinnati Nicholas Longworth sought to
ameliorate the condition of the black man while publicly demonstrating his contempt for Irish anti-Negro hostility. And while Lane Seminary involved itself in the debate between the abolitionists and the
colonizationists, Calvin Stowe and Lane students identified themselves
with the Cincinnati black man to the extent of, in fact, advocating
what today we would call integration and resurrection.

All the river cities developed distinct foreign and Negro quarters.
Of these perhaps Cincinnati's Bucktown and Over the Rhine German
section became the most famous. But the other cities had them, too.
Furthermore, river city employment also became stratified in regard
to nationality and race to the extent that there was a sort of occupational segregation. Thus, in St. Louis, the fur business was largely
in French hands. In Cincinnati pork packing was German, steamboat
serving Negro. And in Louisville the tobacco and bourbon business
was in native American hands.

The truth is that a segregated pattern of housing, occupation, and
religion developed in the river cities in their period of greatest growth
and relative economic power that preceded similar patterns on the
East Coast during their period of greatest immigration at the turn of
the century. The melting pot stopped melting at its inception in the
United States so that virtually from the beginning in the river cities
a majority represented a coalition of minorities. It is also true that
in a later period of river city history these communities went from
having one of the highest foreign-born populations of American cities
to one of the lowest. And it also seems true that the German immi-

25 *Louisville.* American Guide Series. Sponsored by the University of Kentucky (New York, M. Barrows & Co., 1940), pp. 29–30.

grant of the 1830's and 1840's has been the most completely absorbed into the American power structure. But the truth is that this period of absorption, like that of the British royal family, took about 100 years and two wars against Germany.

The sudden and rapid growth of cities in the Mississippi-Ohio Valley from 1800 to 1850 is one of the milestones in the history of the urbanization of the modern world. Although urbanization was proceeding apace on the Eastern Seaboard and although at the same time the overall population of the United States was rural, rather than urban, the river cities grew and prospered in the face of appalling health conditions and poverty among segments of their population and despite slavery, race riots, and violence. Furthermore, they demonstrated that the European rural immigrant was to be attracted to United States urban as well as rural life and that the process of urbanization itself was to create an important part of the nation's capital accumulation that in a later period could be employed in industrializing the new nation.

Economically, the river cities of the period were never really tied to the East; their commercial orientation was with Europe. That part of the Midwestern economy of the time that was not a subsistence one—and a great part of the rural economy was little more— was a commercial one involved in the growing, processing, and shipping of surplus agricultural products to the newly urbanized European countries. The gathering and processing of this produce was the *raison d'être* of the river cities.

Yet, despite this, there was never a question of the subversion of the area, of the detachment from the original country to the East and the formation, as Aaron Burr had dreamed, of a new nation. Despite a European-oriented economy, there were counteracting binding forces that were imprinted on the new Midwestern urban man. A significant factor in this process was the national political parties. Passions over the direction the new nation should take contributed to the growth in depth of the national political parties, so that they reached down into the river cities to embrace every precinct and ward. Other than the political parties, there was little else of an organizational nature that bound the population of the river cities to the majority of the population east of the Alleghenies.

Government, in those days, was so small that its physical presence was not felt as it is today. One could go through life and never meet

a federal government employee or a worker laboring on a government contract or subcontract. The standing Army was small; the
Navy, after the War of 1812, minute. Also, there were no national
associations like Chambers of Commerce or Rotaries or Lions. And
there were no national corporations, the products of which were
nationally advertised and reached into every nook and cranny of the
land. There were virtually no national periodicals. There were only
national political parties designed to elect a President and provide
him with a majority in the Congress. As a national force they were
thus of far more relative importance than they are today.

There were, of course, other factors that bound the river cities to
the nation despite the nonnational character of their economies. A
common history and culture did create in the river cities a feeling
of nationalism that transcended race and religion and disparate
national origins. In each of the river cities the Fourth of July was
the greatest of holidays and created a great stir. Furthermore, its celebration in those days was essentially egalitarian in tone. Also, General
Washington's birthday was celebrated with far more éclat than it is
today, although this holiday had more of a middle- and upper-class
tone and was accompanied by festivities of a different nature, including what we would call, today, debutante balls and jet-set partying.
In addition, the visit to the river cities of national figures such as
Andrew Jackson (the Democrat) and William H. Harrison (the Whig)
created enthusiasm and patriotic hubbub. Men like these became
national symbols that to some extent transcended partisanship, constitutional defects, and economic ties with Europe. Manifestations of
nationalism bound the river cities to a national whole despite the
fact that Philadelphia might be in fact, if not in mileage, more remote
than London or Hamburg.

Then, too, there was something else in those days for the citizen
of the river city that we do not have today that was a supreme
binding force. From the social standpoint it can in a way be regarded
as an equivalent of our national Social Security system or various of
our federal welfare programs—and this was the land vested in the
federal and state governments. Every citizen of the river cities in those
days knew that there was opportunity elsewhere in the new lands.
If he were rich, he could combine with others to organize a land
company. And if he were poor and things weren't going well in
Pittsburgh or Cincinnati or Louisville, he could move somewhere
else and start all over again and, without too much money, acquire

title to land. The assets of government were in truth enormous, and the river city citizen knew this and was not inclined to forgo his right of ownership in such a glorious heritage that was without parallel elsewhere in the world.

But this was a sort of insurance policy in the mind of the river city man. He was not inclined to move elsewhere. His community was too prosperous.

Later, of course, the river cities went into a relative decline, insofar as the nation as a whole was concerned. After 1850, slavery was to divide the nation and the river cities to the extent of civil war. And this war in turn was to afford the country a vivid demonstration on a national scale of the singular importance of a railroad network—the extension of which was to cause the eclipse in relative importance of the river city.

But meanwhile, the river city had already made a significant contribution toward the urbanization of the nation. It had already dealt with problems of the economic, religious, racially oriented, native American and immigrant man both as an individual and as a member of a group. It had already experimented with a wide variety of urban problems and sought solutions both on a municipal basis and on a joint public and private sector basis. It had demonstrated to the world —and this was of supreme importance in the attraction of new immigrants to the nation—that parallel with the wilderness and but a few steps removed from the Indian and the forest primeval, it was possible not only to be urban, but also to be an enormously prosperous and successful urbanite. The existence of urban America did not require, as had been and was the case with Europe, a surrounding countryside that was pacified and had enjoyed centuries of prior cultivation.

The truth was that by 1850 the urban experience of the United States was so rich and so varied that there was no real need to turn to Europe for guidance and example. And later there was an instinctive feeling among the American urbanites that the European Socialist of the 1890's and early 1900's who claimed for himself an urban expertise was in fact a Johnny-come-lately. It was felt that his experience of the urban scene was limited when compared with that of the native American. And to an extent this was indeed the case. For the American experience by 1850 was enormously varied and diverse and unique to the point that there was really not a great deal in the form of inspiration, experimentation, or genuine constructive advice that Europe had to offer.

6

The Transformation
of Slavery in the Cities

by RICHARD C. WADE

Thus, even before slavery had been abolished, a system of segregation had grown up in the cities. . . . [The] whites thought some such arrangement was necessary if they were to sustain their traditional supremacy over the Negroes.

U.S. census figures before 1860 indicate a continuing decline in the importance of urban slaves. From 1820 to 1860 they dropped from 22 per cent to 10 per cent of the total population of Southern cities. The institution, as a viable factor in urban life, fell into disarray. One reason for this was the exposure of the urban Negro slave to the point of view and way of life of the free urban Negro and the urban white man. Slavery once cut off from the prevailing gloom of Southern plantation life simply does not seem to have been able to function with any degree of efficiency despite rather stringent regulations to enforce segregation. This last factor is important in the history of American urbanization. Especially in the last few years there has developed a school of thought in the United States that claims segregation was a post-Civil War urban development. But this is not true. It developed in the South long before the Civil War and was applied to free blacks, as well as to urban slaves, as a means of controlling them.

Richard C. Wade, the author of this selection, is an authority on the history of American urban life. A professor of history at the University of Chicago since 1962, he published *The Urban Frontier* in 1959 and *Slavery in the Cities: The South 1820–1860* (from which this selection has been taken) in 1964. Dr. Wade served as the principal consultant on the historical roots of urban unrest to the Kerner Commission in 1967–68. Born in Des Moines, Iowa, in 1922, he was graduated from the

University of Rochester in 1944 and received his PhD in 1954 from Harvard, where he was a leading student of the late Arthur Meier Schlesinger.

The following selection is Chapter 9 from *Slavery in the Cities: The South 1820–1860,* by Richard C. Wade. Copyright © 1964 by Oxford University Press Inc., it is reprinted by permission.

By 1860 the institution of slavery was in great disarray in every Southern city. The number of Negroes had declined precipitously. Discipline over those remaining proved difficult to sustain. The network of restraint so essential to bondage no longer seemed to control the blacks nor wholly govern the whites. The distance between the races as well as separation of free colored from slave could not be maintained in the kinetic world of the city. In the most dynamic towns the whites overwhelmed the Negro population; even places with a larger proportion of slaves and less impressive growth tended to slough off at least their male blacks. In any case an institution which had been an integral part of urban life in Dixie in 1820 was languishing everywhere in 1860.

The census figures outlined the story. Though the number of slaves rose throughout the South, the proportion living in cities declined. In addition, the Negroes lost their earlier share of the urban population. In 1820, 37 per cent of all town dwellers were blacks; by 1860 that portion had dropped below 17 per cent. Urban slaves fell from 22 per cent to 10. The most dramatic shifts came, of course, in the border area, but everywhere the same pattern appeared. The New Orleans statistics demonstrated the tendency most clearly. In 1820 one out of two residents was Negro; in 1860 only one in seven. To be sure, the black populations of smaller and newer cities, like Montgomery or the Texas towns, showed some vitality, but there is no reason to believe they would not have shared the same attrition as they expanded.

This decline did not stem from any economic reasons. There was plenty of work which whites had traditionally considered appropriate to blacks and particularly suited to slaves. Industrial employment, moreover, had proved feasible in a variety of enterprises. Hiring rates continued to rise throughout the last ante-bellum decades. And, perhaps most conclusively, the price of urban slaves on the market more than matched the general increase. In short, the usual indices suggested the continuing profitability of slavery as an economic institution. "In all departments of mechanical labor, the slaves of the South are profitably employed," the *Richmond Enquirer* asserted confidently in 1853. "As carpenters, as blacksmiths, as shoe-makers, as factory hands, they are far more valuable than field-laborers—indeed, intellectual expertness and manual dexterity are much more important elements in the price of a slave, than mere physical strength and power of endurance." [1] Or, as a visitor put it, "those whom good treatment has rendered most fit for freedom, are the most desired as slaves." [2]

Slavery's compelling problem in the city was not finding work for bondsmen, but controlling them when they were off the job. While busy, in the house or around the yard, on the docks or driving a dray, toiling in a factory or cotton press, they caused little trouble. When the task was finished or the supervision lifted, however, when the slaves became idle or contrived some free time, when dusk fell and the demand for service slackened, then the system weakened. And when the Negroes gathered by themselves, beyond the eye of masters and police, in homes, churches, or grog shops, the "peculiar institution" itself was jeopardized.

It was the total environment rather than industrial or commercial employment which eroded slavery in the cities. The problem was not what happened in the factory or shop but what happened in the back street, the church, the grocery store, the rented room, and the out-of-the-way house. It was not contact with machines or an industrial process which broke the discipline, it was contact with people of all kinds in numerous ways which generated the corrosive acids.

"The city, with its intelligence and enterprise, is a dangerous place for the slave," wrote a shrewd analyst. "He acquires knowledge of human rights, by working with others who receive wages when he receives none; who can come and go at their pleasure, when he from the cradle to the grave must obey a master's imperious will. . . . It is found expedient, almost necessary, to remove the slave from these influences, and send him back to the intellectual stagnation and gloom of the plantation." [3] Bondage "does not thrive with master or slave when transplanted to cities," a Louisiana planter observed, adding

[1] *Richmond Enquirer,* November 29, 1853.
[2] Finch, *An Englishwoman's Experience in America,* 300.
[3] Abbott, *South and North,* 112–13.

that in such surroundings "the slaves become dissipated, acquire the worst habits," and were generally "corrupted." [4]

An editor commenting on the Louisville scene contended that the "negroes scarcely realize the fact that they are slaves" in the city. They became "insolent, intractable, and in many instances wholly worthless. They make free negroes their associates, and imbibe feelings and imitate their conduct, and are active in prompting others to neglect their duty and to commit crime." [5] "The evil lies," a Charleston committee contended, "in the breaking down the relation between master and slave—the removal of the slave from the master's discipline and control, and the assumption of freedom and independence on the part of the slave, the idleness, disorders, and crime which are consequential." [6] Even more directly, a Southerner told a visitor that "the city is no place for niggers. They get strange notions in their heads, and grow discontented. They ought, everyone of them, be sent back on to the plantations." [7]

Slaves, on the other hand, found urban life to their liking. "The negroes are the most social of all human beings," De Bow asserted, "and after having hired in town, refuse to live again in the country."[8] Slavery's most famous refugee to attack the institution in all its aspects made the same point with eloquent simplicity: "Life in Baltimore, when most oppressive, was a paradise" compared to "plantation existence," Frederick Douglass wrote.[9] When masters were forced to sell, their bondsmen pleaded to be kept in the city because—in the words of some Richmond blacks—"they had acquired town habits." [10] And often those sent into the country headed back at the first opportunity to run away. In short, how could you keep them down on the plantation once they had seen Mobile?

The slave's preference was easily understood. Not only was urban life more congenial, but the alternative was especially grim. Solomon Northup found that every Negro sharing his Washington pen "dreaded the thought of being put into the cane and cotton fields." [11] Douglass, too, remembered that it was "a source of deep consternation" to him

4Walker, "Diary of a Louisiana Planter."
5 *Louisville Public Advertiser*, November 30, 1835.
6 Quoted in *De Bow's Review*, XXVI (1859), 600.
7 Abbott, *South and North*, 124.
8 *De Bow's Review*, XXIX (1860), 615.
9 Douglass, *My Bondage*, 235.
10 Lyell, *Second Visit*, I, 209.
11 Solomon Northup, *Twelve Years a Slave; Narrative of Solomon Northup, A Citizen of New York, Etc.* (Auburn, 1853), 62.

and his friends in Maryland that "we should be hurried away to the cotton fields and rice swamps, of the sunny south." [12] A sympathetic Northern traveler caught both the white and Negro perspectives when he observed that "The atmosphere of the city is too life-giving, and creates thought. It is the doom of them all to be sent back to the gloom of the plantation cabin." [13]

II

The cause of slavery's difficulty in the city was the nature of urban society itself. In the countryside physical isolation comprised one dimension of a successful discipline. Another was the simple division between master and slave, with virtually no other important element. The distinction between field hand and house servant, while important to the Negroes involved, constituted no significant fracture in the system. Treatment and comforts might vary, privileges could be more extensive, and everyday tasks quite different, but no area of independence was thus created. Indeed, a house servant often fell more directly under the eye of his owner than the black in the field. Nor did the overseer create a new interest among the whites. Employed by the master, usually a short-term resident, living apart from the colored quarters, and only occasionally a confidant of the owner, the overseer had at most a marginal influence on the structure.

Between black and white the social distance was immense. Slaves were confined to primitive work at worst or acquired rudimentary skills at best. Their contacts with whites were few and seldom lasting. An occasional visitor sometimes broke the isolation; nearby white families were seen just often enough to be recognized; overseers came and went. Except for the infrequent trip to town or a neighboring farm, the possibilities of outside stimuli scarcely existed. Even on small plantations or farms, the contacts with the surrounding world were circumscribed. Indeed, without other slaves about he was deprived of even the most elementary association. Rural life had always involved some social remoteness; for the plantation slave, isolation, next to his servitude, was the most compelling fact of life.

The cities, on the other hand, developed more complex structures. Both white and Negro communities included many different parts, and in the larger places a highly sophisticated system evolved with

---

[12] Douglas, *My Bondage*, 176.
[13] Abbot, *South and North*, 138–9.

almost endless groupings and distinctions. This fragmentation, which, of course, characterized urban life nearly everywhere, had a special significance for slavery. It meant that the great gap between owner and chattel would be filled with all kinds of diverse elements, inevitably disturbing the institution's ordinary relationships. The Louisiana planter who so feared town life saw this process clearly. "The distance is so vast between slave and master" under bondage, he argued, that in the city "the interval is filled up immediately by corrupting influences." And the slaveholder was helpless. He could perceive "the evil of his slave without being able to prevent it," since it sprang from the intractable nature of urban life itself.[14]

III

The most obvious added ingredient in the urban scene was the free Negro. He was, to be sure, also a rural resident, but the distance and detachment of the countryside greatly diluted his influence on slavery. Often living in a remote spot, sometimes as a yeoman, more often a hired hand, he was bound to have a modest role. His opportunity there moreover was limited. Without resources he found it hard to buy land; without many others of his own kind his social life was sparse. Hence he gravitated toward the metropolis.

Freedmen constituted the most highly urbanized group in Dixie. By 1860 they outnumbered slaves ten to one in Baltimore and 9209 to 1774 in Washington. In the deep South, too, their numbers grew with each census. New Orleans always had a considerable contingent; on the eve of the Civil War it exceeded 10,000. Yet even the places which had tried hardest to limit their free colored population could not alter the trend. Charleston had 1475 in 1820 and over 3200 in 1860, while Mobile's figures in the same span were 183 and 817. Across the South nearly a third of the free blacks were found in the larger urban centers. The report of a visitor in 1836 that "the emancipated negroes generally leave the country, and congregate in the cities and larger towns" was a common observation.[15]

The free Negro's position in Southern towns was always precarious, occupying, as one Southerner put it, "a sort of uncertain and undefined position in our midst." [16] His color suggested servitude, but

[14] Walker, "Diary of a Louisiana Planter."
[15] Andrews, *Slavery*, 43.
[16] Quoted in Everett, *Free Persons of Color in New Orleans*, 191.

his status secured a portion of freedom. Hence he suffered many of the inhibitions of his slave brothers while enjoying some privileges denied them. His advantages over the slave were considerable. He could marry, have children, and enjoy something of a normal family life. He could own property, have the right to his earnings, and engage in a few trades forbidden the enslaved. Though the situation was never favorable to either domestic tranquillity or economic advancement, there was at least a measure of independence. And, most crucial of all, in the privacy of the home could be found a seclusion from the constant surveillance of the white world.

Free Negroes learned quickly not to count on much beyond this. "We know full well," the *New Orleans Picayune* wrote with candor, "that the pretence of any real freedom being designed or expected for these negroes is but a sham." [17] In the streets the distinction among colored people was not clear; in the courts the free were sometimes only fined while the slaves were whipped; and legislation increasingly covered all blacks with only nominal regard for status. City ordinances usually handled both categories in a single section. An 1832 Baltimore ordinance dealing with Negro discipline set forth the crucial indentification: "such free negro or mulatto shall be subject to the same punishment, and be liable in every respect to the same treatment and penalty as slaves" and "be guilty of, and convicted of, any offense for which slaves are now punishable." [18]

Despite these obstacles, the free colored of every city struggled to establish a meaningful associational life. They formed congregations and erected churches, established schools and aid societies, and organized improvement projects aimed at bringing some of the better things of life to their members. Occasionally this activity became elaborate, the Negro equivalent of fashionable white life. The Bonneau Literary Society in Charleston, for example, met Wednesday evenings at nine "to further progress in Literary Improvement . . . and the Improvement of our Mental Faculties," [19] while in New Orleans the famous masked balls were carefully planned to emulate the subtlest pretensions of the city's first citizens.

To a few Southerners the presence of free Negroes created no great problem. Indeed, a state legislator from New Orleans called

[17] Quoted in Everett, *Free Persons of Color in New Orleans,* 197.
[18] Baltimore, Ordinances, March 14, 1832.
[19] *Brown Fellowship Society Papers,* September 6, 1833, MSS. (Possession of Mae Purcell, Charleston).

"the better class of our free colored population . . . a powerful check on the turbulence of the more vicious of our slaves." Another, Charles Gayarré, saw them as "sober and industrious mechanics, quiet and useful citizens who are susceptible of noble sentiments and virtues." [20] Similarly, the preamble to a Maryland statute could refer to Baltimore's free blacks as "honest, industrious and peaceable colored persons" as it widened their privileges to form associations for the care of "the destitute of their own color." [21] And a Savannah resident went so far as to say that the "true policy of safety" in the South required emancipation for deserving slaves, since the local experience evidenced the "uniformly quiet conduct" of freedom.[22]

But the common judgment went the other way. A Louisville editor in 1851 came close to the nearly universal view when he stated bluntly that "the free negro question is the most insoluble of all the social problems of the day, and stands as a practical sarcasm on all the theories of abolition and emancipation." [23] A Richmond memorial containing the signature of John Marshall elaborated the ordinary indictment. They numbered "not an eighth part of the inhabitants; yet it would be hazarding little to say that half the criminals tried in the City for the offense of larceny, are free persons of color." In addition, the petitioners said, "their idleness is proverbial; they live, few know in what way, and fewer still know where; their rate of increase far exceeds even that of the slaves, and in a higher degree that of the whites; and whatever energy can be spared from annoying both classes, appears to be expended in multiplying their own number." [24] And a New Orleans editor called the full roll when he spoke of "the absolute idleness, the thriftlessness, the laziness, the dishonesty, the drunkenness, the proneness to vagrancy and vice of the negro when free from all the restraints of servitude." [25]

The central complaint, however, had less to do with the wretchedness of free Negro life, or even with their high crime rate, than with their influence on slaves. Living amongst bondsmen, yet without masters, carrying by color the stigma of servitude, yet without its most humiliating features, shut off from white society, yet released

[20] Quoted in Everett, *Free Persons of Color in New Orleans,* 131.
[21] Baltimore, Ordinances, 1846, 156.
[22] *Savannah Republican,* May 6, 1823.
[23] *Louisville Daily Democrat,* August 5, 1851.
[24] Petition of the Colonization Society of Virginia to the Virginia State Legislature, Dec. 20, 1831, MSS., Virginia State Library, Richmond.
[25] *New Orleans Bee,* April 16, 1858.

from the confinements of slavery, the free blacks were always a disturbing factor. "They are a plague and pest in the community," the *New Orleans Daily Picayune* asserted, because they brought "the elements of mischief to the slave population." [26]

"The superior condition of the free persons of color," a memorial of Charleston citizens argued, "excites discontent among our slaves, who continually have before their eyes, persons of the same color, many of whom they have known in slavery, and with all of whom they associate on terms of equality." The slave saw these blacks "freed from the control of masters, working where they please, going whither they please, and spending money how they please." He thus became "dissatisfied" and "pants after liberty." [27]

But this envy did not split the colored community. "There is an identity of interest between the slave and the free person of color," the Charleston citizens continued, "whilst there is none between the latter class and the whites." And this identity was sustained by many elements: "they are associated by color, connected by marriages, and by friendships. Many of the free negroes have parents, brothers, sisters and children, who are slaves." In case of an insurrection, the document warned, "they would have every inducement to join it." [28]

"The intercourse of free negroes with slaves," wrote a New Orleans paper, "is just as mischievous as letting loose abolitionists among them. . . . If they do not render the slave insubordinate, they make him vicious." This "fact" was "so well understood that in the country" planters could only "with difficulty effect the emancipation of their slaves," and the law usually required that newly liberated slaves be removed from the state.[29] "It is the saucy and insolent air of the *free* negroes," a St. Louis police report declared, "which is most dangerous to the slave population." [30] Whatever the precise formulation of the argument, Southern town dwellers could agree that their free colored residents rendered control over their slaves increasingly difficult.

IV

They could also agree that there were some whites who were al-

[26] *New Orleans Daily Picayune*, March 8, 1856.
[27] *A Documentary History of American Industrial Society*, II, 108–9.
[28] *A Documentary History of American Industrial Society*, II, 109.
[29] *New Orleans Daily Delta*, December 12, 1856.
[30] *St. Louis Daily Pennant*, July 9, 1840.

most as unsettling to the system as freed blacks. These people had found a place at the edge of slavery where their economic life was enmeshed in the irregular relationships bred by the system in its urban environment. Some were grocers who sold to slaves; others ran shops which catered to a colored clientele; still others were ministers who organized Negro churches and sought to bring religion to the enslaved. Port merchants, too, could be included, since their trade brought ships with mixed crews into the harbor. Less easily identified, but also important, were whites sporadically connected with the informal life of town blacks. These interests were obviously quite different, but all developed a stake in the loose form of bondage which evolved in the cities.

The activity of some was illegal because it involved dealing with slaves who did not have the proper papers or permissions. Even ministers tended to allow bondsmen and free blacks to run the colored churches without the careful supervision required by law. And the association of whites in the demi-world of the Negro's night life violated both custom and law. Yet the interstices of slavery were so wide that these relations became a normal part of the functioning of the institution. Despite everything municipal officials could do, there were more whites in this position in the 1850's than ever before. Thus, there arose a white element whose influence, like the presence of free blacks, weakened the system of restraints and exclusions on which slavery rested.

The grocers and the grog-shop operators had the most obvious and deepest stake in the loose enforcement of police regulations. Nearly all dealt occasionally with slaves, and many depended on the trade. Though traffic in any goods was frowned upon, it was the sale of liquor that lay at the center of the controversy. Nearly all whites disliked this commerce; the master because it "led to the corruption of our servants and the loss of property," and others because it resulted in "the unrestrained intercourse and indulgence of familiarities between black and white." In short, the trade created conditions "destructive of the respect and subserviency which our laws recognize as due from the one to the other and which form an essential feature in our institutions." [31]

In every city the suppression of the traffic became a major issue. A Charleston grand jury considered it so important that it proposed

[31] Presentation of the Charleston Grand Jury, May Term, 1846, MSS., South Carolina Archives Division.

that "unprincipled white men" who "interfere between the slave and the owner or employer" ought to be deprived of all civil rights including suffrage. The suggestion was shrewd because it was political power which in the last instance protected the illicit trade. Whenever the public became outraged, the "grocers" acted in concert to control the city government and the police. "The Mayor & Marshall you are aware," wrote a leading Savannah public figure to a friend, "regulate the shopkeepers politically by *not* regulating them as to the Law." [32] Earlier, in 1828, a blue-ribbon citizens committee had tried to crack down and pushed the issue into an election of councilmen. A "Grocer's Ticket" immediately entered the field. Scorning the reformers as "(would-be) gentlemen" and dubbing their program "*pious tampering*," they carried the fight to the voters.[33] The outcome appeared inconclusive, but the ordinance which the committee wanted strengthened remained unchanged. In subsequent years the initial observation of the reform group remained a fact of life in Savannah: "shop keepers in the country can be effectively broken up by the enforcement of the State laws, while one in the city may even yet, before an ordinary jury, justify his act under the present ordinances." [34] A decade later, the grocers, again facing opposition from reformers, easily swept to victory under the banner of "Friends of Civil Freedom." [35]

The same question erupted in Charleston politics in 1834–35, when a new state law was at issue. The editor of the *Courier* summarized the legislation, which embodied a change of emphasis rather than a reversal of long-standing policy. The older statutes, he explained, were designed "to lessen the danger of depredation on the property of owners by making it highly penal to purchase from, or traffic with their slaves. The main object of the new law, is to prevent slaves from being corrupted in their habits, and ruined in their constitutions by the use of intoxicating liquors." [36] Passage of the new regulations followed a vigorous drive by many prominent Charleston people.

The grocers quickly moved to protect themselves. They not only argued their own case in saying that the law would drive out a "hardy and hard-working class" but identified themselves with other interests as well. Since the shops would have to shut down, land-

[32] Shryock (ed.), *Letters of Richard A. Arnold*, 39.
[33] *Savannah Republican*, September 3, 1829.
[34] *Savannah Republican*, July 8, 1829.
[35] *Savannah Republican*, August 29, 30, September 4, 1839.
[36] *Charleston Courier*, April 8, 1834.

lords would be deprived of their rent. Thus, "the loss would fall on a class least able to sustain it—namely, widows and orphans, whose sole income in a great number of cases, arises from this species of property." More subtly, and more significantly, they linked themselves to the entire middle-class by saying that, if the grocers and their kind disappeared, then "society in the South shall contain two classes—the master and the slave—the province of one of which shall be to command and the other to obey." [37] The law remained; so too did the problem; and so too did the grocers.

The shopkeepers often found an ally in those responsible for breaking up the traffic—the police. As early as 1822 a memorial of prominent Charleston residents declared that the City Guard "as now organized, are of little benefit to the city," because "most of them are shopkeepers or retailers of spiritous liquors to the negroes. It is therefore their interest and it is notorious that this interest induces them to permit such of the negroes as are their customers, to pass unmolested through our streets after the bell has rung and the watch has set." [38] In Savannah's election of 1850 Dr. Richard Arnold discovered what this coalition could do. In the campaign he charged "the shopkeepers openly proclaimed that they had a Mayor who suited them very well, and that if elected I would fine every shop-keeper a hundred dollars who might be convicted of breaking the ordinances." On election day the troops moved into action. When the polls opened, the City Guard marched "*en masse* with tickets marked by their officers. . . . The day was then before them to electioneer and bully." When the returns came in he could conclude sadly, "Dr. Wayne's shopkeepers were too strong." [39]

V

The role of the ministers proved more complicated. In stimulating the religious activity of Negroes, they felt they were discharging a public as well as a Christian duty. Believing that a pious slave was a well-behaved, docile, and obedient servant, most felt that the oftener he could be within earshot of the Word of God, the better for master and slave. Yet the elaborate regulations surrounding colored congre-

---

[37] *Charleston Courier,* March 6, 1835.
[38] *A Documentary History of American Industrial Society,* II, 113.
[39] Shryock (ed.), *Letters of Richard A. Arnold,* 46, 39.

gations tended to inhibit rather than encourage an enlarged spiritual life. Hence clergymen tended to bend if not break the law. Their control was formal rather than close; their attendance at meetings casual rather than constant.

But any movement to shut up the churches brought white ministers to the defense of the blacks. *"There is not . . .* sufficient room for their accommodation in the galleries of other churches," five beleaguered Methodist clergymen in Mobile contended, "besides their presence there would be regarded by many as a great evil particularly in the church of which the subscribers are members." The Negroes would moreover regard the action "as a grievance" and "suffer great *injury* in their spiritual interests, an injury that would be irreparable." Pledging "our word and standing in the community . . . that all future *instruction* shall be unexceptional and all *meetings* of colored people under our *direction lawful*," they urged the city council to "take no step to abridge the *present* religious privileges of the blacks in Mobile." [40] Elsewhere the story was the same. White ministers, believing in the necessity of religious instruction to the Negroes, tried to temper the enforcement of laws against colored congregations. Except in Charleston in the 1820's they proved uniformly successful.

A handful of lawyers in every city also discovered an interest in a lax system of slavery. They operated in the crucial intersection of slavery and freedom—the granting of emancipation papers.   The complaint of a St. Louis man explained the practice and detailed the danger. The law permitted a Negro who claimed freedom to bring the case to court. "This is but right, rational and humane," "Topaz" admitted, "but the liberty has become abused, at least in St. Louis, by the ruthless encouragement of those who left-handedly profit by such suits." It worked like this: "Tom wants his freedom, and sallies in quest of legal advice; he states his case, and right or wrong, is flattered to proceed. Pleased with his prospects, he brags to Dick, who after a little scratching of the bump of his reminiscences, takes a notion he has a right to freedom too." Then the hope spreads through the black community. "Fired with untried hope, Dick flies to Ned . . . Ned catches flame and communicates it to Big Bill—Big Bill to little Jim, and little Jim to everything that wears wool." Soon discipline everywhere flags. The slave "grumbles at his master's commands—neglects his duties, and takes his chastisement with the sullen inso-

40 City of Mobile, Papers, Reports, 1840, MSS., Mobile, City Hall.

lence of one who thinks he shall shortly be able to set the white man at defiance." [41]

The lawyer's clients might be slaves whose manumission depended on the action of a municipal body when certain conditions and technicalities were under question. In New Orleans the number was so large that a committee of the city council asserted that everyone was "well aware" there were "persons who speculate and deal" in emancipation papers and made good money at it.[42] Another transaction involved replacing lost documents or establishing the fact that a black was not a runaway. Everywhere a few lawyers discovered a stake in the untidy organization of urban slavery.

Even some masters developed such an interest. Employers of large numbers of slaves in commercial or industrial enterprises increasingly preferred not to house blacks on their own property, and this attitude in turn loosened one of the most intimate bonds. Others found hiring out their slaves profitable and permitting them to live out convenient. These expedients, of course, put a heavy responsibility on public discipline. Yet many owners resented the interference from public authorities that followed. "While loud in their complaints" about lax discipline, a New Orleans editor observed wryly, some masters were "only willing to have every slave not their own arrested." When the police "execute the law vigorously and their heavy hand falls . . . many interfere and by their remonstrances with the officers, dampen their energy and destroy their zeal in the special discharge of their duty." [43]

In a conflict between masters and municipal authority, owners often appeared as advocates of leniency. Before the magistrate they sometimes preferred to pay a fine rather than to surrender their slave for a correction by the jailer. Frequently they complained that the elaborate public discipline confused the bondsmen. "They cannot distinguish why their master has no power to give them his consent to go out and spend an evening with a friend without the fear of the guard house hanging over his head," "A Slave Owner" in Mobile declared. Attacking the entire city code, he concluded with a curious touch of anarchy: "It is human nature, the more stringent the laws the worse they are." [44] Hence even masters occasionally found them-

[41] *Missouri Argus,* January 20, 1837.

[42] Council of the First Municipality of New Orleans, *Journal,* June 9, 1851, MSS., New Orleans, City Hall.

[43] *New Orleans Daily Picayune,* October 6, 1855.

[44] *Mobile Evening News,* January 4, 1856.

selves advocates of a more relaxed regime than local officials believed necessary.

VI

In the metropolis the worlds of bondage and freedom overlapped. The line between free blacks and slaves became hopelessly blurred. Even whites and blacks found their lives entangled in some corners of the institution of slavery. No matter what the law said or the system required, this layer of life expanded. Though much of it was subterranean, at points it could be easily seen. The mixed balls, the numberless grog and grocery shops, the frequent religious gatherings, and the casual acquaintances in the streets were scarcely private. Physical proximity bred a certain familiarity that most residents came to expect. To be sure, when a Richmond officer saw "a white man, walking arm and arm with a black man," he demanded "to know the why and wherefore of such a cheek and jowl business." [45] But occasional friendships that transcended the deference of slavery raised few eyebrows.

What did bother townspeople, however, was the evidence that beyond these visible contacts lay a world of greater conviviality and equality. In this nether world blacks and whites mingled freely, the conventions of slavery were discarded, and the worst fears of Southerners became realized. Not only did the men find fellowship without regard to color in the tippling shops, back rooms, and secluded sheds, but the women of both races joined in. Such mixing engaged a good deal of the private conversation of white people in cities, but its public manifestations were usually found in only police reports and the major's court.

In Mobile, for instance, "two couples, embracing two males and two females, the former in both instances colored, and the latter white," came before the judge on the charge of "amalgamation." They had been found in a bedroom with "only one garment on apiece." One of the women was the "notorious Hoosier Ann"—a certain Ann Fuller—who was no stranger to the police.[46] This episode was not unusual. Five days later, Nancy Bohanan, another white, was picked up for running an "assignation house." "The principal frequenters to this infamous den" were "negro cab drivers, none of whose

[45] *Richmond Enquirer*, August 30, 1853.
[46] *Mobile Daily Advertiser*, October 15, 1859.

names or ownerships could be sworn to." [47]   Not long after, Mrs.
Eliza Crowe, the widow of a "very respectable tailor," came before
the court accused of being with two colored men in her house with
"the door locked." [48] And three days later Julia McCarthy "was found
laying on the same bed with a well known negro driver of a baggage
wagon." [49]

The Richmond newspapers usually carried brief notices of similar
matters "too delicate to dwell on." Yet on occasions they printed a
fuller story, especially when some reform seemed appropriate. "Yester-
day two youthful white girls, not of uncomely features or shape," ran
the court reporter's account in 1859, "were brought before the crowd's
gaze" for "having been caught pandering for lucre's sake to the passions of negroes. These females, depraved in every sense of the word,
are named Betty Moore and Mary Brown." They were sent to jail
"for want of $100 bail." The writer thought "the place for such
creatures should be a house of reform where they could be kept for
a period at industrious pursuits." [50]

Hugh Kelly, who lived in Indiana but commuted to Louisville,
rented a house and for more than a year "made free with a negro
woman, the property of one of our citizens." The affair became
common knowledge in the neighborhood until the police caught him
"between a straw and feather bed" and gave him three months.[51]
Other blacks had better protection than Kelly. When a "handsome"
Negro woman came before New Orleans officials for an illicit alliance,
"at least forty respectable persons came to the Recorder's office to
offer themselves as bail," and she was later released when no witnesses
appeared.[52]

This social underworld encompassed every possible combination
of color and status. The cases brought before New Orleans officials
in a few months in the 1850's illustrate this. "A slave girl and a white
man," ran a typical newspaper account, "were arrested for violating
some of the more prominent of the Ten Commandments."[53] "Frank,
a slave, and Mary Ann Kirvella were arrested for living in a room on
Burgundy Street, in contravention of existing ordinances of good

[47] *Mobile Daily Advertiser,* October 20, 1859.
[48] *Mobile Daily Advertiser,* November 10, 1859.
[49] *Mobile Daily Advertiser,* November 13, 1859.
[50] *Richmond Enquirer,* August 17, 1859.
[51] *Louisville Daily Democrat,* March 10, 1847.
[52] *New Orleans Daily Delta,* August 24, 1855.
[53] *New Orleans Daily Delta,* July 13, 1852.

morals," another recorded.[54] In the Third District, outside the Old Quarter, "two white women have recently been discovered . . . living with negro men," the *Daily Delta* noted with dismay, "in open violation of all social rules. One of them was a runaway slave." [55] Another item suggested the wide compass of these associations: "A young and tolerably good-looking woman of the pave, Brigit Smith, and one of the ugliest of the ugly negro men, named Jack, were brought before Recorder Caldwell this morning . . . for what—we will not say." [56]

Indeed few racial issues produced so much explosiveness. "No subject, political or otherwise, brought forth such a number of persons in many years as this," the *New Orleans Daily Delta* admitted in 1860 in the midst of the "Martin Affair." Thomas J. Martin, a free Negro, had been the city's most sought-after music teacher for twenty years. He had written a successful popular song as well as some serious compositions. In the course of this career, it was belatedly discovered, he had also seduced twenty women—most of them white. After his arrest 2000 people poured into Lafayette Square to protest his transgressions and demand punishment. The newspaper noted that the matter went "much deeper than the first blush would indicate." Moreover, "to trifle with this subject" would be "aiding and abetting of a mischief, a wrong that should be discountenanced by every true Southern man." "Let the amalgamationists say what they want," the editor concluded, but the question was more than "a trifle, a fiarro." [57]

There can be no doubt of the wide extent of this miscegenation. Visitors often commented on it; the newspapers complained about it; the court records teem with it. Even Governor Hammond, who defended the South in general against the charge of racial mixing, admitted its prominence in the cities. The clandestine nature of these attachments makes a more precise generalization risky, but the fear, if not the fact, of "amalgamation," "miscegenation," and "mixing" plainly increased in the decades before 1860. Few defenders, much less advocates, appeared. The public stigma and the hostility of the law made it clear why: those who practised it did not preach it.

New Orleans, with its large population of free and enslaved blacks, had the most famous demi-world in Dixie. The celebrated masked balls and the casual acceptance of colored mistresses seemed to reflect

---

54 *New Orleans Bee,* January 24, 1854.
55 *New Orleans Daily Delta,* July 25, 1852.
56 *New Orleans Daily Delta,* July 16, 1851.
57 *New Orleans Daily Delta,* June 26, 1860.

its Spanish and French roots. Yet that explanation is too facile. The rural areas of Louisiana, some of which reflected similar origins, did not develop the same mores; and, more persuasively, other cities with quite different beginnings did. Actually what visitors noticed about New Orleans was true of urban life throughout the South.

VII

Northern cities, too, had their disorganized elements who left a trail across police blotters, court records, and poorhouse lists. There, too, community leaders, somewhat bewildered by the spread of undisciplined low life, sought some way to introduce system and stability. But, important as this was to civic leaders elsewhere, in the South the problem was greatly complicated by the existence of slavery. On the one hand, the institution required a high degree of order, the careful regulation of Negro affairs, and a fixed status for bondsmen. On the other hand, the city demanded fluidity, a constant re-allocation of human resources, and a large measure of social mobility. Initially, it appeared as though slavery could provide the discipline town life seemed to need. In the long run, however, the force of urbanization loosened the restraints of bondage, smudged the distinctions of status among Negroes, and at points pierced the racial walls of Dixie's cities.

This antithesis was early felt by some municipal leaders. Since slavery was presumed to be an established part of Southern town life for any foreseeable future, none talked about incompatibility. Instead, the dominant race sought to solve it with ordinances, the orderly development of a legal hiring-out system, and a plentiful police force in case of trouble. Yet the acids of urbanization continually eroded the discipline on which bondage rested. Though the disintegration was often hard to gauge, those close to the problem knew it was happening.

To arrest the attrition and handle its consequences, Southern cities moved along three lines. One involved the sale of young male blacks into the countryside. This removed one of the most disturbing elements from the urban scene while meeting a constant demand for field hands in the cotton and cane regions. A second was the tightening of emancipation procedures to stop the accumulation of free Negroes in towns. A third was to develop racial arrangements which took into account the new situation and which embodied most of the features later identified as segregation.

The sale of the men into the cotton and cane country was never an official policy. After the Vesey affair a Charleston spokesman recommended the thinning of the Negro population as a deliberate program, and the *Richmond Enquirer* advocated "reducing surely but quietly, the number of our slaves" following Turner's uprising.[58] But to force owners to this course never seemed feasible. Likewise the widespread interest in attracting white immigrants to Southern cities to replace black labor, even as domestic servants, was not easy to implement. And the high demand for field hands in the new areas furnished a convenient rationale for action that was only partially economic in motivation.

Despite these difficulties the tendency to sell men into the country was pronounced. It was, in fact, the theme of John S. C. Abbott's diary of his Southern trip in 1859. "The slaves in the cities, working in the midst of the conversation of white men, listen eagerly, and gain some information," he noted. "This has alarmed their masters, and they are sending them off, as fast as possible, to the plantations where, as in a tomb, no sight or sound of knowledge can reach them." [59] An examination of real estate conveyances in New Orleans, which list the names and residences of both buyer and seller, confirms the observation. The persistent imbalance between the sexes characteristic of urban Negro population reveals the same tendency. Perhaps, however, the wry observation of the *Daily Crescent* in 1853 describes best the situation: "The whole number of slaves in New Orleans does not exceed 16,000, of which the greater portion are women and children." [60]

While Dixie's towns sloughed off their male bondsmen, they also moved to reduce the number of free Negroes in their midst. This policy involved a change in strategy, for initially emancipation was used as part of a sophisticated control system. "The object of design of such permission," wrote the mayor of New Orleans' Third Municipality, "is to offer a reward to such slaves as would demean themselves correctly, be respectful to the white population or render important services to the state or to their masters." Another object was "to encourage the slave population in imitating the good example and following in the footsteps of those who by an honest, active, and use-

---

[58] *Richmond Enquirer,* October 25, 1831.
[59] Abbott, *South and North,* 124. For further discussion see also 74, 112–13, 139, 175, 190, 321.
[60] *New Orleans Daily Crescent,* June 23, 1853.

ful conduct have succeeded in obtaining their freedom." [61] But every-where the fear of increasing the number of liberated blacks, no matter how well-behaved, overcame the advantages of the selected manumission program. A chorus rose which demanded not only restriction but absolute prohibition.

The case of New Orleans was illustrative, because its policy encompassed both the widest leniency for most of the ante-bellum years and an absolute ban on the eve of war. Through most of the period, under Louisiana law, city councils could grant freedom on petition, and they did so on a substantial scale. In the four years between 1846 and 1850 the First Municipality alone emancipated 321 blacks, while the Second Municipality manumitted at a rate of about 75 annually. The grounds were usually "long important and faithful services" and most carried the notation, "without being compelled to leave the state." [62] Masters wishing to let their slaves go generally got a sympathetic hearing from officials. But not all requests were granted. When, for example, Sara Connor's petition came up for action, a police report disclosed that a few months earlier she had been picked up "in a house on St. John street, dancing, in company with sixteen colored girls, mostly slaves, and about ten or twelve white men." The committee decided that Sara was liberated enough already.[63]

New Orleans' liberal practice obscured somewhat the increasing hostility to emancipation of any kind in Louisiana. The 1830 law required the newly freed Negro to leave the state within thirty days; in 1852 the right to manumit was taken from city officials and given to the legislature. Flooded with petitions, worried about the influence of the unbonded on the slaves, and concerned about rumored insurrections, the state government in 1857 forbade manumission under any conditions. Two years before, a legislator had expressed the tighter attitude: "if slavery is not an evil . . . why should we emancipate under any circumstances in the State of Louisiana?" [64] In 1859

[61] Council of the Third Municipality of the City of New Orleans, *Journal,* January 31, 1848, MSS., City Archives, New Orleans.

[62] Council of the First Municipality of the City of New Orleans, *Slaves Emancipated,* MSS., City Archives, Public Library; New Orleans City Council, *Record of Emancipation,* 1846–1851, MSS., Public Library, New Orleans.

[63] Council of the Second Municipality of the City of New Orleans, Proceedings, April 1, 1851.

[64] Quoted in Everett, *Free Persons of Color in New Orleans,* 154. For an earlier expression of the mounting opposition to routine emancipation see the report of the Judiciary Committee of the Council of the First Municipality

provisions were made for free blacks to choose a master and return to bondage.

Other cities exercised less control over emancipation than New Orleans, but the tendency everywhere was the same. When an owner manumitted, his slave was to be removed quickly from the state. Free colored people from the outside could not become residents, and even Negro sailors arriving in port temporarily on business were kept onboard ships or confined in jail. Though petitions to state legislature often brought relief, the possibility became more remote with each passing decade. By 1860 the percentage of free Negroes among the South's urban population had dropped considerably.

VIII

While Southern cities increasingly moved to reduce their colored population, both slave and free, they also developed a new system of racial deference more appropriate to urban life than slavery in its traditional form. As the institution of slavery encountered mounting difficulties and, as its control over the blacks weakened, another arrangement was devised which maintained great social distance within the physical proximity of town life. Increasingly public policy tried to separate the races whenever the surveillance of the master was likely to be missing. To do this, the distinction between slave and free Negro was erased; race became more important than legal status; and a pattern of segregation emerged inside the broader framework of the "peculiar institution."

In a sense this tendency was always present, though the reliance on traditional controls obscured its importance. The heart of the established system was, of course, the subordination of the slave to his owner. The wide discretion vested in the master made day-to-day discipline almost a private matter. But in the cities a public etiquette was needed to govern the relations of races when the blacks were beyond the supervision of their owners. Increasingly that etiquette required the separation of black and white without regard to legal status. Beginning in only a few areas, the arrangement spread to include the most important public aspects of life.

Taverns, restaurants, and hotels were always off-limits to the

of New Orleans in 1851 when its chairman complained that the full "body" often acted "very harshly" toward petitions for emancipation. June 9, 1851, Journal, MSS., City Archives, Public Library, New Orleans.

Negroes. The laws against trading with slaves, of course, covered all these areas, and their location in the business part of town prevented much laxity. Free blacks fell under the same ban, though by custom rather than by law. In public conveyances this discrimination appeared again. Richmond's ordinances, to cite but one case, prohibited Negroes from "driving, using or riding in any Hackney coach or other carriage for hire unless in the capacity of a servant." [65] In New Orleans the street railway kept separate cars for blacks. And encroachments on this arrangement met with physical exclusion. In 1833, for instance, when "certain colored persons wishing to go to the lake, took possession of the cars appropriated to white people," the conductor evicted them.[66]

Public grounds, however, presented an even clearer case. Savannah's 1827 ordinances, for example, excluded "negroes, mullattoes, or other colored persons" from "the public promenade in South Broad street, or on that leading from thence to the Hospital." And the preamble said why: "for the purpose of protecting the Citizens while engaged in recreation upon the Public Walks, from molestation or intrusion of improper persons." [67]   A section of Richmond's Negro code was entitled "What place slaves not to Walk or be in." The segregated areas included "the grounds adjacent to the City Spring, City Hall, or Athenaeum," as well as "any of the places known as city grounds" and "any public burying ground for white persons." The law relented if the slave accompanied his owner as employer, but the prohibition of free blacks was absolute.[68]

Charleston's regulations kept colored people off the "enclosure of the Garden at White Point" and forbade them "to walk on the East or South Batteries." [69] If attending white children, and if they had a ticket, slaves could enter. Even this variation, however, brought criticism. "It now takes from four to two wenches, *with their attendents* [*sic*], to take one baby in the air," one white wrote indignantly, while taxpayers are "jostled by a succession of darkies" each of whom has "a detachment of 'little niggers' at her heels." [70]

[65] Richmond, Minutes of the Common Council, January 13, 1833.

[66] The Negroes resisted this affront and "went away and armed themselves." They later returned to take a few shots at the conductor. *Niles' Register,* August 24, 1833.

[67] Savannah, Ordinances, August 2, 1827.

[68] Richmond, Ordinances, December 22, 1857.

[69] Charleston, Ordinances, July 30, 1838.

[70] *Charleston Courier,* July 28, 1841.

These measures simply excluded the blacks without providing alternative facilities. It was otherwise in the case of jails, hospitals, and cemeteries. Here the separation was careful and complete, if sometimes painfully contrived. Also, wherever Negroes shared public buildings with whites their quarters were set apart. The division was sometimes by room, at other times by floor. But in every case the segregation was clear and unmistakable.

Prisons presented few problems. Either the blacks had a special jail or they were assigned to a designated section of the same building. Some separate jails had the whipping post in a nearby yard; others, such as Charleston's, adjoined workhouses where colored inmates toiled on tough tasks or kept the treadmill going. When gangs were sent to work on the street or other public projects, officials maintained the same distinction. The new Orleans city council was so anxious in this regard that it furnished different colored clothes for Negro and white prisoners employed on municipal projects.[71]

The same principle governed the organization of poorhouses. The care of the indigent slave, of course, fell to the owner, but free Negroes were the city's responsibility. If the "mandate of the law, the counsel of true wisdom and policy, as well as the dictates of justice and humanity," made them "the fit and rightful objects of poor relief," as a Charleston report observed, it was also "conceded" that they should be "provided for in a place different and separated from . . . the white poor." "The distinction of castes must be strictly and broadly pursued in slaveholding communities," the committee explained.[72] In Baltimore, where the numbers were much greater, a similar practice developed. In the 1830's some mixing occurred because of a continuing space shortage. By 1841, however, the trustees could say that "the colored and white inmates are in general kept separate from each other." Two years later, a new building permitted the removal of white women from the female yard, and thus the Negroes were left with a "comfortable hospital and eating room . . . instead of their being confined exclusively to the garret rooms of the west wing." [73]

Hospitals, too, maintained the pattern. It was most obvious when the institution was initially built for slaves exclusively. Each city had

[71] New Orleans, Ordinances, October 8, 1817.
[72] *Report on the Free Colored Poor of the City of Charleston* (Charleston, 1842), 10.
[73] Baltimore, Ordinances, 1841, Appendix, 98.

at least one of these. But most also established hospitals which admitted both races to separate quarters and facilities. Usually a wing,
or in the case of Louisville, the basement, was set aside for the
blacks.[74] Even in times of emergency, when additional structures were
taken over for hospital use, health officials did not abandon the
practice.

Cultural and recreational enterprises were also segregated when
they did not exclude Negroes entirely. Theatres provided special galleries for colored persons which were often approached through special
entrances. Lyell found the upper tiers of boxes at the New Orleans
Opera House assigned to Negroes.[75] Another visitor reported, "Some
of them were pointed out to me as very wealthy; but no money can
admit them to the pit, or to the boxes." [76] Others, like Thomas L.
Nichols, put a different construction on the segregation, when he referred to the "portion of the house devoted to ladies and gentlemen
of colour" where "no common white trash was allowed to intrude." [77]
But the fact of separation had been part of official policy since the
beginning. As early as 1816 an ordinance established the practice: "It
shall not be lawful for any white person to occupy any of the places
set apart for people of color; and the latter are likewise forbidden to
occupy any of those reserved for white persons, at any public exposition or theatre." [78]

On the stage, of course, no intrusion was permitted. When a Northern newspaper reported that a colored actress had performed in New
Orleans, the *Bee* retorted indignantly: "We beg leave to contradict
and unequivocally this remark. No negress ever has been, or ever
will be permitted to appear on the stage of New Orleans. We are a
slave-holding state, and whatever may be the pretended philanthropy
of our Northern brethren in relation to our conduct, we possess too
much self-respect to submit to any such degrading exhibition." [79] The
prohibition on reading and writing, of course, put libraries off-limits.

Negroes remained as segregated in death as in life. Funerals increasingly became wholly colored affairs. The law usually required a
white minister at the service, and the master and the family sometimes

[74] See, for example, Karl Bernhard, *Travels*, II, 132.
[75] Lyell, *Second Visit*, II, 94.
[76] Pulszky, *Red, White, Black*, II, 101.
[77] Thomas L. Nichols, *Forty Years of American Life* (London, 1864), II,
279.
[78] New Orleans, Ordinances, June 8, 1816.
[79] *New Orleans Bee*, October 13, 1837.

attended, but a petition by Richmond's blacks to the state legislature indicated the reality. The Negroes noted that a new statute, passed in 1832, prohibited slaves and free Negroes from officiating at funerals. As a consequence, they lamented, "many coloured human beings are inter'd like brutes, their relatives and friends being unable to procure white ministers to perform the usual ceremony in the burial of the dead." Eleven clergymen joined in the memorial arguing that the "pressing engagements of white ministers left no time for this function." [80]

The body was finally interred in a segregated cemetery. Sometimes a congregation would set aside space in its church yard for colored members. No doubt, too, though the evidence is scarce, a faithful slave would on rare occasions be buried in the master's plot. But the bulk of urban Negroes, slave and free, rested ultimately in places confined to their own race. Every city maintained at least one extensive "burial ground for negroes," and most churches kept separate cemeteries for black and white. A Charleston directory for 1856 lists fifteen colored graveyards, two owned by the town, one by the Brown Fellowship Society, and the rest by Negro or white congregations.[81] Nowhere else were there so many, but everywhere the distinction was maintained. And New Orleans, with mathematical precision, divided its facilities into three parts: one-half for whites, one-quarter for slaves, and one-quarter for free blacks.[82]

IX

Religious organizations quickly developed segregated facilities without the help of municipal officials and the law. Nearly all Protestant denominations, especially those with large black contingents, either put their colored members in separate galleries during regular services or established special churches for them. This arrangement covered not only Sunday gatherings but prayer meetings during the week and Bible classes as well. The system, however, stemmed less from white design than Negro preference, for whenever the opportunity appeared colored worshippers patronized their own congregations. A Savannah preacher recorded the normal experience in 1819: "There was one

[80] Petition of the Free People of Color to the Virginia State Legislature, Dec. 17, 1834.
[81] *Charleston City Directory*, 233.
[82] New Orleans, Ordinances, March 5, 1835.

side of the gallery [in his church] appropriated for their use, and it was always the most thinly seated part of the church; while there were two respectably large colored churches in the city, with their pastor, and deacons, and sacraments, and discipline, all of their own." [83]

Colored churches, of course, reflected the tendency toward segregation even more clearly. Distrusted by whites, enthusiastically supported by Negroes, they represented the ambiguity of race relations under slavery. Whites developed elaborate devices to keep the races apart in public places and to seal off their own slaves from others in private life; but religious activity fell between these situations. Masters, often considering it a family affair, sought a compromise under one roof. Negroes, on the other hand, finding social as well as spiritual satisfaction by themselves, flocked to separate congregations. Except for some Catholic churches and a few Protestant ones, this combination made Sunday morning one of the most segregated moments of the week.

Slaves were excluded from schools by the legislation against teaching them to read and write, but the pattern of segregation applied to free blacks. Not only could they not attend white classes, but they had to make their own arrangements for education. Even these schools had uncertain careers, being subject to police interference and legal prohibitions as well as financial difficulties. After the Vesey episode, the Charleston grand jury wanted to remove all Negro teachers in private schools, which would have shut them down altogether. "As the Blacks are most carefully excluded from all schools kept by *white* persons, where their persons would be considered as a sort of contamination both by the master and scholars," an English visitor observed, "this bill of the Grand Jury will deprive them at once of all instruction." Indeed, he concluded, "Although they do not avow it (for even the most hardened are sometimes sensible to public shame)," it it was "their real object and intention." [84] If some slaves managed to bootleg a little learning in a free colored school, no black was ever knowingly admitted to a white one.

This exclusion did not, however, exempt Baltimore's large free Negro population from paying the public school tax. As early as 1839, 55 colored leaders asked the mayor to grant them relief, since

[83] Quoted in Albert M. Shipp, *A History of Methodism in South Carolina* (Nashville, 1884), 426.

[84] William Blane, *An Excursion Through the United States and Canada* (London, 1824), 220.

"coloured people are not at all interested in the public schools directly or indirectly." Failing in that, five years later they asked for "two schools in different sections of the city" for their own children. In 1850, 90 Negroes were joined by 126 whites in another petition. Noting that the blacks "are taxed for the support of public schools, into which, for obvious reasons, their children cannot be admitted," it argued that "the true instinct of the white population, as well as the colored, will be promoted by the instruction of the children . . . in such elements of learning as may prepare them . . . with usefulness and respectability, [for] those humble stations in the community to which they are confined by the necessities of their situation." The solution lay in establishing schools for the 20,000 Negro residents. The city refused on the ground that the state would withdraw money from Baltimore's "school fund" if any went to Negro schools.[85]

X

Law and custom sanctioned the segregation of races in public places and accommodations as well as in churches and schools. To disentangle white and black in employment and housing was a different matter. Yet the significant fact is that such a separation took place increasingly often in the last few decades before the Civil War. Under the pressure of white craftsmen, Negroes were pushed out of one line of work after another. With the weakening of the reins of slavery, bondsmen found housing away from their owners and generally in areas of accumulating colored population. Both movements were far from complete, but the tendency was unmistakable.

In employment the clearest manifestation of segregation was the exclusion of blacks, slave and free, from the better jobs. A memorial of Charleston's City Council to the state legislature expressed both the difficulties and the objects of the policy. Noting that "slavery is so interwoven with the constitution of our Society that even if our interests permitted it would be impossible to eradicate it," the petitioners argued that it was "necessary to fix as far as possible the grade of employments" for slaves and "to exclude them by Legislative enactment from all others." [86] Charleston's own ordinances prohibited

[85] City of Baltimore, Petition to the Mayor, January 20, 1839; Petition to the City Council, January 30, 1844; Petition to the Mayor, February 7, 1850; Report of Joint Committee on Colored Schools, February 20, 1850; MSS. Bureau of Archives (City Hall, Baltimore).

[86] Memorial of the City Council to the Legislature of South Carolina, 1826, MSS., South Carolina Archives Division.

teaching slaves "in any mechanic or handicraft trade," though the wording was vague and its enforcement almost impossible.[87]

In Savannah the restrictions were more precise. No Negro could be apprenticed "to the trade of Carpenter, Mason, Bricklayer, Barber or any other Mechanical Art or Mystery." [88] Later, cabinetmaker, painter, blacksmith, tailor, cooper, and butcher were added to the list.[89] Georgia excluded blacks from "being mechanics or masons, from making contracts for the erection . . . or repair of buildings." [90] Though no two cities had the same categories, all tried to keep colored workers out of the higher skills. The fact that practice often belied the law simply underlined the significance of the intent.

If slaves and blacks were still found in many of the better crafts in 1860, they had been pushed out of many of the lesser-skilled jobs. In Baltimore whites took the carting and draying business from them by 1830.[91] A few years later, a visitor could report that "the Irish and other foreigners are, to a considerable extent, taking the place of colored laborers and of domestic servants." [92] In 1823 the City Council of New Orleans directed the mayor "to hire white labor for the city works, in preference to negroes." [93] Two decades later, some prominent citizens there described the extent of the attrition: "Ten years ago, say they, all the draymen of New Orleans, a numerous class, and the cabmen, were colored. Now they are nearly all white. The servants of the great hotels were formerly of the African, now they are of the European race." [94] Even in the home, the displacement occurred with the customary racial rationale. "We have all times spoken against the impropriety of having white and black servants in the homes in the South," the *Richmond Enquirer* explained, "especially so in any capacity where slaves or negroes may be inclined to consider themselves on a par of equality with white servants." [95]

[87] Charleston, Ordinances, October 28, 1806.
[88] Savannah, Minutes of the Council, October 15, 1822, MSS., City Hall, Savannah.
[89] Savannah, Ordinances, November 11, 1831.
[90] Quoted in Lyell, *Second Visit*, II, 81.
[91] *Genius of Universal Emancipation*, January 12, 1828.
[92] Andrews, *Slavery*, 73.
[93] New Orleans, Proceedings, September 13, 1823.
[94] Lyell, *Second Visit*, II, 125. John Milton Mackie found the same thing in Mobile; *From Cape Cod to Dixie and the Tropics* (N.Y., 1864), 158. Though the book bears a later date, this trip took place before the war.
[95] *Richmond Enquirer*, August 27, 1857.

John S. C. Abbott, who toured the South in 1859, found this tendency pronounced everywhere. In Mobile, for instance, he was "surprised to see how effectually free labor seems to have driven slave labor from the wharves and streets." The Irish and Germans, he noted, did the outside work, while white girls moved into domestic service. When he saw New Orleans, he commented, though no doubt with exaggeration, that "hardly a colored face is to be seen on the levee, and the work is done by the Germans and the Irish . . . . Indeed, now, New Orleans and Mobile seem but little more like slave cities than do Philadelphia and New York." [96]

Though the process varied in Dixie's cities and Negroes hung on in many skills, "job busting" became a normal tactic for the growing white labor force faced with traditional colored employment practices. As the black population dropped, white newcomers moved in and took over craft after craft. Occasionally accompanied by violence and usually with official sanction, slave and free colored workers were shunted into the most menial and routine chores. In 1830 Negroes, both slave and free, had been used in a wide variety of employments; by 1860 the number of possibilities had shrunk markedly. The movement toward segregation, so noticeable in other aspects of urban life, was rapidly invading employment.

In housing the same trend was perceptible, though less advanced. The spread of the "living out" system, both in its legal and irregular form, gave slaves some choice of residence. Since the urge to leave the enclosure reflected the freedom from surveillance it entailed, slaves sought spots as removed from whites as possible. For most this meant a retreat to the outer edges of the city or beyond the municipal line altogether. There was seldom any escape from all whites, but there were parts of town with clusters of colored inhabitants. By the 'forties and 'fifties it was apparent in most places that Negroes were settling on the periphery of the cities.

Savannah is a good illustration of this process. The central portion had always been the commercial heart of town. Immediately around it and stretching southward, the substantial and the wealthy built their houses. The best addresses bore the names of eight or ten squares directly away from the wharf toward Forsyth Park. The western and southern edges became the sites for the low-income whites and increasingly for the free colored as well. As slaves moved away from the master's yards, they headed for these areas.

[96] Abbot, *South and North,* 112, 113.

The 1848 census, which listed slaves from their actual place of residence rather than from their master's addresses, revealed the concentrations. Old Oglethorpe Ward on the west had 1327 Negroes to 999 whites. In the same place there were only five brick houses to 451 wooden ones. To the east, Carpenter's Row, Trustees Gardens, and Gilmerville showed the same tendency with fewer numbers. There 300 blacks lived with 182 whites; none of the 127 houses was brick. Significantly enough, Currytown on the southeast edge of the city showed the same characteristics—Negro majorities and wooden dwellings. Elsewhere in Savannah, the figures ran the other way, with white preponderance and large numbers of brick homes.

The movement to the periphery was increasingly common, though in some towns colored concentrations grew up more haphazardly in small enclaves or strips in out-of-the-way places. And the centers of Negro life, formal and informal, followed the people. Colored churches, especially those established after 1840, sought locations in these neighborhoods. Grocery stores and dram shops, too, settled there. Even the cemeteries were put near the living. In Savannah's case, for example, four Negro churches, three Baptist, and one Methodist, were on the west side, while another served the east side. The central city had none. Of 174 "grocers" 101 did business in the outer residential wards, West Broad alone accommodating 19.[97] In Charleston the convergence was on the northern border and the Neck beyond.

In no case did anything like full residential segregation emerge. Few streets, much less blocks, were solidly black. Everywhere some whites occupied nearby dwellings. Still the inclination to cluster here, to concentrate there, was more marked by 1860 than in 1820. The separation apparent in other areas of life was slowly insinuated into housing.

Thus, even before slavery had been abolished, a system of segregation had grown up in the cities. Indeed, the whites thought some such arrangement was necessary if they were to sustain their traditional supremacy over the Negroes. The countryside provided enough room to give meaning to racial separation. The master could be physically quite removed from his blacks, though sharing the same plantation or farm. And together both were isolated from others. In cities these spatial relationships were quite different. Both races were thrown together; they encountered each other at every corner, they rubbed elbows at every turn; they divided up, however inequitably, the limited

[97] *Directory for the City of Savannah to Which Is Added a Business Directory for 1860* (Savannah, 1860), 176–7.

space of the town site. Segregation sorted people out by race, established a public etiquette for their conduct, and created social distance where there was proximity. Urban circumstances produced this system long before the destruction of slavery itself.

Of course, the complete separation of races was impossible in the city, and the practice differed from place to place. In some towns, public conveyances remained mixed; in others Negroes were not excluded from all public grounds; in still others housing continued scrambled. Yet every city developed its own arrangement expressed in the contrived separation of colored and white in countless ways. Though never total, the segregation was so extensive that Negroes were never permitted to forget their inferior position.

XI

The rising incidence of segregation was another index of the increasing weakness of slavery in the cities. Rooted in the white's need for discipline and deference, it developed to take up the slack in the loosening system. It provided public control to replace dwindling private supervision of the master over his slave. To do this, the difference between free and enslaved Negroes had to be narrowed, depriving free blacks of part of their freedom even while permitting a wider latitude to bondsmen. To most whites, however, there seemed no alternative. The old system no longer really controlled; the walls no longer really confined; the chains no longer really held.

The decline of slavery in the cities was the central fact of race relations in the South's cities in the ante-bellum decades. It was also a fact that conditioned Negro life in subsequent generations, for it meant that, when emancipation finally did come, most of the colored population would be in the countryside rather than in cities. Accustomed only to routine tasks, imbruted by the severe limitations of plantation existence, and unused to managing their own affairs, they became free under the most difficult of circumstances.

If the Negro population in the cities had grown in the same proportion as the whites, there would have been present an invaluable pool of potential leadership, for there many blacks, even under slavery, had begun to develop the most important tools of citizenship. There they acquired some skills and learned the rudiments of reading and writing. There, too, many had commenced to manage their own affairs, and in churches they developed a capacity for organization.

In short, the metropolis nourished the literacy and self-reliance needed in a free system.

Observers generally agreed on the other hand that rural blacks plainly bore the mark of their servitude. "The field-hand negro is, on the average, a very poor and bad creature," Olmsted wrote sadly, "much worse than I supposed before I had seen him and grown familiar with his stupidity, indolence, duplicity, and sensuality. He seems to be but an imperfect man, incapable of taking care of himself in a civilized manner." [98] House servants were presumably in a favored condition, but their contacts usually were only somewhat wider, their self-reliance seldom encouraged, and their horizons not appreciably better.

Olmsted found quite the opposite in the cities. "Slaves can never be brought together in denser communities but their intelligence will be increased to a degree dangerous to those who enjoy the benefit of their labor," he observed. "Hundreds of slaves in New Orleans must be constantly reflecting and saying to one another, 'I am as capable of taking care of myself as this Irish hod-carrier, or this German market-gardener; why can't I have the enjoyment of my labor as well as they? I am as capable of taking care of my own family as much as they of theirs; why should I be subject to have them taken from me by those other men who call themselves our owners?' " And the speculation no doubt extended to the next generation: " 'Our children have as much brains as the children of these white neighbors of ours, who not long ago were cooks and waiters at the hotel, why should they be spurned from the school rooms? I helped build the school house, and have not been paid for it. One thing I know, if I can't have my rights, I can have my pleasures; and if they won't give me wages I can take them.' " [99]

Olmsted saw this distinction more clearly than most. But visitors from the North, travelers from abroad, in fact, masters and slaves, also understood the difference. It was an uncomfortable fact for the whites. To them it presaged a wider freedom for the Negro, with all the uncertainties and perhaps chaos that would follow. Hence the response of owners and officials was to tighten rather than adjust, to expel rather than emancipate, to segregate rather than liberate. At the end the "free air of the city" was being increasingly denied to a higher and higher proportion of blacks.

[98] Olmsted, *Back Country,* 432.
[99] Olmsted, *Seaboard Slave States,* 591.

The full significance of the de-urbanization of the Negro under slavery was apparent only much later. Emancipation found him located primarily in the least dynamic area of American life. Capable of simple tasks, familiar only with rural routine, largely illiterate, and unused to managing his own affairs, he faced a long road to full freedom. Ultimately that road carried him to the city. Though confronted by both discrimination and segregation, he could find there the numbers and leadership which could one day spring him loose from the confinements of an earlier bondage.

The recovery of the metropolis began before the First World War. The depression slowed the pace somewhat, but a second global conflict produced an irresistible urban undertow. Colored families had abandoned the land by now or were pushed off it by machines and new techniques. By the thousands each day they flocked to the cities both North and South. There, often amid squalor and deprivation, they began the dramatic rally of forces that would dissolve the walls which for three centuries had kept them outside the promised land of equal rights.

Significantly, among the datelines which reported the new phase of the story were New Orleans, Mobile, Savannah, Charleston, Richmond, Louisville, and St. Louis. A new generation of Negroes pushed aside older leadership and took to the lunchrooms and streets as well as the courts in a drive to desegregate the public life of the South. Though Dixie resisted everywhere, the first breakthrough appeared in the urban areas. Parks, buses, public facilities, and a few schools opened first; commercial enterprises, restaurants, and hotels grudgingly followed. Moreover, the rise of Negro voting in the major cities gradually provided a stable base for further successes.

The characteristic focus of the movement was the churches. Like their ante-bellum predecessors, they were more than religious centers, encompassing in a unique way the whole range of organized Negro life in the city. Their ministers spoke not merely for their own congregations but for the colored community as a whole. And standing in a long Christian and Southern tradition, they commanded respect among important white groups in the city. In the churches the people gathered, heard speeches, and bolstered their morale. Boycotts were planned, discipline established, even demonstrations started from the same sanctuaries. Ironically now, the pattern of social organization born in slavery became the vanguard of a new freedom.

7

Patterns of Mid-Nineteenth-Century Urbanization in the Middle West

by BAYRD STILL

On many a frontier the town builder was as conspicuous as the farmer pioneer. . . .

The spectacular growth of the lake cities—Buffalo, Cleveland, Detroit, Chicago, and Milwaukee—in the decade preceding and the years soon after the Civil War made them harbingers of the urbanization of the country. The combined population of these cities increased by sixteen times their 1840 level, whereas the states in which they were located barely tripled in population. "The town builder was as conspicuous as the farmer pioneer" in this period of American development, and for this reason, the early nature of these communities and the manner in which they changed from village to city are vital to an understanding of modern urban America.

All the lake cities were essentially private in concept, as was Philadelphia in the beginning. Government was limited and for the most part staffed by amateurs. Before the Civil War the emphasis was on trade, but this was to shift to industry after 1865. Meanwhile, railroad construction afforded the lake cities an expanding area of commerce and an increasing scope for their industries. Although they all owed their origins to their accessibility via the Great Lakes, all the lake cities became important railroad cities. As Bessie Louise Pierce has written in the second volume of her definitive *A History of Chicago 1848–1871,*[*] "this vast network of iron was the greatest single factor in the phenomenal commercial development of Chicago during these years."

In some respects all the lake cities reveal a common attitude with the

[*] New York, Alfred A. Knopf, 1940.

agrarian frontier in their emphasis on the importance of the role of the individual in promoting physical and cultural growth and their willing dependence on the East as a transmitter of culture.

Bayrd Still was born in Woodstock, Illinois, in 1906 and received his PhD from the University of Wisconsin in 1933. After teaching at both Wisconsin and Duke, he joined the faculty of New York University in 1947, and he has been head of its history department since 1955. Dr. Still is the author of a number of important historical works including *Milwaukee: The History of a City*, published in 1948; *Mirror for Gotham*, published in 1956; and *The West: Contemporary Records of America's Expansion Across the Continent*, published in 1961.

This essay is reproduced from Volume XXVIII of the *Mississippi Valley Historical Review* with the permission of the Organization of American Historians.

Until recently a persistent preoccupation with the agrarian aspects of the westward march of American settlement has to some extent obscured the fact that the prospect of future towns and cities as well as the promise of broad and fertile acres lured settlers to the "sunset regions." On many a frontier the town builder was as conspicuous as the farmer pioneer; the western city, through the efforts of its founders to extend its economic hinterland, actually facilitated the agrarian development of the West, and the opportunities attending city growth as well as those afforded by cheap farm lands contributed to the dynamic sense of economic abundance felt by Americans of the mid-nineteenth century. As early as 1845 one middle western editor identified this urban growth with the rapid development of the West when he wrote:

> The tide of emigration to the West seems to increase daily. . . . What an enterprising spirit characterizes the American people. . . . This . . . activity and enterprise . . . are the result of free institutions, which give an impetus to the human mind. In no other country have towns and villages sprung up so suddenly as in this. Everything seems to go ahead with railroad velocity. Well might Marryat remark that cities grow up here to more importance in ten years than they do in Europe in a century.[1]

The growth of cities is admittedly a significant aspect of the history

[1] Milwaukee *Daily Sentinel,* May 26, 1845.

of the West. But any precise estimate of the bearing either of urbanization upon the expansion of the American frontier or of the westward movement of population upon city growth in the United States awaits a more adequate exposition of urban development in specific sections of the country than has as yet been set forth.[2]

[2] The following are the most useful titles for making comparative studies of urban development in the Mississippi Valley. Buffalo: Robert W. Bingham, *The Cradle of the Queen City: A History of Buffalo to the Incorporation of the City* (Buffalo, 1931); Henry W. Hill, ed., *Municipality of Buffalo, New York; A History, 1720–1923* (4 vols., New York, 1923); Josephus N. Larned, *A History of Buffalo, Delineating the Evolution of the City* (2 vols., New York, 1911). Cleveland: Elroy M. Avery, *A History of Cleveland and Its Environs* (3 vols., Chicago, 1918); William R. Coates, *A History of Cuyahoga County and the City of Cleveland* (3 vols., Chicago, 1924); Samuel P. Orth, *A History of Cleveland, Ohio* (3 vols., Chicago, 1910). Detroit: George B. Catlin, *The Story of Detroit* (Detroit, 1923); Clarence M. Burton, ed., *The City of Detroit, Michigan, 1701–1922* (4 vols., Chicago, 1922); Silas Farmer, *History of Detroit and Michigan* (Detroit, 1884); Arthur Pound, *Detroit, Dynamic City* (New York, 1940); Robert B. Ross and George B. Catlin, *Landmarks of Detroit* (Detroit, 1898). Milwaukee: William G. Bruce, *History of Milwaukee City and County* (3 vols., Milwaukee, 1922); John G. Gregory, *History of Milwaukee, Wisconsin* (4 vols., Chicago, 1931); Bayrd Still, "The Growth of Milwaukee as Recorded by Contemporaries," *Wisconsin Magazine of History* (Madison), XXI, 1938, pp. 262–292, and "Milwaukee, 1870–1900: the Emergence of a Metropolis," *loc. cit.*, XXIII, 1939, pp. 138–162. Chicago: Alfred T. Andreas, *History of Chicago, 1670–1885* (3 vols., Chicago, 1884–1886); J. Seymour Currey, *Chicago: Its History and Its Builders* (3 vols., Chicago, 1912); Bessie L. Pierce, *A History of Chicago* (2 vols., New York, 1937, 1940), and *As Others See Chicago* (Chicago, 1933). Pittsburgh: Leland D. Baldwin, *Pittsburgh, the Story of a City* (Pittsburgh, 1937); George T. Fleming, *History of Pittsburgh and Environs* (5 vols., New York, 1922); Frank C. Harper, *Pittsburgh of Today, Its Resources and People* (4 vols., New York, 1931); Sarah H. Killikelly, *The History of Pittsburgh, Its Rise and Progress* (Pittsburgh, 1906). Cincinnati: Clara Chambrun, *Cincinnati: Story of the Queen City* (New York, 1939); Henry A. and Kate B. Ford, *History of Cincinnati, Ohio* (Cleveland, 1881); Charles T. Greve, *Centennial History of Cincinnati and Representative Citizens* (2 vols., Chicago, 1904). Louisville: Reuben T. Durrett, *The Centenary of Louisville* (*Filson Club Publications*, no. 8, Louisville, 1893); L. A. Williams and Co., eds., *History of the Ohio Falls Cities and Their Counties* (Cleveland, 1882); J. Stoddard Johnston, ed., *Memorial History of Louisville from Its First Settlement to the Year 1896* (2 vols., Chicago, n. d.). Minneapolis: Norman S. B. Gras, "The Significance of the Twin Cities for Minnesota History," *Minnesota History* (St. Paul), VII, 1926, pp. 3–17; Mildred L. Hartsough, *The Twin Cities as a Metropolitan Market: A Regional Study of the Economic Development of Minneapolis and St. Paul* (Minneapolis, 1925); Calvin F. Schmid, *Social Saga of Two Cities: An Ecological and Statistical Study of Social Trends in Minneapolis and St. Paul* (Minneapolis, 1937). St. Louis: John T. Scharf, *History of St. Louis City and County, from the Earliest Periods to the Present Day* (2 vols., Philadelphia, 1883); Walter B. Stevens, *St. Louis, the Fourth City, 1764–1911* (2 vols., St. Louis, 1911). Memphis: Gerald M. Capers, Jr., *The Biography of a River*

The migrants who poured into the Mississippi Valley in the middle of the nineteenth century built cities as well as cultivated farms. By the seventies, when the American people were first becoming conscious of the drift of population to the city, the Middle West showed a spectacular urban growth. It could then boast seven cities of more than a hundred thousand people,[3] whereas thirty years before only New Orleans had achieved that size. To be sure, the total population of the ten major mid-western cities in 1870 still fell slightly short of the more than 1,800,000 city dwellers then living in New York, Philadelphia, and Boston; but in the rate of their growth the former were putting to shame the cities of the Atlantic coast. Among these mushroom metropolises of the West, the lake cities—Buffalo, Cleveland, Detroit, Chicago, and Milwaukee—rather than the valley cities—Pittsburgh, Cincinnati, Louisville, Nashville, and St. Louis—showed the greatest proportional increase in numbers.[4] By 1870 the five lake cities had attained a combined population of more than sixteen times their total of 1840, although the population of the states in which they were located had barely tripled.[5]

Because of their rapid and parallel growth, a comparative analysis of these five lake cities provides a useful means of studying the nature of the emerging city in the Middle West. With striking similarity, they all limited themselves to those duties of the urban community which were common to eighteenth century cities. They all responded to the democratic movement by extending popular participation in municipal government and then by broadening the authority of the executive or administrative commission. Not only did they rely upon the indi-

Town; Memphis: Its Heroic Age (Chapel Hill, 1939). New Orleans: Henry Rightor, ed., *Standard History of New Orleans, Louisiana* (Chicago, 1900).

[3] St. Louis, 310,864; Chicago, 298,977; Cincinnati, 216,239; New Orleans, 191,418; Pittsburgh, 139,256; Buffalo, 117,714; Louisville, 100,753, *Fifteenth Census of the United States, 1930, Population*, I, 18-19.

[4] Between 1860 and 1870 the total population of the lake cities increased over 100 per cent; that of the valley cities, 60 per cent; that of New York, Philadelphia, and Boston, 20 per cent; that of the United States, 22.6 per cent. *Ibid.*, 12 *et passim*.

[5] Comparative population of the Great Lakes cities:

	1820	1830	1840	1850	1860	1870
Buffalo	2,095	8,668	18,213	42,261	81,129	117,714
Cleveland	606	1,076	6,071	17,034	43,417	92,829
Detroit	1,422	2,222	9,102	21,019	45,619	79,577
Chicago			4,470	29,963	109,260	298,977
Milwaukee			1,712	20,061	45,246	71,440

Ibid., 19. The total population of the East North Central States increased during 1840 to 1870 from 2,924,728 to 9,124,517. *Ibid.*, 11.

vidual to provide most of the services which are demanded today of the city itself but they also expected him to promote the city's growth —a promotion which in every case involved substituting the encouragement of manufacturing for an earlier emphasis on trade. And with equal uniformity they imitated the experience of one another in ordering the details of their municipal life. While it is never too wise to try to compress the variety of human behavior into patterns, the common responses of the five cities suggest the conclusion that these at least are qualities which may well be characteristic of mid-nineteenth century urbanization in the upper Middle West.

A comparative study of the charters under which the Great Lakes cities were governed between 1830 and 1870 discloses the imitation of form and limitation of function in which the powers of the urban community were at that time conceived. These charters were cut from an almost identical constitutional pattern, laid down in the spirit of eighteenth century America. Admittedly the creature of the legislative will of the state, each city nevertheless resorted frequently to the public meeting for the purpose of proposing charter changes and civic improvement.[6] With the advance to city status the meagre functions of the village period—protection against fire, opening and repairing streets, regulating markets, licensing shows, and sinking public wells—were considerably expanded. These functions were enlarged by a uniform extension of regulatory powers, services, and guarantees— additions which were, however, more boldly granted than enforced if one judges from the charges of nonenforcement levied against the city administration by the Milwaukee press.

The first city charters of Buffalo (1832), Cleveland (1836), and Chicago (1837) were strikingly similar in form. The Chicago charter is almost an identical copy of the Buffalo document save for certain local references. In the more than thirty clauses enumerating the powers of the council, the wording of the Chicago charter is different from that of Buffalo in less than half a dozen instances. The Chicago charter added provisions with respect to street lamps and ferries, but lacked the provision for the assize of bread that is found in the Buffalo framework of government. Significantly, the contemporaneous govern-

[6] Chicago's first charter was the result of popular agitation. It was submitted to a mass meeting for popular approval, there slightly altered, and sent to the legislature. Edmund J. James calls it a self-proposed charter, "a practical recognition of local self-government on a large scale." Edmund J. James, *The Charters of the City of Chicago* (Chicago, 1898), 23. Such local participation did not prevent imitation in selecting the form of the charter.

ment of Milwaukee, organized at virtually the same time (1836), was still confined to the restricted duties of a village. Ten years later, however, when it emerged as a city, its citizens sought, and the state legislature granted, an expansion of powers quite similar to those of its sister cities of the Great Lakes. The Chicago consolidation act of 1851 found an echo in a like measure for Milwaukee in 1852 and in a revision of Buffalo's charter in 1853. These charters elaborated rather than expanded the powers of the municipality in ways dictated by closer acquaintance with the problems of city government. Again the customary parallelism in form stands out both in the general pattern of the documents and in the many identical clauses, such as those setting up the fire department and compelling the removal of ill-smelling nuisances.[7]

The advance from village to city brought an extension of municipal responsibilities, but only to an extent normally resulting, especially in America, from the crowding of people into small compass. These new powers were limited in general to the protection of life and property although the results of each extension of authority were recognized as having a bearing on the promotion of trade and hence on the prosperity of the municipality. Concern for securing property against the chronic fire hazard of the western city made possible the enactment of building restrictions and encouraged the organization of fire-fighting facilities. Concern for health prompted the authorities to establish pesthouses, to quarantine immigrants coming through the lake ports, and to abate such nuisances as stagnant pools, foul-smelling substances, and slaughter houses—reforms stimulated not so much by aesthetic considerations as by the prevailing conviction that urban filth and the spread of cholera went hand in hand. While thus exhorting cleanliness, the authorities at the same time, perhaps paradoxically, laid restrictions on wasting water and prohibited bathing in the rivers from which the city water supply was drawn.

In the interests of urban order, the city councils were empowered to provide watchmen and police; to suppress disorderly houses; to impound animals running at large; to prevent immoderate driving, rolling hoops or playing ball in the streets, and the cluttering of sidewalks with snow, dirt, firewood, awnings, or cigar store Indians; to

---

[7] For an example of identical clauses in these city charters see *Laws of the State of New York, 1853* (Albany, 1853), p. 461; *Laws of Wisconsin, 1852* (Madison, 1852), p. 81; and *Statutes of Illinois, Private Laws, 1851* (Springfield, 1851), p. 143.

restrain "runners" for boats and stages; and to curtail city noises. Nor were these idle grants of authority. The Cleveland council, as one of its first acts, passed an ordinance on May 9, 1836, which provided that the streets were to be swept semi-monthly on Friday mornings by the owners or occupants of property; that horses should not be fastened so as to obstruct passage in the streets nor be driven on the sidewalks; and that the huge wooden replicas of boots, saddles, and kettles with which merchants advertised their wares were not to project over three feet into the street. In addition to providing for quarantine and hospitalization of the sick poor, the health ordinances of Milwaukee required that physicians report cases of contagious diseases and that records of burials show the cause of death lest criminal or dangerous causes be left unknown; decreed a fine of ten dollars for refusal to be vaccinated on the request of a physician employed by the city council; set up barriers to the immigration of the diseased, going so far as to empower constables to call upon the aid of bystanders in forcibly keeping immigrants from landing; and banned slaughter houses within the city limits. The Buffalo council prohibited interment within certain limits and ordered that graves be not less than five feet deep. Anti-noise ordinances in Buffalo and Milwaukee prevented the playing of musical instruments on docks or wharves on Sunday, and in Milwaukee the ringing of bells or loud outcries at public sales were forbidden.

In providing for markets and the regulation of traffic in necessary commodities, these western cities followed practices by which frontier and colonial communities had attempted to protect an often insufficient food supply, prevented monopolistic practices detrimental to the public health and security, avoid the competition of foreign vendors and hucksters, and at the same time force competition upon the licensed merchants.[8] In 1849 Chicago had three markets for the retailing of perishable foods. Butchers were forced to hold stalls there until an act of 1851 permitted the establishment of meat shops outside the market.[9] City markets and strict market ordinances were justified as a means of supplying large cities with fresh and wholesome provisions, because leniency in this respect, it was felt, might encourage disease. Vendors of fresh meat, poultry, eggs, butter, lard,

[8] For colonial legislation on this subject consult Henry W. Farnam, *Chapters in the History of Social Legislation in the United States to 1860* (Washington, 1938), 92–115.

[9] Bessie L. Pierce, *A History of Chicago* (New York, 1937–), II, 461, note.

fruit and vegetables were forced to sell their goods at the market during the market hours unless licensed to sell at some other place or in some other way. To guarantee the wholesomeness of the products, cleanliness of the stalls, and orderliness of the market, prohibitions were set up against pitching quoits, the presence of dogs, and the use of obscene and profane language in the vicinity of the market place. Purchasing goods at the markets for resale elsewhere or forestalling country producers for the purpose of buying their produce for resale was prohibited.[10]

Similar regulations for supervising weights and measures affected the purchase of boards, brick, coal, firewood, casks, hay, flour, tobacco, potash, and salted provisions such as fish. According to a Cleveland ordinance of May 8, 1839, vendors of hay without a certificate of weight were subject to a fine of twenty-five dollars. In 1859 Milwaukee farmers opposed as an inequitable tax the weighing charge of five cents per load of wood and twenty-five cents per load of hay—a concession sold by the city to the highest bidder.[11] The assize of bread, customary in the colonial city charter and in early charters in the West, was apparently abandoned in Chicago and for a while in Cleveland, though provided for elsewhere.[12] In these young urban communities, commerce in such necessary commodities as food, fodder, and firewood was of sufficient public interest to warrant close regulation. Other pursuits related to the public welfare were also restricted. For instance, ordinances regulating the fees of hackmen and carters were not unusual. Chapter XIII of the Buffalo ordinances of 1855 stipulated that a hackman might be fined for refusing to carry a passenger or for going by other than the shortest route.

[10] As an example of this type of early municipal regulation see "An Ordinance Relating to the First Ward Market, and to License and Regulate Butcher's Stalls, Shops and Stands for the Sale of Butcher's Meat, Poultry, Game, and Fresh Fish," in *Charters and Ordinance of the City of Milwaukee* (Milwaukee, 1857), 464–465. Of similar nature is a Buffalo ordinance of April 23, 1855, and one in Cleveland, June 3, 1851.

[11] Milwaukee *Sentinel*, January 4, 1859.

[12] An act regulating the "Assize of Bread" seems to have been in force in Detroit as late as 1820. The price of bread was fixed according to a sliding scale based on the price of flour. George N. Fuller, *Economic and Social Beginnings in Michigan, 1805–1837* (Lansing, 1916), 126. A Massachusetts regulation, based on the price of grain plus a reasonable allowance for labor, was abandoned in 1801. Farnam, *Social Legislation to 1860*, 110. The Milwaukee ordinance regulating the manufacture and sale of bread (July 13, 1836) required registration of the baker's place of business, the use of wholesome flour, and the marking of loaves with the weight of the loaf and the initials of the baker. This was virtually the same bread legislation as that of New

Interest in attracting immigrants prompted a Milwaukee ordinance of May 3, 1849, which fixed a maximum charge of ten cents per article on the goods of immigrants and other passengers landed on the piers of the city.

These principal activities of the mid-nineteenth century city were laid down at the inception of cityhood and were based upon the regulations commonly existing during the colonial period. Later amendments elaborated these functions of municipal government as specific problems arose, and occasionally a measure was passed which suggested an expanding concept of city government, as in the Chicago provision of 1851 with respect to planting and preserving ornamental trees along the streets and in the public grounds of the city. In general, however, the close of this middle period saw only a limited expansion of urban responsibilities beyond those assumed with the grant of the original charter. Nor did these differ in any marked way from the eighteenth century pattern of powers granted the government of New York City at the close of the colonial period.

However, in defining the political authority underlying municipal management, these cities, developing in the current of nineteenth century democracy, left eighteenth century limitations far behind. Here again is a striking uniformity of behavior in the five lake cities. Each began its career as a city with a property qualification, in addition to a residence requirement of varying length, for at least one class of voters—whites, aliens, or negroes. Detroit in 1824 required its electors to be freemen who had paid a city tax. Buffalo extended the suffrage to United States citizens but required negro voters to have a freehold estate of $250 on which taxes had been actually rated and paid. A tax qualification was prerequisite to voting in Cleveland in 1836, and Chicago in 1837 expected its voters to be householders or to have paid a city tax of not less than three dollars within the year. As late as 1846 Milwaukee exacted payment of a property tax or required highway or fire duty of male aliens who had declared their intention of becoming citizens. At the outset of cityhood in Chicago, Detroit, and Buffalo, only those owning a freehold estate were eligible for the major elective posts; Milwaukee, having demanded a similar qualification of her village trustees, abandoned this provision upon becoming a city in 1846.

Chicago took the lead in a democratic movement which brought

York in 1839 and of Boston as late as 1834. A similar provision is found in Chapter XXXVII of the Cleveland ordinances as codified in 1877.

by the early fifties the abolition of property qualifications for suffrage and office holding. Milwaukeeans called a proposal to restrict the suffrage to United States citizens an "odious and anti-republican" attempt to deprive "one-half of the citizens of Milwaukee, who will be taxed for the support of the city government, of their right to a voice in electing their officers or making their laws." [13] Like the framers of the state constitutions of the middle period, these mid-western city dwellers believed in representative government closely responsive to the popular will. A proposal to allow aldermen to hold their offices for three years was opposed in Milwaukee as "placing them beyond the reach of public opinion for a time almost equal to an age in older communities." [14] Consequently, annually-elected councils were endowed with wide authority and the power of the executive office was greatly curtailed. In Buffalo the mayor was the creature of the council, and in the other cities little more than a figurehead. Chicagoans in 1840 openly resented the fact that their mayor was given a salary and pointed to Detroit and Buffalo where, they said, the mayors "in fact receive nothing." [15] Adherence to the democratic principle of passing jobs around was the practice if not the provision. In Cleveland between 1836 and 1870 only five mayors succeeded themselves in office, and of the twelve available council positions the yearly average of councilmen who were reëlected was two. A study of the situation in Chicago and Milwaukee shows a similar rotation in office. In Detroit it became necessary to force men by threat or danger of fine to serve once they had been elected, although they were specifically exempted from holding the same office two years in succession. The municipal legislators served without salary, but this did not prevent many of them from amassing fortunes, especially when they held the office of street commissioner.[16] To judge from an analysis of the trades and occupations of those who were councilmen in Cleveland and Milwaukee in the first twenty years of their cityhood, commission merchants, grocers, joiners, builders, masons, and attorneys took a

13Milwaukee *Courier*, January 27, 1845, quoted in Milwaukee *Evening Wisconsin*, October 15, 1895.

14 *Ibid*.

15 Pierce, *Chicago*, I, 328, note.

16 Laurence M. Larson, *A Financial and Administrative History of Milwaukee* (*Bulletin of the University of Wisconsin*, no. 242, *Economics and Political Science Series*, Vol. IV, no. 2, Madison, 1908), 27–28; Milwaukee *Sentinel*, June 27, 1857.

predominantly active part in the government of these young western cities.

Charter changes both in the early fifties and after the financial crisis of 1857 brought some decrease in the amateur management of these governments and a consequent strengthening of the executive arm. In 1852 Milwaukee was provided with an appointed comptroller, soon made elective, to manage city finances. In 1858 the state legislature devised a bicameral council for the city in the hope of retarding hasty legislation. The mayor was granted the veto power in Chicago in 1851 and in Milwaukee in 1859, a negative that was strengthened in the latter city in 1861 and in the former in 1872 by requiring two-thirds rather than a majority of the elected councilmen to override it. The major development in all the Great Lakes cities at the close of the period under discussion was in the direction of establishing boards and commissions as a means of divorcing city management from amateur direction and political interference. This trend, realized in the late sixties and early seventies, was motivated, according to the Milwaukee *Sentinel*, by a feeling that it was inefficient and costly to commit the complicated problems of street improvements and urban services to elected councilmen. It would be better, said the editor, to trust the outlay of great sums of the people's money to "three capable, honest, experienced business men . . . with a moderate compensation for their services, than take the chances under the elective principle of having men of doubtful qualities . . . without compensation . . . under the constant imputation of petty frauds and speculations upon the ward funds." [17] Vesting in the mayor the power of appointing the members of these boards and commissions is an index of the increased prestige of the executive and the decreasing influence of the legislative branch of city government at the opening of the seventies. The Great Lakes cities, growing to maturity in the environment · of nineteenth century democracy, thus broadened the base of urban politics but narrowed the administration of municipal affairs.

These major cities of the Middle West did not "just grow." The promotional activities of the original speculator-founders were only the beginning of a long-time program in which newspaper editors, merchants, and citizens at large combined their efforts to attract

[17] Milwaukee *Sentinel*, April 5, 1869. See also *ibid.*, March 11, 1852, and March 13, 1864; John G. Gregory, *History of Milwaukee, Wisconsin* (Chicago, 1931), I, 253.

settlers and business to a given city and away from its neighboring rivals.[18] The promoters of the embryo village on the east side of the Milwaukee River expended nearly $100,000 laying out streets and effecting other improvements designed to attract the settler. By the exertion of political influence and the donation of land they secured the county courthouse for their growing community. Across the river, the promoters of the "west side" were spending similar sums upon improvements, filling the columns of the Milwaukee *Advertiser* with glowing reports of their city's promise, and, by employing a river boat to meet the lake steamers that touched Milwaukee harbor, pre-ëmpting immigrants possibly destined for their rivals' village. Subsequently many a subterfuge was devised by Chicago and Milwaukee in an attempt to discredit the other in the eyes of European immigrants and eastern capitalists. Only the combination of geography and the railroad left Milwaukee a tired but still confident second in the race. "Forcing" immigrants was accomplished through the use of representatives and promotional advertising in eastern cities. For example, propaganda concerning deaths from cholera, or the absence of them, figured prominently in such campaigns.[19]

The promotion of business in these cities followed a common pattern. A predominant concern for trade and commerce gave way in the middle sixties to the encouragement of manufacturing. Economic developments in Milwaukee and Cleveland substantiate this interpretation. The early interest in trade was reflected by the editor of the Milwaukee *Daily Sentinel and Gazette* in 1846: "It is . . . clearly to the interest of our merchants, millers, forwarders, and business men generally to unite upon some plan for extending and improving roads leading to Milwaukee." [20] Even before this, popular contributions had subsidized a bridge that promised to facilitate the trade of neigh-

[18] The Cincinnati *Gazette,* quoted in the Milwaukee *Sentinel* of June 10, 1859, asserted that a newspaper served the founders of towns by acting as a kind of credential to the reality of the inchoate city, and as a light to direct the pioneer to a new home and to direct business and emigration into new channels.

[19] The Boston *Chronotype,* as quoted in the Milwaukee *Daily Sentinel and Gazette,* August 29, 1846, referred to the "forcing process" as circulating "numberless libels in handbills" in the East. Milwaukeeans claimed that Chicago newspapers were libeling their health record, and Cleveland papers labored during the thirties to deny that the village was sickly.

[20] Milwaukee *Daily Sentinel and Gazette,* March 11, 1846. In his inaugural address, Mayor D. A. J. Upham averred that "the improvements we most need . . . are the roads and facilities of securing trade from the country." *Ibid.,* April 12, 1849.

boring farmers with the village merchants. Plank roads and railroads were heralded as a means of tapping the markets of the hinterland. Connections by rail with the Columbia River, with the Mississippi River (completed by 1857), and with the Minnesota country, and routes eastward by steam ferry across Lake Michigan and by the Detroit and Michigan railroad were only a few of the projects. They were supported by city funds, by loans of city credit, and by popular subscription—contributions often appealed for and given as a matter of civic duty.[21] Clevelanders were equally convinced of the importance of roads and railways for prosperity. The editor of the Cleveland *Daily True Democrat* wrote in 1849: "Let us, like the wise Cincinnati merchants, spend liberally for these [plank] roads and do all to arouse our farmers and everybody to the importance of increasing our facilities for trade and travel and thus make Cleveland the center of a large region." [22] By 1856 it was asserted in the Cleveland *Leader* that railroads were responsible for the city's growth. The establishment of Boards of Trade in Buffalo (1844), Detroit (1847), Cleveland and Chicago (1848), and Milwaukee (1849); the organization and promotional excursions of merchants; the contesting of disputed trade areas through the use of runners and drummers—these activities suggest the early emphasis on trade and commerce as the key to civic prosperity. In 1857, Milwaukee merchants were urged to compete for trade in Iowa and Minnesota where

> already Chicago, St. Louis, Dubuque, Galena, Cincinnati even, have their runners, posters, and advertisements scattered broadcast . . . offering tempting inducements to merchants to come and buy. . . . Now is the time for our merchants, manufacturers, and traders to . . . scatter their cards, handbills, circulars, and advertisements up and down the Mississippi. Let them dispatch some of their shrewdest clerks to La Crosse, Winona, Prescott, Hudson, St. Paul . . . and canvass thoroughly for orders.[23]

[21] The city of Milwaukee soon substituted the issuance of bonds as loans to railroad companies for the earlier practice of buying railroad stock. Substantial security and a popular vote of authorization were required. This popular support was freely given, and by 1858 the loans to railroad companies totaled $1,614,000, all of which was ultimately repaid except two issues of $100,000 each. Larson, *Financial History of Milwaukee*, 74–75. By contrast the city of Chicago had made no railroad investments by 1870, and individual Chicagoans had not found it necessary to invest much in enterprises that eastern capitalists were eager to finance. Pierce, *Chicago*, II, 75.

[22] Cleveland *Daily True Democrat*, June 1, 1849.

[23] Milwaukee *Sentinel*, March 17, 1857.

By 1855, however, Cleveland editors were sounding a warning note. Business men were blinded, they said, "by the belief that commerce alone" would make the city great. The *Leader* asserted in 1856 that "no thinking man with capital will stop here when we have only commerce to sustain us. A manufacturing town gives a man full scope for his ambitions." [24] That newspaper encouraged popular subscriptions to factory enterprises, urged the reduction of real estate prices as an inducement to capital, and agitated for the protection and consumption of home manufactures.[25] An appeal to civic duty attended this promotion as it had the earlier agitation for railroad connections. By the late sixties when Cleveland had become a manufacturing center, earlier arguments used there were being echoed in Milwaukee. Vigorous newspaper agitation, together with the organization of the Milwaukee Manufacturers Association in January 1863, excited industrial ambitions. "Commerce alone can never give us a permanent prosperity," counselled a Milwaukee editor in 1866.[26] By 1872, as a result, one-third to one-half of the working population of Milwaukee was engaged in manufacturing goods valued at $20,000,000.[27] Stimulated by the economic developments of the Civil War period, pressed by the expansion of population into areas farther west of them, and in a sense taking a cue each from the economic experiences of the other, the lake cities had turned by 1870 from an almost exclusive interest in commerce to endorse sentiments to the effect that "a thousand dollars put into manufacturing does more to gather population than a million dollars put into trade." [28]

A major source of the urban services of these young communities developed from the sense of individual responsibility which prompted thousands of city dwellers to invest their savings in the railroads and factories that were supposed to bring prosperity to the urban center. The mid-nineteenth century saw the Great Lakes cities in what might be called the "subscription period" of their municipal growth. Two to three days' work on the streets, for which money payments could be substituted, was expected of all able-bodied men.[29] Street and side-

---

[24] Cleveland *Leader*, October 31, 1855, and March 10, 1856.

[25] *Ibid.*, March 30, 1858.

[26] Milwaukee *Sentinel*, October 20, 1866. See also *ibid.*, April 16, 1869, for an assertion by manufacturers that Milwaukeeans were still putting all their eggs in one basket.

[27] Frederick Merk, *Economic History of Wisconsin During the Civil War Decade* (Madison, 1916), 127.

[28] Cleveland *Leader*, April 10, 1873.

[29] Chicago in 1847 required males between the ages of twenty-one and sixty

walk improvements as well as the eradication of nuisances were to be taken care of individually or charged against the property benefited. For protection against theft and riot Milwaukeeans had to rely upon occasional watchmen, volunteer firemen, and members of free military companies until a night watch and a police force were organized in 1852. As late as 1855 men carried weapons for their own protection, and an ordinance of that year compelled all citizens to aid the police when called upon to do so. In 1837 the Cleveland *Herald and Gazette* referred to the "Mutual Protecting Society," and in 1839 a number of the citizens "with commendable spirit formed themselves into companies for a city watch." In 1859 the merchants of Detroit, where as early as 1825 volunteer watchmen had been mobilized by passing around a subscription paper, subscribed to the support of a patrol for the business district, and the Milwaukee Board of Trade offered a bonus for additional protection in 1860.[30] By the late fifties and early sixties police service was generally provided at city expense, and the management of the police by a commission was agitated or passed in Milwaukee (1864), Detroit (1865), and Cleveland (1866).

Fire protection came also in a major degree from individual contributions of time and money. In the middle thirties Clevelanders were fined when they refused to serve in the bucket line at fires. Local editors appealed to property owners to contribute their share of volunteer firemen and in 1840 congratulated Phoenix Company Number Four for having won the premiums offered annually by the insurance companies to stimulate competitive-minded fire fighters to efficiency and accomplishment. Milwaukeeans from all levels of society were members of the organized volunteer firemen, who met a portion of the costs of their own equipment and whose service exempted them from highway or militia duty. Donations, benefit concerts, and dinners raised $2,500 in 1851 to swell the funds by which the Ocean, Neptune, and Cataract companies of volunteer firemen carried on their work. Despite the pleas of property owners for more efficient service than unpaid volunteers could give, it was not until the appearance of the

to work on the streets three days each year, with commutation at the rate of fifty cents per day. Milwaukee in 1846 required two days' work with commutation at seventy-five cents per day.

[30] Cleveland *Herald and Gazette,* June 28, 1837; Gregory, *Milwaukee,* II, 1123; Milwaukee *Daily Sentinel and Gazette,* April 16, May 20, 1847, and February 6, 1850; Milwaukee *Sentinel,* August 16, 1855, and January 14, 1860; Cleveland *Herald,* November 28, 1839; Clarence M. Burton, ed., *The City of Detroit, Michigan* (Detroit, 1922), I, 406.

steam fire engine in the sixties that professional fire fighters were generally maintained from public funds.[31]

Aside from a meagre and inadequate tax to support almshouses and to furnish medical care for the sick poor, urban relief, too, was provided by individual donation. Invariably the cessation of navigation in the winter season brought demands from the unemployed of the city. Out of public meetings came plans for raising money and organizations for dispensing relief. Mayor D. A. J. Upham of Milwaukee expressed a general opinion in 1849 when he held that private enterprise was best equipped to meet the problem. The Cleveland *Daily True Democrat* said the poor could not be taken care of "unless individual activity and associated effort act." [32] Women's organizations, such as the Martha Washington Society of Cleveland and the Ladies Benevolent Society of Milwaukee, were soon supplanted by more systematically managed relief groups, like the Milwaukee Provident Association and the Cleveland Relief Association. The Milwaukee group advertised its cause as a community responsibility, raised over $20,000 in the five years ending in 1867, and distributed fuel and provisions only after careful investigation of the needy. Private contributions were the chief means of support of the Chicago Relief and Aid Society, incorporated in 1857. Soup kitchens were also subsidized by private gifts and meal tickets were sold to those citizens who wished to offer them to the poor. The Milwaukee women who managed these enterprises trusted "to the benevolence of our citizens . . . for the food to be supplied." [33]

To a large extent the cultural services of the city, beyond the provision for public schools, were the result of support by subscription. Forerunners of the public libraries of the seventies were the membership libraries of such organizations as the Young Men's Associations in Chicago and Milwaukee and the Reading Room Association in Cleveland.[34] Imitating Chicago's example, and realizing that the lack

[31] Cleveland *Herald and Gazette,* December 22, 1837; Cleveland *Herald,* June 24, 1840; Cleveland *Leader,* November 25, 1862, and April 14, 1863; Milwaukee *Sentinel,* January 22, 1852, March 4, 1861, and March 4, 1862; Gregory, Milwaukee, II, 795 ff.; Burton, *Detroit,* I, 402.

[32] Cleveland *Daily True Democrat,* December 20, 1850.

[33] Milwaukee *Sentinel,* November 30, 1857. See also *ibid.,* November 23, 1857, November 12, 1866, and December 20, 1867; Milwaukee *Daily Sentinel and Gazette,* April 12, 1849; Pierce, *Chicago,* II, 445–446.

[34] The Young Men's Association organized in Chicago in 1841 was modeled after a similar organization in Albany. Members were asked to donate books to the library and non-members might use the reading room at a charge of

of private libraries compelled "voluntary association," several Milwaukeeans organized to promote a library in 1847.[35] In canvassing for funds and members they did not neglect to stress community obligation and the example of other cities. The promotional value of good libraries to the city was "a pretty safe index of the mental advancement . . . of a city." They also emphasized the "gallantry of the Association [which] admits even ladies to a full participation of the advantages of membership, with the exception, we think, of voting." [36] Chartered in 1848, the Cleveland Library Association issued stock certificates and charged yearly dues. Soliciting subscriptions in 1851 for a reading room, the editor of the Cleveland *Daily True Democrat* was convinced that "nothing . . . adds so much to the reputation of a city as a good Reading Room and Library." [37]

Many other cultural activities were fostered by subscription. Local musicians and actors volunteered their services in aid of the fire department, orphan asylum, and other causes. The Milwaukee Musical Society when soliciting members in 1857 advised the public that its monthly dues of forty cents plus a two dollar initiation fee were "but a moderate tax to pay towards the support of an organization which ministers so largely to the enjoyment of our citizens and which reflects such credit upon our city." [38] The founders of academies and colleges in asking for endowments also appealed to civic duty.[39] By 1870 the

---

fifty cents a month. By 1847 the library had a thousand volumes, plus current newspapers. Pierce, *Chicago*, I, 286–288. The Cleveland Reading Room Association was supported by voluntary subscriptions. Elroy M. Avery, *A History of Cleveland and Its Environs* (Chicago, 1918), I, 188. Judging from an advertisement in the Cleveland *Herald*, November 30, 1836, dues were five dollars a year.

[35] The charge for life members was twenty-five dollars. Regular members paid an entrance fee of two dollars and fifty cents quarterly thereafter. The sum of $1,513 was collected in the first two months. The association had 810 books at the end of the first year.The librarian donated his services, and the library was open two afternoons a week. By 1867 the association had three thousand members and more than ten thousand volumes. Gregory, *Milwaukee*, II, 1077–1078.

[36] Milwaukee *Sentinel*, December 2, 1857.

[37] Cleveland *Daily True Democrat*, January 29, 1851. "Lucy Ann," having come to Cleveland from the East, wrote to the editor of the Cleveland *Herald*, July 14, 1845, bemoaning the lack of a Young Men's Association or a Reading Room Association. "There are enough young men here to support a . . . library, but . . . they are more fond of riding . . . in buggies, eating ice cream, and smoking cigars . . . than they are of obtaining worth of mind."

[38] Milwaukee *Sentinel*, December 7, 1857.

[39] *Ibid.*, March 4, 1852, November 26, 1853, and August 3, 1855.

beginning of public libraries [40] and the agitation for parks—following New York's example with Central Park—were slight but indicative signs of the role that the urban government was ultimately to play in providing aesthetic satisfaction and social and cultural benefits to its citizens.[41] A Cleveland editor went so far as to start a crusade in 1870 against city noises—"an evil rapidly becoming unendurable." He wrote: "While suppressing so rigorously all offences to the sight and smell, and punishing in general all disturbances of the peace, it would be only consistent to include in the proscription the still greater plague of noise." Yet he concluded a year later that the cure for city noises still lay in the field of individual responsibility: "We have not yet reached that point where the law will guard the nerves of the aged, the tender, and infirm from unnecessary torture." [42] Such a concept of city function did not square with the "subscription period" of city growth.

These striking parallels in the institutional history of the five major cities of the Great Lakes are to be explained in part by the contemporaneous character of their growth, by the common sources from which their population sprang, and by the similarity of the economic forces influencing their behavior. In all five cities, the foreign born provided about half the population, with natives of Germany, Ireland, and Great Britain distributing themselves in nearly uniform proportions, except in Milwaukee where European immigrants were more predominantly German. In the sectional origins of native Americans these cities were also similar. New York, Massachusetts, and Pennsylvania

40 The nucleus of Cleveland's public library was a collection of books provided under the school library law of 1853. A free public library was authorized by an act of 1867 and realized in 1869. According to the Cleveland *Leader*, March 16, 1869, "A free library is proof of the enlightened liberality in a community and of the intellectual culture and refinement thereof." Detroit's public library was formally opened in 1865. Burton, *Detroit*, I, 838. The library of the Young Men's Association of Milwaukee was transferred to the city of Milwaukee in 1878. Gregory, *Milwaukee*, II, 1078.

41 Public parks, according to the press, would counteract "the downward tendencies of city life" (Milwaukee *Daily Sentinel and Gazette*, April 24, 1845); enhance the value of property (Cleveland *Herald*, December 31, 1840); and offset urban congestion as a consequence of which "few grounds around the city remain occupied" (Milwaukee *Sentinel*, December 18, 1865). Detroit was agitating for an extensive park and Cleveland for three of them in 1865. The park question was discussed in a desultory way in Chicago during the fifties and sixties, but not until the late sixties was much accomplished. Pierce, *Chicago*, II, 339–341.

42 Cleveland *Leader*, September 3, October 18, 1870, and May 9, 1871. See also *ibid.*, May 7, 1869.

contributed most abundantly to each of the five cities save Chicago, which drew a large number from neighboring Michigan. The census of 1870 showed as well a remarkable uniformity in the percentages of people engaged in various occupational pursuits. But it was not simply a matter of similar social ingredients, for this municipal development of the Great Lakes area was apparently following a pattern or process not unusual to urban evolution elsewhere. As they grew to comparable size these cities were in many ways merely repeating the experience of the coastal cities half a century earlier. For example, after a generation of city growth the expanded powers of the lake cities in 1870, like those of the seaboard cities in 1800, represented a response more to the problems of size than to any changed philosophy of the functions of urban communities for which a difference in environment or personality might have been responsible. By 1870 each of these lake cities was a more conscious "municipal entity" than in its village period. Commercial regulations for the common good, cooperation through taxes and subscriptions for the promotion and improvement of the city, and the recognition of some of the social responsibilities presented by the interdependence of city life certainly had fostered a group consciousness—a group attitude, however, still very largely articulated by and pivoting around the individual. The "municipal consciousness," twentieth century pattern, was more than a generation in the future. Its full development awaited the flow of population, new economic needs, and changing social philosophy of the late nineteenth and early twentieth centuries.

In these urban centers of the Middle West in the mid-nineteenth century, the houses, to one traveller's surprise, were not "wigwamified," the dress and ornament not "wampumized." [43] As Anthony Trollope said, the "general level of . . . material and intellectual well-being—of beef . . . and book learning" was "no doubt infinitely higher than in a European town." [44] These cities sprang from beginnings closely associated in practice and attitude with the westward expansion of the American people. As they grew, their concern for popular management and their emphasis upon the intrinsic role of the individual in the promotion of the physical and cultural growth of the city reveal attitudes often observed by students of the agrarian frontier. At the same time, they showed a willing dependence upon

[43] A narrative of Nathaniel P. Willis of 1860, quoted in Gregory, *Milwaukee*, II, 1320.

[44] Anthony Trollope, *North America* (New York, 1862), I, 182.

eastern sources in the transmission of culture, a studied imitation of tested forms of municipal practice and urban service, and an expanding assumption of community responsibility. Such influences suggest that in the rise of the larger city in the West, as elsewhere, one sees another—perhaps equally important if less explored—side of American social history in the nineteenth century.

8

Yellow Fever in Memphis
in the 1870's

by GERALD M. CAPERS, Jr.

It became known throughout the nation that life was extremely hazardous in Memphis. . . .

Various American cities have suffered major disasters. Chicago has had its fire, San Francisco its earthquake, Galveston its flood, and New York City its draft riots. Yet curiously, the greatest municipal disaster of all, and the least known, is the Memphis yellow fever epidemic which started with the death of a Mrs. Bionda on August 13, 1878. Before the plague ended with the first October frost, a large part of the white Anglo-Saxon Protestant population had fled, 75 percent of the remaining population had caught the disease, and roughly 25 percent had died. For more than two months the city was paralyzed by panic and death. The epidemic had a lasting effect on the character and nature of the community. A substantial part of the German population left the city, never to return. Since the Catholic population, which was largely Irish, was for the most part too poor to flee, it was severely decimated. Just as the Civil War had "disrupted a *petit noblesse* in the process of aging, so the fever destroyed a second embryonic aristocracy before it cast off its swaddling clothes." The devastating nature of the disaster also served as an inspiration for the development of public health measures throughout municipal America. ". . . it aroused the country to the ever-present threat of disease at the very time that the findings of Pasteur and Koch were being disseminated."

Gerald M. Capers, Jr., the author of this essay, has throughout most of his life been closely associated with the river cities. Born in New Orleans in 1909, he lived in Memphis from 1930 to 1932. He joined the faculty of Tulane University in New Orleans in 1940 and has been chairman of the History Department of Sophie Newcomb College since 1941. Dr. Capers is the author of biographies of Stephen A. Douglas and John C. Calhoun, as well as of a book dealing with the occupation of New Orleans by Federal troops between 1862 and 1865. In 1939 Dr. Capers published *Biography of a River Town*. Chapter 7 of this book, "Sting of Yellowjack," contains additional material on the disaster which overtook Memphis in the 1870's and changed its character.

The following article is reprinted from Volume XXIV (March, 1938) of the *Mississippi Valley Historical Review* with the permission of the Organization of American Historians.

"Memphis astounds me with its rush and roar of business," commented a Kentuckian who visited it in the autumn of 1865. "So soon after the war it is wonderful. I predict that it will be the greatest city in the Mississippi Valley, St. Louis not excepted." [1]

In spite of the obvious enthusiasm of this author, such a prediction was not entirely without foundation at the close of the Civil War; in 1870 it was even less so. During the four years of the vain struggle for independence which cost the South at large so dearly, few southern towns suffered as little commercially as did Memphis. Except for the few months before and after its capture by the Federals in June, 1862, this metropolis of the middle Mississippi enjoyed an almost continuous trade which, abnormal and spasmodic though it was, nevertheless sustained the ordinary economic institutions that otherwise would have ceased to function. According to the estimate of Senator Zachariah Chandler, during the two years following its capture, Memphis was the entrepôt of a contraband trade with the Confederacy valued at from twenty to thirty million dollars; [2] and in 1865 the value of taxable property was set by the local tax assessor at eighteen million dollars, roughly what it had been five years before.[3]

In common with the rest of the state, Memphis was forced by Governor William G. Brownlow, East Tennessee Republicans, carpet-baggers, and scalawags to endure a tragic era no less severe than that to which Congress subjected the rest of the South, yet this

[1] *Memphis Argus,* November 4, 1865. *The Nashville Banner* also commented on this remarkable recovery; *ibid.,* November 7, 1865.

[2] *Congressional Globe,* 38 Cong., 1 Sess., IV, 3324.

[3] *Memphis Commercial,* January 27, 1866. These statistics, due to the increase in prices during the war, represent an actual loss, but a much smaller one than might be expected.

ordeal, too, it survived. At the end of the decade the United States Census revealed that in spite of the catastrophic social changes which war and reconstruction had produced the population of the city had increased from twenty-two to forty thousand. Still the largest inland cotton market in the country, its receipts of that staple were 80,000 bales short of its 1860 peak, though the value of the crop was considerably greater because of the high post-war price.[4] Banking capital was short of the 1860 total by $300,000, but increased insurance funds more than made up the difference.[5] From its harbor were operated eleven steamboat lines employing forty boats, and it led the nation in the manufacture of cottonseed oil with an annual output of 7400 barrels.[6] The pronounced increase in wholesale trade at the end of the sixties foreshadowed its future as a distributing point and dispelled forever its reputation as a "six-months-cottontown," if indeed the commerce of the fifties had not already removed that stigma.[7]   When the Democrats returned to power in Tennessee in 1870 the city had rebuilt its four railroads and had begun construction on new lines to Selma, Alabama, and Paducah, Kentucky. Undoubtedly, by the end of the war decade Memphis had more than regained its lost ground and, in blissful ignorance of the dark days just ahead, it prepared to enjoy a commercial utopia which the recent conflict had only postponed.

Unfortunately the seventies did not fulfill the promise of the sixties. In 1873 the city found itself in the throes of an epidemic of yellow fever which took the lives of 2000 of the 5000 inhabitants who contracted the disease. Again in 1878 the fever came, with 5150 deaths in 17,600 cases; and still a third time, the following year, with 600 deaths in 2000 cases. Considering the size of Memphis at the time, the magnitude and the devastation of these epidemics is without parallel in American urban history, and it is little wonder that the very existence of the city hung in the balance for several years.

Man, prehistoric and modern, has ever regarded plagues with superstition and awe. Since the classic description of the plague in Athens by Thucidydes many epidemics have had their chroniclers, but only the last half-century has possessed the medical knowledge necessary

[4] *Memphis Avalanche*, September 6, 1870. The average price in 1860 was ten cents per pound; in 1870 it varied from thirty-three cents to eighteen cents.

[5] John M. Keating, *History of Memphis* (Syracuse, 1889), I, 611.

[6] *Ibid.*

[7] Extracts from Mississippi papers, quoted in the Memphis *Public Ledger*, September 15, October 11, 1870.

for a scientific study of these catastrophes. Pestilence will probably continue to possess dramatic interest for the layman and scientific interest for the doctor, but the student of economic and social history has an entirely different approach, one which is highly pertinent to a study of Memphis. What effect do epidemics have upon the character and growth of a city, and what part do they play in competition between urban centers?

The health of Memphians, situated as they were in the midst of a swampy region inundated annually by the Mississippi, was wretched throughout the nineteenth century: not until 1900 was it known that the mosquito was the cause of much of its perennial sickness. Germs of exotic diseases, brought to New Orleans from Asia, Africa, South America, and the West Indies, soon found their way up the river. In an age when bacteriology did not exist, no distinction was made between Asiatic cholera and smallpox which were contagious, and dengue and yellow fever which were not transmitted directly. Not only were these diseases common in the valley, but also dysentery, pneumonia, and that chronic ailment of all lowlands, chills and fever. Preventive steps were never taken until pestilence was upon the community, and then quarantine and disinfectant were resorted to desperately, regardless of the nature of the disease. Since the cause of sickness was unknown and its diagnosis therefore unreliable, it is not surprising that the wise sought safety from epidemics in flight rather than in nostrums and medical care.

Sanitary conditions in Memphis during the seventies were perhaps no better than those of the poorest medieval borough. The water supply, which in ante-bellum days had been the Wolf and the Mississippi, consisted of defective wells and cisterns, supplemented in 1873 by a plant reputed to purify river water.[8] Subject to no inspection of any kind, milk was both diluted and polluted; the *Ledger* reported an instance of a live minnow found swimming in one pail.[9] According to the same paper, streets were "huge depots of filth, cavernous Augean stables, with no Tiber to flow through and cleanse them." Avenues, gutters, alleys, front and back yards were full of garbage, refuse, and dead animals that produced a stench which, but for the adaptation peculiar to the olfactory sense, would have driven human life from the town. The whole corporate area with its thousands of "privy vaults"

[8] *Report of the Memphis Board of Health, 1879* (Memphis, 1879), 19–20; Keating, *Memphis,* II, 300.
[9] Memphis *Public Ledger,* September 18, 1867.

drained into Gayoso Bayou, a stream once several miles in length, but which in the seventies had for many years been merely a series of stagnant pools, separated by dams of decaying organic matter and human excrement. Travelers pronounced the city the dirtiest in the country; "I've been to Cairo," facetiously exclaimed one carpet-bagger, "and there's dirt for you. . . . I've been to Cologne where it's pure smell—but they all back down Memphis." [10]

In the absence of reports from an organized board of health before 1879 one can only imagine the high annual toll of endemic diseases prior to that date, but of those which were epidemic there exists the following record:

Epidemics in Memphis before 1880 [11]

1740	Fever	Bienville's army decimated
1827	Dengue	
1828	Smallpox—yellow fever	53 deaths in 150 cases
1832–3	Cholera	Severe
1835	Cholera	350 cases, deaths 55%
1842	Smallpox	
1845	Dysentery	50 deaths in 400 cases
1849	Cholera	1200 cases, deaths 33%
1855	Yellow fever	220 deaths in 1250 cases
1860	Dengue	
1867	Yellow fever	550 deaths in 2500 cases
	Cholera	600 cases, deaths unknown
1873	Yellow fever	2000 deaths in 5000 cases
	Cholera	276 deaths in 1500 cases
	Smallpox	
1878	Yellow fever	5150 deaths in 17,600 cases
1879	Yellow fever	600 deaths in 2000 cases

The entire lower valley was sickly, but its few crowded cities were far more vulnerable than the thinly populated and less exposed districts of the interior. Memphis had suffered almost as much from pestilence before 1870 as had New Orleans, the most plague-ridden town in the nation, yet the press and the loyal citizens on the bluff would never admit that it was abnormally unhealthy. One boast in particular was full of tragic irony—"I honestly believe Memphis," wrote its first historian in 1872, becoming for the moment an apologist, "to be the healthiest place on the river from the mouth of the Ohio down." [12]

[10] *Ibid.*, August 10, 20, 1867, articles entitled "Memphis Mud and Filth."
[11] These statistics, taken from Keating, *Memphis*, I, 677, are only approximate. For a contemporary discussion of disease in Memphis see Denis A. Quinn, *Heroes and Heroines of Memphis* (Providence, 1887), 18.
[12] James D. Davis, *History of Memphis* (Memphis, 1873), 310.

Before proceeding to describe the details of the Memphis epidemics, it is necessary to consider the state of medical knowledge in that age as well as the history and nature of yellow fever. "Negro vomito," as it is more vividly termed in Spanish, ravaged the equatorial and Caribbean regions of the western hemisphere during the four centuries prior to 1900 with an average mortality of more than 50 per cent.[13] Carried by ships along both shores of the Atlantic from Africa to New England, it caused epidemics in cities as far east as Marseilles and as far north as Boston. The West Indies consistently experienced the highest mortality, but Philadelphia, New Orleans, and Memphis suffered from severe attacks on several occasions. Endemic to the tropics, this disease has always been more prevalent in the warmer regions of the temperate zone than in those where the temperature is lower.

Since the Philadelphia plague evoked the interest of Benjamin Rush in the 1790's, American physicians had constantly sought to discover the cause of yellow fever and the means of its propagation. Not until 1900, however, did Major Walter Reed by a series of experiments in Cuba prove that the disease could be transmitted only by the female of that species of mosquito technically known as the *aedes aegypti*.[14] It was announced in 1918 that the bacteria which produced the fever had been isolated, but medical opinion at present rejects this theory in favor of an infilterable virus as the cause.

The pattern of American epidemics has been somewhat as follows: some individual, usually from the tropics, came into port with the germ in his blood-stream. Yellow fever mosquitos proceeded to bite him, and after an incubation period of twelve days the insects by their sting transmitted the germs to other people. This process was repeated wherever those who were thus infected happened to go, as long as the temperature permitted the continued existence of the germ. In the temperate zone the infection can be contracted by no natural means other than the agency of this insect.[15]

Once the fever broke out in a person, it ran its course in a brief period which varied from twenty-four hours to four or five days. In the initial stages the victim suffered from chills, fever, and severe pains in the head and back. Soon these symptoms disappeared and they

[13] *Encyclopedia Britannica* (14th Edition), XXIII, 883.

[14] On Reed's work see *Senate Documents*, 61 Cong., 3 Sess., no. 822.

[15] Yellow fever mosquitos are still numerous in Memphis and elsewhere in the valley, but they are no longer a menace because infected persons are singled out and promptly quarantined.

were followed by sub-normal temperature and pulse beat which gave the patient an impression of convalescence. This was actually the critical stage, for after a brief interval he began to vomit a black substance composed of blood and the acids of the stomach, the only positive sign of the disease. Within a few days he was either dead or on the road to recovery.[16]

The average doctor of the seventies knew little of the cause, symptoms, or treatment of yellow fever, and the public was even more ignorant. Certain individuals made remarkably accurate observations,[17] but no one even remotely associated it with the mosquito. Though a medical student at the University of Pennsylvania in 1803 had proven conclusively that the disease was not contagious in the usual sense of the word, quarantine and disinfectant were still religiously prescribed three-quarters of a century later.[18] Some eminent authorities held that yellow fever was caused by a living organism, permeating the atmosphere under certain conditions, that this organism was received into the blood-stream through the lungs, and that it could be contracted by direct contact.[19] The more popular theory, however, and one which many doctors endorsed, argued that the filth of the city and the decaying wooden pavement had filled the air with noxious poisons. Representatives of the godly, on the other hand, considered the plague divine punishment for the celebration of the semi-pagan festival of Mardi Gras, inaugurated in Memphis early in the seventies.[20]

In a section where all varieties of fever were common, no malady could be positively identified as the yellow pestilence until the unmistakable symptom of black vomit occurred. Inasmuch as the official announcement that the fever was epidemic would create a panic and practically depopulate the town health authorities were hesitant to take such a step until they were certain that the plague was inevitable. By that time hundreds were already infected, and the wholesale flight which followed spread the germs through the surrounding area.[21] As

[16] John P. Dromgoole, *Yellow Fever Heroes, Heroines, and Horrors of 1878* (Louisville, 1879), 16 ff.; Quinn, *Heroes*, 231–234.

[17] See the testimony of various doctors, nurses, and others who had seen the fever at work; Dromgoole, *Yellow Fever*, 19–60.

[18] *Senate Documents*, 61 Cong., 3 Sess., LXI, 207; Dromgoole, *Yellow Fever*, 10. Disinfectants were useless, and a single person with the germ in his blood who passed through quarantine could infect an entire community.

[19] Dromgoole, *Yellow Fever*, 47.

[20] John M. Keating, *History of the Yellow Fever* (Memphis, 1879), 103; Quinn, *Heroes*, 126; Memphis *Public Ledger*, March 1, 1878.

[21] Quinn, *Heroes*, 14–16.

a matter of fact, the medical profession was helpless in the face of the fever. According to the chairman of the New Orleans Board of Health, perhaps the leading authority, it "must run its course, and nothing that we know of can stop its progress." [22] Once the yellow jack struck, the unfortunate community could only wait until the frosts of autumn brought belated relief.

The season of 1872–73 was a calamitous one for Memphis, for the fever scourge was but the last of five major mishaps that occurred within a period of seven months. December found the city in the throes of the "epizootic," an equine malady which paralysed the horse-drawn transportation system and business in general quite as severely as a failure of the supply of gasoline or electricity would tie up a twentieth-century metropolis. In mid-winter also came a severe freeze which suspended traffic on land and river for more than a month and destroyed property worth several million dollars. During the cold weather appeared a violent outbreak of smallpox, followed in the spring by a milder attack of the cholera. This latter infection proved so severe in the rest of West Tennessee that well-to-do Memphians, anxious to secure the services of their own physicians should they be stricken, delayed their departure to watering places until July. Confident at last that no further misfortune could arise, citizens settled down to the lazy existence of the dull midsummer season, awaiting the fall with optimism.[23]

Their troubles were by no means over, however, for a worse fate lay in store for them. Early in August a steamer from New Orleans stopped for provisions alongside Happy Hollow, an under-the-hill community exclusively Irish in composition.[24] When the ship departed several hours later it left behind two sick men who died within several days. Fever broke out immediately in the hollow with an average mortality of two deaths a day, and by the first of September it had reached the top of the bluff.[25] Thence it spread to Pinch, the northern part of the city which was also largely Irish,[26] but it was not until the ninth that the public had any inkling of its danger. When the board of

[22] Quoted in Dromgoole, *Yellow Fever*, 17.

[23] Richard Edwards, *In Memoriam of the Lamented Dead Who Fell in the Epidemic of 1873* (Memphis 1873), 25; *Report of the Yellow Fever Among the Odd Fellows of Memphis* (Memphis, 1874), 3.

[24] Dr. William R. Mitchell in the *Louisville Medical Journal*, May, 1873, quoted in the *Odd Fellows Report*, 3–5. Happy Hollow lay west of Front Street between Poplar and Market.

[25] Edwards, *Epidemic of 1873*, 27.

[26] *Odd Fellows Report*, 5.

health, uncertain for several weeks as to an exact diagnosis, announced on the fourteenth that an epidemic was imminent, an exodus ensued until only fifteen thousand out of a total population of forty thousand were left in the city at the end of the month.[27]

Those remaining, the majority of them Negroes who seemed to have been immune until 1878, had no alternative but to let the fever spend itself, wondering all the while which of their number would be the next victims. The climax came early in October with seventy-one deaths on the fifth and sixty-two on the tenth of the month.[28] Every organization, creed, and nationality obtained donations, largely from outside, and administered to their sick brethren, spending a total of $332,288 in two months.[29] The Howard Association, under the direction of Dr. L. P. Blackburn of Louisville and Major W. T. Walthall of Mobile, erected a hospital and alone spent $124,000 in relief work, but the Catholic priests and sisters bore the brunt of the burden, for it was their communicants who suffered most.[30] Frosts of late October brought welcome respite, and before Thanksgiving the yellow jack had gone into hibernation.

Of the fifteen thousand who braved the peril of the fever, five thousand were stricken and two thousand died.[31] At least half of the victims were Irish-Catholics.[32] Few influential citizens perished since few had exposed themselves to the virus for any length of time. By Christmas most of the merchants had returned and trade was brisk as usual, but in the future they would never be free from the fear that in late summer the plague would strike, swift and deadly, before they could flee.

The first siege of fever in the seventies produced a cautious attitude among inhabitants which was definitely detrimental to the city's welfare. Men would continue to profit from the economic advantages

[27] *Ibid.*, 23; Edwards, *Epidemic of 1873*, 26.

[28] Edwards, *Epidemic of 1873*, 59.

[29] *Ibid.*, 60; *Odd Fellows Report*, 22. These two sources give detailed accounts of the work of all relief organizations.

[30] Edwards, *Epidemic of 1873*, 28–29. Quinn's memoir, referred to above, though it is slightly prejudiced since its author was a priest, is nevertheless the most valuable source for the real story of the epidemics. Better still, it gives a graphic picture of the Irish-Catholics in Memphis and their relations with the Protestants.

[31] *Odd Fellows Report*, 22; Edwards, *Epidemic of 1873*, 59, admits that his estimate of 1664 deaths in 57 days is too conservative. The board of health reported a lower mortality (see James P. Young, *History of Memphis* [Knoxville, 1912], 157), but its figures were always too low: *cf.* Quinn, *Heroes*, 216.

[32] Quinn, *Heroes*, 43; Edwards, *Epidemic of 1873*, 59.

which Memphis offered, but they lived in a temporary world which they must be ready to desert upon a moment's notice. Thus, while the value of annual trade reached seventy-five million dollars in 1875, the value of taxable property dropped from thirty million in 1874 to twenty million in 1878, and in the latter year one-third of this property had been confiscated by the state for taxes.[33] Population should have increased ten or fifteen thousand between 1870 and 1875, but actually it showed no appreciable gain during those years. The panic of 1873 and the mounting municipal debt contributed to this economic stagnation, but without question the fever was the primary cause.

Before the ordeal of 1873 was but a remembered nightmare the scourge again prevailed in what is, relatively, one of the most severe fever epidemics in American annals. In May, 1878, upon a report that the disease was epidemic in the West Indies, merchants unsuccessfully petitioned the authorities to establish a quarantine. On July 26 the newspapers announced that fever had been on the increase in New Orleans for two weeks. Immediately quarantine stations were set up at Germantown on the Memphis and Charleston Railroad, at Whitehaven on the Mississippi and Tennessee, and at the lower end of President's Island in the river.[34] Rumors of a frightful outbreak in Granada, Mississippi, arrived on August 10, and when they were confirmed three days later the bluff community became acutely apprehensive.[35] Little did it suspect that the yellow jack had already entered the city by his usual route from the river, but its sense of security was abruptly shattered by the announcement of the board of health that a Mrs. Bionda, the wife of an Italian snackhouse keeper who catered to rivermen, had died of yellow fever on the thirteenth.[36] Sixty-five new cases were reported during the next two days, and before officials pronounced the plague epidemic on the twenty-third, hundreds of deaths had occurred.[37]

The panic-stricken populace did not wait for an official announcement before acting. On the day of Mrs. Bionda's death began a mad exodus, by rail, by river, on wagon, and on foot, which carried from

[33] Keating, *Memphis*, I, 645; II, 168, reports of the chamber of commerce. The tax rate varied from two to four per cent.

[34] Keating, *History of the Yellow Fever*, 103–106.

[35] *Report of the Central Relief Committee* (Memphis, 1878), 6.

[36] *Ibid.*, 7; Keating, *History of the Yellow Fever*, 107. By August 13 there were already a dozen cases in the city.

[37] Keating, *History of the Yellow Fever*, 149; *Report of the Central Relief Committee*, 7–8; Quinn, *Heroes*, 130.

the town within a fortnight twenty-five thousand of its inhabitants, among them several of its doctors and most of its Protestant ministers.[38] There may have been some excuse for this action since it was mainly the poor Catholics who, because of penury, remained to die in the pest-ridden inferno, yet for months the newspapers denounced the Protestant clergy for their desertion in no uncertain terms.

In the frenzied rush to safety all semblance of courtesy disappeared, nor could police or railroad officials enforce the slightest degree of order. Regardless of age or sex everyone took care of himself, and in numerous instances fathers deserted wives and families. In self-defense many of the neighboring towns established shotgun quarantines and refused to allow trains to stop; in several places they even compelled refugees to camp in the forest without food or shelter.[39] The residents of Jackson, out of fear of infection, not only destroyed every animal which came from Memphis, but in their panic they actually broke to pieces a stove which had recently arrived from the bluff.[40] In spite of his cassock Father Quinn was denied admission to numerous towns in West Tennessee because he was known to have been in Memphis.[41]

About five thousand of the inhabitants, lacking the means of their more fortunate fellows, entered the several camps which had been established at a safe distance in the vicinity.[42] By the middle of September only 19,600 people remained in the city; 14,000 of these were Negroes and most of the whites were Irish.[43] At first the disease had been confined to Pinch, but soon it spread throughout the city in every direction at a rate of hundreds of new cases each day. Five weeks after the existence of the plague had been formally announced the infection had penetrated the suburbs and the surrounding territory within a twelve-mile radius.[44]

"Deaths to date 2250," read a telegram from the relief committee to Booth's Theater in New York on September 20. "Number now sick about 3000; average deaths 60 per cent of the sick. We are feeding some 10,000 persons, sick and destitute. . . . 15 volunteer physi-

[38] Quinn, *Heroes*, 155–156; Keating, *Yellow Fever*, 107–108.

[39] Quinn, *Heroes*, 131–133.

[40] *Ibid.*, 226. Jackson had only eight cases of fever during the epidemic.

[41] *Ibid.*, 27.

[42] *Report of the Central Relief Committee*, 9, 45.

[43] Quinn, *Heroes*, 139. The *Memphis Avalanche* of September 1 stated that there were only 5,000 left. Quinn's figure represents the maximum population, and at times probably not half that number were in the city.

[44] *Report of the Central Relief Committee*, 9, 18; *Memphis Avalanche*, September 3, October 2, 1878.

cians have died, 20 others are sick, and a great many nurses have died. Fever abating a little today, for want of material perhaps. . . . We are praying for frost—it is our only hope." [45]

Soon after the death of Mrs. Bionda, Memphis was converted into one vast hospital that was daily becoming more and more of a charnelhouse. All business ceased, and of the numerous social and economic institutions only the press, telegraph, railroads, steamboats, druggists, undertakers, doctors, and Catholic clergy made any attempt to continue functioning. [46] Every type of organization participated in relief work, but the Howard Association, the Citizen's Relief Committee, and the Catholic Church carried most of the burden. It was as imperative to feed the well as to nurse the sick and bury the dead. Though contributions and volunteers had poured in since quarantine had been lifted on August 16, hundreds died of neglect who might have been saved. The Howards alone furnished twenty-nine hundred nurses and one-hundred-and-eleven ·doctors, and spent over half a million dollars in caring for fifteen thousand persons. [47]

The large number of Negroes, susceptible to the virus for the first time in 1878, [48] could not be induced to leave so long as they were assured free rations. [49] In many cases they were left to care for vacant houses by the owners who had fled to safer regions. Considerable petty thievery went on and there were numerous unfounded tales of rape of white women by Negro men. [50] It was estimated at one time that two hundred tramps were scouring the city in search of spoil. [51] As on all occasions when life is cheap and highly uncertain, debauchery was conspicuous; yet on the whole public order was as well preserved as could be expected, thanks to the efforts of the relief committee and the loyalty of two military companies, composed of Negroes, that were stationed opposite Court Square to preserve order.

The horrors of the epidemic defy description. Bodies were constantly found in an advanced state of decomposition. In one instance workers discovered half a cadaver of a Negro woman covered with dead rats which had eaten the flesh. The county undertaker had four furniture wagons in service all day long, yet at the peak of the pesti-

[45] *Memphis Appeal,* September 20, 1878.
[46] Memphis *Public Ledger,* September 20, 1878.
[47] Keating, *Yellow Fever,* 668; Dromgoole, *Yellow Fever,* 77.
[48] Quinn, *Heroes,* 47; *Memphis Appeal,* September 1, 1878.
[49] Dromgoole, *Yellow Fever,* 74.
[50] Keating, *Yellow Fever,* 113.
[51] *Ibid.,* 130.

lence victims succumbed so fast that scores lay unburied. Hundreds of corpses were interred in shallow gullies with no marks of identification. One party came upon a live infant, coated with black vomit, suckling the breasts of its dead mother. During the duration of the epidemic, with few exceptions, all babies were stillborn. Strange anomalies occurred in the presence of death—strong men turned cowards and lewd women saints.[52]

In the midst of such awful tragedy appeared both the miraculous and the comic. One little girl in her eleventh year, who had been dumb and paralysed for some time, recovered complete possession of her faculties after a long siege of the fever. To ward off disease people drenched themselves with cologne and rosewater, or wore on their persons onions and little bags of assafoetida, that evil-smelling stuff which superstitious folk in the South still use to insure immunity.[53] Men could be seen everywhere wearing sponges on their noses, and the streets were covered with lime for the purpose of disinfection. As the last rites were being said over one Irishman in St. Patrick's Cathedral, the mourners were terrified to see the shrouded figure open its eyes and ejaculate, "What the hell are you doing? "[54]

The early appearance of the epidemic and the unusually hot weather which lasted throughout early autumn accounted for the severe mortality. The following record gives some indication of the progress of the fever:[55]

July 10–Sept. 6	958 deaths	Sept. 13	93 deaths
Sept. 7	97 ,,	Sept. 14	127 ,,
Sept. 8	99 ,,	Sept. 15	98 ,,
Sept. 9	111 ,,	Sept. 16	111 ,,
Sept. 10	99 ,,	Sept. 17	96 ,,
Sept. 11	104 ,,	Sept. 18	68 ,,
Sept. 12	98 ,,	Sept. 19–Oct. 15	50 deaths daily

When frost came in the middle of October and thin ice occurred soon afterwards, the end of the epidemic was announced.

The wild scattering of people which followed the outbreak of the fever in August produced a high mortality in the whole valley.[56]

[52] Dromgoole and Keating recount vivid anecdotes of the plague which would fill a book in themselves.
[53] Quinn, *Heroes*, 191.
[54] Dromgoole, *Yellow Fever*, 68.
[55] Keating, *Yellow Fever*, 109; Quinn, *Heroes*, 115.
[56] *Memphis Avalanche*, September 21, 1878.

Refugees from the city carried the infection as far away as Bowling Green, Kentucky, and Chattanooga, Tennessee, though neighboring towns along railroads were hardest hit. Brownsville reported 844 cases, LaGrange 152, Martin 126, Colliersville 121, and Paris 118.[57] Only those escaped which, like Jackson, refused to admit anyone who had been exposed. As the plague waned in Memphis, more through lack of subjects than for any other reason, the local relief committee began caring for the sick and destitute in the county, and the Howards administered to the entire tri-state region.[58]

According to the medical estimate, which is probably an understatement, in Memphis alone the total mortality was 5150 out of a population that never exceeded 20,000 during the epidemic.[59] Roughly 17,600 of both races were stricken, and of the 7000 whites who remained not more than 200 escaped the fever. Of these whites 75 per cent died in contrast to only 7 per cent of the Negroes.[60] Again the toll was heaviest among the Irish, as is evident from the fact that the Catholic Church lost two thousand of its parishioners, thirteen priests, and thirty nuns.[61]

Immediate signs of recovery were not apparent in the season of 1878–79 as they were following the plague of 1873. Thousands of refugees failed to return, and the public debt became so pressing that the municipality surrendered its charter to avoid bankruptcy, becoming a mere taxing district of the state.[62] In spite of an energetic sanitary campaign during the winter, with the advent of spring sporadic cases of fever appeared in different parts of town.[63] The outbreak which came in the heat of July produced once more the inevitable exodus, and again over half the population fled to Nashville and St. Louis.[64] This attack of the scourge, milder than the last, endured until

57 Dromgoole, *Yellow Fever,* 107–125. In these pages appear reports from all neighboring towns and villages.

58 *Memphis Avalanche,* October 5, 10, 1878; Dromgoole, *Yellow Fever,* 110–116; Keating, *Yellow Fever,* 142–143.

59 Keating, *Yellow Fever,* 116 n.; Quinn, *Heroes,* 216. One undertaker stated that he would testify under oath that more than two hundred were buried in one day, though the highest estimate of the board of health for a single day was little more than one hundred. On September 17 the *Memphis Avalanche* listed the names of 208 persons reputed to have died the previous day, but the estimate of the Associated Press for the same date was 127; Memphis *Public Ledger,* November 26, 1878.

60 Whites, 4204 out of 5600; blacks, 946 out of 12,000.

61 Quinn, *Heroes,* 214.

62 *Acts of the State of Tennessee,* 41 Gen. Assem., chap. X.

63 *Report of the Board of Health, 1879,* 5; Keating, Memphis, I, 676.

64 Memphis *Public Ledger,* September 3, October 18, 1879.

the middle of November, four long months with a mortality of more than six hundred out of two thousand cases.[65] Only the immunity acquired in the previous year saved the town from complete devastation; never did the future seem so dark as in those December days of 1879, when even the most loyal inhabitants were leaving for healthier sites. After three epidemics of such intensity as these, it is remarkable that Memphis did not become, like its ante-bellum rival, Randolph, a forgotten village on the banks of the Mississippi.

Though Memphis suffered much more bitterly than most American cities, unsanitary conditions were general throughout the nation until the end of the century, and every port and river town was at one time or other stricken with devastating epidemics of smallpox, cholera, or yellow fever.[66] Some attempts were made to improve public health, for the federal government had established marine hospitals along the coast and the Mississippi River to confine sailors afflicted with exotic diseases, but as late as 1873 only thirty-two cities in the United States had local boards of health.[67] Yet these boards were helpless as long as medical science was ignorant of the origin of disease, and the seeming apathy of the nation to the menace of pestilence was due actually to a lack of knowledge rather than to a lack of energy or concern.

In the last half of the nineteenth century, as a result of the experiments of European scientists like Louis Pasteur and Robert Koch, preventive medicine made significant advances. The fruits of their research in bacteriology, particularly concerning the germ theory of disease, were introduced to America by young doctors like William Osler, William H. Welch, and Hermann Biggs, who had studied abroad. In the nineties a new public health program was launched under the direction of Biggs, who served as pathologist and director of the bacteriological laboratory of the New York City Health Department from 1892 to 1914,[68] and his methods were soon applied in other cities, particularly in Memphis. In the last decade of the century the scope of the Marine Hospital Service was enlarged and in 1902 it became the Public Health Service.[69]

[65] The secretary of the state board of health estimated the mortality at 587 out of 2,010 cases (whites—470 out of 1,298; blacks—117 out of 702). Quinn, *Heroes*, 214, estimated the dead at 800.

[66] See particularly Thomas J. Wertenbaker, *Norfolk, Historic Southern Port* (Durham, 1931), 206–216.

[67] Henry E. Sigerist, *American Medicine* (New York, 1934), 234, 239.

[68] Charles E. A. Winslow, *Hermann Biggs* (Philadelphia, 1929) is an exhaustive study of Biggs' work in public health.

[69] Sigerist, *American Medicine*, 235–236.

The fever in Memphis was of more than local significance; it was an event of immense national importance, for it aroused the country to the ever-present threat of disease at the very time that the findings of Pasteur and Koch were being disseminated. In his bachelor's dissertation submitted at Cornell in 1882, young Biggs had commented specifically on the Memphis epidemic of 1878, observing that it was "proven to have been due to the filthiness and unpaved streets, insufficient drainage, obstructed and offensive sewers, and the want of proper precautions during the prevalence of the epidemic." [70] The experience of the city was a warning to the nation, and the sanitary campaign upon which it shortly embarked proved an inspiring example.

If Memphis history were to be divided into two periods—and there is ample cause for such a division—then 1880 and not 1860 would be the critical date. The social and economic consequences of the fever epidemics were so far-reaching as to warrant the conclusion that there have been two cities upon the lower Chickasaw Bluff: one which existed prior to the pestilence, and a second metropolis which sprang up like some fungus growth on the ruins of the first. Both possessed certain common characteristics thrust upon them by identity of location—cotton, the Negro, and the river—but the eighties witnessed such a metamorphosis in urban personnel as well as physiognomy that the Radicals who departed at the end of the reconstruction period would hardly have recognized the town in 1890.

While other southern cities were in many cases experiencing a 100 per cent increase during the fever decade, population in Memphis declined from forty to thirty-three thousand. This decrease was confined largely to white inhabitants, for few men of means cared to remain in a town whose future was so perilous. Even the most loyal citizens had to admit that by the close of the decade one-third of the white residents had emigrated.[71] Many refugees remained permanently in St. Louis, and most of those who returned were apparently transient. The amazing extent to which newcomers supplanted the old native stock in the post-fever years is revealed in a census taken in 1918 by the federal bureau of education. Of the 11,871 white parents residing in Memphis forty years after the great epidemic, only 183, less than two per cent, had been born there.[72]

The populace changed not merely in personnel but also in quality.

70 Winslow, *Hermann Biggs,* 41.
71 Calvin F. Vance, *Past and Future of Memphis* (Memphis, 1892), 7.
72 Department of the Interior, *Bulletin of the Bureau of Education,* L, 13.

Among the victims of the three epidemics were thirty-four hundred Catholics, including twenty-four priests and twice as many nuns.[73] Many industrious Germans joined their brethren in St. Louis, and one of their leading clubs in Memphis, the Maennerchor, became virtually defunct for lack of members.[74] Of the once numerous German organizations on the bluff, only Germania Hall remains in the twentieth century. It is significant, too, that after the plague the proportion of Negroes increased until by the turn of the century they constituted half of the total population.[75]

In the history of the city the year 1880 marks a distinct cultural break. It is no wonder, in view of the above statistics, that modern Memphis possesses no aristocracy, no tradition, and little interest in its past. The names of only a few families, like the Topps, McGevneys, Winchesters, McLemores, Trezevants, and Overtons, have appeared consistently in its annals. As the war had disrupted a *petit noblesse* in the process of aging, so the fever destroyed a second embryonic aristocracy before it cast off its swaddling clothes. If the loss of so many Irish was considered by some a good riddance of undesirables, the diminished scope of the Catholic Church was regrettable, for it had served as a check on rural provincialism. The migration of the Germans was much more serious, since it took from the community an influential group which possessed taste in aesthetic matters as well as sober commercial judgment. Qualitatively the cost of the fever is not to be reckoned by the number of victims, but by the intelligent and solid citizens it drove elsewhere.

The old Memphis, with all its filth, was unique; the new city, with all its improvements, was prosaic and in time became a southern Middletown. In losing its filth and some of its notorious viciousness it lost also a certain quality for which paved streets and a sewerage system were by no means complete compensation—that unnamable quality which conspicuously differentiates Boston, Charleston, and New Orleans from Pittsburgh and Kansas City. Once heterogeneous, it became homogeneous and progressive; formerly cosmopolitan, it became hopelessly provincial. Gone were the minority groups necessary to a healthy intellectual atmosphere; and in their places, during the eighties and nineties, came farmers from Mississippi and Tennes-

---

[73] Quinn, *Heroes*, preface, vii; 214.

[74] Keating, *Memphis*, II, 288. Its membership was formerly 350.

[75] The percentage of Negroes in the total population increased from seventeen per cent in 1860 to forty-eight per cent in 1900. The actual numbers were: 1860—3,822; 1870—15,741; 1880—14,986; 1890—28,706; 1900—49,910.

see, a simple and virtuous country folk, but stubborn and often un-lettered.[76]

In 1900, consequently, Memphis presented a strange paradox—a city modern in physical aspect but rural in background, rural in preju-dice, and rural in habit. From each man was demanded allegiance to four conventional ideals: to an unadulterated Protestant fundamental-ism; to a fantastic entity called the Old South; to the principle of white supremacy; and, rather paradoxically, to the Constitution of the United States.[77]

Because of the prosperity that began in the eighties and that made Memphis the third largest city in the South by the end of the century,[78] the theory that the fever may have had dire economic consequences has been generally dismissed. On the contrary, this prosperity came in spite of the pestilence, and but for the pestilence it must have been greater and more permanent. A careful comparison of the growth of Memphis with that of other southern cities during the last century justifies the hypothesis that the plague kept it from becoming a much larger city than it is at present.

On the eve of the Civil War Memphis was the thirty-eighth city in population in the United States. Within ten years it had risen to thirty-second, but during the fever decade it fell to fifty-fifth, and since then it has never been higher than thirty-sixth. Instead of a population of 80,000 in 1880, which from the rate of increase during the past thirty years it had reason to expect, it found itself with only 33,000. In ten fateful years it had lost its superiority over both Nashville and Atlanta, and its position was eventually challenged by those parvenus among southern cities, Birmingham and the Texas towns. The story is clearly told in the following extract from the Federal Census:

GROWTH OF SOUTHERN CITIES, 1860–1930 [79]

	1860	1870	1880	1890	1900	1930
Memphis	22,623	40,226	33,592	64,495	102,320	253,153
Atlanta	9,554	21,789	37,409	65,533	89,872	270,366
Nashville	16,988	25,865	43,350	76,168	80,865	153,866
Birmingham			3,086	26,178	38,415	259,678
Dallas			10,358	38,067	42,638	260,475

[76] Gerald M. Capers, "Where South Met West" (Ph.D. dissertation Yale University, 1936), 321–359.

[77] *Ibid.*

[78] In 1900 New Orleans stood first, Louisville second, and Memphis third. Washington and St. Louis are not considered southern in this estimate.

[79] *Fifteenth Census of the United States*, 1930, I, 66, 224, 1,032, 1,056.

The New South is an offspring of the union of bountiful natural resources and northern capital. Here the deterrent effect of the fever is particularly obvious. In 1870 no southern town was more likely to become the first depot of northern capitalists than Memphis. Better located than either New Orleans or Louisville, the only cities of the western South that outranked it, the town on the bluff possessed commercial and industrial possibilities with which the North, as a result of the profits made by Yankees in the contraband trade of the sixties, was well acquainted.[80]

A decade later the notoriety which accompanied the three fever epidemics had altered this situation completely. It became known throughout the nation that life was extremely hazardous in Memphis, that its taxes were prohibitive, and that its municipal bonds had virtually been repudiated and its municipal charter surrendered. Even in the Gilded Age capital was not unnecessarily reckless, and for a quarter of a century the double stigma of debt and disease kept northern investments in the city at a low figure. It is rather ironical that the largest inland cotton market in the world has not possessed a single cotton mill since 1893, and that the largest hardwood lumber market in the United States manufactured little furniture before 1900.

The industrial handicap has been overcome in the twentieth century, but much of the purely commercial damage arising from the fever remains. The misfortune of Memphis proved the opportunity of St. Louis and Atlanta. The scourge of 1878 drove several firms to St. Louis,[81] and undoubtedly many houses seeking the trade of the lower valley located their headquarters at the mouth of the Missouri, when but for the fever they would have preferred the mouth of the Wolf. The horizontal trade of Memphis suffered as well as the vertical, for northern concerns in search of a location for a single branch office to serve a South that was still moving west chose an inland town in Georgia in preference to a railroad center on the middle Mississippi.

Predictions as to what might have been are but the opinion of an individual, whether he be steamboat captain or historian, but it can

[80] In the seventies the *Iron Age,* a New York industrial journal, made this comment: "At Memphis coal from Kentucky, used with iron ores of like cast, should make it one of our greatest manufacturing centers—coal and iron being obtainable from the Alabama fields cheaper than they can be delivered at St. Louis." Quoted in *Memphis, Past, Present and Future* (Memphis, 1883), 82.

[81] Rice-Stix and Co. was the largest concern to move to St. Louis, but Hill-Fontaine and Co. (cotton); Hill, Ferry, and Mitchell (wholesale shoes); Thomas Hallen and Co. (cotton); and several others joined the exodus after the fever.

be suggested with considerable justification that Atlanta owes its present position as the "New York of the South" more to the work of the *aedes aegypti* in Memphis half a century ago than to any other cause.

9

A Railroad City: The Foundations of Billings, Montana

by WALDO O. KLIEWER

The boom was on! People came so rapidly that the company had difficulty in satisfying buyers.

The founding, early growth, and development of many American cities after 1850 were intimately linked with railroad construction and operation. Previously, the development of American cities had been influenced by topography, the paths of navigable rivers, estuaries, harbors, and natural trade patterns. But since railroads could be built anywhere and could create cities where and when they chose, this was no longer the case. Railroad officials were fully aware of the money to be made out of urban development and growth in the West and energetically pursued this activity. Billings, Montana, is an example of this type of urban development.

Waldo O. Kliewer's essay, republished here with the permission of the *Pacific Northwest Quarterly* from its July, 1940, issue, is an excellent study of the early history of a Western railroad city and affords the modern reader an insight into the intimate connection between the early history of many of our Western cities and the railroads. All footnotes in the original essay have been omitted because of the limited availability of this material. Information on Mr. Kliewer is not available.

It is often forgotten that most of the early settlers of American Western cities did not arrive by covered wagon, but came on the steam cars. They got off the trains where they did as a result of highly organized and loudly promoted schemes for urban development initiated by railroad officers and directors.

By 1877 the development of mining had brought a considerable population to western Montana, but settlement in the eastern plains region was still sparse. After 1877 cattlemen became permanent settlers. As their number increased, the demand for supplies, communication facilities, and transportation became greater and stage lines appeared. A stimulant to traffic along the Yellowstone River was the advent of the steamboat on that stream. Until the railroad arrived, steamers came within a few miles of the present site of Billings, most of them landing their cargo at Huntley, ten miles down the river. The steamer *Josephine* was the only boat to reach a point on the river due south of Billings, half a mile west of the present "South" bridge. As the stage lines prospered and population increased, post offices were opened along the way, and around these points trading posts and villages appeared.

One of these was the village of Coulson, located about two miles east of the present site of Billings. Early in the winter of 1876–1877, P. W. McAdow came to this location, took up a land claim, and a little later opened a store. He was the first settler in the vicinity. It was here that the ferry to Fort Custer crossed the Yellowstone. A post office was established and a telegraph line running from Miles City to Bozeman was erected by the army for the accommodation of Forts Keogh, Custer and Ellis. By 1880 Coulson contained a two-storey hotel, a little general store, a post office, a telegraph office, several saloons, and a little saw mill. About fifty people resided there at that time.

The population of eastern Montana gradually increased, but in spite of this the country remained somewhat savage. From time to time the ranches in the vicinity of Coulson were raided by Indians, and on once occasion a saloon in Coulson was attacked and burned.

The village of Coulson seemed destined to grow and prosper. But the approach of the Northern Pacific construction force during the winter of 1881–1882, although bringing the promise of prosperous times, brought into existence a competitor—the town of Billings. In January, 1882, Coulson acquired a newspaper, the *Post*. The editor of this journal was certain that Coulson would be made the center of the new town and envisioned the time when it would be the shipping point for Montana cattle. Later, as Billings grew, he voiced the hope that Billings and Coulson would be "one." An effort was made to tie the two villages together by running a hack between them.

When the Billings "boom" was well under way, the little village finally gave up. The *Post* was the first to desert for the better location. The brewery, hotel, three general stores, five saloons, and thirty other buildings were either vacated or moved to Billings. Coulson gradually disappeared, first becoming a ghost town, and then vanishing so completely that nothing remains to mark its original location.

I

Before 1882, the Northern Pacific Railroad Company was aware of the fact that a town was to be erected somewhere in the vicinity of Coulson, although the exact location was not known. Several capitalists became convinced that it would be profitable to invest in land and in a townsite in the Yellowstone Valley if the railroad would cooperate. The idea first occurred to Herman Clark, general contractor on the Northern Pacific. He secured the support of T. F. Oakes, vice president of the Northern Pacific, and Frederick Billings, former president of the road and one of the largest and most influential stockholders in the railroad company at that time.

After satisfactory arrangements had been made with the railroad company, those interested organized and incorporated themselves as the "Minnesota and Montana Land and Improvement Company" under the laws of the state of Minnesota, the papers being filed in the office of the Secretary of State on March 24, 1882. The authorized capital of the company was $200,000. The charter members were Herman Clark and John B. Westbrook of Miles City, and Thomas C. Kurtz of Moorhead, Minnesota.

The contract of April 1, 1882, between the Northern Pacific Railroad Company and Herman Clark, embraced 29,394.22 acres in and around the townsite of Billings for a consideration of $113,558.86. This contract was assigned (date unknown) to the land company. On March 21, 1883, the railroad company made two conveyances to the land company: one covered Section 3–1S–26E and Section 33–1N–26E on which the townsite of Billings was located; the other took in the balance of the lands included in the contract.

The townsite was laid out in the fall of 1881. It was located on the north side of the Yellowstone River, on a gently sloping plain near the eastern end of the valley. This plain, known as Clark's Fork Bottom, is sixty-five miles long and from four to ten miles wide. The plain, or bench, as it should be called, is high enough to be out of reach of the flood waters of the Yellowstone, which occasionally spread out over the bottom lands near the river. On both sides of the river, at the eastern end of the "bottom," where the town is located, rise "precipitous bluffs and rugged cliffs of a yellowish sandstone formation," which narrow the valley down to a mere gap about a mile wide just below the present eastern border of Billings. Herman Clark suggested naming the town Billings, after Frederick Billings, and the suggestion was adopted.

The choice of this location for Billings was due neither to the topography nor to the proximity of natural resources, but was the result of a peculiar fact connected with the government survey of the region. A town was to be founded somewhere in the Clark's Fork Bottom. In looking over the survey map of the county, engineers found that the base survey line east and west through Montana cut through the Yellowstone Valley near where they wanted to start the town. The alternating townships which had been deeded to the railroad lay side by side across this line, instead of cornering together as they did elsewhere. "We will put the town where this line crosses the railroad track, and get two adjoining sections," they said, and that is the way the site was selected. Another reason for the choice of this location was the necessity of a division point here for the railroad. The distance from the last division was already too great, and, as the railroad ran through Indian land south of the river before crossing at Coulson, it was impossible to locate a town any sooner.

The company had extensive plans. After contracting for every alternate section of each side of the right of way and the two townsite sections, Herman Clark set about dividing the site into streets, avenues, and parks on a scale for a city of twenty thousand inhabitants. The next step was to get inhabitants to populate both the townsite and the farm land adjacent to it. Lots and farm land were advertised as far east as St. Paul, and whole blocks were sold in Chicago and New York. According to reports, Mr. Clark arranged to form a settlement of not less than a thousand inhabitants in the vicinity of Coulson. He planned to erect "seven or eight or nine" saw mills there and construct an irrigation ditch sixteen miles long. It would cost more than $60,000 and irrigate both the townsite and the entire Clark's Fork Bottom. He planned to start a bank for the convenience of settlers and men doing business in that vicinity and for the purchase of bullion from the gold mines. He intended also to make the new town the shipping point for Montana cattle, to build railroads to the mines, to engage in stock raising, to assist settlers in securing stock, and in every way to encourage immediate settlement of the community. At this time Coulson held high hopes because of the overtures the land company was making to J. J. Alderson to buy forty acres of land adjoining the townsite on the southeast. Alderson demanded more money than the company offered and the deal was dropped since the company already owned a townsite that extended up on the rim rocks beyond the present city limits.

Herman Clark arrived in April and stated that he planned to erect a brick foundry to take care of building materials for the machine shops, round house, a "mammoth" hotel and other buildings. He stated to the editor of the *Post* that a colony of 450 families from Wisconsin was soon to arrive, to take advantage of his promise to any new settler "to fence and break his land, erect him a house and furnish him one hundred head of sheep or cattle as he selects."

The boom was on! People came so rapidly that the company had difficulty in satisfying buyers. The demands for lots were so pressing that Herman Clark carried on transactions until G. B. Hulme, the agent for the company, arrived in April. He was immediately besieged by anxious would-be purchasers who had already chosen their lots. Considerable dissatisfaction was experienced by applicants who were too late to secure locations on the main avenues parallel to the right-of-way. This led to charges of favoritism and unfairness. Information was received that large blocks of lots had been sold to people in St. Paul and other places in the east before the agent arrived. Prospective buyers feared that the choicest lots had been sold or promised to friends of Herman Clark. He informed them, however, that the choicest lots had been held for those who intended to build immediately and that it was not to the company's interest to have the land purchased by speculators.

Within a few months the company sold almost all of its two sections. The price of lots averaged around $100 and the choice business locations sold for as high as $500. Dwelling lots, located on the other edge of the site, sold for as low as twenty-five dollars. The "trafficing [*sic*] in town lots" constituted a large share of the business and amusement of the citizens. Lots changed hands rapidly and huge profits were made by early investors. People came in so rapidly from the end of the railroad and from other parts of the Territory that the *Herald* complained that it took "a very likely reporter nowadays to 'keep track' of all the arrivals" in Billings. Usually the first act of the new arrival was "to draw from his pocket a well-wrinkled and perhaps dirty plat of the town and . . . hunt for 'his lot.' " If the lot was satisfactory and located in the business section, lumber was hauled to the location and in less than a week a new building was ready for occupation and immediately opened for business.

The prairie on which this sudden and profitable boom took place presented a beautiful picture when viewed from the bluffs on either side of the river, but on closer inspection the mirage dissolved. The spot on which the present depot is located was on the edge of an alkali flat. West and north of that spot and almost continuously up the valley was pasture land; closer to the river the grass had grown tall enough to make hay; the whole prairie was treeless except for the line of cottonwoods and willows on the banks of the Yellowstone. The eastern part of the town was a "dreary expanse, white with alkali flats." The location of the engineers' headquarters was an "oasis of sagebrush" surrounded by patches of alkali and swampy land. The residential district was located on flats on the southeast edge of the site of the present city, but very shortly afterward that section was abandoned.

Buildings went up as rapidly as carpenters could put planks together. The *Post* moved into a frame structure next to the Metropolitan Hotel and shortly afterwards competition developed with the publication of the *Herald*. New business houses appeared so rapidly that it was impossible to make a record of them all. Billings lacked a good hotel until late in November. The old engineers' headquarters building had been used exclusively for the construction engineers till that time, but when the construction crews had passed out of range of the town, the building was moved to the railroad right-of-way in the center of Twenty-Eighth Street and became the Headquarters Hotel, the city's leading hotel until it burned down ten years later.

Real estate values soared. Lots originally costing $250 now sold for as high as $1500. Many of the owners were not residents of Billings. On June 3, 1883, it was estimated that there were approximately 500 people in the new town, and that 2000 people owned the lots in the townsite. By that date fifty houses had been completed and forty-seven tents housed those who had not found shelter in permanent buildings.

The continued and lasting qualities of the boom depended not alone on the business establishments in town, but also on the successful colonization of the land belonging to the land company. The promises made by Herman Clark brought some immigrants into the valley during the first months of the boom. They came by railroad to the end of the track and made their way to Billings in wagons or on foot. Freighting companies were swamped with business. With the exception of the farmers, Herman Clark, and a few others, the general opinion of the townspeople and the ranchers in the vicinity of Billings was that the irrigation project, begun by the land company, was no more than a "harebrained" scheme which was to be used to entice settlers to buy the land so that the company could realize huge profits on its holdings. It is true that until the railroad came, and for some time afterwards, the land was little used for farming, but the faith placed in irrigation by Herman Clark, instilled faith in others. Farmers gradually moved in but it was some time before farming became an important factor in the development of the town. The railroad company failed to cooperate with the land company and did little to encourage farmers. Instead it concentrated on the cattle industry. After the cattle industry had suffered several severe reverses due to hard winters, farming became one of the important economic factors in the growth of Billings and the Yellowstone Valley.

By the middle of June, 1882, Billings was still booming, but the first rush was past and civic-minded people began to see that improvements must be made if the town was to continue to prosper. The *Post* urged that the town be incorporated because the hot weather had arrived and "many matters needed attending to if the health of the population was to be protected." A very serious drawback was the lack of a water supply. Water was hauled in carts from the Yellowstone River and delivered around town in barrels. The *Post* of June 10 challenged someone to organize a company and dig an artesian well, but the challenge was not accepted until the next spring.

Coupled with the water problem was the ever-present danger from fire, the dread enemy of tent and shack towns without adequate fire protection. The *Post* and *Herald* both urged immediate action to forestall a disastrous fire but nothing was done at the time. The shortage of water also made it impossible to keep the streets free of dust, which rose in clouds whenever a vehicle passed through town. The *Post* suggested that the town be incorporated so that the "nuisance" could be "abated" by gravelling the streets.

The *Post* estimated on June 26th that Billings had a population of 800 people. As the town grew, an embarrassing situation developed. All of Billings' residents had to go to Coulson to get their mail; even local newspapers had to be registered in Coulson. A group of citizens met early in June and formulated a petition which was sent to the post office department, and in July, Colonel L. Whitney received notice of his appointment as postmaster. On August 4, 1883, the first mailbags were delivered at the door of the new post office. The mail was brought by stage from Miles City until several weeks after the arrival of the railroad.

The railroad survey through the valley had started the boom. The arrival of the track and trains in Billings stimulated it still further.

II

Early in August, 1882, the railroad track reached the Yellowstone. It was not until August 22, however, that the trains crossed the bridge and entered Billings. Instead of the boom collapsing when the railroad crews had gone on up the valley, activity more than doubled. The following figures of the growth of housing illustrate this: April 26, two houses; May 26, fifty-one houses; June 26, eighty-one houses; July 26, 124 houses; and on October 7, 250 houses. These figures do not include the still considerable population living in tents.

To maintain a permanent growth, the town had to have a solid group of industries to back the boom growth. This was furnished chiefly by the railroad, together with the cattle industry. On September 11, the first shipment of cattle was made. By October about three hundred and thirty-four carloads had been shipped east. After the season was over and the ranchers had bought their winter supplies, a let-up in business was felt. Advertisements in the local papers had brought in sufficient trade during the boom. Now it became evident that if the town was to continue its rapid growth, definite efforts must be made to obtain more trade by reaching farther into the territory adjacent to Billings. Attempts were made to incorporate the town and to create a new county with Billings as the county seat, but these were unsuccessful at the time. An attempt was also made to organize a board of trade to further the interests of the town, but this did not succeed until the following March. On November 2, however, a citizens' committee was appointed to take the place of a board of trade. Its first duty was to look after building a road to the Mussel Shell region lying to the north. The local papers and ranchers in that territory had been urging some action, so a plan was drawn up whereby subscriptions were taken from the ranchers and business men who hoped to receive benefits from the road. By November 11, almost all of the amount needed had been subscribed and work was begun.

A special committee was appointed in November to investigate and report on the best method to prevent fire in Billings. It was voted to assess everyone in the city according to property valuations in order to raise sufficient funds to buy the hook and ladder equipment necessary to build up a fire company. Citizens began immediately to sign up for the volunteer company but no efficient organization was completed at the time. The committee also attempted to get under way plans for a city jail, a system of wells to provide a better water supply, and a petition to the territorial legislature for a charter of incorporation for the town.

The arrival of winter brought an end to the boom, but the town continued to grow slowly. The creation of Yellowstone County, with Billings a county seat, gave the town a good start in the new year, but more important than this was the formation of a board of trade. On March 2, 1883, H. H. Mund, chairman of a committee appointed to study the problem of forming a board, offered a draft constitution at a public meeting. Article I of the constitution set forth the objects of the board as follows: "To facilitate and promote the business interests and general welfare of the town of Billings; to create harmony and good feeling among its business men and to form a body devoted to the advancement of any enterprises for the common good." On March 10, the organization of the board was completed at its first meeting.

Numerous problems awaited the newly formed board. It first turned its attention towards attracting more business to Billings by means of wagon roads, railroads, and mail lines running in all directions. It had been rumored for some time that the Northern Pacific was going to build a branch line, to be known as the "Benton Branch," from Billings to Fort Benton, tapping the coal region in the Bull Mountains some fifty miles north of Billings. The Board of Trade was very active in trying to get this line actually started. Much interest was also shown in the proposed wagon roads to the Clark's Fork, Maginnis, and Baker mining districts. Even with the poor roads, bull trains came in frequently, carrying silver bullion to the railroad and carrying back supplies.

The receipt of a letter from Otto Franc, a rancher in the Stinking Water district of northern Wyoming, revived interest in that territory. Much of that region was served by Cheyenne and the Union Pacific, but was closer to Billings. The main obstacle was crossing the Stinking Water River, so the cattlemen, the merchants, and the Northern

Pacific, in an attempt to get the trade of this region, agreed to raise $2000 with which to build a bridge. When the news of this plan reached Cheyenne, the Union Pacific put forth every effort to keep it from being successful. The plan did fail, but this was due to disagreement as to the amount each group should contribute. Even without the bridge, however, Billings received much trade from this territory.

The efforts of individual merchants to draw trade from a larger territory were important in bringing about the growth and prosperity which Billings enjoyed in 1883. They no longer waited for the ranchers to come and get their supplies, but sent freight wagons into the hills. H. Clark & Co. was the largest commercial establishment and took the lead in these activities. This company, headed by Herman Clark, president of the land company, had a decided advantage over other establishments because of its extensive freighting outfit which enabled it to carry goods directly to the doors of the cattlemen and traders located as far as 175 miles from Billings.

Billings became the center of the stock-raising industry of Montana and also a very important wool market. Cattle-raising was the leading industry of the territory. Billings became a real "cow town." The ranch foremen went there for their annual meetings preparatory to holding the spring round ups. The winter of 1882–1883 was mild, and the cattle industry flourished. Cattle shipments in the fall of 1883 were far greater than those of 1882. The local stockyards were continually filled with incoming young cattle to stock up new ranches or with fat cattle ready for shipment to eastern markets. Since the railroad was very largely dependent for its profits on cattle shipments, it did everything possible to aid this industry. Before the season was over nearly 20,800 head had passed into and out of Billings, and more than 600,000 pounds of wool had been shipped east.

Even though the cattlemen, sheepmen, the railroad, and most of the people in Billings ignored the possibilities of agriculture, there were some individuals who joined Herman Clark in his efforts toward its development. The most important result of those efforts was the irrigation canal built by the land company. H. M. Rowley, an engineer who had taken part in the platting of Billings, was put in charge of construction. When completed, the canal was thirty-nine miles long and cost approximately $125,000. The water was turned into the ditch in July but did not reach Billings until September 14, 1883. The citizens were more interested, however, in the abundance of water for fire protection, for watering the dust in the streets, and for growing

trees and lawns, than in the importance of the canal in the development of agriculture, which in later years became the chief support of
the city.

III

Much of Billings' prosperity was due to the activity and interest of
the land company. Without this company, growth would have been a
great deal slower. In the spring and summer of 1883, the townsite
company and the land company profited greatly from the boom in
real estate values. Business men who had failed to locate in the heart
of the town due to short-sightedness or bad luck accused the land
company of having misrepresented the facts to them. Everyone tried to
guess where the center of town would be, and as there was nothing
but the plat to go by, the "center" was hard to find. Speculators supposed that it would be close to the new depot, so all concerned attempted to find out where that was to be located. When the railroad
first reached Billings, a box car was used as a depot, but a short time
later a freight house was built and a portion of it was used temporarily
as a depot. This freight house was located in block 110 on 27th Street.
A plat and an architect's picture of the townsite hung in the office of
the townsite company and this gave the impression that the depot
would be located opposite block 112. Herman Clark, president of the
townsite company, had contracted to build a depot at a cost of approximately $60,000 as part of the agreement drawn up when the
townsite was turned over by the railroad company. When this fact
became known and the depot was not forthcoming, the owners of lots
located in the vicinity of block 112 became worried. Rumors were
floating around that the depot plans had been changed and that now
it was to be erected opposite block 109 on 28th Street. The old
Headquarters Hotel was moved west opposite block 109 and used
temporarily as a depot, and the lots in that vicinity increased in value.
The town grew rapidly around that location, while the lots near block
112 remained unoccupied. Lot holders and business men became
indignant.

In the spring of 1883, R. J. Anderson brought suit against the land
company for damages amounting to $20,000 on the grounds that the
company had not fulfilled its agreement to build the passenger depot
according to the plans in the original plat. The railroad company also
started suit for failure to build the $60,000 depot; the land company

immediately erected one in block 112, but when it was finished it cost only $10,000 instead of the amount agreed upon. The railroad company refused to accept this in fulfillment of the contract, so after its completion it stood empty, being used only as a public hall for dances and other gatherings. When the passenger trains arrived they halted momentarily in front of the new depot, announced "Billings" and then pulled up to the depot and hotel on 28th Street in block 109. The buildings that could be moved easily were relocated further west. When the present depot was built, it was located about eighty feet west of the exact spot where the old depot was built in 1883. The dispute started by Anderson was soon forgotten, the city and county rising above the disappointment which this episode created, and the general consensus favored rather than opposed the land company.

IV

The activities of the Board of Trade, the land company, the railroad company, H. Clark and Company, and other business groups brought results. Many changes took place in Billings. New firms established themselves; older establishments changed locations, enlarged their buildings, changed policies, and added new departments. In September, 1883, the *Herald* made a survey of building progress and found that the total expenditure for buildings under construction and for those proposed was about $150,000. These new buildings were very much in contrast to the shacks, tents, and wooden structures of the 1882 boom days, since they were constructed almost entirely of brick and stone.

Early in April, 1883, an attempt was made to establish an electric light plant in Billings but nothing came of the plan. Late in 1883, an attempt was also made to have a telephone exchange established, but all that came out of this scheme was a single wire system installed by individual merchants from their business establishments to their homes. Cancellations of mail increased so rapidly that early in 1884 the Billings post office was changed from fourth to third class.

As early as 1882, mention had been made of the possibilities of establishing a meat packing plant. Everyone was aware of the value of such a project located in the heart of the cattle country. The Northern Pacific was establishing refrigeration plants at points along the road and the rumor was spread that it intended to locate a plant at Billings. The Board of Trade investigated the matter and reported that the proper procedure was to offer assistance to the Marquis de Mores, who, in cooperation with the Northern Pacific, was erecting slaughtering houses in the Dakotas and was rapidly expanding his business westward. An offer was made to the Marquis and he accepted it, but he postponed building from year to year until finally the idea was abandoned entirely.

In the spring of 1883, the street railway, started in 1882, was completed. The citizens were proud of this addition to their town at first and the company experienced little difficulty in selling shares of stock. A regular schedule was worked out and the street cars, drawn by horses, left from in front of P. W. McAdow's store. The route ran down Minnesota Avenue to 18th Street, out 18th Street to 4th Avenue, and down 5th Avenue to Coulson, a total of about two miles. As an added incentive to customers, a beer garden was established in Coulson and all passengers were given one free glass of beer as a premium for each ticket purchased. After two seasons, difficulties made it necessary to sell the road. The people now discovered that it had been merely a scheme to boom the McAdow addition lying southeast of town.

During the last week of March, 1883, the Artesian Well Company was organized in an attempt to relieve the acute water problem faced by Billings until the irrigation canal was completed. The people of Billings showed their interest by purchasing all the stock that was offered for sale. Actual operations were not started until August, after shareholders had been assessed two dollars per share. Good progress was made in drilling but several additional assessments were necessary to raise money to continue operations. When the drill reached the depth of 900 feet, flowing water had not been reached. The stockholders were called upon for further funds, but sufficient money was not forthcoming. The operations ceased and in March, 1885, the apparatus of the company was sold.

In spite of the very satisfactory economic growth during 1883, many of the townspeople became discouraged because it did not match the boom period of 1882. The *Post* and the *Herald* bolstered up the courage of the citizens by pointing to the many achievements, to the sound foundations on which the town rested, to the fact that sound, steady growth was better than boom growth. The gloom was gradually dispelled and the year 1884 began with an optimistic note. During that year freight shipped to and from Billings increased considerably. The cattle shipments more than doubled; the county assessment for the year increased 30 per cent over the previous year. The idea of a railroad to the Bull Mountain coal fields was discussed, only to lie dormant for twenty-five years before it was realized.

The building record for 1884 was quite satisfactory, mainly because of fire. In July, block 110 was completely destroyed and the new buildings erected were of brick and stone instead of wood. Again in May, 1885, fire broke out, this time in block 111, and all the buildings except the Park Hotel were destroyed. Then in July, block 110 was again "singed." This was followed by great building activity, which gave the town more permanent structures. Billings now settled down to a steady growth for the next few years. Growth was slow but evident until the hard winter of 1886–1887, which wiped out over half of the cattle on the ranges and had a definite retarding effect.

V

Billings was faced with numerous problems as it gradually became more permanent and more populous. It had to obtain an adequate and healthful supply of water, to supplant the muddy water of the Yellowstone, and to provide some sort of protection from the hazard of fire. No provisions had been made to dispose of sewage or garbage and certain sections of the town were very unsightly. Neither were there any means of caring for the streets during muddy or extremely dry weather. No sidewalks had been built and during the wet season it was almost impossible to get around. These problems were not adequately solved until the town was incorporated.

At first the residents depended on the water of the Yellowstone River, brought to them in water wagons and in barrels. Later some of the merchants put in surface wells. The town anxiously awaited the completion of the artesian well, but when the water in the completed irrigation ditch reached town, in September, 1883, interest in the well lagged. The Artesian Well Company failed in its undertaking and the town continued to use the ditch and surface water until 1885. In June of that year plans were laid for a privately owned water plant to supply the city, but while those plans were being developed, Prentiss and Martin arranged to buy from the Northern Pacific several tanks of water weekly and this they resold to the citizens for fifteen cents a barrel. After considerable investigation and preparation, the Billings Water Power Company was organized by Henry Belknap, P. W. McAdow, H. H. Mund, and H. M. Rowley. The site for the plant was located on the P. W. McAdow farm next to the river, near the present location of the 7X Dairy. The water was taken from the river, carried a distance of 4,000 feet in a canal, and then dumped back into the river, giving a fall of thirteen feet. It was not until the summer of 1886 that the project was completed. The water was pumped to the corner of Minnesota Avenue and 27th Street through 8-inch pipe and from there in smaller pipes to the settled parts of the town. A 48-inch turbine wheel was ordered and plans were also laid to establish a power plant.

As long as the water system was incomplete, the volunteer fire department was severely handicapped and practically helpless against a real fire. No serious fires occurred until July 14, 1884, when McKee's Bank Exchange caught fire. Before the fire was brought under control, the whole block, the center of the town, was in ruins. A regular fire company was now organized, but this company was also handicapped by lack of water and tools. A bill was proposed in the Territorial Legislature in January, 1885, to enable the county commissioners to levy a special tax on all of the original townsite and all of the additions, the proceeds to be used to provide better fire protection. The bill passed but meantime two disastrous fires had occurred. The Billings Roller Rink on the south side burned to the ground and only the efforts of a bucket brigade saved the Headquarters Hotel and other buildings. This was in March, and in May another fire broke out and destroyed all but the Park Hotel in block 111. Then in July several buildings were burned in block 110, including the old log court house. Insurance companies threatened to withdraw from Billings unless adequate fire protection was provided at once. As a hose company was out of the question, a hook and ladder company was organized in September, with a membership of fifty men. This company did valiant service until it was replaced by a hose company when the water system was completed in 1886.

The disposal of garbage was another problem which was not solved until incorporation was completed. Refuse was permitted to collect in back yards during the winter and when the spring thaws occurred "the stench in certain localities was very offensive" and was injurious to the health of the citizens. The Board of Trade appointed a committee to deal with this problem. A slough east of town near the railroad bridge was chosen as the proper place to haul accumulated refuse and garbage. The sheriff of the county was asked to notify all persons to remove their garbage or face legal proceedings. These efforts brought no results. After incorporation the *Post* published several scorching editorials on the subject. . . .

The care of the streets presented another problem. In the spring frequent rains or melting snows often made the streets into a quagmire. The mud was "almost too deep to wade, and hardly deep enough to swim." All social functions were cancelled during the worst periods, because there were almost no sidewalks. Attempts were made to get business men to build walks in front of their establishments but not until after incorporation was it possible to obtain uniform action.

The difficulty that the Board of Trade experienced in trying to enforce regulations necessary to the welfare of the town and its citizens led to the second attempt to incorporate. The election held in November, 1883, showed that the general opinion was against any change. The reasons for the negative vote were the fear of additional expense to residents, who felt that the county officials were already taking care of the duties that would have to be transferred to city officials if incorporation took place, and the knowledge that licenses and fees would be increased by a city government.

On January 19, 1885, a group of citizens meeting to consider again the question agreed on a bill and a franchise charter which was sent to the Territorial Legislature for consideration. There was considerable discussion and protest over the franchise charter which stated that . . . the franchise was given to women. . . .

The Legislature did not change this provision and passed the bill on March 10, 1885. A commission of five men was elected by the people to take care of official business until the first election was held April 6. On April 2, the charter was presented to the people for their approval. Only 122 votes were cast and the charter was adopted by a majority of four votes.

On April 6, when the city officials were elected, less than a thousand votes were cast.

The population of Billings during the boom period included more of a "farseeing, enterprising and thrifty class" than usually fell to the lot of towns along the railroad. During the construction period a certain amount of riff-raff drifted into town, but this was only temporary, for as soon as the road was completed far enough up the valley, this class drifted on to live off the wages of the men building the road. Speculators, transients, and the like became scarce and men like Rowley, Belknap, Babcock, Clark, Mund, McAdow, and Camp became more numerous. Many of the business men were engaged in the retail trade, since Billings was chiefly a trading center. Another group was engaged in furnishing entertainment, such as saloons, pool halls, dance halls and skating rinks. A third group obtained a livelihood by working in the railroad shops.

The cowboys constituted the wildest element. They poured into Montana in increasing numbers, as cattle ranches sprang up all through the region from which Billings got much of its trade. . . .

The country peace officers had little difficulty in keeping the peace. Occasionally there were disputes between the Indians and the cowboys, ranchers and merchants. Then too, a "tin-horn" gambler occasionally drifted into town and fleeced an innocent victim. . . .

The saloons and pool rooms took care of the social desires of the residents during the boom period, but as the town became more permanent other means of recreation and entertainment were provided. In August, 1882, McKee's large building was turned into an "Opera House" and used by road companies such as the Boston Comic Opera Company which presented the "musical extravaganza, the Magic Doll and the Loan of a Lover" which was the first presentation of its kind in the new town. In October a variety theatre was opened. A group of young men organized the Billings Social Club and sponsored dances every two weeks during the winter months. The churches entertained another group of society by giving tableaux, bazaars, suppers, and socials.

Late in January, 1883, a literary society was formed. . . . Billings did not lack musical entertainment either. The town's Brass Band, the German Orchestral Band, McKee's Italian Band, an independent brass band, a male quartette, and the Military Band from Fort Custer participated in the entertainment at social functions.

During the summer of 1883, as more travelling troupes visited Billings, a call went out for a public hall which would accommodate any and all that cared to attend. The old Opera House and the Variety Theatre were used frequently, but "more advanced civilization" demanded something which would encourage respectable entertainment to come to Billings and which would make it possible for ladies, who had previously been "debarred," to attend. Rockwell and Mains leased the Meyer Block and converted it into a rink but erected a stage so that it could be used for other entertainment as well. It was in this hall that Gerald Panton became the "hero" of the skating enthusiasts. He defeated "all comers" in the eastern part of the state. A purse was attached to these races, winner taking all. As an added feature to this type of entertainment, a tug of war, with oysters as the prize, was frequently held. The rink was used occasionally too for magic lantern shows. . . .

The Fourth of July Celebration was always an important event of the year. The celebration of 1884 was typical. In the forenoon, Judge Platt read the Declaration of Independence, and Mr. J. R. King made a patriotic speech. In the afternoon a baseball game and horse races furnished entertainment. In the evening a "brilliant display of fireworks" and a "grand ball" at the new depot completed the day's fun.

By September, 1882, it had become evident that a school must be provided to educate the children, who were rapidly increasing in number. A meeting held on September 13 adopted a petition asking the county commissioners of Custer County, of which Billings was at the time a part, to establish a school district for the Billings community. The petition was not answered favorably, so subscriptions were taken up among the residents until sufficient funds were obtained to operate a free school for a period of six months. School began in October and was held in Foster's building for one week and then moved to Breauchaud's building near the Congregational Church. No building was purchased because a new county was going to be created and because Frederick Billings had promised to donate $4,000 to aid in erecting a permanent building. The hope that the new building would be ready by the time the six-month free school term expired was not realized.

Billings was located in the third school district of Custer County. This district was fifty-five miles long and thirty miles broad, reaching from Pompey's Pillar to Canyon Creek and containing 216 children of school age. After Yellowstone County was created, the commissioners divided the county into six separate districts, locating schools at Junction, Billings, Newman, Canyon Creek, Park City, and Columbus. . . .

On the same day that the boundaries of the district were accepted, the trustees drew up plans to float a bond issue of $8,000 to be added to the $4,000 promised by Frederick Billings. The bond issue, when presented to the people, was carried with only one dissenting vote. Late in August the contract for the new building was let. The old St. James Restaurant located on Minnesota Avenue, which had been occupied by the subscription school in 1882, was again rented and used until February, 1884, at which time the new building was ready for occupation.

This first public school in Billings opened on Monday, September 17, 1883, with Hattie Graham in charge. On the opening day fifty-six pupils reported for instruction, but by October 4, seventy-five were enrolled and it was found necessary to hire Rose Camp to take care of the additional pupils. The Congregational Church donated the use of its chapel, where the forty-five pupils instructed by Miss Camp reported.

The school board had difficulty raising enough money to take care of the current expenses of the school. It issued a call for an election to be held in November to authorize the raising of an additional $1500. When the measure was brought before the people, it passed unanimously. Late in November it was necessary to move from the chapel to the old building formerly used by the *Post*. This building was occupied only a short time, for on December 7 it was destroyed by fire. The work on the new building, a two story stone and brick structure, located on a plot of ground 300 feet square; twenty-two lots had been given to the district by Kurtz & Foster and two more were purchased from F. B. Kennard. The actual cost to the taxpayers was only $8,000 because of the gifts of Frederick Billings and Kurtz & Foster. Early in February the building was ready for occupation.

The school continued to grow, and when it opened in the fall of 1884, three teachers were required to supervise the 130 pupils enrolled. In March, 1885, it was again found necessary to go to the people for permission to raise additional funds to finance the school. A special tax was voted to raise $2,500 to pay the outstanding debts and to help defray the expenses for the current year. The citizens were almost unanimously in favor of the additional tax as it became evident that the ordinary taxes were insufficient to take care of the rapidly growing school.

The first religious services in Billings were held by the Congregational church under the direction of Rev. B. F. Shuart. He began his work in the early spring of 1882. Later in the year a small frame structure was erected on the lots now occupied by the same congregation. At the back of this building a lean-to was erected which served as a parsonage. In October, 1883, plans were made to erect a new building, since the old one was inadequate. Frederick Billings donated $12,000 to the cause and the land company and the owners of the

Foster Addition donated the lots. By November, the completed church was occupied and dedicated.

Within six months after Rev. Shuart began his work, three other organizations appeared. Rev. W. W. Van Orsdel held the first Methodist services in town. It was not until 1885, however, that a Methodist church was erected. The Episcopal church was first represented by Rev. W. Horsfall. Services were first held in the old railroad depot, then in an empty store, then in a hotel parlor. In 1886 a church building was erected on the lots donated by the land company on the south side of 29th Street. The first Catholic mass was held by Father Palladino in the early summer of 1883, but it was not till 1887 that a building was erected.

The two sources of information most valuable in compiling this record were the newspapers, the *Post* and the *Herald*. They played an important part in the early development of the town. . . .

The Coulson *Post* was founded by A. K. Yerkes, who was sole owner and editor of the paper. He purchased the plant and equipment from the Yellowstone *Journal* (Miles City) and freighted the outfit to the village of Coulson, where late in January, 1882, he issued the first number of the *Post*. In June, after taking an active part in booming Coulson, he moved the plant to Billings and the name of the journal changed to the Billings *Post*. Shortly after this move, he sold out to J. D. Matheson, who was sole owner until the *Post* was merged with the *Herald* and the *Rustler* to form the *Gazette* in 1885. The *Post* was definitely a Republican paper. It had about 3000 readers "more or less" who paid the sum of three dollars per year when they were able. Matheson at one time advertised that he would accept cord wood from those who had offered to give that instead of the three dollars.

The second paper in Billings, the *Herald*, was established in June, 1882, by Alexander Divine and E. A. Bromley, in the fourth building erected in Billings. In November, 1882, Bromley retired and Divine assumed full control. A daily *Herald* was begun in April, 1883, and Billings boasted its first daily paper. In May, 1883, Divine sold a half interest to J. D. Matheson and they published the weekly and daily in partnership. After giving the daily a fair trial it was found that the advertising public would not give the necessary support and it was discontinued January 16, 1884, but the weekly continued. In September, 1884, J. D. Matheson sold his interest to C. S. McFarlin. Divine and McFarlin then conducted the *Herald* until late in April, 1885, when the consolidation took place.

In April the proprietors of the *Herald* and the *Post*, together with some other citizens, formed a joint stock company, called the Gazette Publishing Company. This company purchased the plant of the *Daily Rustler*, which came into existence briefly in 1884, and combined it with the plants of the *Herald* and *Post*. The Gazette Publishing Company secured the franchise of the Associated Press and issued a morning paper with full press dispatches known as the *Gazette*. They also issued a weekly named the *Montana Stock Gazette*, which was devoted particularly to the expanding cattle interests. The three plants were moved into one building on May 2nd, but that night the building was destroyed by the worst fire the town had experienced. A small hand press that was saved was used to carry on until a new plant arrived. A brick building was erected and publication continued uninterrupted. In October, 1885, Divine and McFarlin withdrew and J. D. Matheson purchased their stock and became sole owner. He conducted both papers until January, 1887. The *Gazette* is now one of the leading papers in the state.

10

The Secret City:
The Withering of Hope

by CONSTANCE McLAUGHLIN GREEN

The deterioration of Negro status sprang from a complex of causes, but the common denominator was the steady paring down of incentive.

In 1937 advocates of a deeper study of American race relations secured the sponsorship of the Carnegie Corporation of a "comprehensive study of the Negro in the United States, to be undertaken in a wholly objective and dispassionate way as a social phenomenon." This resulted in the publication in 1944 of Gunnar Myrdal's *The American Dilemma* which demonstrated the ambivalence of American society, dedicated, on the one hand, to the equalitarianism of the Declaration of Independence and committed, on the other, to practices quite at variance with equality. From the standpoint of historiography Myrdal's book laid one of the foundations for a new school of American historical writing that concerned itself with a historical examination of the American dilemma and the inequities and inequalities of American urban and rural life. *The Secret City: A History of Race Relations in the Nation's Capital* by Constance McLaughlin Green is an expression of this post-Myrdal approach to historical writing which has opened up a whole new dimension of consideration for the American historian.

Chapter VII, "The Withering of Hope, 1879–1901," reproduced here from this book, deals with the blacks of Washington, D.C., during the period 1879–1901 and represents an important contribution to our knowledge of the history of the American capital, a large percentage of the population of which has been black from the beginning. *The Secret City* by Constance McLaughlin Green was published by the Princeton University Press in 1967. The following selection is reprinted by permission of Princeton University Press.

Constance McLaughlin Green was born in Ann Arbor, Michigan, in 1898 and educated at Smith, Mount Holyoke, and Yale. She has taught history at the University of Chicago, Mount Holyoke, and Smith and received the Pulitzer Prize for history in 1963 for her two-volume history of Washington, D.C. Among her other books are *American Cities in the Growth of the Nation* and *The Rise of Urban America.* She has also written histories of Holyoke, Massachusetts, and Naugutuck, Connecticut.

"We live," wrote the famous army surgeon Dr. John Shaw Billings, "in a fortunate time and place—in the early manhood of a mighty nation, and in its capital city, which every year makes more beautiful and richer in the treasure of science, literature and art." White Washington in the 1880's enjoyed a material prosperity and amenities richer than any the city had ever known before. For Negroes the satisfactions of life diminished steadily after 1878. Between white and colored people such tolerant friendliness as survived the seventies slowly disappeared. The change was gradual enough to permit colored people for a time to persuade themselves that a year or two would suffice to reestablish them on the footing they had attained earlier. Not until the autumn of 1883 did they clearly sense how much the atmosphere had chilled in a decade, and not until the 1890's did they realize that no effort of theirs was likely to restore warmth to the city's race relations.

In 1888 the Washington *Elite List,* a forerunner of the *Social Register,* carried the names of five or six Negroes; by 1892 they had been dropped. After John Forney of the *Chronicle* retired, the white press, increasingly critical of Negroes' "shiftlessness" and the high rate of crime among them, gradually reduced other news about them to an occasional facetious comment on a colored social gathering. Exasperation or disgust blotted out compassion for the great mass of blacks, while white people's interest in the careers of gifted Negroes became so condescending as to be insulting, the more so as the condescension was unconscious. By the mid-nineties a reader of the white newspapers might have supposed that Washington had no colored community, let alone three virtually separate Negro communities. White people, in short, in the course of the twenty-odd years resolved the problem of race relations by tacitly denying its existence.

How to explain so drastic a shift in attitude? The two decades under scrutiny encompassed a period of far greater national change than was apparent to Americans experiencing it. It was marked by an inundation of foreign immigrants, by a concentration of wealth in the hands of a half-hundred daring and often ruthless industrialists and railroad executives, by an accompanying decline in the influence of a somewhat bewildered middle class, by violent conflicts between labor and capital, by the "rise of the city" in a formerly agricultural nation, and finally by the emergence of the United States as a world power. Of those factors several had less direct bearing on life in the national capital than in other cities. Relatively few foreign-born came to Washington. Being nonindustrial, the city escaped the full force of labor battles and kept some aspects of its bucolic past. To outsiders the District seemed singularly placid, untouched by the intensely competitive spirit of the rest of the country. Nevertheless, as the capital Washington was highly sensitive to new political winds, of which a wooing of the newly industrializing South was one of the strongest. Ostensibly in a position to mould American public opinion and guide public policies, in actuality the city was a follower, "yr obdt servant," accepting the standards of behavior of communities whose votes in national elections counted heavily. Along with the "bloody shirt" Washington rapidly discarded concern for racial justice. Colored men were economically too insecure to affect the climate of opinion in a nation increasingly dedicated to material progress and all too ready to embrace the thesis of Social Darwinism about the "survival of the fittest."

In Washington, where Negroes had made greater strides than any-where else in the United States, local disenfranchisement abruptly ended political associations between Negroes and whites. Social inter-course, only beginning to develop in 1870, consequently died out for want of nourishment from natural, day-by-day encounters of fellow citizens with obvious common interests. As time went on, the failure of the bulk of the city's black population to evince a sense of responsi-bility disillusioned formerly well-disposed whites who professed to think they had more than discharged their obligations to colored people. That disillusionment fed racial hostility as surely as racial dis-crimination undermined Negroes' determination to help themselves. The result was a vicious spiral. Whites concluded that most Negroes would never make good citizens, and Negroes, feeling themselves steadily shoved further into a corner by prejudice, ceased to stand up for one another and let the fight degenerate into that of each for himself. The exceptions were too few to alter the large picture. Well-educated aristocrats of predominantly white blood drew further away from the darker-skinned middle-class families, while the gulf separating both groups from inarticulate blacks widened. Except as seen in all Negroes' search for *"whiteness*—the ability to pass unnoticed in the crowd, the power to avoid humiliation and abuse," a community in the sense of people united by common aspirations and cultural identity fell apart before it had outgrown infancy. The biological accident of pigmentation created growing resentments which colored people directed at each other more bitterly than at whites. By the 1890's most Negroes in the District were adhering to the social pattern common in the deep South: conflict within the caste and compliance with or carefully concealed hostility toward the white group outside.[1]

For upper-class Negroes civil rights were still the key to progress. During the Hayes administration violations of the antidiscrimination laws apparently multiplied but were either too trivial or too skillfully cloaked to lead to court action. The *People's Advocate* initially urged Negroes to concentrate on fair play: instead of suing white proprietors for refusing them accommodation, first file complaints against Negro barbers who refused to serve other colored men. Two years later the editor doubted the wisdom of those tactics. "A respectable colored lady or gentleman, unless it happens to be a man like Frederick Douglass, John F. Cook, or Register Bruce [former United States Senator from Mississippi], is not readily accommodated, if at all, in the eating establishments, no matter how genteel he may be in appearance or in manners." The result was "more or less friction between the keepers of these saloons and a class of our citizens rapidly growing in wealth and intelligence." Washington Negroes nevertheless still relied upon patience to destroy prejudice.[2]

In the summer of 1883 a Negro visitor from Connecticut sued a Washington restaurant owner under the criminal section of the federal Civil Rights Act. Newspapers throughout the country discussed the case, partly because it was only the second criminal suit to be brought under the act of 1875, partly because the argument for the defense

[1] A. Hunter Dupree, *Science in the Federal Government,* p. 230; Pauli Murray, *Proud Shoes, The Story of an American Family,* p. 53; see John Dollard, *Caste and Class in a Southern Town*; Albion Davis and G. and M. Gardner, *Deep South.*

[2] *People's Advocate,* 5 Jul, 15, 29 Nov 1879, 10 Jul 1880, 6 Aug 1881 (hereafter cited as *Advocate*).

had an ominous logic: a government which sanctioned separate colored schools could not reasonably require a restaurant proprietor to seat Negroes in a dining room with whites; he had offered to serve the colored man in the pantry. The judge reviewed all earlier decisions in local civil rights cases, noted that several verdicts had been adverse to the plaintiffs, but in this case found against the defendant and fined him $500.

It was at best a Pyrrhic victory. It strengthened white animosities already heightened by the discovery that federal courts outside the District of Columbia rarely heard civil rights cases, and it inspired pronouncements that the judge's interpretation of the law would force restaurant owners either to accept an exclusively black clientele, or see their business ruined, or both. Negroes native to the District were ironically rewarded for their past forbearance by repeated statements citing their eight-year failure to sue under the federal law as proof that the color line was unobjectionable to them. Two months after the decision of August 1883, the United States Supreme Court declared the Civil Rights Act unconstitutional in the states, although it might still be binding in the District of Columbia and United States territories. Ignorant blacks were badly frightened, expecting to see the whipping post brought back at any moment. Educated Negroes in Washington were angry. Frederick Douglass, with more passion than accuracy, called the decree a deliberate repudiation of a law that had won general public acceptance. Only George Richardson, a teacher in the colored high school, told the Bethel Literary and Historical Association that the court ruling, however distressing to colored people, was "severely and equitably just." Negroes would have to count on demonstrating to the states that colored people were citizens worthy of the same treatment as whites. In any case, the local laws were in force. But no one favoring racial legal equality pretended that the court decision was not a serious setback.

The Bethel Literary and Historical Association, founded in 1881 by Bishop Daniel Payne of the African Methodist Episcopal Church, frequently debated the question of what course Negroes should pursue. Alexander Crummell, rector of St. Luke's Episcopal Church, whom many people considered the foremost Negro intellectual of his time, in 1875 had called it a "heresy" for colored Americans to forget "that they ARE colored people." On coming to Washington in 1873 after spending twenty years as a missionary in Liberia, he had discarded his advocacy of colonization, but he preached a gospel of Negro uniqueness. Negroes, " 'a peculiar people' in this land," must strive for racial organization as a distinct entity in the nation. Other speakers at Bethel Literary sessions insisted that racial solidarity and economic chauvinism were destructive, underscoring Negro differences from other Americans; colored people ought rather to aim at obliterating the factors that set them apart and seek social assimilation into white America. But John Cromwell of the *Advocate* in addressing himself to the thesis of Negro advancement by self-improvement pointed out that "the material defect in the individual development theory is that the white people will not let you get rid of the idea of race."

The Negro press took special note of Frederick Douglass' about-face. In 1866 he had told white paternalists to leave the Negro alone to find his own level; by the mid-1880's he had become convinced that the race problem was the white man's problem which Negroes could not and should not have to solve. When he married a white woman in 1884 and some of his associates angrily accused him of lacking pride of race, he brushed their criticism aside as an impertinence. Race pride and race solidarity he contended were fallacies. He wrote in the AME *Review* in 1889: "Our union is our weakness," breeding a cultural provincialism in an oppressed people. "A nation within a nation is an anomaly. There can be but one nation . . . and we are Americans." Yet in the capital most colored leaders veered increasingly toward a form of Negro nationalism.[3]

Between 1884 and the turn of the century most of the few civil rights suits filed in the District of Columbia were dismissed; only two or three were successful, such as the case against a lunchroom proprietor who had not posted a price list and had overcharged a Negro outrageously by demanding fifty cents for three eggs, two biscuits, and a cup of coffee. In the 1880's barrooms generally served colored customers, but lunchrooms and ice cream parlors usually excluded them, a source of particular irritation to "genteel" Negroes. The genteel plainly indicated their readiness to have vulgar blacks denied service. Petitions submitted to Congress in 1886 asked for stronger local laws extended to areas not covered in the municipal and territorial acts, but new laws seemed unlikely to improve white tempers. Congress dismissed all proposals for racial legislation, whether bills forbidding miscegenation or those demanding a change in the District Medical

[3] *Ibid.*, 3 Mar, 25 Aug 1883; Washington *Bee*, 4 Aug, 8 Sep 1883, 28 Apr 1884; *Star*, 7, 13, 16, 18, 24 Aug, 17, 24 Oct 1883; John Cromwell, *History of the Bethel Literary and Historical Association*; August Meier, *Negro Thought in America, 1880–1915*, pp. 42–43, 53–55, 75–77.

Society's discriminatory rules. In 1896 the Supreme Court struck a deadly blow at all American Negroes by ruling in the famous Plessy versus Ferguson case that separate but equal accommodations met every requirement of the Fourteenth Amendment. Four years later a suit against the owner of the Washington Opera House for refusing to let a colored man occupy the orchestra seat he had paid for netted the plaintiff damages of one cent.[4]

Nor were Negroes guiltless. A number of Negro-owned barber shops and some hotels and restaurants run by colored men would not accept Negro customers. A circular of 1888, for example, announced: "Preston's Pension Office barber shop, first class in every particular. Devoted *Strictly to White Trade*. The rumor that this shop has been serving any Colored Trade is false in every particular." The white press called attention to such incidents. "The refusal is based, of course," remarked the *Star*, "not on color prejudice, but on the business consideration that the best paying class of customers can be retained only by excluding those who for any reason are objectionable to their fastidious notions." [5] After the founding of the short-lived Afro-American League in 1890, a Washington branch sent delegates to its national conventions, but disunity, lack of a positive program to combat racism, and the magnitude of the problem stripped the organization of effectiveness. Its successor, the Afro-American Council, which came into being in 1898, was largely controlled by Booker T. Washington, whose seeming subservience to whites alienated Negro militants. As Jim Crow laws began to multiply in the Southern states, Negroes in the District realized they were far better off than most of their race; but they saw that the local antidiscrimination laws had come to be more honored in the breach than in the observance.

Chance, moreover, played into the hands of segregationists. In 1901 Congress accepted the first part of a codification of District law but left "the second or municipal part" to be revised and adopted later. Although Congress specified that existing police regulations, unless expressly repealed, should continue in force—a stipulation that meant the civil rights laws were still valid—the fact that the published code

---

[4] *Star*, 8, 22 Nov 1884, 4 Feb, 10 Dec 1887, 18 Feb 1888; *Cong Rec*, 47C, 1S, pp. 1408–10, 1839; ptn, S49A-H63, 28 Jan 1886; S. Rpt 1050, 52C, 1S, Ser 2915; *Bee*, 1884–1899, 24 Nov 1900. As virtually every issue of the *Bee* carried items relevant to the topics discussed in this and in the next chapter, citations represent a mere sample.

[5] *Star*, 12 Dec 1887; *Bee*, 21 Jul 1888.

contained no mention of the antidiscrimination ordinances encouraged white men to ignore them.[6]

Washington's old, well-established colored families such as the Cooks and the Wormleys had reason for a time to believe that they and distinguished later arrivals such as Frederick Douglass and ex-Senator Blanche K. Bruce could enjoy some rights not specifically protected by law. Good manners, professional status, and money made them acceptable residents of any locality provided they did not obtrude themselves socially upon white people. But cultivated Negroes, even those who looked almost white, discovered that each passing year made it harder for them to purchase or rent comfortable houses without paying exorbitant prices; by the 1890's they could rarely buy at all in a conveniently located, orderly neighborhood. In 1892 John Lynch, a successful building contractor, put up a handsome house for himself in the most fashionable section of New Hampshire Avenue, but Mary Church Terrell's *A Colored Woman in a White World* tells of endless humiliations in the course of her house hunt. Yet her husband was a *cum laude* graduate of Harvard, a respected lawyer, principal of the M Street High School, and after 1896 a member of the Board of Trade; she herself was a graduate of Oberlin, an accomplished linguist, and one of two women before 1900 to be appointed to the school board.

Rising rentals hastened the exodus of Negro householders who in the seventies had lived along 16th Street a few blocks above Lafayette Square and out beyond Scott Circle. As the real estate boom in northwest Washington gained momentum, colored people moved farther from the center of the city. Whether sheer economics or, as rumor had it, combinations of real estate agents kept respectable Negroes from moving into desirable localities, the result was the same. It did not mean that clear-cut solid black belts arose outside of which Negroes could not find housing; some intersprinkling of white and Negro dwellings continued down into the 1930's. But by 1900 the barrier of caste, seemingly collapsing in the late 1860's, had become stronger than ever. The one notable exception lay in the Board of Trade, the

---

[6] *Colored American*, 9 Apr 1898; *Bee*, 16 Nov 1889, 27 Aug 1898; August Meier, "Booker T. Washington and the Negro Press," *Journal of Negro History*, XXXVIII, 85, n; *Cong Rec*, 56C, 2S, pp. 3497, 3586, 3603; Walter S. Cox, "Attempts to Obtain a Law Code for the District of Columbia," CHS *Rec*, III, 127–32; Phineas Indritz, "Post Civil War Ordinances Prohibiting Racial Discrimination in the District of Columbia," *Georgetown Law Journal*, XLII, 196–201.

city's principal business organization: James T. Wormley was a charter member; Dr. Charles Purvis, head of Freedmen's Hospital, George F. Cook, superintendent of the colored schools, and Robert Terrell were elected in the mid-1890's.[7]

Disregard of civil rights as a rule affected only upper-class Negroes. The workings of the criminal law, on the other hand, touched the lives of countless blacks living on a bare subsistence level. Of those some were undoubtedly vicious; and some, though vaguely well-intentioned, took to thieving, drunkenness, and disorderliness as the easiest way to blunder through a world that offered them at best very little. In a city where only one person in three was colored, the number of Negro arrests exceeded the number of white every year after 1889. People as ignorant of their rights as of their obligations were, to be sure, in some measure at the mercy of the police, and police brutality was all too common. The *Bee*, founded in 1882, asserted that policemen, particularly the Irishmen on the force, frequently clubbed Negroes savagely when arresting them, and the dark-skinned man was always the first suspect when a crime occurred. Officers "delight in arresting every little colored boy they see on the street, who may be doing something not at all offensive, and allow the white boys to do what they please." The severity of the sentences magistrates imposed on Negro misdemeanants seemed often to reflect white men's aversion to the entire race. Calvin Chase, editor of the *Bee*, as a boy having seen his father shot down in cold blood and his white assailant go unpunished, was vitriolic about Washington police methods. But more temperate men than he believed that racial equality before the law had largely disappeared by the end of the century.[8]

Despite the decline of Negroes' legal position, political preferment for colored men fell off surprisingly little. Frederick Douglass kept his post as Marshal of the District through President Hayes' administration, while the lucrative position of District Recorder of Deeds continued to go to Negroes. President Garfield, moreover, appointed ex-Senator Bruce of Mississippi Register of the Treasury, a place that

[7] *Advocate*, 8 Sep 1883; *Star*, 4 Feb 1887; Edward Ingle, *The Negro in the District of Columbia*, in *Johns Hopkins University Studies in Historical and Political Science*, 11th Series, nos. III and IV, pp. 50–51, 90 (hereafter cited as Ingle, *The Negro in D.C.*); Coroner's maps in Comrs Rpts, 1882, p. 508, 1890, p. 826, 1900, p. 826; Joseph W. Moore, *Picturesque Washington*, p. 139; Mary Church Terrell, *A Colored Woman in a White World*, pp. 113–19; membership lists in *Rpts B/Tr*, 1897, 1899; *Colored American*, 26 Mar 1898; *Bee*, 1898–1901.

[8] *Star*, 15 Mar 1882, 27 Oct 1887, 1 Jan 1897; *Chronicle*, 10 Mar 1895, 7

would be filled by a Negro for the next thirty-two years. Garfield's assassination and President Arthur's failure to give colored men much consideration, it is true, hurt their prospects and shut off talk of appointments to the Cabinet, but during the 1880's a half-dozen Negroes had administrative assignments of some importance, and more clerkships and custodial jobs than formerly went to colored men. Both before and after the introduction of competitive civil service examinations, colored employees feared for their jobs when a new administration took over, but even the shake-up anticipated during Grover Cleveland's first term did not cut the number of Negroes on the federal payroll; on the contrary, scrupulous fairness in grading examinations enabled more Negroes than ever before to enter government service. In 1891 out of 23,144 federal employees in Washington, nearly 2,400 were colored; they held 337 of the 6,120 jobs in the Interior Department, and 127 ranked as copyists, "transcribers," and clerks. At the Library of Congress Daniel Murray was one of nineteen assistant librarians, only seven of whom drew an annual salary larger than his $1,400. Negroes rarely encountered overt hostility from fellow white employees. Negroes got far less consideration from the District commissioners. In 1879 one appointment out of fifty to the police force was colored, none to the fire department. Later policy gave Negroes some of the jobs but never established a stable ratio of colored to white. Outside the colored school system, in 1891 Negroes held only 25 District positions above the rank of messenger and day laborer,

Cleveland's second administration, troubled as it was by country-wide unemployment, saw a drop in Negro preferment and the dismissal of "surplus" Negro clerks. Republican prosperity, launched with the election of William McKinley, failed to restore the earlier proportion of colored employees, in spite of the liberal attitude of Secretary of the Treasury Lyman Gage and his top assistants. The falling off in other departments, if less pronounced than white men expected, was at once a bitter disappointment to Negroes and a gloomily foreseen development in keeping with trends in other areas of American life.[9]

Jun 1896; *Sentinel,* 15 Oct 1892, 25 Nov 1893; *Bee,* 6 Aug 1887; Ingle, *The Negro in D.C.,* pp. 100–01; William J. Simmons, *Men of Mark, Eminent, Progressive and Rising,* pp. 118–19; Elizabeth M. Chapin, *American Court Gossip, or Life at the Nation's Capital,* pp. 36–40.

[9] Laurence John Wesley Hayes, *The Negro Federal Government Worker, A Study of His Classification Status in the District of Columbia,* 1883–1938, pp.

Negro pride was badly hurt, moreover, when the new president of Howard University filled seven out of nine faculty vacancies with whites. A worse humiliation befell at the outbreak of the Spanish-American War. Independent companies of colored Civil War veterans had organized in the late 1860's and 1870's, formed into battalions in the mid-1880's, and had been incorporated into the District National Guard in 1887. Until then they had paid all their own expenses, recruited student cadets, and periodically held competitive drills. Thus a dozen times a year every old soldier relived the glory of the days when he had served his country on active duty. When the commanding general in 1891 mustered out the colored battalions as supernumerary, an appeal to the President had reinstated them, whereupon they were consolidated into the First Separate Colored Battalion of the District National Guard. That the battalion appeared at every drill and ceremonial occasion thereafter made the rebuff harder to bear when in 1898 General George Harries refused to enroll the unit for active service with the District regiment sent to Cuba. Colored men felt that their loyalty and efficiency had been impugned.[10]

The collapse of earlier hopes for political and legal equality might have distressed Negroes less had their economic opportunities widened consistently. With the District's colored population growing from the 59,000 of 1880 to 90,000 twenty years later, Negroes trained in the professions seemingly should have found abundant openings. Besides more than four hundred colored teachers, Washington in 1900 had fifty qualified physicians, ten professionally trained dentists, over ninety ministers, and some thirty lawyers. The colored press usually put the totals in each category very much higher. Negro doctors, barred from the District Medical Society, formed the Medico-Chirurgical Society in 1884, the first Negro medical association in the United States. But except for the pastors, including those without much schooling, colored professional men faced hard sledding. About ten applicants for every teaching post in the school system created intense competition. Relatively few Negroes could afford to pay

22–25 (hereafter cited as Hayes, *Negro Govt Worker*); Cleveland *Leader,* 7 Nov 1884; *Nation,* XCVII, 114; *Sentinel,* 10 Apr 1880; *Advocate,* 3 Dec 1881; *Bee,* 1882–1901; *Star,* 9 May 1883, 2 Feb 1887; Ingle, *The Negro in D.C.,* pp. 48–49: Rpt Sec/Int, 1895, p. 724, Ser 3383; *Official Register of the United States,* 1891, p. 18.

10 Hilyer, *Directory,* pp. 150–57; Capt George W. Evans, "The Militia of the District of Columbia," CHS *Rec,* XXVIII, 95–105; *Bee,* 3 Jul 1897, 13 Jan 1900; Fleetwood Mss.

doctors', dentists', and lawyers' fees, no matter how modest, and a discouragingly large proportion of the colored people of means preferred to deal with white men. The *Colored American*, in 1898 the *Bee's* new competitor, observed that colored people in Washington went to a colored doctor "only when we wish to run a bill we do not intend to pay." Conversely, several Negro physicians refused to attend impoverished colored patients, "the back door trade." Inexperienced lawyers, in a frantic scramble to find clients, hawked their services about the Police Court.

Colored business enterprises also suffered from Negroes' reluctance to patronize men of their own race. The failure of the Freedmen's Bank in 1874, although due primarily to white exploitation, had shattered confidence in their capacity to handle finances. A colored savings bank opened in 1888 increased the list of its depositors yearly, but for commercial purposes Negroes used white banks. As in other American cities, Negro merchants had enormous difficulty in competing with white for the colored trade and could rarely cater successfully to both races.[11] The career of John A. Gray, a restaurant owner and one-time member of the territorial governor's council, illustrates some of the hazards. "He kept one of the first houses in the city," reported the *Bee*. "He first opened it for white people and was having a success until the Negroes kept clamoring for a respectable place to go. He opened his house to the hightoned colored people and in less than a year they broke him up." Undeterred by the refusal of white merchants to employ Negro clerks, colored families persisted in trading at white shops. Prices were often lower there, and service and the selection of goods better, but investigation revealed a more basic and pettier reason: in the city's colored business world the "great impediment has been jealousy and a dislike to see each other succeed."

Caterers were one of the few groups able to avoid the complications of seeking mixed or purely colored patronage, for the business, unique

---

[11] *Colored American*, 14 May 1898; W. Montague Cobb, "Washington, D.C.," in Dietrich C. Reitzes, *Negroes and Medicine*, pp. 193–94; Walter L. Fleming, *The Freedman's Savings Bank*, pp. 53–99, 129–30; W. E. B. DuBois, ed., *The Negro in Business, The Report of the Fourth Conference for the Study of Negro Problems, held at Atlanta University*, 30–31 May 1899, pp. 13, 28–29, 56–61 (hereafter the special studies and the reports of the proceedings of the conferences at Atlanta University every May from 1896 to 1916 are cited only by title, conference number, and date); *Advocate*, 30 Aug 1879; *Bee*, 31 Jul 1886; Ingle, *The Negro in D.C.*, pp. 91–92; John H. Harmon, Arnett G. Lindsay, and Carter G. Woodson, *The Negro as a Businessman*, pp. 34, 51–55; Hilyer, *Directory*, pp. 4, 38, 62, 73–74.

to Washington, depended solely upon a white clientele. Unlike the modern term, catering in the capital of the 1880's and 1890's meant delivering hot meals twice a day to people living in rented rooms who wished to escape from the restaurant or dismal boardinghouse table by breakfasting and dining in their rooms. The best caterers charged from $25 to $30 a month per person. Those with fast teams of horses could deliver well-cooked dishes in specially constructed double-racked tin containers before the food cooled. A skillful caterer with a clientele of fifty to a hundred families could clear a considerable sum in a year, despite the decline of his business in the months between congressional sessions. Since the enterprise, however profitable, smacked of menial service, white men rarely competed.

A few Negroes made money in fields considered wholly dignified, notably real estate, building, and selling life insurance or shares in benefit and relief associations. James Wormley, owner of the famous Wormley House, left an estate of over $150,000; his sons, after nearly doubling their inheritance, so gossip said, by betting on President Harrison's election in 1888, put the family fortune into the construction business. Negroes who had owned local real estate before the war and had hung on to it through the disasters of the board of public works era and the Freedmen's Bank failure might be very well off indeed, although the number whose holdings were ever extensive was certainly small. District tax collector John F. Cook, himself said to be the largest taxpayer of his race, reported in 1887 two local colored men worth $100,000, two worth $75,000, a flour merchant worth $50,000, and some forty men with property valued at a figure between $10,000 and $25,000.[12]

While the lack of racial solidarity hurt the Negro professions and business enterprises, the increasing hostility of white workingmen and the bars erected by labor organizations severely handicapped the lower-class Negro. An analysis of 1881 attributed the troubles of Philadelphia's colored workmen to foreign immigrants: "Southern cities were built by colored mechanical labor. In this city twenty years before the late war, it was no unusual thing to find a majority of colored mechanics engaged in all the leading trades. . . . But Irish emigration [*sic*] was destined to strike a blow at the colored mechanic, from which it will take years for him to recover." Negroes in Washington looked

12 *Bee*, 22 Oct 1887, 17 Nov 1888, 12 Jan 1889, 12 Jul 1890; Cleveland *Leader*, 5 Jan, 7 Apr 1883; *Star*, 23 Oct 1884, 18 Apr 1926; Simmons, *Men of Mark*, pp. 249–50; Harmon et al., *Negro as Businessman*, p. 91; Hilyer, *Directory*, pp. 3–4, 104–09.

upon Irishmen as enemies, but foreign immigrants in the capital were too few in the last decades of the century to be a determining factor in the local labor market.

In the early eighties the local carpenters' union drew no official color line, and one of the two mechanics' unions had mixed membership, but white mechanics made life for their colored fellows miserable in a dozen ways, and, by refusing to accept colored apprentices, the unions gradually excluded all Negroes. A colored lodge of the Knights of Labor, organized in 1884 as the Thad Stevens Assembly, fell apart before the Haymarket tragedy in Chicago two years later undermined the national brotherhood. In 1886 a Negro waiters' union appeared, but within a decade colored men found that occupations "which by common consent were regarded as belonging to them, such as waiters and the like, are now being monopolized by the whites." Booker T. Washington's exhortations to Negroes to think less about political equality and more about acquiring competence as workers fell on sterile soil in the District; here economic independence appeared to be unattainable merely by hard work.[13]

To combat trade union discrimination, "the curse of which has more than any other, fettered the energies of the colored people," and to recapture civil rights, nonsegregated schools still seemed to some Negroes the first essential; only early association of the races would induce a "more generous spirit" in white men. But the opposition of other Negroes strengthened as the colored school system expanded and the number of teaching posts grew. The opening of a colored high school nine years before the city had a white high school weakened the integrationists' contention that the white schools invariably provided a quality of education superior to anything available in the colored. In actuality the Miner Fund, not tax money, initially supported the colored high school as well as the Negro normal school. The question of mixed schools revived in 1881 and 1882 when the school trustees allowed two or three very light colored children to attend white schools. While Negro advocates of separate systems insisted that more money and Negro trustees less prone to toady to whites and less ready to show favoritism would correct every shortcoming in the colored schools, the *Star* declared school integration a "purely sentimental" notion:

[13] *Advocate*, 21 Apr 1882; *Bee*, 1 Jan 1897, 8 Oct 1898; *Star*, 26 Jul 1885; Simmons, *Men of Mark*, pp. 270–72; *Sentinel*, 30 Mar 1889.

There is a small sprinkling of colored children in the white schools, but for the most part the colored people prefer to have their separate school organization with a superintendent and teachers of their own race ; just as they prefer to maintain their own . . . benevolent and social associations. The colored schools get their full share of school moneys ; and in proportion to numbers are supplied with better school accommodations than the whites. For various reasons the colored children get on better in schools of their own. One is that they are spared the disadvantageous competition with white children of their own age who have had greater opportunities at home and else-where for advancement in their studies. Again were the schools to be merged it would necessarily throw 165 colored teachers out of em-ployment, as it could not be expected that the white school popula-tion of the District—outnumbering the colored about two to one—should give up their teachers to make room for colored teachers. . . . Better let well enough alone.

Somewhat later, at two lively sessions of the "Bethel Literary," George W. Cook of Howard University, George T. Downing, and Dr. Charles Purvis vainly opposed John Cromwell and other proponents of ethno-centrism.

The census figures on the percentage of adults unable to write sug-gest the handicap under which the children of hundreds of Negro parents labored :

	1880	1890	1900
White	5.4	2.67	1.86
Colored	59.3	39.4	30.47

From the mid-1880's onward one group of colored people argued that vocational training was a wiser goal for the Negro schools than a more literary education; a curriculum like that of the white schools should wait until the economic level of the average colored family had risen enough to enable Negro children to benefit from academic courses. In the 1890's Booker T. Washington, by then head of Tuskegee Insti-tute in Alabama, began to popularize that thesis among white people who saw in it a way to create a permanent, docile working class. Dissi-dents in Washington, although believing the plan equivalent to giving up the fight for racial equality and accepting a position of inferiority for decades to come, had to abandon the campaign for integrated schools. The issue dropped out of sight in Washington for fifty-odd years. But more than one colored aristocrat, unwilling to subject his children to a segregated system, had them taught at home and then sent them to boarding schools and colleges in New England.[14]

Meanwhile Negroes who were determined to develop an independent school system as good in every particular as the white vigilantly watched the school board's every act. Hypersensitive to any possible slight, they criticized so persistently, and sometimes so unfairly, that the board president in 1899 resigned in protest at their nagging. But the fact remained that salaries were nearly 10 percent lower and teaching loads heavier in the colored than in the white schools. At an annual salary of $750 a colored high school teacher earned $74.54 less than his, or more often her, white counterpart, and the differential for grammar and primary grade teachers was as great or greater. In 1890 white classes averaged forty-one children to a teacher, the colored forty-seven. Otherwise the two systems ran generally parallel. In 1892 a well-equipped, roomy colored high school rose on M Street. Despite Negro complaints about favoritism in teaching appointments on the part of Superintendent George F. Cook, some of the Negro schools made a good showing. Insofar as the limited resources at his disposal permitted, he introduced the innovations in teaching methods begun by Superintendent William Bramwell Powell in the white schools in the late 1880's. Like Powell, Cook sought to encourage pupils to reason rather than depend solely upon memory; he added classes in nature study and manual training to the curriculum and arranged field trips for pupils and teachers to the Library of Congress, the Smithsonian Institution, the zoo, and other places where children could learn by observation. Thanks to the insistence of a group of colored women, in 1896 the school board opened both Negro and white kindergartens.

Lower standards obtained in the colored grade schools than in white, but in examinations given all high school students in 1899, the colored high school scored higher than either the Eastern or the Western high schools. At the M Street High School a dedicated and stimulating faculty fostered students' intellectual ambitions. Twenty of the thirty regular teachers had degrees from top-flight Northern colleges and universities and five others had graduated from Howard, a far larger proportion of highly trained talent than the white high schools could claim. Still when Congress reorganized the entire sys-

---

[14] *Advocate*, 25 Feb 1882; *Star*, 14 Sep 1881, 22 Feb 1882; *Bee*, 30 Dec 1882, 10, 17, 24 Mar 1884; *Rpt School Trustees*, 1882, pp. 29, 33, 67; Booker T. Washington, *Up from Slavery*, p. 91; Ingle, *The Negro in D.C.*, pp. 34–37, 103; Cromwell, *History of the Bethel . . . Assoc*, pp. 5–7.

tem early in 1901, Negroes acquiesced in having a white superintendent put over the head of the colored school system. Fortunately, the new assistant superintendent, Winfield Scott Montgomery, a Phi Beta Kappa of the class of 1878 at Dartmouth and a gifted teacher, spent no time in protecting his own dignity. Under his enlightened direction the colored schools during the next decade would achieve an excellence well beyond that of Negro schools in other cities.[15]

Unhappily, in the late nineteenth century relatively few Negro children stayed in school beyond the fourth grade, and of those who finished the eighth grade, still fewer, especially of the boys, went on. "There are inducements to keep white children in the white High School," remarked the *Bee*. "Our colored citizens should see to it that some effort be made to keep their boys in the schools." Quite apart from their poverty, the seeming futility of acquiring more than an acquaintance with the three R's deterred many Negro families from making the effort. They saw well-educated girls, barred from suitable occupations by an inflexible caste system, drift into the life of the *demi-monde* and Negro college graduates forced for want of something better to take jobs as waiters and hotel bell boys. It is not surprising that 325 of the 367 undergraduates at Howard University in 1898 were enrolled in its secondary school; as none of the 42 taking the college course were white, the original ideal of a biracial institution vanished.[16] And the university had only partly recovered from the financial reverses of the mid-1870's.

Long before the Negro intelligentsia saw that public schooling in itself was unlikely to elevate greatly the general level of Negro society, Washington's colored aristocrats had begun to detach themselves from the Negro rank and file; for their own reassurance they felt they had to sharpen class distinctions. Educated colored men in other cities also defended the thesis that the social equality of all Negroes was a concept destructive to racial progress. In 1880 a letter to the *Advocate* declared that Frederick Douglass, John F. Cook, and others to whom the community had once looked for leadership "have shown conclusively how little they care whether other colored men sink, as long

15 Lofton, "Separate but Equal," pp. 164–87; *Bee*, 11 Feb 1888, 20 Aug 1897; *Rpts School Trustees*, 1890, 1892, pp. 153–202, 1899, pp. 273–97; Hilyer, *Directory*, pp. 161–63.

16 *Rpts School Trustees*, 1880, p. 152, 1886, p. 13, 1892, p. 17; *Report of the Board of Education of the District of Columbia*, 1901, pp. 140–43 (hereafter cited as *Rpt B/Ed*); *Bee*, 14 May 1887; W. E. B. DuBois, ed., *The College-Bred Negro* (Fifth Atlanta Conference, 1900), p. 16.

as they swim." Calvin Chase of the *Bee*, not himself one of Washington's "first families" but occupying a place in the upper stratum of the rank just below, alternately defended the "exclusive set" and attacked it for a snobbery that he believed originated in the determination of the Lotus Club after 1863 to force contrabands to keep to themselves. Later societies heightened that snobbery. "The Monday Night Literary is a caste organization," wrote Chase. "There is more intelligence excluded than there is in the association . . ; there are few holding clerkships who belong." Members had ceased to give New Year's Day receptions because they did not want to meet "objectionable upstarts."

The Negro press repeatedly insisted: "There is more discrimination among the colored people than there is among the white against the colored." A petition complained to Congress in 1896 that only daughters of "the favored few" were admitted to the colored normal school. "The would-be leaders, . . . John M. Langston excepted, have taken no interest in the general welfare of the masses of our people; political office by all means, after that, their wish is total exclusion from their race and to be white." Yet many of that small group composing the highest circle of Negro society were indeed nearly white, and a number of them had personal distinction as scholars, office-holders, and professional men. They were certainly culturally closer to the white community than to the lower-class Negro. In displaying an ungenerous attitude toward their inferiors, they were behaving like most self-made white men who reached positions of eminence in the face of enormous obstacles.[17]

The *Sentinel*, Washington's German-American newspaper edited by a former abolitionist, presented the tolerant white man's view of the Negro's position in 1883:

> The colored people of Washington enjoy all the social and political rights that law can give them, without protest and without annoyance. The public conveyances are open to them, and the theatres, the jury box, the spoils of party power are theirs. Many of these men are wealthy. . . .
>
> But the color line is rigidly drawn in what is known as society.

[17] *Advocate,* 4 Dec 1880; *Star,* 11 May 1880; *Bee,* 10 May 1884, 18 Sep 1886, 18 Sep 1887; ptn, H54A-H7.6, 2 Jun 1896; see illustrations accompanying the articles on Washington Negroes in Simmons, *Men of Mark;* Richard Bardolph, "The Distinguished Negro in America, 1770–1936," *American Historical Review,* LX, 527–47.

Wealth, learning, official place, give no colored family the right or privilege of entering the best or the commonest white society on terms of equality or endurance. In this respect the colored race lives as separate and exclusive a life as in the days of slavery, and as a drop of African blood was once held to make a man a negro, so now it taints him and makes an immutable barrier against social recognition.

Blanche K. Bruce lives in a handsome house that he [Mr. Bruce] owns on M. Street. It is richly furnished. . . . Mrs. Bruce is a handsome woman, with not a suggestion of her race in her face, and whose manners are regarded as the consummation of ease, grace and courtesy. She dresses as richly and handsomely as any woman in the city. In official circles Mr.Bruce is received in courtesy and as a political equal, but there the line is drawn.

Envious Negroes, averred the *Sentinel*, considered this exclusive set not good enough for whites and too good for its own race, but the next lower rank of Negro society was equally cut off from the class below. Government clerks formed the basis of the second stratum. "They are well dressed, seem to prosper and are happy. For the great bulk of the colored population—the servants, laborers and the poor— they have sympathy, but have no more social relations than a white family would." Those at the base of the social pyramid "in the main are thriftless, living from hand to mouth; happy if they do nothing, happy if they get a job. Their social instincts are gratified by the organization and maintenance of societies of all sorts, benevolent, patriotic, social and economic. There are nearly one thousand of these organizations, supported almost entirely by the laboring colored people." [18]

That portrayal, if in any degree fitting the Washington of 1883, was too simple and too cheerful in tone to describe the Negro community a decade or more later. Before the end of the century the class structure resembled a pyramid less than a truncated cone capped by a needle. From the strata below, the Negroes who danced on the point of the needle appeared to be not angels, but scarcely more accessible than heavenly creatures. Of the District's 700 octoroons and 1,100 quadroons, those who had, in addition to light color, the qualifications of antiquity of family, money, education, and honorable occupation belonged to the aristocracy; "honorable occupations" included the professions, political posts of more than trivial importance, banking, real

[18] *Sentinel,* 22 Dec 1883.

estate brokerage, and businesses not tinged with menial service. Washington's Negro "Four Hundred," as the *Bee* dubbed the aristocrats, probably numbered not more than ninety to a hundred families.

The middle class in the 1890's apparently derived mainly from the District's 18,000 mulattoes. Only less fully than the Four Hundred with their very light skins and generally non-Negroid features were the mulattoes conscious of gradations of color: those of "doe-nut or ginger-cake color . . . said those blacker than themselves should be ignored." The relative flexibility of the middle class permitted the occasional acceptance of exceptionally able, ambitious, full-blooded Negroes. But even a well-qualified government clerk, if a newcomer to the city, could not hope for immediate entree to upper-middle-class circles. Whether the barber, the caterer, the livery-stable man, the oyster-house owner, or the proprietor of any other small business was acknowledged as upper or lower middle class evidently depended upon the extent of his business success as well as his nativity and his complexion. Warnings frequently appeared in the *Bee* about unsuitable marriages between scions of established families and those of doubtful antecedents who wormed their way into the "social circle" by joining a "tony" church, by enrolling for a few weeks in one of Howard University's professional schools, or by making a specious show of great wealth. Differentiations among the "masses," that is, chiefly the city's thousands of full-blooded Negroes, were not a topic the press bothered to explore.[19]

Nor did any observer analyze the family structure of colored Washington. The infrequent mention of colored women except in the *Bee*'s society columns suggests that the matriarchy common among Negroes in the Southern states had slight hold in the District. Apparently during the Reconstruction era colored men able to support their families had been the acknowledged heads of their own households and, as voters and sometimes officeholders, had commanded a status as clearly denied their wives and mothers and daughters as in the white family of the Victorian era. When hard times and racial prejudice left Negro workingmen unemployed, their women could usually still find work as domestic servants, and, as the family breadwinners, might then assume matriarchal authority, just as they were obliged to do when husbands or fathers deserted them. But not until social workers began

[19] *Bee*, 30 May 1885, 8 Jun 1889; W. E. B. DuBois, ed., *The Negro in Business* (Fourth Atlanta Conference, 1899), pp. 13, 19–20; *Eleventh U.S. Census, 1890, Population,* 1, 397.

to report upon what they found when they walked into colored homes in the late 1890's did the role of the colored woman as the backbone of the indigent colored family evoke comment.

From 1884 to 1898 Washington's Negro press was the *Bee*. It prided itself on its sting aimed at the shoddy and evil. Yet back-biting and destructive jealousy of one class and of one Negro toward another was a striking feature of the paper's reporting. Let anyone get his head ever so little above his associates, and his individual accomplishments and former services were forgotten in vitriolic attacks upon his real or imagined self-seeking. Instead of applauding a colored man who won recognition, especially from whites, his fellows at once set to work to belittle him and accuse him of sycophancy and putting on airs. The *New National Era* had eschewed that line, and the *People's Advocate*, which ceased publication in 1884, pursued it very little. The *Bee*, without wholly abandoning a crusading point of view, indulged in more sweeping condemnations of individual Negroes and organizations the longer it ran. Its publisher obviously thought scandal and malicious gossip sold better than other news. A comment on a problem affecting Washington as a whole was a rarity.

Booker T. Washington, after some months at the Baptist Wayland Seminary in 1878–1879, decided that Washington was no place for a Negro who wished to dedicate his life to helping his race; here false standards and selfishness predominated. Among immigrant minorities and among the Jews in the District, mutual helpfulness was the rule. Not so among Negroes. The pressures of caste which kept the gifted colored man from going as far as his talents would otherwise permit split colored Washington into jealously competing fragments, with results damaging to every Negro. Congress, noted a Philadelphia journal, was naturally disinclined to do anything for Washington's colored people because their squabbling made them ridiculous: rivals claimed "that this one's father was a horse thief, that one doesn't know who his father was, another is too black, another is too light and therefore does not represent the race, another does not belong to the best families and still another is an interloper." Bitterly the *Bee* asked in 1887: "Who of our so-called colored representative men can point to a single thing of a public character beneficial to the colored people established and fostered by them? To their shame and to the humiliation of the race the record is a blank, and with all our boast about our wealthy . . . men the race is dependent upon the charity of whites." Yet if "you talk to our people about an excursion down the river in August, or a cake walk in December, they will listen to you and will no doubt purchase several tickets." And a large part of the funds of the mutual benefit societies, in which much of the social life of working-class Negroes centered, went for elaborate funerals rather than help for the living.[20]

The assertion that well-to-do Negroes never lifted finger for the needy was, of course, an exaggeration. John F. Cook, for years an active member of a citizens' relief committee, was also a trustee of the Home for Destitute Colored Women and Children, while a dozen public-spirited Negro women served on the board of manageresses. Caroline Taylor, who founded the Home for Friendless Girls in 1886, also organized an Aid Society at the Berean Baptist Church. About the same time, two or three Negro women opened a free kindergarten and day nursery for the children of working mothers, and in the 1890's the newly organized Colored Women's League expanded the program. Although Alexander Crummell, rector of St. Luke's, was more concerned with developing character in his people than with their material progress, he raised a considerable sum of money for the Episcopal Freedmen's Aid Society by sale of copies of one of his sermons. In 1887 the Colored Baptist Home Mission Society was "putting shoes on the feet of the poor, clothing on them, and giving immediate aid," but $95.72 represented the total sum collected in the course of several months from Washington's thirty-five colored Baptist churches and the members of the society.

In 1893 a severe depression again swept over the United States. As was true in the mid-1870's, Washington's colored people were hit harder than white. Negro volunteers worked with the Associated Charities, and the "Hill Group" on 6th Street, moved by the suffering of the poor at the foot of the hill, distributed food and fuel in that neighborhood. A good many relatively well-to-do individuals gave help without working through any organization, just as desperately poor Negro families often took care of the children of even poorer neighbors. From a mother-child center, opened in 1895, came the Southwest Social Settlement, and that year Miss Amanda Bowen, assisted by funds from the Metropolitan African Methodist Episcopal Church, launched the Sojourner Truth Home for Working Girls. Three years

[20] Jesse Lawson to Booker T. Washington, 6 May 1902, Booker T. Washington Mss; Washington, *Up from Slavery*, pp. 88–90; *Cong Globe*, 41C, 2S, p. 842; Ingle, *The Negro in D.C.*, p. 109; Philadelphia *Odd Fellows Journal* quoted in *Bee*, 23 Feb 1901; *Bee*, 15 Jan 1887, 12 Nov 1898.

later the Colored Women's League undertook "rescue work" among young women. A study prepared for a conference on Negro problems held in Atlanta in 1898 listed thirty-eight Negro churches in Washington which spent $4,300 for charity, contributed to the support of eighty-three benevolent and missionary societies, and supplied twelve workers in the slums and the jail. The individual generosity of Professor William Hart of Howard University made possible the Hart Farm School for colored boys. And in 1900 a colored woman started the Stoddard Baptist Home for aged Negroes.

Yet the overall record of Negro charities, while not "blank," was distinctly thin. The impressively long list of welfare projects at the end of the century was deceptive, for most of the undertakings were small-scale and short-lived unless white people came to the rescue. Unhappily, numberless whites were extraordinarily myopic; prone to think charity must go only to the "worthy" lest it nurture pauperism, they were chary of helping struggling Negro organizations. The white women whom Mrs. Grover Cleveland interested in the Home for Friendless Colored Girls raised only $150 for it in two years of soliciting. The uncooperativeness of many well-to-do Negroes annoyed ordinarily open-handed whites. "We all know," a white woman told a congressional committee, "that a good deal of what was good in the race has gone and they are now in a state of transition." What exasperated whites failed to take into account was that the social pressures that fostered philanthropy in the white community could not operate effectively among people who felt their precarious position in the city's overall social structure progressively and inescapably weakening. And white people probably attributed larger resources to prosperous Negroes than they actually possessed.[21]

Negro pastors and Negro churches which in earlier years had not

---

[21] Katherine Hosmer, "What Women Have Done in Washington City Affairs," *Municipal Affairs*, II, 514; W. E. B. DuBois, ed., *Some Efforts of Negroes for Their Own Social Betterment* (Third Atlanta Conference, 1898), pp. 14, 36–37, 57–59; *Bee*, 14 May 1887; Cleveland *Leader*, 29 Feb 1884; *Advocate*, 5 Feb, 20 Nov 1881; *Anl Rpt of the Home for Destitute Colored Women and Children*, 1891; Inabel Lindsay, "Participation of Negroes in the Establishment of Welfare Services, 1865–1900, with special reference to the District of Columbia, Maryland and Virginia," pp. 124–59, 164, 170–73 (dissertation, Univ of Pittsburgh, 1958); S Doc 185, 55C, 1S, Joint Select Committee to Investigate the Charities and Reformatory Institutions in the District of Columbia, Pt. 1, pp. 56, 100–01, 155, 197, 310–17, 396–402, 554, Ser 3565. For a fuller account of white neglect of Negro needs, see Green, *Washington, Capital City, 1879–1950*, pp. 67–74.

only provided spiritual leadership but taken an active part in lightening parishioners' material distress apparently lost sight of both goals as congregations vied with each other in building big, costly edifices. Between the worldliness of the sophisticated churches and the excessive otherworldliness of those wedded to a somewhat primitive, highly emotional religion teaching that only heaven or hell in the hereafter mattered, the efforts of the handful of selfless civic-minded Negroes met with defeat. Proposals to turn over to the National Colored Home the proceeds of Emancipation Day celebrations fizzled because the money from ticket sales went into the pockets of "sharks" or for the rental and elaborate decoration of floats for the parades. Lack of funds threatened to close the Sojourner Truth Home three years after it opened. A small indebtedness, which modest gifts could have wiped out, shut down the colored YMCA. According to one critic of his people, when Negroes contributed to any good works their motive was notoriety, not Christian charity. Such behavior was characteristic of the *nouveaux riches* the world over, but the small public-spirited minority in colored Washington sadly admitted that the generosity that had once distinguished the community was rarely in evidence at the end of the century.[22]

Negroes with means could scarcely plead ignorance of the want existing about them, for destitution was nearly as widespread as in post-Civil-War years. In the early nineties, amid the enormous prosperity of much of the city, 16,000 persons, the great majority of them colored, were without visible means of support; in 1870 the number had been little greater. Until 1897 the police were responsible for reporting cases of illness and desperate want and for distributing relief; Negro distrust of the police was an obstacle, but the health department defended the system on the grounds that it hastened investigations of complaints and lessened demands upon doctors to care for malingerers. The police found Negro families eking out existence by picking spoiled food from garbage cans and dumps. Households in the Negro slums were ridden with illness; a report of 1891 described a one-room shanty in which beside a dead infant lay five adults and six children stricken with influenza. Four-fifths of the patients at Freedmen's Hospital were indigents; of the 17,048 persons to whom the District's seven public dispensaries ministered in 1891, over 12,000

[22] Lindsay, "Negro Welfare Services," pp. 105–18; *Advocate*, 5 Apr 1884; *Bee*, 1887–1901; Ingle, *The Negro in D.C.*, pp. 95–100, 107; Carter G. Woodson, *The History of the Negro Church*, pp. 224–30; Hilyer, *Directory*, pp. 30, 136–48.

were colored. The most conscientious physician could do little more than palliate momentarily the miseries he encountered daily.

In twenty years the colored death rate dropped to 28.12 per thousand from the 40.78 of 1876, but Negro mortality always greatly exceeded and in most years was double that of whites. Infant mortality, high for whites, was 338.5 per thousand for Negroes in 1890 and in 1900 was still 317. The occasional charge that Negro "ignorance and indifference" was to blame was a part-truth. A larger cause, the health officer argued, was the foulness of the alley tenements in which thousands of Negroes lived.[23]

Neither poverty nor illness, however, prevented Negroes from enjoying themselves at times. The gift of laughter, that capacity to create and delight in moments of gaiety in the midst of suffering and want, is a Negro characteristic that down to the present day confuses and baffles white people. As W. E. B. DuBois sardonically put it, "that we do submit to life as it is and yet laugh and dance and dream is but another proof that we are idiots." With a light-heartedness that sobersided white Washingtonians called irresponsible, colored families not always able to feed themselves joined in church sociables and in club and fraternal society celebrations. The lower down the economic ladder, the more pleasure members of a society took in giving it a high-sounding name, such as "Grand Ancient Order of the Sons and Daughters and Brothers and Sisters of Moses of the USA and the World at Large." A funeral, always an occasion, usually called for lavish spending on carriages and clothes. Noisy picnics complete with bands to furnish music took place on Sundays, in the 1880's frequently at the "Manor," once the house and grounds of a wealthy mayor of the city, where the National Red Cross Headquarters now stand; when a proprietor of the beer hall there closed the place in 1887, colored picnickers were allowed to use the Schuetzenverein park. Mutual benefit societies arranged excursions down the Potomac until the steamboat lines, adopting the pretext that every boat was already chartered, refused to sell Negroes tickets.

For lower-class Negroes the great event of the year was the annual District Emancipation Day parade on April 16. Every colored organization in the District usually took part. Despite a downpour of rain, in

[23] *Star,* 15 Mar 1882; Comrs Rpts, 1887, pp. 16–17, 1889, p. 14, 1890, pp. 639, 756–57, 845–47, 1895, pp. 9–13; H Ex Doc 1, 51C, 1S, p. 94; *Chronicle,* 11 Sept 1899; *Eleventh U.S. Census,* 1890, *Population,* 1, Pt. 11, 20; *Twelfth Census,* 1900, *Population,* Pt. II, 22; W. E. B. DuBois, ed., *Mortality Among Negroes in Cities* (First Atlanta Conference, 1896), pp. 8, 18–19, 20–28.

1883 the procession was a mile and a half long; among the scores of societies parading in dress array were the Chaldeans, the Knights of Moses, the Osceolas, the Galilean Fishermen, the Sons and Daughters of Samaris, the Solid Yantics, the Lively Eights, and the Celestial Golden Links. White onlookers, watching the elaborately decorated floats and the thousands of Negroes marching on foot to the accompaniment of twelve brass bands, were impressed, amused, or indignant at the money poured into the display. Sophisticated Negroes sensitive to white ridicule protested now and again that a church service would mark the day more fittingly. "The thought is already gaining ground," wrote Frederick Douglass in 1886, "that tinsel show, gaudy display and straggling processions, which empty the alleys and dark places of our city into the broad day-light of our thronged streets and avenues, thus thrusting upon the public view a vastly undue proportion of the most unfortunate, unimproved, and unprogressive class of the colored people, and thereby inviting public disgust and contempt, and repelling the more thrifty and self-respecting among us, is a positive hurt to the whole colored population of this city. These annual celebrations of ours . . . should bring into notice the very best elements of our colored population." But until the school board voted in 1899 not to dismiss the colored schools for the day, the parade on April 16 was more important to most of colored Washington than the Fourth of July and Christmas and New Year's combined.[24]

Few middle-class Negroes were in a position to carp at the extravagances of their social inferiors, for display was an essential ingredient in most of their own pleasures. Below the thin top crust all Negro society was as intent upon keeping up with the Joneses as were ambitious, socially insecure whites. Booker T. Washington spoke with dismay of seeing "young colored men who were not earning more than four dollars a week spend two dollars or more for a buggy on Sunday to ride up and down Pennsylvania Avenue in, in order that they might try to convince the world that they were worth thousands." Plug-hatted "dudes" carrying canes swaggered about the streets to impress their fellows. Clothes were all-important. At a club party "young gentlemen and ladies in and just leaving their teens, assembled, dressed in full reception style, the young gents in full dress suit, the ladies in every ornamentation art or fancy could give. One lady of family remarked, 'they are all plebians, too!' " Plebeians as well as aristocrats still attended the theatre occasionally, but, as time went on, evening parties at home or concerts at the churches became a more customary form of entertainment. Athletics had not yet begun to loom large, although Negro bicycle clubs appeared in the eighties, and in the nineties colored cyclists held races at the Park Cycle Track. The Cadet Corps drills, begun in 1883, invariably attracted large crowds.

After the Lotus Club disappeared, for a year or two the Monday Night Literary Society embraced the most distinguished of the Negro intelligentsia, but the Bethel Literary and Historical Association soon overshadowed the older clubs by supplying the principal forum for enlightened discussion of race problems; the most notable Negroes in the country spoke before it. On three or four occasions learned white men, such as the meteorologist Cleveland Abbe of the Weather Bureau, lectured on scientific topics, but racial themes, including Negro history, were more compelling. As the sessions were open to every interested person, they gave unknown newcomers a chance to try their wings. There Kelly Miller, in the mid-1880's a student at Howard, emerged from obscurity by challenging some of the radical statements of the eminent Bishop Benjamin Tanner. Indeed the three factors which, despite manifold discouragements, made Washington a center of Negro civilization were government employment, Howard University, and the Bethel Literary and Historical Association. The creative and performing arts, on the other hand, played a minor part in community life, although proponents of an all-inclusive cultural nationalism sometimes talked of Negro artistic potentialities. The church choral societies earned modest fame, and the Treble Clef Club, founded in 1897, stimulated interest in classical music, but local talent focussed its attention chiefly on practical affairs.

The Negro newspapers gave a great deal of space to society weddings; the list of presents, often with the donors' names attached, might fill over a column. The gowns, "a Worth dress of canary silk" or a "crimson velvet entrainee," were described in the same detail with which white society reporters wrote of the costumes at White House receptions. Even after discounting the braggadocio of the Negro press, the evidences of Negro wealth and taste were unmistakable— beautiful jewelry, handsome clothes, well-furnished houses tended by Negro servants, and expensive summer holidays. Every June the exodus began with "Saratoga trunks" packed for Newport, Harpers Ferry, and Cape May. In 1886 the *Bee* reported: "Mr. Richard S. Locke of Washington who spends his summers at Nonquitt Beach [Massachusetts] has sold his beautiful yacht; Mr. Locke is the only gentleman of color that ever owned a yacht at Nonquitt." By and large, the higher a Negro's social standing, the more exactly his diversions corresponded to those of white people of similar position. Well-bred colored people in the mid-1880's sometimes joined the gatherings on the White House lawn on summer afternoons to hear the Marine Band play, but by the 1890's they avoided mingling with whites even on such informal social occasions.[25]

In 1900 Andrew Hilyer of the then eight-year-old business-promoting Union League compiled a "directory" to take stock "after a generation of freedom . . . [to] see just what is the actual status of the colored population of Washington, the Capital of the Nation, . . . where the conditions are the most favorable, to see what is their actual status as skilled workmen, in business, in the professions, and in their organizations; in short, to make a study, at first hand, of their efforts at social betterment." Frankly intended to overcome Negro hostility to Negro enterprise, the slim booklet assembled a wealth of specific information and offered a judicious appraisal of what fuller cooperation thenceforward could mean. But while seeking to encourage by pointing to past accomplishments, the analysis was too honest to hold out golden hopes.

Washington Negroes whose memory stretched back into the late 1860's had little cause for optimism. Since the days when they had shared in governing the city and the territory and the wall of caste had appeared to be crumbling, their bright prospects had darkened and then all but vanished in the shadows of a new and mounting racism. The *New National Era* had marked 1870 as the high point for the Negro community and saw the shrinkage of its horizons as beginning with the creation of the territorial government.[26] Witnessing the inexorable narrowing of their world after 1874, the wisest colored people doubtless knew that the splintering into mutually jealous groups had further reduced the elbow room for all contestants and had multiplied the difficulties of combatting white prejudice. Washington's reviving racism was the harder to fight because the white community,

[25] Cleveland *Leader,* 7 Apr 1884; Washington, *Up from Slavery,* pp. 88–89; *Advocate,* 1880–1884; *Bee,* Apr 1883 and 1884–1901; Francis Cardozo, Jr., to Booker T. Washington, 8 Aug 1902, Booker T. Washington Mss; Cromwell, *History of the Bethel . . . Assoc*; Mrs. E. T. Williston, "History of the Treble

increasingly oblivious to the existence of any other, recognized no opponent. The few white Washingtonians who acknowledged Negro citizens' potentialities were prone to dismiss the possibility of any injustice by declaring the capital "the colored man's paradise."

The very light-colored Negro with three-fourths or seven-eighths white blood might find an answer for himself by passing permanently into the ranks of whites. Miscegenation, not unlawful in the District of Columbia and far more common than most people realized, eased the process for the stranger, but for a member of any well-known local family passing was difficult. In any case, it left the larger problem unsolved: how Negroes were to live with dignity in a white world. Voluntary isolation might protect individuals from some humiliations but would scarcely ensure long-term progress for the race. Preoccupation with these questions stripped colored Washington of interest in the well-being of the city as a whole.

In 1901 for white Washingtonians the future stretched out in an ever-widening vista of prosperity and orderly living in a beautiful city whose national and world importance could only expand. The difference between that picture and what perceptive Negroes could envisage for their own people was heightened by the contrasts between their status then and that of a quarter century before. True, some families had made money in the interval, and others had achieved a modicum of financial security. Negroes who worked in government offices usually received civil, if impersonal, treatment from their white fellows. Moreover, a careful unobtrusiveness permitted well-dressed Negroes to hover in the background at the reception celebrating Washington's centennial. But sensitive men and women found that concession a poor substitute for friendliness. Fortunately they could not foresee that events in the next fifteen years would force colored aristocrats and middle-class Negroes into a psychological ghetto along with ambitionless blacks.

While the most easily observed factor in the progressive disintegration of Washington's Negro world was the failure of economic opportunity to keep pace with the growth of the colored population and with the spread of education, that material loss was itself rather a manifestation than a cause of the change. The wealthy Negro knew all too well that financial security provided no safeguard against endless

Clef" appended to program, *Treble Clef Club,* 16 May 1923 (Music Div., L.C.); *Post,* 3 Aug 1902.

[26] Hilyer, *Directory,* pp. 3–5 and *passim; New National Era,* 25 Jun 1874.

humiliations and frustration. The deterioration of Negro status sprang from a complex of causes, but the common denominator was the steady paring down of incentive. With the dwindling of the attainable external rewards for continuing the struggle, only the strongest individual able to draw upon deep inner resources could withstand the ceaseless battering of his self-respect.

11

The Intellectual Versus the City:
The Outlines of a Tradition

by MORTON and LUCIA WHITE

. . . American intellectuals . . . created no solid tradition of love for the American city.

Parallel with the growth of American cities and the urbanization of the country has been a continuing intellectual antipathy to the city. Many of America's most highly regarded thinkers and poets have been antiurban. Jefferson, Emerson, Thoreau, Whitman, Henry James, Henry Adams, Theodore Dreiser, and even the urban architect Frank Lloyd Wright have been hostile to the city. The consequence of this has been that the American cities have had to depend for the most part on Chambers of Commerce, boosters, civic groups, and literary sentimentalists for their defense. This prevalence of antiurbanism among the intellectual elite of the country may well have contributed to the flight to the suburbs of the educated middle classes. It is not without significance that Shaker Heights outside Cleveland, Mariemont, outside Cincinnati, and now Reston and Columbia outside Washington, D.C. (all planned suburbs carved out of pastureland), are built around ponds somewhat reminiscent of Thoreau's beloved Walden. Certainly, if one accepts the Actonian view that ideas "are not the effect, but the cause of public events," the continuing American intellectual hostility to the cities has been of great importance in their evolution and present predicament. Clearly this peculiar aspect of American urbanization requires profound consideration.

The following essay, which was published as the last chapter, "The Outlines of a Tradition," by Morton and Lucia White in their book *The Intellectual Versus the City,* is one of the few works that has examined the city from the point of view of the American philosophic tradition. It was copyright © in 1962 by the President and Fellows of Harvard

College and the Massachusetts Institute of Technology and is reprinted here by permission of the publishers.

Morton White is a professor of philosophy at Harvard. Born in New York in 1917, he was educated at the College of the City of New York and at Columbia. He has been a Guggenheim Fellow, a member of the Institute for Advanced Study at Princeton, and a Fellow of the Center for Advanced Study in the Behavioral Sciences at Stanford. In 1949 he published *Social Thought in America ;* in 1950, *Religion, Politics and the Higher Learning ;* and in 1956, *Toward Reunion in Philosophy.* Lucia White did her graduate work at Columbia and has worked as a medical and psychiatric social worker.

. . . it will now be useful to recapitulate the history of more than a century and a half of reflection on American city life and to highlight certain stages in the development.

The story opens with a relatively irenic age so far as the literature on the city is concerned. It is a period in which the American city, being very small and as yet nothing like a dominant force in our national life, aroused little hostility and little ideological debate between leading writers. To demonstrate this, one need only recall the views of Franklin the city-builder, of Crèvecoeur the celebrant of rural life, and of Jefferson the most articulate of American eighteenth-century writers on the problems of urbanization. Franklin, the bustling, busy urbanite, felt no inconsistency about being an agrarian pamphleteer; Crèvecoeur, the sentimental agrarian, was able to admire the American cities he knew; and the polemical Jefferson himself came at the end of his life to think that America might well have cities, in spite of his earlier attack on them in the *Notes on Virginia.* He despised the manners and principles of the urban mob as he knew it in Europe, and he hoped to keep that mob from crossing the Atlantic intact. He viewed the city as a cancer on the body politic, but he was conciliatory about the claims of the city in his later years. Not out of any love for it, but out of concern for the national interest. The country and its yeomen Jefferson loved all his life. In his old age he felt himself forced to accept the manufacturing city as a necessity after the War of 1812. This shift was made easier because Jefferson was not imprisoned by any elaborate philosophical framework that prevented him from recognizing the economic and political values of the city as an instrument of national defense and welfare: no metaphysical preconceptions forced him to view the city in a hostile manner. On the contrary, his later acceptance of the city's claims allowed him to adopt an attitude toward it which was more typical of the Enlightenment whose child he was.

However, the very War of 1812 that led Jefferson to reassess his views was followed by an enormous expansion of the American city, inaugurating a major phase of urban civilization between the Revolution and the Civil War. By 1860, the urban population was eleven times what it had been in 1820. This age of urban expansion, as William Dean Howells later observed, was not that of the statesman or the politician in the history of popular ideals, but rather that of the literary man. And the literary man had fallen under the spell of romanticism, which in America, as in Europe, entailed a variety of anti-urbanism that was not merely a human response to the horrors of the Industrial Revolution, but a theorem in a philosophical system which deprecated artificiality and science, feared technology as the enemy of sensibility, and regarded the American city as a threat to basic values. Emerson was the high priest of this movement. In his first philosophical work, *Nature,* he assailed the city at the very mid-point of the interval in which the urban population had increased eleven times. He shared Jefferson's dismay about aspects of city life which had become even more troubling in the second quarter of the nineteenth century. Communing across the Atlantic with writers who had already confronted a more fully developed city, he derived from them a metaphysics which permitted him to view the city as artificial and curtailed, unnatural, inferior to the wilderness, and destructive of poetry, philosophy, and solitude.

We know, of course, that Emerson, who was wary of consistency, also extolled the application of science and the virtues of civilization, the need for sociability and the advantages of specialization in spite of his distrust of science, his passion for the wilderness, and his desire to live the life of the whole man. But the preponderant impression he gives is that of one who feared the city, harped on the failings of State Street's commercialism, shuddered when he approached New York, regarded the city as a haven of liars and as a place of debased moral standards. His friend Thoreau and other associates in the transcendentalist movement went even further in their distaste for the city, for they were more opposed than Emerson to civilization as such. Thoreau's *Walden* is a prose poem in praise of the isolated individual, living in nature and free of *all* social attachments. The intellectual conversation and genial clubbiness that Emerson admired so much could not lure Thoreau into Boston. He was, as Henry James said, essentially a sylvan personage.

No matter how much they feared the effects of urbanization, romancers who followed Jefferson in our story had seen only the American beginnings of a troubling development. But like Jefferson they saw disturbing omens in the streets of Liverpool, London, Paris, and Rome of what might come to America. And being romancers, they characteristically resorted to the dream as a vehicle for expressing their feelings. Unlike Schiller, that avatar of romanticism in his "Greetings to the New Century," they did not flee from the realities of urban life to *happy* urban dreams. Their dreams of the city were rather nightmares in which they confronted ghostly cities, cities of crime, sin, poverty, and degradation. When they luridly portrayed foreign cities, they expressed their anxieties about what the American city might become. These pictures carried the American romancers' greetings to the new century that would begin in America with the Civil War. In these pictures they sketched the urban scenes they forsaw with a dread such as the prescient de Tocqueville, with a fuller knowledge of European cities, had voiced in 1835. While Hawthorne advocated the more dramatic course of purifying cities by burning them to the ground periodically, de Tocqueville urged the creation of a national armed force that would be able to repress the excesses of the urban rabble. So, pre-Civil War optimists and pessimists, deists and transcendentalists, empiricists and idealists, all composed their ideological differences while joining in an intellectual crusade against the American city. Even before the really great burst of post-Civil War urbanization began, the nation had been treated to a morbid critique of the city by its literary men, its philosophers, and its most penetrating visitor.

When Howells came to the Civil War in his illuminating tale of American images of greatness, he noted a brief period in which the military man took the national stage before being rudely replaced by the urban millionaires. At the time, the literary man was also forced to take a back seat, but from this position he was still able to witness an urban spurt whose magnitude exceeded anything his predecessors had seen or complained about. Between 1860 and 1900, the urban population quadrupled as the rural population merely doubled: between 1790 and 1890, the urban population increased one hundred and thirty-nine times while the total population had grown only sixteen times. The countryside was being drained of people; New England farms were being deserted; and the elevated railroad, trolley cars, cable cars, subways, telephones, and skyscrapers began to move into the city, bringing in their jarring wake what was then nervously called "American nervousness." New York had become the metropolis, and from that point on, when a writer referred indefinitely to the American city, he invariably referred to Manhattan. Some of the first writers to react sharply to this new world were, as Daniel Aaron has pointed out, men who looked at civilization with agrarian eyes—Walt Whitman and Mark Twain.[1] The same Whitman who was enchanted by Broadway in 1868, and who wrote "Crossing Brooklyn Ferry," looked through his "moral microscope" in 1871 and saw "cities, crowded with petty grotesques, malformations, phantoms, playing meaningless antics." [2]

But for purposes of this story, even more interesting responses to the new city may be found in the writings of Henry Adams and Henry James, who reacted less with pre-war agrarian feeling than with a respect for the values of urban civilization itself. Adams and James were members of cultivated families, one with Boston and the other with Albany wealth in his background, and for both of them the new American city created profound spiritual problems. Because they lived in the period of the American city's undisputed supremacy, they could no longer speak of it as a remote phenomenon of the future or as something in Europe alone. They were refined, civilized, indeed urban men, whose distress with the American city was more significant because they were not opposed to cities in principle. They, therefore, demonstrate what a hard time the American city suffered at the hands of nineteenth-century American intellectuals. For here at last were two *city* types, neither of them professional romanticists or agrarians, who found the American metropolis sadly wanting in different ways. Adams in old age succumbed to the virus of anti-Semitism in his discussion of the city's defects, and to nostalgia for the days of the Virgin in medieval France. James was dismayed by the lack of historic monuments, by the decline of civility, by the absence of organic social relations, by the absence of elevating conversation, and by the absence of the King's English. In New York, where he found all these things wanting, he longed for the whole national consciousness of the Swiss and the Scot, and he too looked at the past as a place

1 Aaron, *Men of Good Hope*, p. 172.
2 *Ibid.*, for quotation from Whitman.

of refuge from the chaos he saw. One must not forget, of course, that James' novel *The Princess Casamassima* represents a marvelous effort to penetrate the depths of London, and that his admiring essay on that city was an effort to express his love for it and its people. But the more one remembers James' concern with London, the more one realizes how very different his attitude toward the American city was. After his harsh handling of the Boston reformers in *The Bostonians,* the American city did not provide him with any serious material for a full-length novel because, as F. O. Matthiessen has pointed out, he found neither the uptown nor the downtown of New York sufficiently interesting. In *The Princess Casamassima* he saw the crushing, oppressive effects of the British metropolis, but he could never bring himself to feel much affectionate concern for those who lived in the American metropolis.

On the other hand, the literary realists and naturalists, Howells and Norris and Dreiser, who expressed a sympathetic interest in the inhabitants of the American city, could be as devastating as James in their estimate of the city itself. Dreiser came to Chicago and then to New York in a state of awe and wonder, with great expectations; but he ended his life thinking that New York was a handsome woman with a cruel mouth. Norris left New York City in disgust for California. And William Dean Howells shared the anti-urbanism of Henry George, Laurence Gronlund, Tolstoy and William Morris. In spite of Howells' democratic socialism, realism, and scientific attitude, even he finally called for the dismantling of the American city and its replacement by curiously blank capitals to which officials and artists would make periodic visits. The predominant form of social life in his utopia would be that of villages and hamlets in which neighborliness and close family ties would unite all in a spirit of love. The traveler from Altruria told his American friends, "I do not think you will find anything so remarkable in our civilization, if you will conceive of it as the outgrowth of the neighborly instinct. In fact, neighborliness is the essence of Altrurianism. If you will imagine having the same feeling toward all," he explained to Mrs. Makely, the New York socialite, " as you have toward your next door neighbor."

Howells' book of 1894 continued with an exchange which outlined about a half-century of thinking on city life by sociologists and social workers. In response to the Altrurian's praise of neighborliness, Mrs. Makely exclaimed: "My next door neighbor! . . . But I don't *know* the people next door! We live in a large apartment house, some forty families, and I assure you I do not know a soul among them." The Altrurian looked at her in puzzlement as Mrs. Makely went on to admit that "sometimes it *does* seem rather hard. One day the people on the same landing with us, lost one of their children, and I should never have been a whit the wiser, if my cook hadn't happened to mention it. The servants all know each other; they meet in the back elevator, and get acquainted. I don't encourage it. You can't tell what kind of families they belong to." The Altrurian persisted and asked, "But surely you have friends in the city whom you think of as your neighbors? " And Mrs. Makely persisted and said, "No, I can't say that I have . . . I have my visiting list, but I shouldn't think of any-body on *that* as a neighbor." At this point Howells reports that the Altrurian looked so blank and baffled that he, Howells, could hardly help laughing. The Altrurian then said that he would not know how to explain Altruria to Mrs. Makely. But Mrs. Makely had a ready urban answer: "Well . . . if it's anything like neighborliness, as I've seen it in small places, deliver me from it! I like being independent. That's why I like the city. You're let alone." And now a lonely coun-try lad breaks into the exchange to report: "I was down in New York, once, and I went through some of the streets and houses where the poor people live . . . and they seemed to know each other, and to be quite neighborly." At which point the irrepressible Mrs. Makely asks him whether he would like to live all messed up with other people in that way. And he replies, "Well, I thought it was better than living as we do in the country, so far apart that we never see each other, hardly. And it seems to be better than not having neigh-bors at all." [3]

Howells' Altruria, then, was somewhere between an isolated farm and an overcrowded tenement, neighborly and friendly, bent on com-bining the best of both worlds. But while Howells called for the removal of cities so that genuine neighborliness could be encouraged, a generation of reforming social workers, social scientists, and social philosophers all set themselves the task of accomplishing the same result within the city as it was known in the twentieth century. They did not adopt Howells' drastic methods of city destruction; they did not abandon the American city to its fate in the manner of Henry Adams, Henry James, and Theodore Dreiser. They wanted to be neighborly while they were let alone. Their patron saint was Henry James' brother, William, who was not driven by the sight of the

3 Howells, *A Traveler from Altruria*, pp. 123–124.

American city to Europe or to the past. William James' hope and optimism allowed him to view the urbanization of America in a way that might encourage Americans to do something about urban problems. He did not worship the great cities of Western Europe. The blackness and the age of everything in Florence disgusted him in 1875 and the yellow-brown, stale spaciousness that he saw in London in 1889 filled him with a desire never to see England's capital again. With Emerson he looked to an American future, but the future he saw, unlike Emerson's, was filled with people in American cities living decent lives. Even New York at the turn of the century could send William James into ecstasy while it made his brother shiver and caused his friend William Dean Howells to call for its destruction. Skyscrapers, noise, movement, the subway—all were viewed by William James with characteristic whoops of pleasure.

There was, however, a deeper strain in James' thinking which was even more important in forming the attitudes of a whole generation of younger thinkers, among them Dewey, Jane Addams and Robert Park; and that was James' hatred of bigness, his great need for communication, hs desire to go behind the faces of men, to overcome blindness about other people's thoughts and feelings. It was James' outgoing and yet penetrating spirit that heralded a pragmatic phase in urban thinking, in which educators, sociologists, and social workers joined forces in an effort to check the uncontrolled growth and impersonality of the American city. One dominant note in their typically progressive thinking was opposition to giantism, the desire to cut this vast force down to manageable size. And their conception of size was affected by a certain degree of nostalgia for the American village. They did not flee the metropolis for this village, but they wanted to decompose the city into spiritual units that would emulate village life. This is evident in Park's idealization of the primary group, in Jane Addams' hope that the settlement house would help fill the urban void, and in Dewey's plea for a revival of localism in his *Public and its Problems*. All of these figures in the Age of Reform stressed the importance of community and communication in re-creating a livable urban life, but they sought to inject into the city the kind of face-to-face community they knew in their own small villages and towns in the nineteenth century, before the radio, the automobile, the airplane and television made less neighborly forms of communication possible. Josiah Royce, on the other hand, looked to the province as a place in which the self-estrangement of the Hegelian spirit might be diminished.

The cause of communitarianism was not helped by the rushing development of technology. The forces for localism or provincialism were not favored by the march of Megalopolis from the centers of cities, through its suburbs, into the countryside and on to the outskirts of other cities, as it surrounded 31,000,000 people in a supercity along the eastern seaboard by 1960. No wonder Frank Lloyd Wright saw the primary group and face-to-face relations as a thing of the past. No wonder he spoke in strident tones about the search for village-scale community as a lost cause in the middle of the twentieth century. For him the American city had come to an end, brought there by the evolution of the forces that had once ushered it into existence. Technology, which had brought men together into cities would now disperse them, he warned—gradually by means of urban sprawl, instantly by bombs. Wright's Broadacre City was a return to the model of the self-sufficient homestead distributed uniformly over the vast, continental United States. With Wright this tale of more than a century and a half of intellectual anti-urbanism reached a climax.

In this narrative of anti-urban attitudes in America, a number of complaints and fears have persisted throughout the one hundred and seventy-five year period. Fears and doubts about the activities of the city mob, and about the unwieldy and corrupt political character of the city, continue from Jefferson through the early twentieth-century reformers and social critics. Also, distrust of commerce and disapproval of the accumulation of money, those evils continuously condemned by classical, biblical, and medieval writers onward, are still prominent and persistent in the minds of our nineteenth-century thinkers. Those who are burdened with this ancient distrust divide into the romantically inclined, who would most of the time imaginatively dispense with commerce and technology, and the more realistic reformers, who look for social control of both while being ready to recognize their benefits. As American intellectuals came in contact with the industrialization of the city, they issued a series of complaints about the bad city air, the dust, the noise, the dirt, the miserable crowding, the accumulated poverty and beggary, the monotony of the buildings—looking like senseless chunks—and the monotony of the industrial jobs. As industrialization increased and after attempts to grapple with its biological and social effects, we find the reformers questioning whether the modern city is not too complex and too big to deal with effectively.

There are some striking shifts from the early reflections on the city to the later ones. The view that the city is artificial in its very nature and essence is mostly abandoned. Meanwhile, Jefferson's early view is sustained and elaborated: that the city is a malignant social form; over and over again the figure of the city's being a cancer or a tumor is used. The other shift of concern is from the fear of earlier thinkers about city people being especially vulnerable to infections and communicable diseases, a fear which medical science has so rapidly been making obsolete.

Complaints about the modern American city which emerge after the Civil War are: that it is not civilized enough and is too provincial compared to cities in Europe; that the modern commercial and industrial city destroys valuable forms of social life and substitutes nothing as socially valuable in their place; that city life is *too* mobile, both physically and socially; that life in the city is also too spectatorial but that there is too little that is especially worth looking at, little that is sensuously pleasing or artistic. And finally, after the Civil War, there is a great deal more complaint about the difficulties the individual encounters in the modern city. Our writers suggest that being alone in this kind of city has terrors that the country, or the country town, as they knew it, did not possess. They mention over and over again that there is in the city too much impersonality, too little genuine communication, too many immigrants, too many complete strangers, and too little continuity of face-to-face relations for the sound and full development of character. Although the large majority of our thinkers after the Civil War chose to live in cities for long periods in their lives, and were stimulated and fascinated by the freedom and variety of social life there, by the unexpected opportunities, by the range of human adaptations and achievements, still they all expressed grave psychological reservations about modern city life; and many of them were as much repelled by the smell, the sight, and the sound of our commercial and industrial cities as by the way of life they represented.

Considering the tidal wave of forces that rapidly inundated American cities during about a century and a half, it is no wonder that they should not have taken on all the characteristics of stable social settlements. Instead they retained or developed many of the characteristics of the socially fluid frontier. The vast, unsettled continent of the United States was continuously inviting the population to disperse westward into rural areas, while at the same time the combined forces of capitalism, industrialization, rapidly increasing population, and immigration from the ends of the earth were producing urban concentration. After the Civil War, while people began pouring into the cities, the autonomy of cities was being more and more undermined, not only by the advance of nation-wide capitalism and industrialization, but also by the full development of the national state. Moreover, an increasingly strong undertow in the direction of suburban dispersion began in the early years of the twentieth century to drain the vitality of the central city, and to create ill-defined metropolitan areas. And finally, the rapid technological advances in building, transportation, and communication hastened the detachment of individuals from any one fixed, permanent locality or social group.

Confronted with these constantly shifting urban developments over the relatively short span of a century and a half, American intellectuals developed conflicting or antipathetic attitudes and created no solid tradition of love for the American city. Instead they celebrated life in the wilderness, on Virginia farms, in exurban Concord, in isolated Walden, in nineteenth-century London, in the English countryside, in conversational Washington, in American villages and suburbs, in primary groups, in Broadacre City. The celebration of the city was left to chambers of commerce, to boosters and to literary sentimentalists from Dr. Holmes to O. Henry. To the most gifted intellectuals— by literary and philosophical standards—New York was certainly not what London was to Dr. Johnson, what Paris was to a long line of French writers, what Athens was to Aristotle. If distinguished American intellectuals came to the American metropolis to live, they did not always stay to live the good life; and some of them sedulously avoided our urban centers.

Readers who may feel that this story is based on an excessively narrow selection of writers and thinkers should remember that they represent some of our most distinctive intellectual and literary movements: the empiricism of the Enlightenment, transcendentalism before the Civil War, realism and naturalism in literature, post-Civil War pragmatism, idealism and naturalism in philosophy, and functionalism in architecture. Readers who think that we have not aimed high enough in our choice of American intellects should remember that other readers will find in these pages the names of our greatest philosopher, our greatest political thinker, our greatest essayist, our greatest theorist of education, our greatest novelist, our greatest historian, our greatest autobiographer, our greatest social worker, and our greatest architect*—most of them worrying or throwing up their hands about one of the most distinctive features of our national life. And that is a fact worth recording and pondering.

---

* The authors are referring here to the entire book, not this one chapter—Ed.

12

The Church and the City

by ROBERT D. CROSS

It was clear from the start that the response [of religion to the city] would be remarkably multiform.

Parallel with the growth of American cities has been the development of urbanized religion. A knowledge of the true nature of the church in the American city—an understanding of what it is and what it is not, of what it has been and of what it has not been—is of great importance in understanding the American city. The church has always played a significant role in the life of the urban American, and it has also, from time to time, been a decisive factor in influencing the conduct of urban government. As the American has become more and more urbanized there has been continuing controversy about the proper role of the church. Although no definitive solution has evolved, the multiform character of the American urban church is in itself a testimony of the strength and vitality of the church as an urban institution.

Dr. Robert D. Cross, president of Swarthmore College, has written a succinct and informative summary of what happened between the close of the Civil War and the onset of World War I to the church in the American city. First published in 1967 as an introduction to an anthology titled *The Church and the City 1865–1910,* it is a highly useful and informative historical essay on the religious aspects of urban life.

Dr. Cross was born in Grinnell, Iowa, in 1924, and was educated at Harvard, where he also served as a teaching fellow from 1949 until he joined the faculty at Swarthmore in 1952. Later he taught at Columbia and served as chairman of the history department there from 1964 to 1967. During World War II, Dr. Cross was a pilot in the USAAF. He is also the author of *The Emergence of Liberal Catholicism.*

The following selections from the introduction to *The Church and the City 1865–1910,* edited by Robert D. Cross, copyright © 1967, by the

Bobbs-Merrill Company, Inc., are reprinted by permission of the publisher. A few short excisions have been made, and the footnotes have been renumbered accordingly.

I

In the fifty years between the close of the Civil War and the onset of World War I, American cities grew rapidly. Although early in the nineteenth century religious spokesmen like Lyman Beecher had been aware of the need to "evangelize" the growing city populations, most had been preoccupied with the challenges and opportunities presented by the "frontier." The emphasis shifted after the Civil War. A flood of books with titles like *The Challenge of the City, The Redemption of the City, If Christ Came to Chicago,* and *Christianity's Storm Centre: A Study of the Modern City* demonstrated how acute the problem had come to seem.[1] It was not, of course, in the bookstore that religion's response was most authoritatively rendered, but in the behavior of the churches—not only the churches which found the community in which they were established swelling into a metropolis, but also the new churches of one kind or another appearing in the cities. No more in this era than in any other in American history was all religious life lived within the churches; then as always there were sturdy individualists to whom religion was gravely important but to whom church membership seemed an irrelevance if not a spiritual handicap. But for the vast majority of religiously concerned Americans, the churches were the normal vehicle of religious life, making the conduct and welfare of these churches the best barometer of American religion's response to the city.

It was clear from the start that the response would be remarkably multiform. There were already in the 1840's many mansions in American religion; each variant form reflected a unique set of notions not only about church membership and organization and worship, but also about the church's proper role in "the world." [2] Furthermore, in

---

[1] Josiah Strong, *The Challenge of the City* (New York: Missionary Education Movement, 1907); Charles H. Sears, *The Redemption of the City* (Philadelphia: Griffith and Rowland Press, 1911); William T. Stead, *If Christ Came to Chicago* (Chicago: Laird and Lee, 1894); Charles Stelzle, *Christianity's Storm Centre: A Study of the Modern City* (New York: Fleming Revell, 1907).

[2] Two useful nineteenth-century surveys of the range of religious organization are Robert Baird, *Religion in the U. S. of A.* (Glasgow: Blackie, 1844) and Daniel Dorchester, *Christianity in the United States* (New York: Hunt

practice if not always in ecclesiastical theory, initiative in responding to new situations rested mostly in the hands of the local church. When such a varied and decentralized institution was confronted with the fact of city growth, dynamic both in its pace and in its apparent unpredictability, it is hardly surprising that church life in the cities was soon almost incredibly diverse in character. (So diverse, in fact, that for many years it was regarded as simple chaos, a judgment of God upon American religiosity.) About the turn of the century, churchmen like H. Paul Douglass began to survey the urban scene more matter-of-factly, and to discern patterns in the kind of religious responses they found.[3] In recent years, such churchmen have been joined by professional sociologists, and together they have evolved quite sophisticated typologies—never in the belief, however, that any typology could do full justice either to the whole range of response or to the uniqueness of the individual churches.[4] Still, these efforts at classification make it possible now to distinguish four general modes of churchly response.

Transformations include the changes that took place in long-established churches when the towns in which they stood rapidly expanded into cities. Suddenly they found themselves "downtown" churches with a conspicuous location, an equally conspicuous loss of neighborhood membership, and consequently a pressing need to redefine their mode of preaching to the community.

Transplantations characterize the attempts—always unsuccessful in the long run—to create, in the midst of a city, churches identical to warmly remembered ones in town or country. Immigrant groups usually created "ethnic churches," and migrants from the American countryside often founded "village churches" in a fond attempt to create at least one bulwark against urban demoralization.

Adaptations, by far the largest category of urban churches, resulted from single-minded attempts to cope with some specific challenge of the city. Viewed from the perspective of the traditional church in America or Europe, these adaptations seemed heretical for their emphasis or over emphasis on some belief or practice. (1) Neighborhood

and Eaton, 1888). The classic analysis of the correlation in America between sectarian difference and social attitude is H. Richard Niebuhr, *The Social Sources of Denominationalism* (Hamden, Conn.: Shoe String Press, 1954).

[3] Typical of Douglass' many works on urban religion is his *One Thousand City Churches* (New York: George H. Doran, 1926).

[4] A good summary and critique of seven of the most widely accepted typologies is Frederick A. Shippey, "The Variety of City Churches," *Review of Religious Research,* II (Summer, 1960), 8–19.

churches, on the way to becoming the "suburban church" of the mid-twentieth century, defined their ambit in terms of a neighborhood that was not the whole of a community, nor even a cross section of it, but a highly stratified segment. (2)   Some churches came to specialize as centers of revivalist exhortation. (3) Adventism, always stimulated by untoward developments in the surrounding culture, was given renewed expression by Charles Taze Russell and the group that came to be known as Jehovah's Witnesses. (4) A congeries of short-lived but intense Pentecostal churches matched the Witnesses' hostility to the culture in which they found themselves, but drew upon the opportunities the city offered for an autonomous religious life. (5) Christian Science exemplified the special anxiety of city-dwellers about health and well-being, and their receptivity to "new thought" which offered a gnostic solution to uncertainties about both this world and the next.

Reintegrations were typified by the "institutional church," which self-consciously sought to restore the old identification of the church with the whole community. Since the population of most cities was far too large for a single congregation to encompass, the institutional church resolved at least to draw its membership from a real cross section of the city, not simply some congenial social class or ethnic group. "Transplanted" or "adapted" churches might in time follow the path of "reintegration"; in the late nineteenth and early twentieth centuries, however, it was the churches "transformed" by urbanization into downtown churches which were most likely to make this transition.   But there was nothing inevitable about it, even for the "transformed."

II

The churches located near the center of a growing city faced a difficult choice. Almost inevitably, the bulk of the congregation of "Old First Church"—of "Center Church"—of "Trinity Church"—moved to less crowded, more fashionable neighborhoods; their former homes were made over into places of business, or were subdivided into boarding houses, or were replaced by barracks and tenements to accommodate a flood of new inhabitants. Many of the newcomers were immigrants from Europe, deterred by language and faith from joining the old church on the green. Others, fresh from the American countryside, were nearly as uprooted psychologically, and at least as unlikely to find the old church a purveyor of the kind of religious life they had been accustomed to. Some were the "derelicts" that find shelter in the heart of large cities. In the middle of the nineteenth century, the old churches in the southern reaches of Manhattan found themselves surrounded by Irish and German Catholics, by people from the provinces, by a large fraction of the Negro population, and by the city's professional criminals. In the area known as the Five Points, all of these lived in close proximity, physically near the old churches, but in spirit hopelessly remote. Some of the congregations, in despair, sold their buildings to commercial enterprises (or, occasionally, to immigrant religious groups) and built new churches "uptown" or in the suburbs. Those that resolved to stay where they had always been encountered the vicissitudes of the "downtown" church.

In most "downtown" churches the number of religious services declined; even so, attendance became increasingly sparse. By the end of the century, it had become conventional for city newspapers to note the meager congregations at Sunday morning services in the famous old churches. Budgets were met by income from property, from pew rents, and from the large donations of the few wealthy families that maintained a traditional loyalty; some contributions also came from parvenus seeking the prestige which conspicuous support of the older churches—Trinity, Brick Presbyterian, Temple Emanu-El—still brought. Great emphasis was placed on church architecture, on carefully elaborated ritual and liturgy; organized religion would thus demand respect from the passer-by, even if it did not bring in flocks of members. It became increasingly important to have a minister of high social standing; Episcopalians, Reformed Jews and others frequently imported them from Europe. Dignity, social grace, learning, and eloquence were required of him. It would be an especial accolade for the church if ceremony and sermon were so distinguished that prominent visitors to the city regarded a visit to the church as one of "the things to be done." Such visitors fit easily into Sunday congregations made up not of the families of the neighborhood but of a handful of individuals from various parts of the city.

Under such circumstances, it would have been miraculous if the minister proved a pastor to his neighborhood. Phillips Brooks, of Trinity Church, Boston, was admirably suited by the remarkable sweetness of his character to be such a pastor. But his influence extended little beyond the narrow circle of his upper-class Episcopalian congregation. Much the same might be said about Morgan Dix of Trinity Church, New York, and about Gustav Gottheil of Emanu-El.

Priests to their "own" people, they felt little incentive to explore the way religion affected, or failed to affect, the rest of the city.

Though the downtown church of the late nineteenth century touched the lives of a far smaller percentage of the population than had its ancestor on the village green, it preserved, simply by staying in the center of the city, a potential for future importance which the churches which moved uptown or to the suburbs decisively abdicated. Its location gave it the moral right, and its financial resources gave it the means, to experiment with new techniques of "churching" the urban population. An easy but in the long run unsuccessful mode was to support a flock of mission churches or chapels. Premised, tacitly, on the belief that different social classes "do not like to worship together," such colonialist enterprises sometimes developed into viable churches —especially if they were planted in the midst of a population group so bound together by a common foreign language, national consciousness, or color as to be able to resist the disintegrating forces in urban life. More often, the life of a mission church was short, and marred by feelings of dependence and hostility. . . .

The major alternative to creating separate chapels was to make unusual efforts to attract to the downtown churches themselves the large unchurched population. As early as 1856, the New York Sunday School Union had tried to allocate to each downtown church responsibility for a certain territory of the city; members of that church were to visit each person in the area at least weekly in order to bring him into active church life. Essentially similar plans were experimented with in other cities before the Civil War; and the Home Evangelization program, the Evangelical Alliance, and the Federation of Churches and Christian Workers in New York made brave efforts in the late nineteenth century. On the whole, they were no more successful than had been the chapels and mission churches.[5] Only very slowly some of the downtown churches came to realize that the transformation worked on society by the city was so intense that the character of the church had to be transformed if a genuine reintegration of church and culture was to be accomplished. The institutional church, about which more will be said later, emerged between 1890 and 1910 as the most ambitious attempt at this larger task.

[5] The failure of most earlier efforts is discussed in Walter Laidlaw, "A Cooperative Church Parish System," *American Journal of Sociology,* III (May, 1898), 795–808.

III

Just as some of the older residents tried to preserve what they remembered as the major characteristics of their churches, so many of the newcomers tried to transplant the rural or small-town church into their new environment. Especially in the first years of industrial cities like Holyoke, Massachusetts, in the mid-nineteenth century, or Gastonia, North Carolina, in the 1920's, a high percentage of the Protestant population was right off the farm, and right out of the rural churches.[6] For them, the old-time religion was the strongest surrogate of the continuity they wished to preserve with their former lives. In the churches they built and supported, they tried to keep much the same patterns of service. They wanted no doctrinal or theological concessions to the spirit of the times, or the ethos of city culture; "you have to carry a bucket of blood into the pulpit to satisfy these people," a Gastonia minister remarked.[7]

Baptists and Methodists predominated in the countryside, and so it was natural that the bulk of the transplanted churches were of these denominations. But a sizeable number of the emigrants to the cities brought with them such a compelling concern for "perfection" that many "holiness" churches were also founded. The origins of such churches lay in the revivalism of the early and middle nineteenth century. As Timothy Smith has shown, the ardent search for God's grace not only led many leaders of the old Calvinist faiths—like Charles G. Finney—to stress the possibility of perfectionism; it also gave renewed intensity to Methodist belief in sanctification through the benefits of the "second blessing."[8] The National Holiness Association represented a massive attempt to foster personal holiness. Most of its leaders were Methodists, and most hoped to intensify religious life within Methodist churches, rather than to create a new denomination. But like earlier awakening or reform movements in American Protestantism, the holiness group encountered opposition within the settled churches. Not all bishops, conferences, or ministers could approve of the emotionalism the holiness meetings engendered and found praise-

---

[6] The situation in Holyoke is referred to briefly in Constance M. Green, *Holyoke* (New Haven: Yale University Press, 1939). For Gastonia, see Liston Pope's excellent study, *Millhands and Preachers* (New Haven: Yale University Press, 1942).

[7] Pope, *Millhands and Preachers,* p. 88

[8] Timothy Smith, *Revivalism and Social Reform* (New York: Abingdon Press, 1957).

worthy. Churches, whether in the country or the city, sometimes bog-
gled at the willingness of the holiness advocates to experiment with
new measures of preaching revival, of seeking out converts, and of
caring for the needy. As a result, the late nineteenth century saw
the gradual, often reluctant, coalescence of new denominations, such
as the Church of the Nazarene and the Church of God.[9] Some migrants
to the city had made the transition before leaving the country; for
them, membership in a holiness congregation was completely natural,
an act that reaffirmed a previous commitment. Others left the countryside before breaking with an older denomination, but, faced in the
city with the need to affiliate with a different congregation in any
event, chose a holiness group as best fulfilling long-cherished preferences. For both, the holiness congregation was a kind of transplantation—a re-creation of the rural past.

A similar spirit characterized the attempts of immigrant groups to
preserve unmodified in American cities the religious life they had
known in European villages. Such people were doubly alienated from
the "downtown" churches they encountered. So, within a few months
of the arrival of the first sizable numbers of Jews from Eastern
Europe, New York was dotted with synagogues, each seeking to re-
create the special religious life of a *shtetl*, or small village. Those
Lutherans from Germany or Scandinavia who settled in the cities tried
to find, in churches effectively limited to members speaking the mother
tongue, something of the church life they remembered. Catholic immigrants, belonging to a Church which in theory organized local
churches by territorial rather than ethnic boundaries, were not always
so successful in finding churches limited to their own "kind." [10] But
by the end of the nineteenth century, many American dioceses had
provided "national" parishes which encompassed all those speaking
a similar foreign language. In those national parishes where the Church
could also provide a priest of the same nationality, parishioners were

[9] Timothy Smith, *Called Unto Holiness. The Story of the Nazarenes: The
Formative Years* (Kansas City: Nazarene Publishing House, 1962) is the best
study of a holiness group's development. Professor Smith regards the Nazarenes
as more of a creative adaptation to city needs, and less of a transplantation
from the countryside, than I.

[10] The much controverted "Cahenslyite" episode in American Catholic history turned around the reluctance, or the inability, of Irish-American bishops
to provide immigrant Catholics with parishes and priests of their own nationality. See Document 7, and Colman J. Barry, *The Catholic Church and German
Americans* (Washington: Catholic University Press, 1953).

able to enjoy the round of services and festivals cherished in the old country.

Such churches were inevitably transient. Sometimes, a peculiarly rigid social-economic structure such as prevailed in a small Southern industrial city would keep a group together for a generation or more; sometimes the centripetal forces of a foreign-language ethnic group enabled its members for a period of time not only to renounce the opportunity to scatter through the whole city but also to resist temptations to adapt their "country" church to city life. (Of course, the country churches willy-nilly made some adaptations immediately; the very determination to transplant and maintain an institution exotic to the city created a beleaguered spirit which they had not previously had.) But usually within a decade or so, the transplanted churches from the country, like those older churches which had experienced the transformation of their community into a city, were forced to make much more radical adaptations. Though at any given moment a considerable proportion of a city's churches might be striving to remain country churches, a growing number had adapted in dramatic fashion.

IV

The much more complex, heterogeneous life of the cities produces institutions that are far more specialized than those which flourish in rural culture. Furthermore, just as city-dwellers expect of such institutions rather precise intellectual and moral services, so the leaders of such institutions come to approximate functionaries with highly specialized skills. So it was with most of the churches which adapted to the ways of city life in late nineteenth-century America. Compared with the traditional churches, many of these adaptations—even some of those the age most admired—seem almost grotesque, heretically preoccupied with responding to some limited aspect of urban life, and stressing some limited theme in the churches' armory of beliefs and modes of worship.

The "neighborhood" church neatly illustrates both the plausibility and the peril of adaptation. As Springfield, Massachusetts, grew from a frontier town to a considerable city and its population spread out away from the original cluster on the Connecticut River, those who thought of themselves as Congregationalists but did not wish to journey into the centre of town to "Old First Church" founded successively a North and a South Congregational Church, a Faith Church, a Hope Church, until more than a dozen neighborhood churches had been created. Such cellular division was sometimes justified as creating new, reasonably sized and reasonably located churches, each as concerned as the original church with the total gospel of the Church to the World. But Springfield was not, any more than were other cities, a cluster of generally similar neighborhoods, but an area that was highly stratified according to income, class, and ethnic group. As a result, each new congregation tended to be markedly segregated, and thereby highly susceptible to a very specialized notion of the nature of the Church and of its proper relations with the World. An extreme but illuminating example of the neighborhood church was Plymouth Congregational, founded in the 1840's in the City of Brooklyn, for many decades a suburb for up-and-coming New Yorkers. For forty years its minister and central figure was Henry Ward Beecher.

Perhaps because of his expansive, ebullient personality, perhaps because he was the son of Lyman Beecher, one of the great churchmen of the prewar years, but mostly because of the demands of his congregation, Beecher enjoyed a singularly close relationship with his flock. Instead of speaking from a pulpit far back from or high above the congregation, Beecher had one constructed as much in the center of the church as possible. His sermons frequently elicited emotional outbursts. At the weekly prayer meeting, he delighted to emphasize his communion with his people by sitting on a chair where he could share rather than direct the flow of testimony. Everything about his role militated against prophetic preaching against the sins of his people. It was not that Beecher felt inhibitions about the subjects to which the minister ought to address himself. Shrugging off the tradition that enjoined the minister to concentrate on simple evangelical truths, Beecher claimed the right and duty to speak on politics, economic life, the most recent innovations in the world of culture—all the themes of interest to his congregation. But the evils which excited his alarm were those that came from without the circle of his congregation's lives, and threatened their social and psychological well-being. The old doctrines of hell and eternal damnation, for example, seemed increasingly incongruous to both Beecher and his thriving, prospering people, and Beecher soon avowed that the God they all worshipped was a God of love, who would not conceivably deal harshly with creatures made in His own image. "You are Gods," he once told his congregation; "you are crystalline, your faces are radiant." [11] Aware that the

---

[11] Constance Rourke, *Trumpets of Jubilee* (New York: Harcourt Brace, Harbinger edition, 1963), p. 129.

newly bruited doctrines of Darwinism threw into doubt the power of God as well as His amiability, Beecher was not long in assuring his people that evolution, rightly construed, implied only that God chose to create by retail, rather than wholesale. (The metaphor, no less than the sentiment, was harmonious to the sensibilities of his bourgeois audience.) Equally important, he vindicated the righteousness of middle-class economic behavior against the polite innuendos of the wealthy, and the protests and occasionally obstreperous revolts of the poor. Justifying the *douceurs* of prosperity, he slashed at the immoralities that luxury induced in the wealthy; preaching a Protestant ethic of hard work, he denounced working-class demands for better wages and living conditions, as evidence of unfitness to live. If few neighborhood or suburban churches were so imaginatively and fulsomely served as was Plymouth Congregational, most of them encountered a version of the Gospel so edited and distorted as to be almost a parody. Many developments in American culture helped promote this kind of Christianity, but it could hardly have been sustained in the churches if the sociology of metropolitan life had not produced parishes so stratified and so unrepresentative of the full spectrum of potential churchgoers. . . .

For former country folk deprived of a genuinely country church and not yet settled into a neighborhood church, revivalism often afforded a consoling sense of continuity. (It had been one of the strong appeals of the transplanted holiness churches, but it also proved powerful even when sharply separated from regular congregational life.) To church leaders it seemed wholly natural that revivals, which had played a crucial part in bringing religion to the unchurched West, should be used to Christianize the "city wilderness." As early as 1857, the Baptist minister, Henry Clay Fish had exclaimed, "What can save our large cities, but a powerful revival of religion?" [12] Superficially, at least, the city seemed an even easier place to conduct a revival than the open country, where the people had to be collected, housed, and supervised, or the small town, where the numbers available were strictly limited. But early nineteenth-century revivalists had noticed that their success was greater in small towns than in cities. To Finney, city people were too engrossed in worldly ambitions; "see how crazy these are who are scrambling to get up . . . ," he said, "enlarging their houses, changing their styles of living. . . . It is like climbing up [the] masthead to be thrown off into the ocean. To enjoy God you

[12] Smith, *Revivalism and Social Reform*, p. 49.

must come down, not go up there," as the city continually tempted.[13] By the 1840's, however, it appeared that the right kind of revival could "succeed" in the great city. Emphasis upon the theological niceties of a single denomination was inappropriate for a heterogeneous city audience; furthermore, the newspapers and other impersonal modes of communication on which a city revival depended for its notoriety were not inclined to herald purely sectarian efforts. As a consequence, revivalism developed in considerable autonomy from the congregations existent in the city. Churches developed, like Tremont Temple in Boston, which offered a steady fare of revival services. Inevitably they came to place emphasis not on the continuing religious life of their audiences, but on the success of the revivals in producing numerous convictions of sin.

The dramatic but curiously limited effect of urban revivalism was perfectly illustrated by the career of its greatest exponent, Dwight L. Moody. After a pious upbringing in East Northfield, Massachusetts, he sought a business career in Boston. When converted, he felt that the cities in England and America were his destined field; "if we can stir them, we shall stir the whole nation," he said.[14] Never ordained as a minister, he felt no obligation to any denomination, and preferred to conduct his revivals in a special tabernacle rather than a church. He recognized that careful planning was necessary to provide the advance publicity; to secure the necessary funds; to coordinate the ushers, choirs, and auxiliary ministers; to keep the meeting to a brisk schedule of sermon, gospel hymn, and exhortation; to obviate—and if necessary to suppress—hysterical outbreaks. He would no doubt have been gratified by the contemporary's observation that Moody made the business of revivals businesslike.[15] His goal was so simple that it was easy to pursue it matter-of-factly. He once defined his duty as to ask at least one stranger a day, "Are you a Christian?" By the end of his life, he had asked several million, with an energy and persuasiveness unsurpassed in his era. Speaking as he felt he was to people no more than a generation away from active church life, he did not imagine that complicated arguments were necessary; the main task would be to confront as many hearers as possible with the challenge: were they for or against Christ?

[13] William G. McLaughlin, *Modern Revivalism: Charles Grandison Finney to Billy Graham* (New York: Ronald Press, 1955), p. 119.

[14] *Ibid.*, p. 166.

[15] Gamaliel Bradford, *Dwight L. Moody, A Worker in Souls* (New York: George H. Doran, 1927), pp. 227–263.

Concentrating on this one task, he made no effort to respond to the peculiar difficulties of urban culture. "The old-time religion" was "good enough" for him; knowing the Bible, he saw no need to read or consider Darwin. A natural kindliness made him worry about difficulties of the poor in keeping warm in the winter, but he refused to be distracted from his revivalist efforts into any prolonged consideration of the social-economic order. Critics of a later era could without much difficulty construct from Moody's occasional remarks a ready acquiescence in *laissez faire,* but his attitude was less affirmation than simple indifference. No doubt his aloofness to worldly concerns was strengthened in Moody by a belief in an imminent Second Coming. (But even those revivalists without millennial expectations showed far more interest in the moment of grace than in the subsequent life of the faithful in the world.) . . .

Like the neighborhood church, too, revivalism appealed only to special segments of the city population. Moody believed that the poorer classes were those most cut off from religion; he made them the target of his revivals, and when he founded the Moody Bible Institute in 1886 he charged its students to devote their lives to evangelizing the poor. Yet, like most other urban revivalists, he drew most of his audiences from the middle and lower-middle classes, especially those who in their own lives or family traditions had had some contact with organized Protestantism. When he tried to conduct a revival on Fourteenth Street and Second Avenue in New York, the attendance was so sparse that he sent out men to try to round up listeners from the nearby cafes. " 'Don't you want to come up to the church . . .and hear Dwight L. Moody preach?' the chairman said to four men who sat at a cardtable near the door. 'Who the hell is Moody?' one of them replied. And that was all there was to it." [16] Moody's complete defeat on the Lower East Side neatly symbolized the limits of revivalism's ability even to begin the process of reestablishing the old church order among the city's poorer people.

The striking growth of what came to be known as Jehovah's Witnesses demonstrated that many of those whom revivalism could not reach sought a more radical rejection of contemporary culture than men like Moody demanded. In the 1840's pre-millennialism had attracted a large following; when William Miller's predictions of a day of judgment had not been fulfilled, some had been disillusioned, but a variety of adventist churches remained in existence. Then in 1872, Charles

[16] The incident is recounted in Stelzle, *A Son of the Bowery,* p. 119

Taze Russell, dissatisfied not only with his early Congregationalism but also with the "infidelity" to which "science" and "modern thought" had led him, found in the eschatological promises of the Bible a guarantee that Christ would soon return to rule on earth. In that overwhelming perspective, the creeds and practices of the churches seemed worse than temporizing; not preaching the truth, they were necessarily diabolic agencies. Zion's Watch Tower Society, which Russell organized in 1884, tolerated no compromise with the world, no participation in rituals or worship which tried to sanctify modes of accommodation. Society members were to devote all their efforts to "witnessing" and "publishing" Christ's imminent coming. Free of the need to follow conventional modes of action, Russell was able to develop modes of "evangelism" peculiarly suited to the masses of unchurched city dwellers. He developed an illustrated lecture, or sermon, "The Photo Drama of Creation," and transcribed his words on to phonograph records that could be played to many more people than Moody could ever have reached, and in situations and places where neither Moody nor any other regular revivalist would ever have been accepted.[17] Unencumbered by a theological tradition (Russellites declared for example that the Trinity was a vulgar error), he could depict "the divine plan of the ages" with the clarity of an architectural drawing; even the barely literate could see in the chart which prefaced most collections of Russell's writings the point in history where mankind stood. Though the movement avoided stipulating an exact day in which Christ would sit in judgment, 1914 was generally thought to mark the beginning of Christ's reconquest of the world. As important as the danger was the promise, epitomized in the slogan made popular by the Witnesses in the twentieth century, that "millions now living will never die." Simple in the demands they made upon the believer, unqualified in the denunciations they uttered against the government, the other churches, indeed modern culture generally, Jehovah's Witnesses exerted a growing appeal to the lower social and economic classes in American cities. By the twentieth century, observers recognized that the Witnesses were proselyting successfully among the habitués of city missions, which apparently could reach down-and-outers, but could not mold them into any kind of church.[18]

[17] Charles S. Braden, *These Also Believe. A Study of Modern American Cults and Minority Religious Movements* (New York: Macmillan, 1949), p. 361.

[18] Theodore Abel, *Protestant Missions to Catholic Immigrants* (New York: Institute of Social and Religious Research, 1933), pp. 54–55.

Symbolically, when Jehovah's Witnesses established themselves in Brooklyn, they turned a former mission of Plymouth Church into their headquarters. Though they did not themselves develop congregational life of the once familiar type, they made out of one strain of traditional religion an adaptation to felt needs that was more viable than either the mission ventures of transformed churches or the adaptations of revivalism.

The Witnesses were held to their single religious purpose first by the charismatic leadership of Russell and later by a highly centralized organization dominated by "Judge" Rutherford. In marked contrast were the flock of largely autonomous local groups which began to appear, as it seemed, spontaneously in many of the large cities about the turn of the century. Sharing with the Holiness churches an almost unlimited trust in the leadings of religious emotion, and with the Witnesses a strong conviction of a not too distant Second Coming, these churches were often lumped with Holiness groups and the Witnesses as manifestations of Pentecostalism. But while all did indeed believe that the special gifts of the Pentecost would be bestowed on men again, both Witnesses and Holiness groups remained extremely wary toward contemporaries claiming the gift of "tongues" and of healing.

The gift of tongues, or *glossolalia*, was not only an easy development of the hyper-excitement of the protracted religious meetings these groups treasured; it met the needs of simple, untutored people anxious to take a leading part in meetings.[19] Honorific distinctions in favor of a professional minister disappeared; formal training, logic, even Biblical scholarship lost most importance. Above all, command of the language, which more than anything else inhibited European immigrants and slow-speaking country folk from masterful participation in urban culture, now was irrelevant, for might not God choose to speak through His people in any language, any accent? . . .

One of the prized Pentecostal gifts was that of healing. Like the gift of tongues, it proved to have extraordinary appeal to the lower-class folk who flocked into "storefront" churches. But the conviction that organized religion should assume responsibility for bodily ailments was not confined to any one sect or any one social class. In the Episcopal Church, a group of ministers led by Drs. Elwood Worcester and Samuel McComb of Emmanuel Church, Boston, began to treat parishioners suffering from "functional nervous disorders." But

[19] See F. G. Henke, "The Gift of Tongues and Related Phenomena at the Present Day," *American Journal of Theology*, XIII (1909), 196–201.

the shining example of the attempt of religion to guide the faithful to victory over illness was Christian Science. It was the achievement of Mary Baker Eddy that the Church of Christ (Scientist) which she founded in 1879 was premised on the guidance given by the Scriptures to "Science and Health."

The central strategy of Christian Science was a denial of the reality of matter; for this there were abundant precedents in American transcendentalism, and Mrs. Eddy not surprisingly always had to cope with numerous competing brands of gnosticism. But Mrs. Eddy had unusual powers both of inspiration and organization. Students spoke "of a certain spiritual and emotional exaltation which she was able to impart . . . , a feeling so strong that it was like the birth of a new understanding and seemed to open to them a new heaven and a new earth." Those who "were imaginative and emotional, and especially those who had something of the mystic in their nature, came out . . . to find that for them the world had changed. They lived by a new set of values; the color seemed to fade out of the physical world about them; men and women became shadow-like. . . . The reality of pain and pleasure, sin and grief, love and death, once denied, the only positive thing in their lives was their belief. . . ,[20] Once Mrs. Eddy became convinced that the only way to preserve the purity of this gospel against the distortions of her "enemies" (whom she believed informed with "malicious animal magnetism") was to establish a church, she created an institution which placed all power in her hands, and which made the study of her words the primary religious duty. She built and ruled so well that at her death in 1910 her church was able to survive her.

It was, however, a church with a very special appeal as well as a very special doctrine and government. Most of the members had not long before been members of the older Protestant churches; most were middle or upper-middle class; almost all were living in cities; the preponderance of woman members was exceptional, even for the American churches.[21] All of this seemed reasonable and natural to

[20] Quoted in Georgine Milmine, "Mary Baker Eddy," *McClure's Magazine,* XXIX (July, 1907), 108–109.
[21] See David O. Moberg, *The Church as a Social Institution* (Englewood Cliffs, N.J.: Prentice-Hall, 1962), p. 396; see also the perceptive English study, Bryan R. Wilson, *Sects and Society. A Sociological Study of the Elim Tabernacle, Christian Science, and Christadelphians* (Berkeley: University of California Press, 1961), p. 350.

Mrs. Eddy. Though she would have denied that Christian Science was simply an adaptation of Protestantism, she always believed that a sound Protestant background was virtually a prerequisite for seeing the light. Christian Science, like Beecher's Plymouth Church, purveyed a singularly straitened version of Christianity to a peculiarly middle-class segment of the urban population.

V

By the last decades of the nineteenth century there was an enormous variety of urban churches—downtown, country, immigrant, neighborhood, revivalist, Witnesses, Pentecostal, Christian Science; but those which were churches were not urban in anything but location, and those which were urban were not churches, at least in the traditional sense of being the religious expression of the community. Many prominent churchmen made no secret of their sense that the many expedients did not constitute a triumph of religion in its new tasks.

Among Catholic leaders, much of the discontent focused on the difficulties posed for the Church by the ethnic heterogeneity of the city. Once these were overcome it was plausible to imagine that urban Catholic churches would suffer none of the distortions obvious in Protestant adaptions. Parish boundaries seldom coincided with lines dividing social classes, so that most parishes would come closer to approximating "the whole Church in microcosm" than the average Protestant downtown or neighborhood church. The Church's hierarchical structure seemed also to guarantee that no parish, whatever its social composition, would become too parochial in outlook. Furthermore, by the late nineteenth century, urban Catholic parishes had begun to develop that bewildering array of parochial schools, sodalities, confraternities, and societies—something for every condition of man—for which the modern American Catholic parish is famous. Yet, as a few of the more "Americanist" clergy recognized, the typical urban parishes fell short in two ways of being the authentic voice of their communities—as by ancient rural custom, and theological claim, they ought to be. Recoiling from the city because it was not the country, and because it seemed, to a Catholic population still of immigrant stock, formidably "American," they tended to remain aloof from attempts to civilize the city. Also, obsessed by the dangers to the faith engendered in a religiously heterogenous city, most Catholics contented themselves with resisting error; they were almost sectlike in their disposition to preserve Catholicism from contact with the non-Catholic world.[22]   Though Protestants regularly hailed the success of Catholics in transcending the social divisions rending urban Protestantism, the more perceptive Catholics were anything but satisfied with the Church's response to the city.[23]

A growing number of Protestant leaders concluded that churches could not simply react to urban life; if they hoped to re-establish the harmonious relationship between religion and culture, they would have to take an active responsibility for reshaping that culture, even if that required marked departures from the usual modes of church action. In reaching this perception, churchmen were aided not only by their recognition of the partial failures of the city churches, but also by the partial successes of such enterprises as the YMCA and the Salvation Army. Though making no claims to being churches, such responses to what Aaron Abell has felicitously called 'the urban impact" demonstrated that religion could be presented to some elements in the city, only if the men of God would seek to meet certain creaturely needs.[24] Equally influential was the gradual formulation of a "social gospel"—what Henry May and Charles Hopkins have ably discussed in terms of the Protestant churches, but which had parallels in Catholicism and Judaism as well.[25] Finding its great appeal among those least trammeled with congregational responsibilities—among seminary teachers, bishops, and denominational officials—the social gospel gave sanction to those ministers and laymen anxious to redefine the gospel to meet specifically urban needs.

This attitude was especially attractive to Episcopalians, who maintained a disproportionate number of "downtown" churches; who had, as a church, never acquiesced completely in the "denominational" assumption that the responsibility for the welfare of society could be shared with other religious organizations; and whose parishes frequently included enough of the city's wealthiest citizens to permit very

[22] Robert D. Cross, *The Emergence of Liberal Catholicism in America* (Cambridge, Mass.: Harvard University Press, 1958), especially chapter 2.

[23] Robert D. Cross, "The Changing Image of the City among American Catholics," *Catholic Historical Review*, XLVIII (April, 1962), 33–52.

[24] Aaron I. Abell, *The Urban Impact on American Protestantism* (Cambridge, Mass.: Harvard University Press, 1943).

[25] Charles H. Hopkins, *The Rise of the Social Gospel in American Protestantism* (New Haven: Yale University Press, 1940); Henry F. May, *Protestant Churches and Industrial America* (New York: Octagon Books, 1963). For some reverberations in the Catholic Church, see Abell, *American Catholicism and Social Action* (Garden City, N.Y.: Doubleday, 1960).

costly innovations in the ministry to the city. St. George's, for example, on the East Side of New York, had been surrounded by new immigrants, few of them Episcopalian. The handful of wealthy members, including J. P. Morgan, invited to the pulpit the Reverend William S. Rainsford, an English cleric of considerable experience with the problems of London and Toronto as well as New York. Determined to preside over a community church, even if that required using much of the church's resources to create the community, Rainsford soon had developed a parish program to meet the social and economic needs of every sort and condition of urban man. He attained notoriety by his proposal to establish, as an alternative to the saloon, a church club where the workingman could enjoy his glass in edifying circumstances; more important were his programs of industrial education. That such enterprises were not simply alternatives to church life—like the earlier ventures of city missions, or the Salvation Army and YMCA— seemed demonstrated when the membership of St. George's grew from 200 to 4,000, with much of the increase coming from people of humble circumstances, both foreign-born and American. This mode of reintegrating church and community became celebrated as the institutional church.

Although the majority of institutional churches grew out of "downtown" Episcopal and Congregational churches of high social standing and low membership, Grace Church in Philadelphia illustrated that a city Baptist church might also become "institutional." In 1882, Russell Conwell brought to the pastorate of Grace no majestic ecclesiastical tradition, but the conviction that churches to succeed must prove more relevant to social problems than they had been to him as a country boy seeking his fortune in the city.[26] As an adjunct to Grace Church, he built Samaritan Hospital, and also Baptist Temple, eventually the center for Temple College and for a whole complex of recreational and social clubs. Grace Church soon claimed to have the largest congregation in the United States. . . .

. . . commitment to the social gospel involved the institutional churches in some of the ambiguities of that movement. Faith that a program of action satisfactory to all social classes could be agreed on was soon shaken by the intransigence of the congregations. Early in the twentieth century, Charles Stelzle became convinced that the institutional church would never even consider the socialistic ideas which,

[26] Agnes R. Burr, *Russell H. Conwell and His Work* (Philadelphia: John Winston, 1917).

he thought, were talismanic to many city workers; his own inability to get support from the Presbyterian Church for radical congregational experiments was paralleled in subsequent decades by the rebuffs many social gospelers received from their denominations.[27] Most congregations would endorse the social gospel only if it did not involve pronounced departures from middle-class values.

Conversely, to the extent that institutional churches committed themselves to programs of more or less radical social action, they did so on the assumption—explicit in Rainsford's case—that either a healthy community would be swiftly restored, or that the state would see its duty and relieve the churches of their social responsibilities. Either eventuality was conducive of disillusion. As the municipalities, or private agencies like the settlement houses, increased the range of community service, the institutional churches lost much of their sense of mission. Perhaps more ominous was the discovery that social amelioration did not by itself automatically produce a population naturally inclined toward congregational life. The dawning realization that alienation from the churches was not simply a by-product of problems of society was central to the neo-orthodox revolt of the 1930's from the social gospel on which the institutional churches were premised.

VI

For all its limitations, the institutional church constituted the most coherent effort to re-establish the congregation as the normal vehicle of religious life in the city. Its obvious successes encouraged churches threatened by a changing city environment not to desert to the suburbs. Its very willingness to experiment with new modes of evangelism made it an important precedent for contemporary enterprises like the East Harlem Protestant Parish, with its determination to construct a congregational life in a demoralized neighborhood.[28] On the other hand,

[27] For the history of the later years of the Social Gospel, see Paul A. Carter, *The Decline and Revival of the Social Gospel* (Ithaca, N. Y.: Cornell University Press, 1956) and Donald Meyer, *The Protestant Search for Political Realism* (Berkeley: University of California Press, 1960).

[28] For the implications of the experience in this parish, as seen by one of its leaders, see George R. Webber, *The Congregation in Mission* (New York: Abingdon Press, 1964). For contemporary Catholic concern about the urban parish, see Dennis Clark, *Cities in Crisis* (New York: Sheed and Ward, 1960), and the references in Cross, "The Changing Image."

the institutional church has never been so generally accepted as to preclude the continued existence—and in some cases the steady growth —of more specialized adaptations to the urban scene.

The number of neighborhood churches has increased during the twentieth century. As suburbia has grown more rapidly than center-city, new congregations have been established at an astonishing rate, each usually drawing on a highly stratified segment of the population. The consequence has been much like that exhibited in Beecher's Plymouth Church; within the last decade some Protestant, Catholic, and Jewish spokesmen have gloried in the obvious vitality of these churches, while others have deplored the "suburban captivity." [29]

The relatively steady abandonment in many suburban churches of traditional theology in favor of a gospel of social adjustment and mental health has further narrowed the gap separating them from the gnostic cults once represented almost exclusively by Christian Science, but now including New Thought, Unity, Psychiana, and I Am. Of these, only Christian Science maintains any semblance of congregational life, but the strong group indentification of their members renders these cults almost as close to the old church order as many of the suburban churches.

The rural churches established in the cities in the late nineteenth century have been markedly affected by urban life. The Church of God (Anderson, Indiana), for example, one of the larger holiness bodies, has steadily accommodated to the religious diversity of the city by shedding its hostility to other denominations. As members slowly abandon their peculiarities of dress and expression, the church concentrates on maintaining the allegiance of the younger generation; it

relaxes its program of grab-him-by-the-lapel evangelism, puts robes on the choir and candles on the altar, divides the chancel, replaces folding chairs with oaken pews, and calls a college-trained minister. . . . It moves out of its plain rectangular white frame building into a stone gothic or redwood contemporary structure. It is now respectable.[30]

[29] Representative views are those of Andrew Greeley, *The Church and the Suburbs* (*New York*: Sheed and Ward, 1959); Albert J. Gordon, *Jews in Suburbia* (Boston: Beacon Press, 1959); and Gibson Winter, *The Suburban Captivity of the Churches* (Garden City, N.Y.: Doubleday, 1961).

[30] Val B. Clear, "The Urbanization of a Holiness Body," *The City Church,* IX (July-August, 1958), 2–3, 7–11.

Such transformed churches, of course, do not appeal so strongly any more to the migrants from the countryside. But with the restriction in the 1920's of immigration from abroad, and with the reduction of the American rural population, the number of country folk in the city has decreased; the likelihood has therefore decreased of creating a church which continues the special version of religious life cherished in one's own country or region. However, the ability of revivalists like Billy Graham to mount revival crusades demonstrates that there are still many people in the cities who are not completely satisfied with the ethos of the city churches.

Meanwhile, the probability has steadily grown that newcomers will be attracted to one of the cultic or Pentecostal groups authentic to the cities. Some of these groups owe their existence to a charismatic leader like Daddy Grace or Father Divine; others are sustained by a special myth like that which connects the "Black Jews" with the Lost Tribes; still others have stressed a single doctrine like the rapidly growing Jehovah's Witnesses, or a single gift, like some of the healing cults.[31] In 1958, Henry Van Dusen, President of Union Theological Seminary, estimated that a third of all believers now adhere to radical sects or cults, and that, taken together, they comprise the most rapidly growing component of American religion.[32] About the same time, two sociologists noted how Puerto Rican migrants to New York, not strongly drawn to the Roman Catholic parishes, have flocked into Pentecostal churches. Not only do these churches offer a stringent moral code in reassuring contrast to the apparent normlessness of the city; they also provide frequent meetings, in which newcomers are welcomed, in which the modes of worship are simple, and in which participation in songs and "tongues" is warmly cherished. "The first time I went there, I was impressed by the way everyone shook hands with me," reported one member. Another said that "I was sick, they came to my home to say a prayer for me." "I used to go to the Catholic Church," a third explained; "there nobody knew me. . . . Now in my church they call me sister." [33] Such testimonies reaffirm

[31] See G. Norman Eddy, "Store-Front Religion," in Robert Lee (ed.), *Cities and Churches, Readings on the Urban Church* (Philadelphia: Westminster Press, 1962). See also Elmer T. Clark, *The Small Sects in America* (Nashville: Cokesbury Press, 1937).

[32] "The Third Force in Christendom," *Life*, XLIV (June 9, 1958). p. 23.

[33] Renato Poblete and Thomas F. O'Dea, "Anomie and the 'Quest for Community': The Formation of Sects among the Puerto Ricans of New York," *American Catholic Sociological Review*, XXI (Spring, 1960), 18–36.

that a need for congregational communion continues to be a strong theme in American religious life. Under the social confusions, the economic difficulties, and the psychological tensions engendered by urban life, congregationalism has developed in ways often unfamiliar and almost always profoundly unsatisfactory to leaders whose ideal has remained the village church on the green.

13

Streetcar Suburbs: The Consequences

by SAMUEL BASS WARNER, Jr.

. . . the suburbs offered a physical demonstration that the rewards of competitive capitalism might be within the reach of all.

The close mesh of urban development and technological advance is an integral pattern in our history. Much of the technology was itself a product of the city within which industrial activity and intellectual creativity have been concentrated.

The thirty years following the Civil War saw a marked acceleration and clear convergence of technology and urbanization. The shape and character of the modern American city were largely cast in that period. With the invention of the elevator and the electric light, with a new capacity to control disease and dispose of wastes, with the ability to provide water, gas, and electricity to a wide public, and with the beginnings of new forms of communication such as the telephone and telegraphy, life in the American city changed profoundly.

In this new texture of the city an important dimension was provided by the streetcar, for it made it possible to transport people within cities. By 1882 there were more than 400 streetcar companies in the nation, with 18,000 horse-drawn cars carrying 1.2 billion passengers a year. By 1890 electric trolley lines were superseding horsecar lines as they transported more than 2 billion passengers.

More than any other force the streetcar made possible the metropolitan suburb and ended the dependence of the middle and the laboring classes on walking distance between home and place of work. The streetcar introduced for much of the populace a new flexibility and mobility. It altered patterns of land use, and industrial and residential location, and it brought a general outward shift of population and merged the peripheral town and central city.

These changes were easily apparent in Boston after 1870. Samuel Bass Warner, Jr., in *Streetcar Suburbs* (1962) has made a detailed study of how three formerly independent towns—Roxbury, West Roxbury, and Dorchester—coalesced with the old "pedestrian" city of Boston as new traffic axes and geographical bindings were created by the streetcar. In this particular instance—rather uncharacteristically in the Northeast—the towns were politically absorbed into Boston as well. In an unusually suggestive and well-written monograph Mr. Warner fits the streetcar into the web of factors that make up the modern metropolis in America, one of whose main features is the residential suburb.

This essay, the final chapter in the book, is reprinted with the permission of the Harvard University Press, copyright 1962 by the President and Fellows of Harvard College and the Massachusetts Institute of Technology. A sketch of Mr. Warner's career is included in the introduction to Chapter 2.

Two qualities mark off the Boston of 1900 from all preceding eras: its great size and its new suburban arrangement. In 1850 the metropolitan region of Boston encompassed a radius of but two or three miles, a population of two hundred thousand; in 1900 the region extended over a ten-mile radius and contained a population of more than a million. A change in structure accompanied this change in scale. Once a dense merchant city clustered about an ocean port, Boston became a sprawling industrial metropolis. In 1850 it was a fairly small and unified area, by 1900 it had split into two functional parts: an industrial, commercial, and communications center packed tight against the port, and an enormous outer suburban ring of residences and industrial and commercial subcenters. By examining in detail the method of building one part of the great outer suburban ring, this book has attempted to discover something about the society that underwent this transformation, and to elicit some of the consequences of this new physical arrangement of people.

In Roxbury, West Roxbury, and Dorchester the parade of 23,000 new houses arranged by grid streets and frontage lots, the regular progress from one architectural style to the next, the constancy of basic house design, and the clustering of buildings by the income levels of their owners witness uniformity of behavior among individual decision makers.

Both positive and negative factors contributed to the uniformity of decisions of the 9,000 private builders. Positively, these middle class homeowners and amateur investors shared a sympathy for the suburban style of living which was then developing in metropolitan Boston. There existed a consensus of attitude which made each decision maker to some degree favorable to the new shingle and later colonial revival styles of architecture. This same consensus caused each man to build houses much like those of his neighbors and to seek to locate in a neighborhood or on a street which was popular with families of an income similar to his own. Finally, this same consensus encouraged each man to seek and to perpetuate the new suburban environment which emphasized the pleasures of private family life, the security of a small community setting, and the enjoyments of an increased contact with nature. The strength of this consensus grew with the passage of time. Every year more and more middle class families lived in the suburbs. Every year, too, the streetcar and utility networks brought a steady increase in land available for settlement so that successively closer approximations to the desired environment became possible.

Negatively, suburban builders were repelled by conditions in the central city. The unending immigrant invasion, the conversion of old houses and the encroachment of industry and commerce heightened the contrast between the new suburbs and the central city. Negatively, too, the limited financial position of homebuilders disciplined their choices of houses and neighborhoods and controlled their methods of land division.

The policies of the large institutions concerned with building supported and disciplined these individual choices. The role of the larger agents was essential. At the municipal scale, utilities had to be laid before most men would be willing to build. Adequate streetcar service also preceded homebuilders and their customers. At the neighborhood scale the arrival of new families attracted by a new improved transportation service, or the expansion of adjacent neighborhoods, or the departure of old families because of housing obsolescence, all encouraged one kind of building and discouraged others. At his peril a man built cheap rental units in outer suburbs, or expensive singles in old inner suburbs. The patterned spread of various kinds of new construction bears witness to the power of the informal neighborhood regulation of building. It was a power based upon the sensitivity of individual landowners to the economic standing of their neighbors.

The behavior of the large institutions concerned with suburban building also encouraged individual landowners to repeat in their building the popular suburban architecture, engineering, and economic grading of neighborhoods. Late nineteenth century Boston was a fast-growing metropolitan society made prosperous by the new industrial technology and propelled by the energy of thousands of individual capitalists. The middle class was one of the principal beneficiaries of this prosperity, and its well-being and rapid enlargement gave this large segment of Boston society the confidence to stress its equalitarianism and the willingness to exploit each new technological device. The rise of thousands of families of the most diverse ethnic backgrounds to a middle class competence, like their quick adoption of each new invention, was taken as proof of the success of the society.

The City of Boston and the later metropolitan boards enthusiastically adopted the new sanitary engineering. These institutions undertook to see that all new neighborhoods would be built to the latest standards, and at great expense attempted to service the old parts of the city. This enormous undertaking not only made the new devices available to Boston's homeowners, but also stimulated the universal acceptance of middle class criteria for home services. In the suburbs all the new regulations for plumbing, gas fitting, and building and fire safety were perhaps more important as official affirmations of middle class norms than for policing an occasional offender. With the cooperation and example of the large institutions almost all new suburban building from 1870 to 1900 included safe construction, indoor plumbing, and orderly land arrangement. From the prosperity of the middle class and its enthusiastic acceptance of the new sanitation and transportation technology came the popular achievement of the late nineteenth century suburbs: a safe environment for half the metropolitan population.

The orientation of the large institutions toward the benefit of the suburban builders also assisted the small landowners. The street railways and other utilities rapidly extended their service to outlying metropolitan villages. In so doing they encouraged private development of distant land. This policy was aimed at taking advantage of the general growth of the city, but it also reflected a belief that public agencies should assist private undertakings. Similarly, the Park Department carefully avoided land which was thought to be suited to private construction, taking instead the marshes and uplands at the edge of areas then building. In effect, the Park Department landscaped the margins of private developments. In the new neighborhoods the City of Boston built schools at a very rapid rate and its official architecture and landscape design mirrored the fashions of private builders.

Public policy held installation charges for new utilities and streets to below cost, much of the expense being borne by general taxation and general rates. When the city bargained with gas and electric companies for the extension of its lighting it often bargained in behalf of residential users as well, endeavoring to see that they too would be connected to the new lines and served at reasonable rates.[1] The combined effect of all these policies was to greatly assist the individual builder to develop the vacant land outside the old city.

At the level of homeowners' decisions the class character of neighborhoods played a more supportive than immediately disciplinary role. Though the migration of various income groups ultimately determined the uses, rents, and fate of neighborhoods, at the moment of construction the power of regulation lay only in the example set by the behavior of others. The presence of houses of similar cost and style encouraged a man to build his own house in keeping with existing ones. No laws, however, prevented him from building something different.

The variety of ethnic backgrounds of families living within the surrounding houses also encouraged the builder of a new house to minimize any ethnic hostilities he might possess. If no Catholic, Methodist, or Episcopal church yet existed in his neighborhood the presence of recently built churches and schools all over the suburbs allowed a new resident to expect one soon. Just as curbs and gas lights might still be a few years in coming to his street, so, too, the arrival of his particular church, club, and school, was merely a matter of time.

To all these characteristics—the speed of building, the mass arrival of new families, the separation of families by economic class, the universality of the new high standards of light, air, land, and sanitation—must be added the effect of the omnipresent newness. Whether a man lived in a lower middle class quarter of cheap three-deckers, or on a fashionable street of expensive singles, the latest styles, the freshly painted houses, the neat streets, the well-kept lawns, and the new schools and parks gave him a sense of confidence in the success of his society and a satisfaction at his participation in it. These physical expressions gave him the willingness to abide by the rules of the society whether the rules took the form of building regulations or the less specific directions of group imitation. The very extent of newness in the suburbs, which by 1900 dwarfed the old central city, made these areas a source of pride for Boston's metropolitan society. Today

[1] *Boston Transcript,* March 6, 1893, p. 1.

suburbs are increasingly assigned all the evils of American society; but in the late nineteenth century they created a widespread sense of achievement.

The general contemporary satisfaction with suburbs came from their ability to answer some of the major needs of the day. To be sure, the costs of new construction were such as to exclude at least half the families of Boston; but the suburban half, the middle class, was the dominant class in the society. To middle class families the suburbs gave a safe, sanitary environment, new houses in styles somewhat in keeping with their conception of family life, and temporary neighborhoods of people with similar outlook. In an atmosphere of rapid change, the income-graded neighborhoods rendered two important services to their residents. Evenness of wealth meant neighbors who would reinforce an individual family's efforts to pass on its values to its children. The surrounding evenness of wealth also gave adults a sense of a community of shared experience, and thereby gave some measure of relief from the uncertainties inherent in a world of highly competitive capitalism.

In addition to benefiting their own residents, in one important way the suburbs served the half of Boston's population which could not afford them. The apparent openness of the new residential quarters, their ethnic variety, their extensive growth, and their wide range of prices from fairly inexpensive rental suites to expensive single-family houses—these visible characteristics of the new suburbs gave aspiring low-income families the certainty that should they earn enough money they too could possess the comforts and symbols of success. Even for those excluded from them, the suburbs offered a physical demonstration that the rewards of competitive capitalism might be within the reach of all.

The rendering of these important social services gave Bostonians of the late nineteenth century a confidence that at least in the suburbs they had struck a successful compromise among the conflicts then active in their society. The suburban city, however, was a compromise which had all the faults of its virtues. Many of the same devices that gave power and dynamism to its building contained within them unresolved conflicts. These conflicts, in turn, worked to destroy much of what the suburb hoped to achieve.

Homeownership was one suburban goal, but the high down payments and short-term, nonamortizing mortgages of the unregulated mortgage market restricted homeownership to one quarter of Boston's families. A pleasant landscape was another goal, but the lack of training and limited financial capabilities of subdividers condemned the new streetcar suburbs to the progressive destruction of their natural setting. Under the grid street and frontage lot system of land division natural contours were thrown away for the short-term advantages of easy marketing and cheap utility and street construction. Once all the narrow lots had been occupied, a band of tiny front lawns and a row of street trees was about all the verdure a suburban development could offer.

The suburb, the home of property owners and settled family life, was thought by contemporaries to be an environment that encouraged individual participation in community life. Compared to transient conditions in older parts of the city the suburbs were more conducive to integration of the individual into some sort of community activity.[2] Their physical arrangement, however—the endless street grids and the dependence upon the downtown for work and shopping—failed to provide local centers where all the residents of a given area might, through frequent contact, come to know each other and thereby be encouraged to share in community-wide activities.

Aside from class segregation there was nothing in the process of late nineteenth century suburban construction that built communities or neighborhoods: it built streets. The grid plan of the suburbs did not concern itself with public life. It was an economically efficient geometry which divided large parcels of land as they came on the market. The arrangement of the blocks of the grid depended largely upon what farm or estate came on the market at what time. The result was not integrated communities arranged about common centers, but a historical and accidental traffic pattern.

Where a railroad station and arterial streets came together, stores, churches, and sometimes schools were built to serve some of the needs of the residents of the area. In Dorchester, for example, there were historic village clusters that grew with the increase of population around them: Meeting House Hill, Harrison Square, Codman Square, Lower Mills. Other clusters—such as Fields Corner, Grove Hall, and Columbia Square—were largely the work of the new streetcar transportation network. Most characteristic of the new suburban order was the commercial strip which followed the main transportation lines

[2] Josiah Quincy, *Moderate Houses for Moderate Means, A Letter to Rev. E. E. Hale* (Boston, 1874); Woods and Kennedy, "The Zone of Emergence," chapters on Dorchester and Roxbury.

and had no center at all. Washington street, Dorchester, from Codman Square to Grove Hall lacked any historic center. It was simply a long row of little stores which served those passing by and those living in the houses behind.

This centerless tendency was intensified by the Boston School Department's building policy which placed schools on inexpensive land on the side streets. In this way the schools formed partial centers by themselves which were often isolated from the commercial and social centers. The most dramatic example was the placing of Dorchester High School in Ashmont with the consequent destruction of the town's old educational center at Meeting House Hill. Roxbury High School was similarly mislocated. In West Roxbury, however, the school building policy maintained the historic center at Eliot Square. By this municipal money-saving policy the child of the suburbs was isolated from the center of his community in the same way his mother was separated from her husband's work.

An amorphous and weak neighborhood structure was the consequence of compounding communities with a mix of side-street grids, commercial strips, and small historic centers. A family living near the corner of Tonawanda street and Geneva avenue in central Dorchester during the 1890's shopped locally on Geneva avenue, and went to Boston for major purchases. If they happened to be Congregationalists their church stood on their corner. The father went to Boston on the Old Colony Railroad or took the streetcar down Dorchester avenue. The children went to primary school, however, in a different neighborhood on the other side of Dorchester avenue. If the family was not Congregational they had to go to a third neighborhood for church, and, of course, social clubs were scattered through the town. A similar family living twelve doors up Tonawanda street had an entirely different orientation. Its business area lay along the Washington street strip.

As a result of the centerless character of most suburbs, community life fell into fragments. Groups formed about particular churches, clubs, schools, and ward club rooms; rarely did any large fraction of the population of a suburban area participate in any joint endeavor. When, through accident, the historic political boundaries of a town coincided with the building pattern of a new suburb local politics provided a framework for community activities. Nevertheless, even these conditions were unfavorable to the development of meaningful community life. The limited subject matter of town politics, and the frequently narrow income band of the residents of new bedroom suburbs, together generated an enervating parochialism which hung heavy over such community life as existed.[3]

In 1900 the new metropolis lacked local communities that could deal with the problems of contemporary society at the level of the family and its immediate surroundings, and it lacked a large-scale community that could deal with the problems of the metropolis.[4] As a result Boston community life fell into a self-defeating cycle. Each decade brought an increase in the scale and complexity of economic and social life; each decade's problems demanded more wide-scale attention, more complex solutions. Because of the physical arrangement of the new metropolis, each decade also brought an ever greater fragmentation of community life into town and ward politics, church groups, clubs, and specialized societies of all kinds. The growing parochialism and fragmentation resulted in a steady relative weakening of social agencies. Weakness, in turn, convinced more and more individuals that local community action was hopeless or irrelevant. From this conviction came the further weakening of the public agencies. The self-defeating cycle, begun by the streetcar metropolis, has continued with increasing severity to this day. It has proved, both for the metropolis and its constituent political units, an iron cycle, a cycle which once established, is difficult to break.

The inattention of late nineteenth century Bostonians to the fragmentation of their community life was not an accidental oversight, it was a matter of principle, the principle of individualistic capitalism. Above all else the streetcar suburbs stand as a monument to a society which wished to keep the rewards of capitalist competition open to all its citizens. Despite ignorance and prejudice, during this period

[3] Even the most active municipal government in the metropolitan region, the City of Boston, undertook to deal with a rather narrow range of subject matter in its municipal affairs. Matthews, *The City Government* of Boston, pp. 174–182; Quincy, *The Development of American Cities*.

The limitation of municipal subject matter was reflected in the city's expenditure patterns: in the period 1868–1871 Boston spent 62.0 percent of its budget on real estate affairs (water, sewers, streets, and public grounds); in the period 1883–1886, 50.4 percent; in the period 1903–1906, 52.2 percent (included rapid transit). Huse, *The Financial History of Boston*, p. 366.

[4] Contemporary recognition of the problem of the scale of governmental units: Sylvester Baxter, *Greater Boston; A Study for a Federated Metropolis* (Boston, 1891); Massachusetts Metropolitan Commission, *Report to the Massachusetts Legislature* (Boston, 1896), pp. 17–19, 33–34.

of mass immigration, the suburbs remained open to all who could meet the price.

By 1900 about half the families of metropolitan Boston had come to share this new environment. The wealth brought to the society by its industrial technology, and the special practices of suburban building, made this mass achievement possible. The manner in which the nineteenth century building process physically separated the metropolitan population into two sections—the middle class section of families who could afford new construction, and the lower class section of families who could not—assisted some of the open equalitarian goals of the capitalist society. In the suburbs families of similar economic standing lived next to each other, and their similarity of economic position helped them to learn to ignore their differences of religion and national background. The great extent of the new suburbs, moreover, left room for fine gradations of the middle class population. Middle class families were free to choose among hundreds of possible locations, free to find a neighborhood which suited both their ethnic feelings and their progress up the economic ladder.

The infrangible and enduring problems of the suburbs also derive from the principle of open capitalist competition. At any moment in the late nineteenth century half the metropolitan society was not successful, half the society remained apart from the achievements of the suburbs. The process of new construction, since it was tied to the abilities of individual builders erecting houses for their own immediate use or profit, took no effective responsibility for the lower income half of the society. As a result, contemporary progress in housing for lower class families was slow and uncertain, limited to slight improvements in sanitation, structural safety, and fire prevention.

By sheer enlargement of their numbers, and by the obsolescence of middle-income structures, low-income groups could and did reach the new suburbs. Most often, however, they could occupy them only by destroying much of what the suburb had achieved. Because the latecomers possessed but small sums for rent, secondhand houses in the suburbs often had to be divided and redivided so that a single became a double or a triple, to a two-family house was added an attic apartment, and so forth. Even where slightly higher incomes made division of structures unnecessary the cost of maintaining old wooden houses often prevented the newcomers from keeping up their houses and lots to the level originally intended. Though not included in their rent bills, the progressive deterioration of their environment was one of the prices of low-income tenancy.[5]

Neither the architecture nor the land planning of the new suburbs took any account of the possible subsequent users. A satisfactory single-family house brought, when divided, two or three cramped and mean apartments, each one often well below the building's original standards for light, air, and sanitation. The reduction in floor area per person brought an immediate and obvious retreat from the norms of the first owner. The garden setting of the street often disappeared under the feet of running children; back yards and porches filled with the overflow and trash from the houses; planted playgrounds required tar to support increased use; and the large country parks grew to weeds because of lack of time and interest among their new users.

By assigning building to the activities of thousands of individual middle class landowners the metropolitan society allowed itself to build a physical environment which would become, by its own terms, the unsatisfactory home of half its members. By this means also the society received a physical plan which was destructive to its democratic processes. The essence of the new metropolitan plan was the separation of the vast areas of new construction from the old central city.

The literature of late nineteenth century reformers tells the consequences of this division. For the middle class the inner area of low-income housing became an unknown and uncontrolled land. Here, in one ward vice and drunkenness flourished out of reach of middle class supervision; in another ward nationalist demagogues, institutionally isolated from the rest of the metropolis and responsible only to the majority of the ward, held free rein in the search for their own profit. Such troublesome manifestations of the divided society gave much concern to contemporaries. They were but symptoms of the serious consequences of the physical division of classes.

Most important, the concentration in a solid two-mile area of foreign languages, poverty, sweatshops, and slum housing gave the suburban middle class a sense of hopelessness and fear. Much of the work of reformers in the twentieth century progressive era had to be devoted to the task of educating the middle class to the conditions of modern

[5] Woods and Kennedy, "The Zone of Emergence," chapters on Roxbury and Dorchester; Wolfe, The Lodging House Problem, pp. 1–26, 34–37.

industrial cities. It was a task undertaken with the middle class faith that through knowledge would come a willingness to take action.[6]

Opposing reformers' goals of knowledge and action stood the structure of the streetcar metropolis which had damaged the fabric of the society. In part the rural ideal bore responsibility for the arrangement of the metropolis, for it had encouraged middle class families to seek escape from the conditions of modern industrial life into an isolated family environment. More important, the dominant ideal of individualistic capitalism with its accompanying unwillingness to bring private profit to account had caused the economic division of the society. The slums and the suburbs were the physical expression of this division. The conditions of the central city which so dismayed the middle class were the product of its failure to control the distribution of income, its failure to regulate housing and working conditions, its failure to develop an adequate welfare program for the sick and unfortunate, and its failure to devise a community program for integrating the thousands of new citizens who every year moved to the metropolis. These things, neglected, bore a harvest of middle class fear. From fear came the late nineteenth century paradox of the growth of an economically integrated regional city of over a million inhabitants accompanied by an increase in the parochialism of its political and social units.

In 1870 many middle class suburbanites regarded Boston as their achievement, something they wished to join in order to create a political union of homes, jobs, and community. Such sentiment gave popularity to the mid-century annexation movement. From about 1850 to 1873 almost every city and town around Boston had an annexationist group, and the question of the advantages and disadvantages of union with Boston was seriously debated. In 1868 Roxbury joined Boston; in 1870 Dorchester, and in 1873 Charlestown, Brighton, and West Roxbury, voted for unification.

The year 1873 marked the end of the annexation movement. That year the residents of Brookline voted to remain separate. This political

---

[6] One of the basic attempts of the nineteenth century settlement house movement was to discover the facts of the existence of "the other half." In Boston, the first fruit of this effort was Woods, *The City Wilderness* (1898). The title meant to convey both a sense of social disintegration and the fact that to middle class Bostonians this was an unknown land. The same tone follows through all this group's work, *Americans in Process* (1903), and "The Zone of Emergence" (c. 1912). For the general reform background: Arthur Mann, *Yankee Reformers in an Urban Age* (Cambridge, 1954), espec. 126–200.

defeat, and the Depression of 1873–1878 ended public concern over the metropolitan expansion of Boston. With the return of prosperity, however, the movement never revived. Instead, the legislature created in the late 1880's and early 1890's three specialized state-managed agencies which undertook to serve metropolitan needs for water, sewer, and park building.

The sudden and permanent collapse of the annexation movement had two causes: the first concerned municipal services; the second, the idea of community. During the middle years of the nineteenth century some of the larger and more prosperous of the peripheral towns and cities had built their own waterworks and expanded their street and educational services so that they approximated some of the high standards of Boston. In 1870 Charlestown, Cambridge, and Brookline had satisfactory independent waterworks. These same towns and Dorchester and Roxbury possessed advanced educational facilities. Other towns, however, lacked the tax base and access to the rivers and lakes necessary for high-quality municipal service. The metropolitan agencies, by building a unified drainage and water supply for the whole metropolis, put all the region's towns in a position to meet modern municipal standards.

The motive of services having been withdrawn, there remained only the idea of community. Annexation debates had always concerned themselves with this question. Annexationists appealed to the idea of one great city where work and home, social and cultural activities, industry, and commerce would be joined in a single political union. Boston, they said, would share the fate of Rome if the middle class, which heretofore had provided the governance of the city and the force of its reforms, abandoned the city for the suburbs.[7]

Opponents of annexation countered with the ideal of small town life: the simple informal community, the town meeting, the maintenance of the traditions of rural New England. They held out to their audience the idea of the suburban town as a refuge from the pressures of the new industrial metropolis. Nor were the opponents of annexa-

[7] Boston City Council and Roxbury City Council, *Reports in Relation to the Annexation of Roxbury, etc.*, Roxbury City Document no. 3 (Boston, 1867); John H. Clifford, *Argument on the Question of the Annexation of Roxbury to Boston before the Legislative Committee, Thursday, February 23, 1865* (Boston, 1867); Nathaniel W. Coffin, *A Few Reasons in Favor of the Annexation of a Part of the Town of Dorchester to the City of Boston* (Boston, 1867); Committee in Favor of the Union of Boston and Roxbury, *Report* (Boston, 1851).

tion slow to point out that the high level of city services maintained by Boston meant higher taxes, and further, they frankly stated that independent suburban towns could maintain native American life free from Boston's waves of incoming poor immigrants.[8]

As early as 1851 West Roxbury estate owners led a successful move to separate the rural part of the town of Roxbury from its industrial half. In 1873 middle class Boston commuters who had moved to West Roxbury reversed this decision by a close vote, and the town joined Boston. The new commuters wanted the high level of services offered by Boston, and they were confident that the middle class could govern the enlarged city to its own satisfaction.

By the 1880's, with but one exception, no suburban town ever again seriously considered annexation.[9] The segregation of the metropolitan population brought about by the interaction of the expansion of street railway transportation and the suburban building process had by the mid-1880's given a permanent set to political life. In the face of the continually expanding size of the metropolis, by contrast to the continual waves of poor immigrants that flooded the central city and destroyed its old residential neighborhoods, the new suburbs offered ever new areas of homogeneous middle class settlement. Here, most immigrants spoke English, most were Americanized, and here the evenness of income lessened the scope of political conflict. It was already apparent in the 1880's that to join Boston was to assume all the burdens and conflicts of a modern industrial metropolis. To remain

[8] Josiah Quincy, Sr., *Annexation of Roxbury and Boston. Remonstrance of Bostonians Against the Measure* (Boston, 1865); *Considerations Respectfully Submitted to the Citizens of Boston and Charlestown on the Proposed Annexation of the Two Cities* (Boston, 1854); Arthur W. Austin, *Address at the Dedication of the Town-House at Jamaica Plain, West Roxbury* (Boston, 1860); Rufus Choate, *Speech on Application of Samuel D. Bradford and Others to Set Off Wards 6, 7, & 8 of the City of Roxbury as a Separate Agricultural Town* (Boston, 1851); B. W. Harris, *The Annexation Question, Closing Argument for the Remonstrants Against the Annexation of Dorchester to Boston* . . . (Boston, 1869); Roxbury Committee Opposed to the Annexation to Boston, *A Word for Old Roxbury* (Roxbury, 1851), *Another Word for Old Roxbury, In Reply to the Report of the Committee in Favor of Annexation* (Boston, 1852); Alfred D. Chandler, *Annexation of Brookline to Boston* (Brookline, 1880), pp. 15, 18.

[9] Review of the whole late nineteenth and early twentieth century metropolitan government movement, a movement that was always alive but never in danger of being achieved: Joseph H. Beale, "The Metropolitan District," *Fifty Years of Boston* (Elisabeth M. Herlihy ed., Boston, 1932), pp. 116–127. Complete bibliography of the metropolitan and annexation pamphlet literature: Katherine McNamara, *The Boston Metropolitan District* (Cambridge, 1946).

apart was to escape, at least for a time, some of these problems. In the face of this choice the metropolitan middle class abandoned their central city.

Very soon the middle class began to reap the harvest of its action. Already by 1900 Boston was something to be feared and controlled. Many of its powers of self-government had been taken from it by the state or voluntarily abandoned by tax-conscious voters to put a check on demands for public improvements.[10] Beyond Boston the special suburban form of popularly managed local government continued to flourish. In suburbs of substantial income and limited class structure, high standards of education and public service were often achieved. Each town, however, now managed its affairs as best it could surrounded by forces largely beyond its control. New transportation, new housing, new industries, new people, the great flow and vigor of the metropolis, lay beyond the knowledge and competence of these individual agencies. In the years to come World Wars and depressions would unleash antidemocratic forces that threatened the foundations of the society: its democratic institutions, its property, its ethnic harmony, the chance of each citizen to prosper through capitalist competition. Confronting these challenges stood a metropolitan society physically divided by classes, politically divided by about forty parochial institutions. So divided, the society denied itself the opportunity to end, through common action against common problems, the isolation of its citizens and the fear they held toward each other. So divided, the metropolis was helpless to solve its own problems.

During the years 1870 to 1900 industrial capitalism was, comparatively, a new thing, and a mass suburban metropolis like Boston had never existed before anywhere in the world. To rely on individual capitalists, to expect that each man building for himself would build a good environment for a democratic society was perhaps a reasonable error to have made. Today, some of the problems confronting the streetcar city have been solved or passed by. Except for the American Negro, immigration conditions are over. The automobile allows a less rigid class arrangement and less dense housing than was possible under streetcar transportation. Zoning, large-scale subdivision planning, and new financial institutions have made suburban building somewhat more orderly, and have opened homeownership to a greater

[10] Loss of Boston's home rule: Henry Parkman, Jr., "The City and the State, 1880–1930," *Fifty Years of Boston*, pp. 128–147.

proportion of the society. Most important of all, the great twentieth century national reforms of progressive taxation and labor, factory, and welfare legislation have allowed more widespread participation in the profits of industrialism.

Despite these changes the two great problems first met in the streetcar city remain unsolved. Even by popular standards one enormous segment of the population still lives in an unsatisfactory physical environment. More serious, because it is a condition which affects all others, the growing metropolitan society as a whole remains shut up in an ever larger number of specialized social and political units, its citizens isolated from one another, its society needlessly uncontrolled because of the weakness of its agents.

LOCATION OF METROPOLITAN POPULATION, 1850 AND 1900*

Location	1850 Inhabitants	Percent	1900 Inhabitants	Percent
Living in the pedestrian city, two-mile radius: Boston, Roxbury, Cambridge, and Charlestown	187,676	66.6	504,553	44.2
Living in the peripheral towns of the early railroad and omnibus era. Two- to three-mile radius: Brookline, Chelsea, Dorchester, and Somerville	20,726	7.3	195,349	17.1
Subtotal. Pre-streetcar metropolis, three-mile radius	208,402	73.9	699,902	61.3
Living in the new suburbs, railroad and streetcar commuters. Three- to ten-mile radius: Quincy to Lynn	73,664	26.1	441,642	38.7
Total, ten-mile metropolis	282,066	100.0	1,141,544	100.0

* Due to the irregularities of town boundaries this table shows approximate shifts in population only. Especially the growth of the peripheral towns is overstated since all these towns but Chelsea had boundaries that stretched from two to five miles from Boston's City Hall.

Source: J. D. B. DeBow, *Seventh Census* (Washington, 1853), pp. 50–52; U.S. Census Office, *Twelfth Census* (Washington, 1901), I, 198–201.

14

Beyond the Melting Pot

by NATHAN GLAZER AND DANIEL PATRICK MOYNIHAN

Ethnicity is more than an influence on events; it is commonly the source of events.

Just as the major concepts of the progressive historians of a generation ago, such as Frederick Jackson Turner, Charles A. Beard, and Vernon L. Parrington, have been subject to reevaluation during recent years, heretofore widely accepted notions with regard to the evolution of urban America have also been subject to reappraisal. In 1963 the Joint Center for Urban Studies, a cooperative venture of the Massachusetts Institute of Technology and Harvard University, published *Beyond the Melting Pot* by Nathan Glazer and Daniel Patrick Moynihan. This book consisted of an examination of the Negroes, Puerto Ricans, Jews, Italians, and Irish and the role of their ethnicity in the complex life of New York City. The authors concluded that "the notion that the intense and unprecedented mixture of ethnic and religious groups in American life was soon to blend into a homogeneous end product has outlived its usefulness, and also its credibility. . . . The point about the melting pot is that it did not happen."

Nathan Glazer was born in New York City in 1923 and educated at the College of the City of New York, the University of Pennsylvania, and Columbia. Formerly a professor of sociology at the University of California (Berkeley) and previously an editor and member of the faculties of Smith, Bennington, and the University of Chicago, he is now on the Harvard faculty. He is the author of a number of books, including *American Judaism* and *The Social Basis of American Communism*. He is also a co-author, with David Riesman, of *The Lonely Crowd*.

Daniel Patrick Moynihan was born in Tulsa, Oklahoma, in 1927. He studied at City College, New York, Tufts, and the Fletcher School of Law and Diplomacy. Dr. Moynihan has combined a career in government, both federal and state, with an active interest in politics. Since 1966 he has served as director of the Joint Center of Urban Studies of the Massachusetts Institute of Technology and Harvard University. In 1965 as Assistant Secretary of Labor he prepared a report on the Negro family which has had great influence on thinking. In December, 1968, President-elect Nixon appointed Dr. Moynihan principal staff officer in the White House of the Cabinet-level Council on Urban Affairs. He has recently been named Counselor to the President.

The following selections from *Beyond the Melting Pot* which Dr. Moynihan co-authored with Nathan Glazer were copyright © 1963 by the Massachusetts Institute of Technology and the President and Fellows of Harvard College. They are reprinted here by permission of the publishers.

The idea of the melting pot is as old as the Republic. "I could point out to you a family," wrote the naturalized New Yorker, M-G. Jean de Crèvecoeur, in 1782, "whose grandfather was an Englishman, whose wife was Dutch, whose son married a French woman, and whose present four sons have now four wives of different nations. *He* is an American, who leaving behind him all his ancient prejudices and manners, receives new ones from the new mode of life he has embraced . . . Here individuals of all nations are melted into a new race of men. . . ." [1] It was an idea close to the heart of the American self-image. But as a century passed, and the number of individuals and nations involved grew, the confidence that they could be fused together waned, and so also the conviction that it would be a good thing if they were to be. In 1882 the Chinese were excluded, and the first general immigration law was enacted. In a steady succession thereafter, new and more selective barriers were raised until, by the National Origins Act of 1924, the nation formally adopted the policy of using immigration to reinforce, rather than further to dilute, the racial stock of the early America.

This latter process was well underway, had become in ways inexorable, when Israel Zangwill's play *The Melting Pot* was first performed in 1908. The play (quite a bad one) was an instant success. It ran for months on Broadway; its title was seized upon as a concise evocation of a profoundly significant American fact.

[1] J. Hector St. John Crèvecoeur (Michel-Guillaume Jean de Crèvecoeur), *Letters from an American Farmer*, New York: Fox, Duffield & Co., 1904, pp. 54–55.

Behold David Quixano, the Russian Jewish immigrant—a "pogrom orphan"—escaped to New York City, exulting in the glory of his new country:

> . . . America is God's Crucible, the great Melting Pot where all the races of Europe are melting and reforming! Here you stand, good folk, think I, when I see them at Ellis Island, here you stand in your fifty groups with your fifty languages and histories, and your fifty blood hatreds and rivalries, but you won't be long like that brothers, for these are the fires of God you've come to—these are the fires of God. A fig for your feuds and vendettas! German and Frenchman, Irishman and Englishman, Jews and Russians—into the Crucible with you all! God is making the American.
>
> . . . .
>
> . . . The real American has not yet arrived. He is only in the Crucible, I tell you—he will be the fusion of all the races, the coming superman.[2]

Yet looking back, it is possible to speculate that the response to *The Melting Pot* was as much one of relief as of affirmation: more a matter of reassurance that what had already taken place would turn out all right, rather than encouragement to carry on in the same direction.

Zangwill's hero throws himself into the amalgam process with the utmost energy; by curtainfall he has written his American symphony and won his Muscovite aristocrat: almost all concerned have been reconciled to the homogeneous future. Yet the play seems but little involved with American reality. It is a drama about Jewish separatism and Russian anti-Semitism, with a German concertmaster and an Irish maid thrown in for comic relief. Both protagonists are New Model Europeans of the time. Free thinkers and revolutionaries, it was doubtless in the power of such to merge. But neither of these doctrines was dominant among the ethnic groups of New York City in the 1900's, and in significant ways this became less so as time passed. Individuals, in very considerable numbers to be sure, broke out of their mold, but the groups remained. The experience of Zangwill's hero and heroine was *not* general. The point about the melting pot is that it did not happen.

Significantly, Zangwill was himself much involved in one of the more significant deterrents to the melting pot process. He was a

2 Israel Zangwill, *The Melting Pot,* New York: Macmillan, 1909, pp. 37–38.

Zionist. He gave more and more of his energy to this cause as time passed, and retreated from his earlier position on racial and religious mixture. Only eight years after the opening of *The Melting Pot* he was writing "It was vain for Paul to declare that there should be neither Jew nor Greek. Nature will return even if driven out with a pitchfork, still more if driven out with a dogma." [3]

We may argue whether it was "nature" that returned to frustrate continually the imminent creation of a single American nationality. The fact is that in every generation, throughout the history of the American republic, the merging of the varying streams of population differentiated from one another by origin, religion, outlook has seemed to lie just ahead—a generation, perhaps, in the future. This continual deferral of the final smelting of the different ingredients (or at least the different white ingredients) into a seamless national web as is to be found in the major national states of Europe suggests that we must search for some systematic and general causes for this American pattern of subnationalities; that it is not the temporary upsetting inflow of new and unassimilated immigrants that creates a pattern of ethnic groups within the nation, but rather some central tendency in the national ethos which structures people, whether those coming in afresh or the descendants of those who have been here for generations, into groups of different status and character.

It is striking that in 1963, almost forty years after mass immigration from Europe to this country ended, the ethnic pattern is still so strong in New York City. It is true we can point to specific causes that have served to maintain the pattern. But we know that it was not created by the great new migrations of Southern Negroes and Puerto Ricans into the city; nor by the "new" immigration, which added the great communities of East European Jews and Italians to the city; it was not even created by the great migration of Irish and Germans in the 1840's. Even in the 1830's, while the migration from Europe was still mild, and still consisted for the most part of English-speaking groups, one still finds in the politics of New York State, and of the city, the strong impress of group differentiation. In a fascinating study of the politics of the Jacksonian period in New York State, Lee Benson concludes: "At least since the 1820's, when manhood suffrage became widespread, ethnic and religious differences have tended to

---

[3] Joseph Leftwich, *Israel Zangwill*, New York: Thomas Yoseloff, 1957, p. 255.

be *relatively* the most widespread sources of political differences." [4]

There were ways of making distinctions among Welshmen and Englishmen, Yorkers and New Englanders, long before people speaking strange tongues and practicing strange religions came upon the scene. The group-forming characteristics of American social life—more concretely, the general expectation among those of new and old groups that group membership is significant and formative for opinion and behavior—are as old as the city. The tendency is fixed deep in American life generally; the specific pattern of ethnic differentiation, however, in every generation is created by specific events.

We can distinguish four major events or processes that have structured this pattern in New York during the past generation and whose effects will remain to maintain this pattern for some time to come—to be replaced by others we can scarcely now discern. These four formative events are the following:

First, the shaping of the Jewish community under the impact of the Nazi persecution of the Jews in Europe and the establishment of the state of Israel; second, the parallel, if less marked, shaping of a Catholic community by the reemergence of the Catholic school controversy; third, the migration of Southern Negroes to New York following World War I and continuing through the fifties; fourth, the influx of Puerto Ricans during the fifteen years following World War II.

THE JEWS

Developments within the Jewish community have had the most immediate significance. A fourth of the city is Jewish; very much more than a fourth of its wealth, energy, talent, and style is derived from the Jews. Over the past thirty years this community has undergone profound emotional experiences, centered almost entirely on the fact of Jewishness, has been measurably strengthened by immigration, and has become involved in vast Zionist enterprises, the rationale of which is exclusively Jewish. There are two aspects of these developments as they affect melting pot tendencies, one negative, the other positive.

The negative aspect has prevented a change that might otherwise have occurred. Prior to the 1930's Jews contributed significantly to the ethnic pattern of New York politics by virtue of their radicalism.

---

[4] Lee Benson, *The Concept of Jacksonian Democracy*, Princeton, N.J.: Princeton University Press, 1961, p. 165.

This kept them apart from the Catholic establishment in the Democratic party and the Protestant regime within the Republican party but did give them a distinct role of their own. At the time of *The Melting Pot* there were, to be sure, a great many Democratic and Republican Jewish merchants and businessmen. Most East Side Jews probably voted the Tammany ticket. But indigenous Jewish politics, the politics of the Jewish Daily Forward, of the Workmen's Circle, and the needle-trades unions were predominantly socialist. The Russian Revolution, in which Russian Jews played a prominent role, had a strong attraction for a small but important number of their kinsmen in New York. It would appear, for example, that during the 1930's most Communist party members in New York City were Jewish.[5] It must be stressed that the vast majority of New York Jews had nothing whatever to do with Communism. Some of the strongest centers of anti-Communist activity were and are to be found within the New York Jewish community. Nonetheless there was an ethnic cast to this form of political radicalism in New York, as there had been to the earlier Socialist movement.

Both Socialism and Communism are now considerably diminished and both have lost almost entirely any ethnic base. But just at the moment when the last distinctly Jewish political activity might have disappeared, a transcendent Jewish political interest was created by the ghastly persecutions of the Nazis, the vast dislocations of World War II, and the establishment of the State of Israel. These were matters that no Jew or Christian could ignore. They were equally matters about which little could be done except through politics. From the beginnings of the Zionist movement a certain number of New York Jews have been involved on that account with the high politics of the nation. Since the mid-1930's, however, this involvement has reached deeper and deeper into the New York Jewish community. They are the one group in the city (apart from the white Protestant financial establishment) of which it may fairly be said that among the leadership echelons there is a lively, active, and effective interest in who will be the next U.S. Secretary of State but one . . . or two, or three.

In a positive sense, events of the Nazi era and its aftermath have produced an intense group consciousness among New York Jews that binds together persons of widely disparate situations and beliefs. A

[5] See Nathan Glazer, *The Social Basis of American Communism*, New York: Harcourt, Brace & World, 1961, Chap. IV.

pronounced religious revival has occurred. Among those without formal religious ties there is a heightened sense of the defensive importance of organized Jewish activity. Among intellectuals, the feeling of Jewishness is never far from the surface.

Now, as in the past, the Jewish community in New York is the one most actively committed to the principles of racial integration and group tolerance. But open housing is something different from the melting pot. There is no reason to think that any considerable portion of the Jewish community of New York ever subscribed to Israel Zangwill's vision of a nonreligious, intermarried, homogeneous population, but it surely does not do so today. To the contrary, much of the visible activity of the community is aimed in directions that will intensify Jewish identity: Jewish elementary and secondary schools, Jewish colleges and universities, Jewish periodicals, Jewish investments in Israel, and the like. In the meantime, Jewish politicians make more (or at least not less) of the "Jewish" vote.

This is not to say the Jewish community of New York has been *created* or *maintained* by these events of the thirties or forties: that would be too narrow a view of Jewish history, and would ignore the group-making characteristics of American civilization. But the Jewish community was *shaped* by these events. Moving rapidly from working-class to middle-class occupations and styles of life, many alternative courses of development were possible. Within the frame set by these large social movements, the historical drama shaped a community intensely conscious of its Jewishness. Religion plays in many ways the smallest part of the story of American Jews. In New York City in particular the religious definition of the group explains least. Here the formal religious groups are weakest, the degree of affiliation to synagogues and temples smallest. In a city with 2,000,000 Jews, Jews need make no excuses to explain Jewishness and Jewish interests. On the one hand, there is the social and economic structure of the community; on the other, ideologies and emotions molded by the specific history of recent decades. Together they have shaped a community that itself shapes New York and will for generations to come.[6]

THE CATHOLICS

Outwardly, events since World War I have brought Catholics,

[6] For the complex interplay of religious, ideological, and socioeconomic factors within the American Jewish community, see *American Judaism* by Nathan Glazer, Chicago: University of Chicago Press, 1957.

notably the Irish Catholics, ever closer to the centers of power and doctrine in American life. But following a pattern common in human affairs, the process of closing the gap has heightened resentment, among some at all events, that a gap should exist. Here, as in much else concerning this general subject, it is hardly possible to isolate New York events from those of the nation generally, but because New York tends to be the center of Catholic thinking and publishing, the distinction is not crucial. The great division between the Catholic Church and the leftist and liberal groups in the city during the period from the Spanish Civil War to the era of McCarthy has been narrowed, with most elements of city politics converging on center positions. However issues of church-state relations have become considerably more difficult, and the issue of government aid to Catholic schools has become acute.

Controversy over church-state relations is nothing new to the American Catholic Church. What is new, however, and what is increasingly avowed, is the extent to which the current controversy derives from Catholic-Jewish disagreements rather than from traditional Catholic-Protestant differences. Relations between the two latter groups have steadily improved: to the point that after three centuries of separation Catholics in the 1960's began increasingly to talk of the prospects of reestablishing Christian unity. In general (there are, of course, many individual exceptions) the dominant view within Protestant and Catholic circles is that the United States is and ought to be a Christian commonwealth, to the point at very least of proclaiming "In God We Trust" on the currency and celebrating Christmas in the public schools. However, as this *rapprochement* has proceeded, within the Jewish community a contrary view has arisen which asserts that the separation of church and state ought to be even more complete than it has been, and that the "Post-Protestant era" means Post-Christian as well, insofar as government relations with religion are concerned.

The most dramatic episode of this development was the decision of the United States Supreme Court on June 25, 1962, that the recitation of an official prayer in the New York school system was unconstitutional. The case was brought by five parents of children in the public schools of the New York City suburb of New Hyde Park. Two of the parents were Jewish, one a member of the Ethical Culture Society, one a Unitarian, and one a nonbeliever. Before it concluded, however, the principal protagonists of the Catholic-Jewish controversy in New York City were involved. The attorney for the Archdiocese of

New York, for example, argued in the Supreme Court for a group of parents who supported the prayer. The response to the decision could hardly have been more diametrical. Cardinal Spellman declared, "I am shocked and frightened. . . ." The New York Board of Rabbis, on the other hand, hailed the decision: "The recitation of prayers in the public schools, which is tantamount to the teaching of prayer, is not in conformity with the spirit of the American concept of the separation of church and state. All the religious groups in this country will best advance their respective faiths by adherence to this principle." The American Jewish Committee, the American Jewish Congress, and the Anti-Defamation League of B'nai B'rith strongly supported the Court. Only among the Orthodox was there mild disagreement with the Supreme Court decision.

Although the argument could certainly be made that the American Catholic Church ought to be the first to object to the spectacle of civil servants composing government prayers, and although many Catholic commentators noted that the decision strengthened the case for private Church-sponsored schools, the general Catholic reaction was most hostile. The Jesuit publication *America,* in an editorial "To our Jewish Friends," declared that Jewish efforts to assert an ever more strict separation of church and state were painting the Jewish community into a corner, where it would be isolated from the rest of Americans.

Significantly, Protestant reaction to the decision was mixed. The Brooklyn *Tablet* took the cue, stating that the crucial question raised by the decision was "What are the Protestants going to do about it? For, although this is a national problem, it is particularly a Protestant problem, given the large Protestant enrollment in the public schools. Catholics have been fighting long—and sometimes alone—against the Church-State extremists. May we count on Protestants to supply more leadership in this case? If so, we pledge our support to join efforts against the common enemy: secularism." [7]

The subject of aid to Catholic schools is only one aspect of the more general issue of church-state relations, and here again the ethnic composition of New York City tends to produce the same alignment of opposing groups. There are elements within the Jewish community, again the Orthodox, that favor public assistance for religious schools, but the dominant view is opposed. In 1961 the New York Republican party at the state level made a tentative move toward the Catholic

---

[7] Quoted in the *New York Herald Tribune,* July 2, 1962.

position by proposing a Constitutional amendment that would have permitted state construction loans to private institutions of higher learning, sectarian as well as secular. Opposition from Jewish (as well as some Protestant) groups was pronounced, and the measure was beaten at the polls.

The situation developing in this area could soberly be termed dangerous. An element of interfaith competition has entered the controversy. As the costs of education mount, it becomes increasingly difficult to maintain the quality of the education provided by private schools deprived of public assistance. It is not uncommon to hear it stated in Catholic circles that the results of national scholarship competitions already point to the weakness of Catholic education in fields such as the physical sciences. The specter is raised that a parochial education will involve sacrifice for the students as well as for their parents.

There is understandably much resentment within Catholic educational circles at the relative crudity of most such observations. At the same time this resentment is often accompanied by an unmistakable withdrawal. In a thoughtful address calling for more meticulous assessment of the qualities of Catholic education, Bishop McEntegart of the Diocese of Brooklyn went on to state that "Judgment on the effectiveness of an educational system should be something more profound and more subtle than counting heads of so-called intellectuals who happen to be named in Who's Who or the 'Social Register.' " [8]

Whether the course of the controversy will lead Catholics further into separatist views of this kind is not clear. But it is abundantly evident that so long as Catholics maintain a separate education system and the rest of the community refuses to help support it by tax funds or tax relief, a basic divisive issue will exist. This will be an ethnic issue in measure that the Catholic community continues to include

---

[8] *The Tablet*, February 17, 1962. In an address given in Washington on April 30, 1962, Very Reverend William F. Kelley, S.J., President of Marquette University, implicitly proposed a secondary role for Catholic education. As reported in *The Washington Post*, Father Kelley suggested that Catholic schools leave "research and the exploration for new knowledge" to "research institutes" like Hopkins, Harvard, and M.I.T., it being "perfectly respectable and professionally honorable" to concentrate on the transmission of the knowledge of the past:

It is an entirely sound plan to be trailing along at a respectable distance with a trained and educated citizenry competent to appreciate and consume the discovery of the successful investigator. Let us remember that if there are no followers, there can be no leader.

the bulk of the Irish, Italian, and Polish population in the city, at least the bulk of those affiliated with organizations taking a position on the issue. If, as may very well happen, the Catholics abandon elementary and even secondary education to concentrate on their colleges and universities, the larger issue of church-state relations will no doubt subside.

But it is not the single issue of school aid, no matter how important and long-lived it is, that alone shapes the polarization between the Jewish and the emerging Catholic community. There have been other issues in the past—for example, the struggle over the legitimacy of city hospitals giving advice on birth control, which put Jews and liberal Protestants on one side and Catholics on the other. There are the recurrent disputes over government censorship of books and movies and magazines that have become freer and freer in their handling of sex and sexual perversion. This again ranges Jewish and Protestant supporters of the widest possible freedom of speech against Catholics who are more anxious about the impact of such material on young people and family life. One can see emerging such issues as the rigid state laws on divorce and abortion.[9]

Many of these issues involve Catholic *religious* doctrine. But there exists here a situation that is broader than a conflict over doctrines and the degree to which government should recognize them. What is involved is the emergence of two subcultures, two value systems, shaped and defined certainly in part by religious practice and experience and organization but by now supported by the existence of two communities. If the bishops and the rabbis were to disappear tomorrow, the subcultures and subcommunities would remain. One is secular in its attitudes, liberal in its outlook on sexual life and divorce, positive about science and social science. The other is religious in its outlook, resists the growing liberalization in sexual mores and its reflection in cultural and family life, feels strongly the tension between moral values and modern science and technology. The conflict may be seen in many ways—not least in the fact that the new disciplines such as psychoanalysis, particularly in New York, are so largely staffed by Jews.

Thus a Jewish ethos and a Catholic ethos emerge: they are more strongly affected by a specific religious doctrine in the Catholic case than in the Jewish, but neither is purely the expression of the spirit

9 See *A Tale of Ten Cities,* Albert Vorspan and Eugene Lipman, New York: *Union of American Hebrew Congregations,* 1962, pp. 175 ff.

of a religion. Each is the result of the interplay of religion, ethnic group, American setting, and specific issues. The important fact is that the differences in values and attitudes between the two groups do not, in general, become smaller with time. On the contrary: there is probably a wider gap between Jews and Catholics in New York today than in the days of Al Smith.[10]

NEGROES AND PUERTO RICANS

A close examination of Catholic-Jewish relations will reveal some of the tendency of ethnic relations in New York to be a form of class relations as well. However, the tendency is unmistakably clear with regard to the Negroes and Puerto Ricans. Some 22 per cent of the population of the city is now Negro or Puerto Rican, and the proportion will increase. (Thirty-six per cent of the births in 1961 were Negro or Puerto Rican.) To a degree that cannot fail to startle anyone who encounters the reality for the first time, the overwhelming portion of both groups constitutes a submerged, exploited, and very possibly permanent proletariat.

New York is properly regarded as the wealthiest city in the nation. Its more affluent suburbs enjoy some of the highest standards of living on earth. In the city itself white-collar wages are high, and skilled labor through aggressive trade union activity has obtained almost unprecedented standards. Bricklayers earn $5.35 an hour, plus 52c for pension, vacation, and insurance benefits. Electricians have a nominal twenty-five hour week and a base pay of $4.96 an hour plus fringe benefits.[11] But amidst such plenty, unbelievable squalor persists: the line of demarcation is a color line in the case of Negroes, a less definite but equally real ethnic line in the case of Puerto Ricans.

The relationship between the rise of the Negro-Puerto Rican labor supply and the decline of industrial wages is unmistakable. In 1950 there were 246,000 Puerto Ricans in the city. By 1960 this number had increased by two and one-half times to 613,000, or 8 per cent. In 1950 the average hourly earnings of manufacturing production

[10] Gerhard Lenski, *The Religious Factor*, New York: Doubleday, 1961, gives a great deal of evidence to the effect that value differences between Catholics and white Protestants and Jews (the latter two often linked, but not always) in Detroit have increased as the groups move from working-class and immigrant generation to middle-class and later generations. Parochial schooling plays some part in these differences. For an interesting evocation of the milieu in which Jewish-Catholic political cooperation flourished, see *Al Smith*, by Oscar Handlin, Boston: Little, Brown, 1958.

[11] U.S. Bureau of Labor Statistics data for October, 1962.

workers in New York City ranked tenth in the nation. By 1960 they ranked thirtieth. In the same period comparable wages in Birmingham, Alabama, rose from thirty-third to tenth. In 1959 median family income for Puerto Ricans was $3,811 as against $6,091 for all the city's families (and $8,052 for suburbs of Westchester). In 1962 average weekly earnings of manufacturing production workers were 19 per cent higher in Birmingham than in New York City, 15 per cent higher in New Orleans, and almost 10 per cent higher in the nation as a whole.

These economic conditions vastly reinforce the ethnic distinctions that serve to separate the Negro community and the Puerto Rican community from the rest of the city. The Negro separation is strengthened by the fact that the colored community is on the whole Protestant, and much of its leadership comes from Protestant clergy. Thus the Negroes provide the missing element of the Protestant-Catholic-Jew triad.

Housing segregation, otherwise an intolerable offense to the persons affected, serves nonetheless to ensure the Negroes a share of seats on the City Council and in the State Legislature and Congress. This power, as well as their voting power generally, has brought Negro political leaders to positions of considerable prominence. Following the 1961 mayoralty election, Mayor Wagner appointed the talented Harlem leader, J. Raymond Jones, as a political secretary through whom he would deal with all the Democratic party organizations of the city. Puerto Ricans have only begun to make their influence felt, but they are clearly on the way to doing so.

Their fate gives them an interest in the same issues: the housing of the poor in a city of perpetual housing shortage; the raising of the wages of the poorly paid service semiskilled occupations in which most of them work; the development of new approaches to raising motivation and capacity by means of education and training in the depressed areas of the city. They live adjacent to each other in vast neighborhoods. And they cooperate on many specific issues—for example, in fighting urban renewal programs that would displace them. But there are deeply felt differences between them. The more Americanized group is also more deeply marked by color. The furtive hope of the new group that it may move ahead as other immigrants have without the barrier of color, and the powerful links of language and culture that mark off the Puerto Ricans, suggest that, despite the fact that the two groups increasingly comprise the proletariat of the city, their history will be distinct.

Thus the cast of major characters for the next decades is complete: the Jews; the Catholics, subdivided at least into Irish and Italian components; the Negroes; the Puerto Ricans; and, of course, the white Anglo-Saxon Protestants. These latter, ranging from the Rockefeller brothers to reform district leaders in the Democratic party are, man for man, amongst the most influential and powerful persons in the city, and will continue to play a conspicuous and creative role in almost every aspect of the life of the metropolis. . . .

THE FUTURE

We have tried to show how deeply the pattern of ethnicity is impressed on the life of the city. Ethnicity is more than an influence on events; it is commonly the source of events. Social and political institutions do not merely respond to ethnic interests; a great number of institutions exist for the specific purpose of serving ethnic interests. This in turn tends to perpetuate them. In many ways, the atmosphere of New York City is hospitable to ethnic groupings: it recognizes them, and rewards them, and to that extent encourages them.

This is not to say that no individual group will disappear. This, on the contrary, is a recurring phenomenon. The disappearance of the Germans is a particularly revealing case.

In terms of size or the achievements of its members, the Germans ought certainly to be included among the principal ethnic groups of the city. If never quite as numerous as the Irish, they were indisputably the second largest group in the late nineteenth century, accounting for perhaps a third of the population and enjoying the highest reputation. But today, while German influence is to be seen in virtually every aspect of the city's life, the Germans *as a group* are vanished. No appeals are made to the German vote, there are no German politicians in the sense that there are Irish or Italian politicians, there are in fact few Germans in political life and, generally speaking, no German component in the structure of the ethnic interests of the city.

The logical explanation of this development, in terms of the presumed course of American social evolution, is simply that the Germans have been "assimilated" by the Anglo-Saxon center. To some extent this has happened. The German immigrants of the nineteenth century were certainly much closer to the old Americans than were the Irish who arrived in the same period. Many were Protestants, many were skilled workers or even members of the professions, and their level of education in general was high. Despite the language difference, they did not seem nearly so alien to the New York mercantile establishment as did the Irish. At the time of their arrival German sympathies were high in New York. (George Templeton Strong was violent in his support of doughty Prussia in its struggle with imperial, tyrranical France.) All of this greatly facilitated German assimilation.

In any event, there were obstacles to the Germans' becoming a distinct ethnic bloc. Each of the five groups we have discussed arrived with a high degree of homogeneity: in matters of education, skills, and religion the members of the group were for the most part alike. This homogeneity, as we have tried to show, invested ethnicity with meaning and importance that it would not otherwise have had. But this was not so with the Germans, who were split between Catholics and Protestants, liberals and conservatives, craftsmen and businessmen and laborers. They reflected, as it were, an entire modern society, not simply an element of one. The only things all had in common were the outward manifestations of German culture: language for a generation or two, and after that a fondness for certain types of food and drink and a consciousness of the German fatherland. This was a powerful enough bond and would very likely be visible today, except for the impact of the World Wars. The Germanophobia of America during the First World War is, of course, notorious. It had limits in New York where, for instance, German was *not* driven from the public school curriculum, but the attraction of things German was marred. This period was followed, in hardly more than a decade, by the Nazi era, during which German fascism made its appearance in Jewish New York, with what results one can imagine. The German American Bund was never a major force in the city, but it did exist. The revulsion against Nazism extended indiscriminately to things German. Thereafter, German Americans, as shocked by the Nazis as any, were disinclined to make overmuch of their national origins.

Even so, it is not clear that consciousness of German nationality has entirely ceased to exist among German-Americans in the city, or elsewhere. There is evidence that for many it has simply been submerged. In New York City, which ought logically to be producing a series of Italian and Jewish mayors, the political phenomenon of the postwar period has been Robert F. Wagner.

It is even possible that the future will see a certain resurgence of German identity in New York, although we expect it will be mild.

The enemy of two world wars has become an increasingly powerful and important ally in the Cold War. Berlin has become a symbol of resistance to totalitarianism; Germany has become an integral part of the New Europe. Significantly, the German Americans of the city have recently begun an annual Steuben Day Parade, adding for the politicians of the city yet another command performance at an ethnic outing.

Despite this mild German resurgence, it is a good general rule that except where color is involved as well the specifically *national* aspect of most ethnic groups rarely survives the third generation in any significant terms. The intermarriage which de Crèvecoeur described continues apace, so that even the strongest national traditions are steadily diluted. The groups do not disappear, however, because of their *religious* aspect which serves as the basis of a subcommunity, and a subculture. Doctrines and practices are modified to some extent to conform to an American norm, but a distinctive set of values is nurtured in the social groupings defined by religious affiliation. This is quite contrary to early expectations. It appeared to de Crèvecoeur, for example, that religious as well as national identity was being melted into one by the process of mixed neighborhoods and marriage:

> . . . This mixed neighborhood will exhibit a strange religious medley, that will be neither pure Catholicism nor pure Calvinism. A very perceptible indifference even in the first generation, will become apparent; and it may happen that the daughter of the Catholic will marry the son of the seceder, and settle by themselves at a distance from their parents. What religious education will they give their children? A very imperfect one. If there happens to be in the neighborhood any place of worship, we will suppose a Quaker's meeting; rather than not shew their fine clothes, they will go to it, and some of them may attach themselves to that society. Others will remain in a perfect state of indifference; the children of these zealous parents will not be able to tell what their religious principles are, and their grandchildren still less.
>
> Thus all sects are mixed as well as all nations; thus religious indifference is imperceptibly disseminated from one end of the continent to the other; which is at present one of the strongest characteristics of the Americans.[12]

If this was the case in the late eighteenth century, it is no longer. Religious identities are strongly held by New Yorkers, and Americans

[12] de Crèvecoeur, *op. cit.,* pp. 65–66.

generally, and they are for the most part transmitted by blood line from the original immigrant group. A great deal of intermarriage occurs among nationality groups of the three great religious groups, of the kind Ruby Jo Kennedy described in New Haven, Connecticut under the general term of the Triple Melting Pot,[13] but this does not weaken religious identity. When marriages occur between different religions, often one is dominant, and the result among the children is not indifference, but an increase in the numbers of one of the groups.

Religion and race seem to define the major groups into which American society is evolving as the specifically national aspect of ethnicity declines. In our large American cities, four major groups emerge: Catholics, Jews, white Protestants, and Negroes, each making up the city in different proportions. This evolution is by no means complete. And yet we can discern that the next stage of the evolution of the immigrant groups will involve a Catholic group in which the distinctions between Irish, Italian, Polish, and German Catholic are steadily reduced by intermarriage; a Jewish group, in which the line between East European, German, and Near Eastern Jews is already weak; the Negro group; and a white Protestant group, which adds to its Anglo-Saxon and Dutch old-stock elements German and Scandinavian Protestants, as well as, more typically, the white Protestant immigrants to the city from the interior.

The white Protestants are a distinct ethnic group in New York, one that has probably passed its low point and will now begin to grow in numbers and probably also in influence. It has its special occupations, with the customary freemasonry. This involves the banks, corporation front offices, educational and philanthropic institutions, and the law offices who serve them. It has its own social world (epitomized by, but by no means confined to, the *Social Register*), its own churches, schools, voluntary organizations and all the varied institutions of a New York minority. These are accompanied by the characteristic styles in food, clothing, and drink, special family patterns, special psychological problems and ailments. For a long while political conservatism, as well as social aloofness, tended to keep the white Protestants out of the main stream of New York politics, much in the way that political radicalism tended to isolate the Jews in the early parts of the century. Theodore Roosevelt, when cautioned that none

---

[13] Ruby Jo Reeves Kennedy, "Single or Triple Melting Pot: Intermarriage in New Haven," *American Journal of Sociology*, Vol. 58, No. 1, July, 1952, pp. 55–66.

of his friends would touch New York politics, had a point in replying that it must follow that none of his friends were members of the governing classes.

There has been a resurgence of liberalism within the white Protestant group, in part based on its growth through vigorous young migrants from outside the city, who are conspicuous in the communications industry, law firms, and corporation offices of New York. These are the young people that supported Adlai Stevenson and helped lead and staff the Democratic reform movement. The influence of the white Protestant group on this city, it appears, must now grow as its numbers grow.

In this large array of the four major religio-racial groups, where do the Puerto Ricans stand? Ultimately perhaps they are to be absorbed into the Catholic group. But that is a long time away. The Puerto Ricans are separated from the Catholics as well as the Negroes by color and culture. One cannot even guess how this large element will ultimately relate itself to the other elements of the city; perhaps it will serve, in line with its own nature and genius, to soften the sharp lines that divide them.

Protestants will enjoy immunities in politics even in New York. When the Irish era came to an end in the Brooklyn Democratic party in 1961, Joseph T. Sharkey was succeeded by a troika (as it was called) of an Irish Catholic, a Jew, and a Negro Protestant. The last was a distinguished clergyman, who was at the same time head of the New York City Council of Protestant Churches. It would have been unlikely for a rabbi, unheard of for a priest, to hold such a position.

Religion and race define the next stage in the evolution of the American peoples. But the American nationality is still forming: its processes are mysterious, and the final form, if there is ever to be a final form, is as yet unknown.

15

The Fragmented Metropolis:
Los Angeles, 1850-1930

by ROBERT M. FOGELSON

. . . the unique dispersal of Los Angeles reflected not so much its chronology, geography, or technology as the exceptional character of its population.

A true canvas of the American city includes not only the town grown large, or the tenement, or the three-decker house, or a simple cleavage between the inner city and the dormitory suburb. There has also been—especially in Southern California, in the Southwest, and in Florida—the sprawling and dispersed city with floating mercantile and political cores and great decentralization of both business and domicile.

More than any other major city Los Angeles is characterized by the detached or semidetached single family dwelling. As James Q. Wilson has stressed, "A house was, as a Catholic might put it, the outward and visible sign of inward grace. There was no anonymity provided by apartment buildings or tenements or projects. . . . A strong, socially reinforced commitment to property was thus developed." *

Robert Fogelson in *The Fragmented Metropolis* seeks to show how Los Angeles developed this special pattern, in which there is an effort "to join the spirit of the good community with the substance of the great metropolis." Professor Fogelson argues that Los Angeles has largely failed in this quest—that the dispersion, the single-family subdivisions, the failure of electric railways, and the isolated enclaves of ethnic minorities brought on a bland middle-class way of life, much irresponsible privatism, little popular involvement in politics and social change, and nativism.

* James Q. Wilson, "A Guide to Reagan Country: The Political Culture of Southern California," *Commentary* (May, 1967), p. 39.

312

Though Fogelson is not always successful in wedding current planning concepts to his material and places too heavy a burden of responsibility on the failure of transit systems in Los Angeles, he has drawn on a wealth of historical, economic, architectural, and planning sources to write one of the few satisfactory treatments of urban sprawl. In addition, he gives a compelling account of how Los Angeles, with a number of disadvantages such as the lack of a natural harbor and easy sources of water, overcame the rivalry of a better-situated San Diego and the preeminence of San Francisco to become in our day the second largest metropolitan complex in America.

Professor Fogelson, who trained under Oscar Handlin at Harvard, has been the Samuel Stouffer Fellow at the Harvard-MIT Joint Center for Urban Studies and is now teaching American history at Columbia University. This chapter is reprinted with the permission of the Harvard University Press, copyright 1967 by the President and Fellows of Harvard College. Illustrations and graphs have been omitted.

THE URBAN LANDSCAPE

Urbanization had an overwhelming impact on the landscape of greater Los Angeles. Before 1885 the region was predominantly rural. Flocks of sheep foraged on the Santa Ana plain, and thousands of acres went uncultivated in western Los Angeles. Immense wheat fields covered the San Fernando Valley ranches, and corn stalks grew tall on the El Monte farms. Vineyards were planted symmetrically in eastern Los Angeles, and orchards were tended in clusters in the San Gabriel Valley.[1] These flourishing valleys and the nearby mountains overwhelmed small settlements such as Anaheim and Pasadena. Even in Los Angeles, then the section's first and the state's third city, more than 90 per cent of its thirty-six square miles were rustic.[2] Everywhere bountiful gardens relieved the severe earth, fragrant fruits diluted the pungent mesquite, and agriculture imposed its quiet on the region.

[1] Isaac W. Lord to Mrs. Nealy, March 17, 1876, Lord Letterbrook, p. 130, Lord Papers; Los Angeles *Journal,* November 2, 1879; Brewer, *Up and Down in California,* p. 13; Smith, *Adobe Days,* chap. ix; Robinson, *Ranchos Become Cities,* pp. 86–90, 182–184.

[2] "Map of the City of Los Angeles California by H. J. Stevenson, U.S. Dept. Surveyor, 1884," Department of Water and Power Files; Salvator, *Los Angeles in the Sunny Seventies,* p. 124; Thompson and West, *Los Angeles,* illustration facing p. 16.

Nowhere did the population, facilities, and businesses of the region's urban centers intrude much upon the sights, smells, and sounds of the agrarian environment.

Immigration and enterprise, of course, created a market for residential and commercial property after 1850; but the transformation of rural land into urban property was the responsibility of private enterprise not municipal authority. Corporate utilities provided service only when convinced that anticipated revenues justified initial expenditures; they made commitments cautiously even under favorable circumstances. Individual developers undertook improvements only when confident that current demand exceeded existing supply; thus their activities were limited to the minor booms of the early 1870's and 1880's.[3] For these reasons the transformed portion of Los Angeles did not extend more than two miles from the town's center before 1885.[4] And since many landholders found agriculture sufficiently profitable and conversion prohibitively expensive, subdivision proceeded sporadically and erratically even in central Los Angeles.

The separation of homes from stores and shops accompanied the expansion of Los Angeles. Unsuccessful Americans, unassimilated Chinese, and unadjusted Mexicans still rented rooms in dilapidated and overcrowded adobes and shacks amid rundown hotels, gambling dens, and houses of prostitution near the old plaza. But prosperous and respectable native Americans and European immigrants who refused to live there purchased lots and erected houses on outlying tracts in the southern and western flats and the northern and eastern hills.[5] At the same time many businessmen moved from central to southern Los Angeles. While retailers followed the residential subdivisions, wholesalers pressed towards the railroad station; while professionals concentrated in the Temple Street vicinity, craftsmen spread all over the south-central section. These enterprises extended over only a few blocks, but, dominating the town's economy, they formed its principal commercial center in 1885.[6]

3 Los Angeles *Herald,* December 10, 1877.

4 "Map of the City of Los Angeles California, 1884"; "Map of the City of Los Angeles California, 1876."

5 Los Angeles *Daily News,* March 8, 1869; Los Angeles *Herald,* December 28, 1873; Los Angeles *Star,* April 25, 1874; Newmark, *Sixty Years,* p. 112; Salvator, *Los Angeles in the Sunny Seventies,* p. 136; Woods, *Pacific Coast,* pp. 27–29; James J. Ayres, *Gold and Sunshine: Reminiscences of Early California* (Boston, 1922), pp. 225–226.

6 Jackson A. Graves, *My Seventy Years in Southern California 1857–1927*

Incipient industrialists who considered this district too congested and costly sought larger and cheaper parcels elsewhere. Some attempted to exploit local water power and obviate high-priced coal by constructing plants close to the Los Angeles River. Others followed their lead when the Southern Pacific routed its main line alongside the river. By 1885 a small but active manufacturing complex—made up of a gas plant, flour mills, rail yards, and slaughterhouses—had emerged there.[7] Land-use segregation did not encompass the agricultural (and thus the largest) portion of Los Angeles, however. Nor was it complete, extensive, and irreversible elsewhere. The poor and the minorities still lived in the old business center, the residential, commercial, and manufacturing areas were not yet far apart, and the inclinations of the town's entrepreneurs alone sanctioned this arrangement. From the perspective of the people of Los Angeles, however, land-use segregation was desirable and deserved encouragement.

The developers shaped the town's layout as well as its land-use. They favored the traditional American gridiron—an arrangement of perpendicularly intersecting streets—which simplified subdivision and, they believed, reduced expenses and facilitated marketing. "I have planned for straight lines and not for curved ones in the street alignments," a civil engineer reported to a San Gabriel Valley subdivider. "The advantages gained are economy of survey and platting and probably better sale for the property than if it were cut up on curves."[8] The developers divided the rest of the land into suburban lots, from 5,000 to 7,000 square feet in size and twice as deep as wide, which fronted on narrow thoroughfares and supplied space for modest houses surrounded by front lawns, small gardens, and rear yards. The developers covered the tracts with streets and lots, reserving little or no property for community purposes, and disposed of their holdings as rapidly as possible, permanently relinquishing responsibility for the subdivision's future.

The purchasers or contractors who designed the buildings faithfully reproduced the picturesque patterns then prevailing in the

(Los Angeles, 1927), pp. 105–115; George William Baist, *Baist's Real Estate Atlas of Surveys of Los Angeles* (Philadelphia, 1889), pp. 4–6.

[7] Los Angeles *Star*, July 16, 1870; Los Angeles *Herald*, February 4, 1877, Los Angeles *Evening Express*, July 26, 1880; Baist, *Real Estate Atlas* (1889), pp. 36–39, 51, 61, 64.

[8] William Hamilton Hall to J. de Barth Shorb, January 4, 1892, Shorb Papers. For a protest against the gridiron pattern, see Los Angeles *Herald*, April 24, 1890.

United States. Distinguished by wide verandas, wooden shingles, bay windows, and mansard roofs, their Victorian homes looked like country cottages fashionable in both the Pacific Northwest and northern California. Replete with Corinthian columns, iron façades, Renaissance cornices, and ornamental towers, their business blocks closely resembled commercial edifices familiar in Seattle and Sacramento alike.[9] While southern Californians boasted of their unique climate, history, and resources, nothing in the setting, structure, and materials of their architecture evoked these features—except, ironically, the deteriorating Mexican adobes. With its rustic landscape, limited dispersal, segregated land-use, gridiron layout, and picturesque aesthetic, Los Angeles differed little in appearance from the typical town of the late nineteenth-century American West.

After 1885 Los Angeles became increasingly urban. As a result of the prodigious growth of the population, the widespread demand for property, and the marked advance of industry, herds were moved out of the region, crops were harvested for the last time, and orchards were relentlessly destroyed. Henceforth the landscape of greater Los Angeles was dominated by homes, offices, stores, and factories; streets, sidewalks, and railways; and water mains, gas pipes, electric lines, and sewers. The cities covered the countryside; Anaheim spread over the southeastern plain, Pasadena extended to the Sierra Madre Mountains, and the amount of land subdivided in Los Angeles proper increased more than one hundredfold.[10] Even in the distant eastern San Gabriel and western San Fernando valleys, which were still cultivated, and the steep Hollywood and Baldwin Hills, which were yet

9 Carr, *Los Angeles,* pp. 136–137; Lord Letterbook, pp. 49–50, Lord Papers; Thompson and West, *Los Angeles,* illustrations facing pp. 38, 44, 60, 76. See also, Harold Kirker, *California's Architectural Frontier: Style and Tradition in the Nineteenth Century* (San Marino, 1960); Vincent J. Scully, Jr., "Romantic Rationalism and the Expression of Structure in Wood: Downing, Wheeler, Gardner and the 'Stick Style,'" *Art Bulletin,* 35: 121–142 (1953).

10 Wm. H. Babcock & Sons, *Report on the Economic and Engineering Feasibility of Regrading the Bunker Hill Area* (Los Angeles, 1931), plate 2; Baker, *Rapid Transit System for Los Angeles,* plate 2; Olmsted Brothers and Bartholomew and Associates, *Report to the Citizens Committee on Parks, Playgrounds and Beaches Los Angeles Region* (Los Angeles, 1931), plate 16; Metropolitan Surveys, *"Industrial Guide" and Street Index of Los Angeles and Its Environs* (Los Angeles, ca. 1935), Los Angeles Chamber of Commerce Files; Jackson A. Graves, *California Memories 1857–1927,* 2d ed. (Los Angeles, 1930), pp. 5–6; Regional Planning Commission County of Los Angeles, *Report of a Highway Traffic Survey in the County of Los Angeles* (Los Angeles, 1934), passim.

wasteland, the services and facilities requisite for development were available by 1930.

Although Los Angeles had to expand into a vast urban center—after all, two million new inhabitants and a billion dollars of additional business had to be provided with adequate transportation, water, utilities, property, and buildings—it did not have to emerge as the dispersed metropolis par excellence. Yet with far fewer people and much less manufacturing than metropolitan Chicago and Philadelphia, greater Los Angeles, as Table 1 reveals, encompassed many more square miles. Also, with slightly more persons and much less industry than metropolitan Detroit and Boston, it numbered far fewer residents per square mile. Moreover, whereas the population ratio of central city to outlying suburbs exceeded sixteen to one in Pittsburgh and reached twenty-three to one in St. Louis, it came to fewer than three to one in Los Angeles.[11] In 1930, therefore, the structure of greater Los Angeles differed radically from that of the typical American metropolis—a divergence not wholly attributable to the material progress of southern California.

TABLE 1. Area and Density of Selected Metropolitan Districts, 1930

Metropolitan district	Population (in thousands)	Area in sq. miles	Population per sq. mile	Population per sq. mile in central city	Population per sq. mile outside central city
New York	10,901	2,514	4,336	23,179	1,001
Chicago	4,365	1,119	3,890	16,723	1,077
Cleveland	1,195	310	3,852	12,725	1,230
Milwaukee	743	242	3,076	14,056	824
Philadelphia	2,847	994	2,865	15,242	1,035
Detroit	2,105	747	2,819	11,375	881
Boston	2,308	1,023	2,257	17,795	1,560
Minneapolis-St. Paul	832	525	1,584	8,384	231[a]
St. Louis	1,294	822	1,574	13,475	573[b]
Los Angeles	*2,319*	*1,474*	*1,572*	*2,812*	*1,045*
San Francisco-Oakland	1,290	828	1,563	15,105	509[c]
Pittsburgh	1,954	1,602	1,201	13,057	815

Source: U.S. Bureau of the Census, *Fifteenth Census of the United States: 1930. Metropolitan Districts* (Washington, 1932), pp. 35, 49, 57, 73, 115, 129, 131, 140, 159, 165, 171, 193, 203, 215.

[a] Excluding St. Paul.
[b] Excluding East St. Louis.
[c] Excluding Oakland.

[11] *Fifteenth Census: 1930. Metropolitan Districts*, pp. 10–12, 35, 39, 73, 115, 165, 171.

Los Angeles' chronology contributed to this incongruity. The metropolis grew slowly in the era of the horse car, rapidly during the period of the electric railway, and even faster in the age of the private automobile. But so did Detroit and Minneapolis which, as Table 1 indicates, were less extensively and less evenly dispersed. Los Angeles' geography also expedited dispersal. The southern and western plains extended to the ocean and the northern and eastern valleys to the mountains; so no natural barriers concentrated settlement. But, except for Lakes Michigan and Erie, respectively, greater Milwaukee and Cleveland were likewise unobstructed, and they too far exceeded Los Angeles in over-all and differential densities. Hence neither timing nor nature fully accounted for the physical uniqueness of the Los Angeles landscape.[12]

Changes in the operation, management, scope, and regulation of transportation and utilities also removed restraints on expansion in Los Angeles. The connection between electric railways and real estate subdivision and the subsequent monopolization of the street and interurban lines by Huntington and Harriman spurred the creation of an extensive radial transit network. Municipalization of the waterworks supplanted a private company, responsible to its stockholders and devoted to profits, with a public department, responsive to the community and committed to expansion. The highway authorities and Metropolitan Water District supplemented the corporations and the city by providing motor thoroughfares and domestic water to places off the railroads and outside Los Angeles. And both local and state commissions compelled the gas, electric, and telephone utilities to serve customers whenever they deposited funds to construct additions to the distributing systems.[13] These improvements were permissive not compulsory, however; they encouraged but did not compel subdivision.

Differences in kind among the developers fostered dispersal in

12 *Ibid.*, pp. 56–57, 114–115, 128–129, 130–131, 214–215. Although these figures are somewhat misleading because the central cities vary so much in territory, the description presented here, even adjusted for Los Angeles' vast corporate expanse, requires little change.

13 . . . It should be stressed, if only to correct a common misconception, that residential dispersal in Los Angeles was not due to the automobile. That pattern was fixed by the radial routes of the electric railways fully ten years before the widespread ownership of the motor car. The automobile certainly contributed to urban sprawl, but largely because it fit so well the existing pattern of residential dispersal and the prevailing notion of the good community.

Los Angeles too. There were still operators who relied upon persuasion instead of capital, amateurs who converted property in their spare time, and promoters who marketed small and cheap subdivisions. But now there were also investors such as Henry E. Huntington who possessed funds to undertake almost any project, professionals such as H. J. Whitley who made development their life's work, and entrepreneurs such as Robert C. Gillis who transformed whole sections of Los Angeles into exclusive suburbs.[14] Wealthier, more capable, and more imaginative than their predecessors, they gave an entirely new dimension to subdivision. Nevertheless, like the companies and agencies that extended facilities under pressure from consumers and voters, the Huntingtons, Whitleys, and Gillises transformed real estate according to the preferences of their prospective purchasers.

Hence the unique dispersal of Los Angeles reflected not so much its chronology, geography, or technology as the exceptional character of its population. It was not like Chicago—a typical concentrated metropolis—inhabited largely by impoverished and insecure European immigrants, who, in their attempt to find work and fellowship, were confined to the city's teeming tenements and crowded ghettos.[15] The model of the dispersed metropolis, Los Angeles was populated principally by native Americans with adequate resources and marketable skills, who faced the problems of adjustment confidently because of a common language and similar background. Relatively affluent and secure, the native Americans had a much wider choice than the European immigrants of housing and communities—to both of which, as newcomers in quest of a well-rounded life more than a remunerative occupation, they gave an extremely high priority.

Moreover, the native Americans came to Los Angeles with a conception of the good community which was embodied in single-family houses, located on large lots, surrounded by landscaped lawns, and isolated from business activities. Not for them multi-family dwellings, confined to narrow plots, separated by cluttered streets, and interspersed with commerce and industry.[16] Their vision was epitomized by

[14] Santa Monica Land and Water Company Corporate Records, Santa Monica Land and Water Company Files; Huntington Land and Improvement Company Ledgers and Journals, Huntington Land Companies Files; Los Angeles Suburban Home Company Minutes, Whitley Papers.

[15] Bessie L. Pierce, *A History of Chicago*, III (New York, 1957), passim; Homer Hoyt, *One Hundred Years of Land Values in Chicago* (Chicago, 1933), chaps. iv, v.

[16] Los Angeles *Examiner*, April 11, 1924; Los Angeles *Herald*, March 21, 1891; Mrs. Ernest T. Emery Diary, passim, Special Collections Division,

the residential suburb—spacious, affluent, clean, decent, permanent, predictable, and homogeneous—and violated by the great city—congested, impoverished, filthy, immoral, transient, uncertain, and heterogeneous. The late nineteenth- and early twentieth-century metropolis, as the newcomers in Los Angeles perceived it, was the receptacle for all European evils and the source of all American sins.[17] It contradicted their long-cherished notions about the proper environment and compelled them to retreat to outskirts uncontaminated by urban vices and conducive to rural virtues. And though native Americans everywhere shared these sentiments, they formed a larger portion of the populace in Los Angeles than in other great metropolises. Here then was the basis for the extraordinary dispersal of Los Angeles.

The developers, who were predominantly native Americans, responded sympathetically. "I can't understand why anyone should oppose the expansion of the city," one remarked. "If people did not go into the outside tracts that are being opened up they would be forced into apartments." Even more important, they knew that these preferences generated profitable opportunities in subdivision, particularly in the outlying sections where real estate was still inexpensive. For these reasons they transformed southern California's vast countryside into Los Angeles' sprawling suburbs. The purchasers subsequently constructed houses there, and by 1930 Los Angeles, as Table 2 shows, had more single-family and fewer multi-family dwellings than any comparable American metropolis—except to some extent Philadelphia.[18] Since most newcomers preferred to rent accommodations until they decided where in the metropolis to settle, however, only slightly more than one-third of them owned their homes.

The developers realized that a homogeneous population and compatible land-use were no less essential than a proper layout to the suburban vision. To this end they devised appropriate deed restrictions. These not only prohibited occupancy by Negroes and Orientals in most tracts and, in the more exclusive ones, fixed minimum costs for houses so as—in one developer's words—"to group the people of

University of California Library, Los Angeles; *Cahuenga Suburban,* April 1895, Cole Papers; Agricultural Department of Los Angeles Chamber of Commerce, *What the Newcomer Should Know About the Small Farm in Los Angeles County* (1927).

17 *Report of the Housing Commission of the City of Los Angeles* [1909–1910], p. 26; Finck, *Pacific Coast Tour,* pp. 31–33.

18 *Fifteenth Census: 1930. Population. Volume VI,* p. 72; George William Baist, *Real Estate Atlas of Surveys of Los Angeles* (Philadelphia, 1921), passim.

TABLE 2. Families and Dwellings in Selected Cities, 1930

City	Number of families (in thousands)	Number of dwellings (in thousands)	Per cent of total dwellings		
			1-family	2-family	3-or-more-family
Los Angeles	*369*	*301*	*93.9*	*3.8*	*2.4*
Philadelphia	458	398	91.6	6.1	2.3
San Francisco	179	119	88.3	5.9	5.9
Washington	126	85	87.9	8.0	4.1
Baltimore	194	163	86.7	10.8	2.5
Detroit	370	263	79.7	15.5	4.8
Pittsburgh	155	117	77.4	18.0	4.5
Cleveland	222	146	69.2	23.2	7.6
St. Louis	215	141	64.1	29.1	6.8
New York	1,723	557	52.8	24.5	22.7
Chicago	843	403	52.0	28.9	19.1
Boston	179	89	49.5	25.5	25.0

Source: U.S. Bureau of the Census, *Fifteenth Census of the United States: 1930. Population. Volume VI. Families* (Washington, 1933), p. 72.

more or less like income together." They also forbade commercial and industrial activities in most subdivisions, and, again in the more fashionable ones, outlawed all but the single-family houses deemed— by most Los Angeles residents—"the foundation of this country's security." (Whereas the restrictions on use, though not on race, normally expired after one or two decades in ordinary developments, they usually extended in perpetuity in more pretentious ones.) In short, deed restrictions were employed by the subdividers to ensure that most of greater Los Angeles' suburbs would stay strictly homogeneous and purely residential.[19]

Los Angeles' extraordinary dispersal was thereafter accelerated by its populace's extreme mobility. At first most newcomers found the entire region as enchanting as one woman who confided in her diary that "[southern] California seems so pretty all over that it is hard to say which is the best part." [20] But, guided by tangible considerations such as climate, topography, accessibility, and price, they eventually selected a subdivision, purchased a lot, and built a house. They rarely

[19] "Tract No. 6753. Restrictions for the Huntington Palisades," Santa Monica Land and Water Company Files; Huntington Land and Improvement Company Minute Book C, Huntington Land Companies Files; "Tract 6882. Protective Restrictions Palos Verdes Estates, Los Angeles California," City Hall, Palos Verdes Estates; Los Angeles Suburban Homes Company Minutes, February 8, 1912, Whitley Papers. See also, Siegfried Goetze, "Towards Better Housing in Los Angeles," Lissner Papers; Charles H. Cheney to Edgar F. Conant, October 8, 1928, Palos Verdes Homes Associations Files.

[20] October 22, 1905, September 24, 1906, Mrs. Ernest T. Emery's Diary.

remained there long, however. It was not just that the influx of Mexicans, Japanese, and Negroes and the expansion of commerce and industry threatened the homogeneity and rusticity of many subdivisions. It was also that the native Americans felt little attachment to neighborhoods which, like themselves, were so new as to be devoid of any meaningful institutional ties. Thus, so long as the real estate market remained active, these people moved time and again to more prestigious, though no less homogeneous and rustic, suburbs elsewhere in Los Angeles.[21]

The aspirations of the Mexicans, Japanese, and Negroes who initially settled in the central Los Angeles ghetto also fostered residential dispersal in outlying parts of the metropolis. Although the colored minorities there lived in houses and not tenements, they, no less than the white majority, preferred modern homes in suburban settings. But developers only subdivided tracts for them which, as a result of inferior drainage or other disadvantages, were not otherwise marketable. Hence colored people with funds and determination had no alternative save to attempt to enter the few subdivisions where deed restrictions had never been applied or had already expired. But there they often encountered the opposition of white landowners who explained that, though they had—as they put it—no objection to colored people "in their place," "they must not crowd us out and lower the value of our property." [22] Still, they sometimes secured houses outside central Los Angeles, and, as their white neighbors fled in panic, other colored people succeeded them, forming suburban enclaves and furthering residential dispersal in greater Los Angeles.[23]

Los Angeles' unmatched residential dispersal was only one manifestation of the community's antiurban ethos. Its unprecedented business decentralization was another, though it was barely evident as late as 1920. By then suburbanization had brought about a

[21] J. R. Douglas, "Report on Conditions Affecting the Real Estate Business in Los Angeles" (1923), Security-First National Bank Research Department, Los Angeles; Bessie Averne McClenahan, *The Changing Urban Neighborhood: From Neighbor to Nigh-Dweller* (Los Angeles, 1929), pp. 35, 47, 84.

[22] Bessie Averne McClenahan, "The Changing Nature of an Urban Residential Area" (University of Southern California Doctoral Dissertation, 1928), p. 218.

[23] Kiyoshi Uono, "The Factors Affecting the Geographical Aggregation and Dispersion of the Japanese Residences in the City of Los Angeles" (University of Southern California Masters Thesis, 1927), pp. 124ff; J. Max Bond, "The Negro in Los Angeles" (University of Southern California Doctoral Dissertation, 1936), pp. 68ff.

thorough, extensive, and permanent land-use segregation in the metropolis. For the thousands of Mexicans, Japanese, and Negroes who lived amidst commerce and industry in the small ghettos of central Los Angeles and San Pedro there were a million white Americans who resided in the suburbs sprawling north to Hollywood, east to Pasadena, south to Long Beach, and west to Santa Monica. Moreover, greater Los Angeles extended so far into the countryside that only electric trains and motor cars connected its homes, stores, and factories—a pattern not only preferred by the populace and imposed by the developers, but also sanctioned by city and county authorities. Land-use segregation was characteristic of other American metropolises, however, and so the uniqueness of Los Angeles' landscape had not yet extended by 1920 beyond its residential dispersal.

Here as elsewhere, the downtown district dominated the region's business. It was clearly the locus of employment; according to a traffic survey conducted in January 1924, 1.2 million persons a day, or more than the entire population of the city, traveled to and from the section bounded by Temple, Figueroa, Pico, and Los Angeles Streets.[24] It was also the center of commerce. "It is a common sight on the highways," a utility company executive observed in 1915, "to see large trucks . . . headed for some town outside Los Angeles crowded, filled to the brim, but returning empty." [25] As the focus of Los Angeles' economy, moreover, downtown expanded from a few small shops and offices covering several blocks in 1885 to many large mercantile and professional buildings spread over a square mile in 1920—the most concentrated section in southern California.[26] And though most people took more pride in the outlying residential suburbs than the central business district, they believed that it had achieved a position in Los Angeles comparable to the Loop in Chicago and Lower Manhattan in New York.

Downtown also steadily shifted south and west, and its center moved from Spring and Third in 1885 to Sixth and Hill in 1920. New buildings there gained the retail trade, a banker noted in 1909, because shoppers encountered congestion further north and east.[27]

[24] Kelker, de Leuw & Company, *Report and Recommendations on a Comprehensive Rapid Transit Plan for the City and County of Los Angeles* (Chicago, 1925), p. 37, plate 17.

[25] California Railroad Commission, *Archives,* Application 1,424, Reporter's Transcript, pp. 1,163–1,165.

[26] Babcock & Sons, *Regrading the Bunker Hill Area,* plate 29.

[27] Jackson A. Graves to I. W. Hellman, November 15, 1909, Graves Papers;

The extreme fluctuations in values that accompanied this movement sorely distressed property owners, and they called on private enterprise and public authority to anchor the central business district. The construction of financial houses on Spring, utility headquarters on Fifth, department stores on Broadway, and (incipiently) a civic center at Temple permanently fixed downtown Los Angeles' location in the 1920's.[28] In the meantime, however, its function changed. Between 1885 and 1920 . . . office buildings and department stores increased their share of downtown space at the expense of hotels and stores. These changes notwithstanding, the central business district still held more than three-quarters of Los Angeles' commercial and professional enterprise in 1920.[29]

Industry, by contrast, was not concentrated downtown. This was not because the small manufacturers who operated lofts found land there too expensive. Although some who did moved to the depressed district north of Temple Street and the rundown section south of Pico Street, over half of the city's lofts were still located in the central business district in 1920.[30] It was rather because the large industrialists, who, unlike merchants, lawyers, and small manufacturers, derived few advantages from a central location, required more space than was available downtown at any price. They preferred to locate in the vicinity of the original industrial district in southeastern Los Angeles which was served by the Southern Pacific, Santa Fe, and Pacific Electric and consisted of large undeveloped tracts. When the Goodyear Tire and Rubber Company decided to establish its Pacific coast branch facilities in Los Angeles, for example, it transformed an immense parcel south of downtown and west of the railroad tracts into a massive manufacturing center.[31]

see also, Los Angeles *Times,* July 25, 1909; Los Angeles *Examiner,* November 17, 1911.

[28] Harrison Lewis to F. E. Lee, February 6, 1919; John P. Kennedy to Robert C. Gillis, March 19, 1926, Gillis Papers; Los Angeles *Examiner,* May 1, 1914, May 14, 1915.

[29] Babcock & Sons, *Regrading the Bunker Hill Area,* plates 4, 6; Baist, *Real Estate Atlas* (1921), pp. 2, 3.

[30] Babcock & Sons, *Regrading the Bunker Hill Area,* plates 4, 9; Los Angeles Department of Water and Power, "City of Los Angeles and Vicinity Showing the Percentages of the Areas Occupied by the Different Classes of Improvements as of Jan. 1925," Department of Water and Power Files; Baist, *Real Estate Atlas* (1921), pp. 2, 3.

[31] Hugh Allen, "California," p. 80; Frank G. Mittelbach, "Dynamic Land Use Patterns in Los Angeles. The Period 1924–1954," in possession of the author, Real Estate Research Institute, University of California, Los Angeles.

For other heavy industries, the waterfront district was the choice location. It had not only immediate access to the harbor and direct contact with the transcontinental lines, but also abundant water and power, adequate rail and truck connections, and inexpensive acreage, factors that strongly attracted industrialists. When the Ford Motor Company decided to abandon its downtown automobile factory, for instance, it bought property at Long Beach large enough to house its sprawling assembly plant and close enough to the water to receive parts by ship.[32] Manufacturers were able to exploit inexpensive acreage here by virtue of the existing rail transportation and public utilities, but they were unable to build plants elsewhere in the metropolis because of the absence of these facilities. Just as commerce was concentrated in the central business district until 1920, industry, while somewhat decentralized, was confined to the downtown, southeastern, and waterfront vicinities.

Business centralization was thus far compatible with residential dispersal in Los Angeles—as in other American metropolises—because of its land-use patterns, transport facilities, and utility services. The scattered suburban population did not form a large enough market for outlying retail enterprises, and the radial electric railways, which did not supply cross-town service, provided swift and inexpensive transit in and out of downtown. Hence the metropolis' merchants felt little incentive to relocate stores and found little difficulty in attracting customers. Moreover, the transcontinental railroads (and, less important, the Pacific Electric) did not operate freight trains everywhere in Los Angeles. Nor did the private companies and public agencies distribute utilities throughout the entire metropolis. Thus, as the existing industrial districts contained enough acreage at reasonable prices, the manufacturers, like the merchants, found centralization profitable as well as obligatory.

These conditions changed soon after 1920. The retail market grew prodigiously in the suburbs, reflecting not so much the increase of immigration—which was accompanied by the expansion of territory—as the changes in the character of the populace. First, in response to the influx of single persons, entrepreneurs erected outlying apartment houses. Their proportion of new construction advanced . . . from

---

[32] "The Reminiscences of Mr. M. L. Wiesinger," p. 51, Ford Motor Company Archives, Oral History Section, Dearborn, Mich. See also, Kelker, de Leuw & Co., *Rapid Transit Plan for Los Angeles,* plate 9; Department of Water and Power, "City of Los Angeles . . . Jan. 1925."

8 per cent in 1920 to 53 per cent in 1928.[33] An extremely small fraction of all housing in Los Angeles, apartment houses were so concentrated as to raise densities in communities such as Hollywood and on thoroughfares such as Wilshire Boulevard. Second, in response to the wealth of many residents, developers created very exclusive subdivisions such as Beverly Hills and San Marino which had enormous purchasing power.[34] Although the subdividers restricted business there, they reserved lots along major arteries for commerce. Nonetheless, these changes were essentially permissive. They generated opportunities for mercantile enterprise in the suburbs, but they did not compel established businesses to desert downtown.

The failure of the electric railways, however, did just that. The street and interurban lines were heavily congested as early as 1910: "There are times in the rush hours," the Los Angeles *Examiner* reported "when every foot of trackage in the business district is covered with trolley cars." [35] Subsequently, the electric railways had to share the surface with private automobiles, the number of which in Los Angeles County soared from under 200,000 in 1920 to over 500,000 in 1924. By then 262,000 motor cars traveled in and out of downtown everyday and, with the trains, so tightly jammed the streets that, as distraught witnesses complained to the California Railroad Commission, it was very hard to reach the central business district.[36] The municipal authorities attempted to alleviate this congestion, but to little avail. And in time the electric railways, plagued by automobile competition that increased their expenditures and reduced their revenues, so curtailed service and raised fares that the car supplanted

[33] *Annual Report. Department of City Planning. Los Angeles* [1923–1930], p. 61. Los Angeles Department of Water and Power, "City of Los Angeles and Vicinity Showing the Percentages of the Area Occupied by the Different Classes of Improvements as of January 1934," Department of Water and Power Files.

[34] W. R. Ferrell, "The Merchants' Map of the Los Angeles Market" (1930); Division of Business and Market Research of the Los Angeles *Examiner*, "Los Angeles Metropolitan and ABC City Market by Family Expenditures" (ca. 1935), Los Angeles Chamber of Commerce Files.

[35] Los Angeles *Examiner*, November 17, 1911; see also, Los Angeles *Times*, July 25, 1909; Automobile Club of Southern California, *A Report on Los Angeles Traffic Problems with Recommendations for Relief* (Los Angeles, 1922), passim.

[36] "In the Matter of . . . Railway Service in the Hollywood District of the City of Los Angeles," California Railroad Commission, *Archives, Case* 1602, Reporter's Transcript, pp. 128ff; Kelker, de Leuw & Co., *Rapid Transit Plan for Los Angeles*, p. 36; Baker, *Rapid Transit System for Los Angeles*, plate 9.

the train as the principal means of transportation in Los Angeles.[37]

The central business district profoundly felt the repercussions. Since at least twenty autos were required to convey as many people as one train, traffic became heavier, travel took longer, and parking space became scarcer. The optimists predicted that these troubles, delays, and expenses would discourage drivers and compel them to ride the railways again. Others disagreed, arguing that the residents, faced with these alternatives, would avoid downtown before they returned to the trains.[38] The pessimists proved more perceptive. Between 1923 and 1931, while the population within ten miles of the central business district expanded 50 per cent, the number of people entering downtown Los Angeles increased only 15 per cent. "The automobile has brought a distinct change in the city building," a visitor who observed these trends predicted. "The day is not far distant when vehicular congestion will be so great down town that enterprising merchants will be establishing great department stores in outlying business centers where shoppers can be conveniently served." [39]

The triumph of motor transport facilitated the decentralization of industry too. The extensive county highway and city street systems enabled manufacturers—long dependent on the railroads—to move freight throughout the region by trucks. Widespread automobile ownership, combined with sprawling suburban subdivisions, also rendered hitherto remote and still cheap residential locations accessible to the working force.[40] The expansion of utility facilities undermined another basis for industrial concentration. The municipal authorities provided inexpensive water and power throughout the city, and regional districts and private companies supplied service at slightly higher rates elsewhere. Hence, when rapid industrial development in the 1920's made land in the still desirable downtown, southeastern, and waterfront sections extremely expensive, the industrialists had a far greater choice of sites.

[37] *Annual Reports of the Traffic Commission of the City and County of Los Angeles [1925–1930]*; Olmsted, Bartholomew and Cheney, *Major Traffic Street Plan*, pp. 11–16.

[38] Hale H. Huggins, "Decentralization of Shopping," *Los Angeles Realtor*, 3: 4 (January 1924); "In the Matter of the Application of Los Angeles Railway Corporation, for an Order Readjusting Rates . . .," California Railroad Commission, *Archives*, Application 13, 323, Reporter's Transcript, pp. 594–596.

[39] Stanley McMichael, "Los Angeles as It Appears to an Eastern Realtor," *Los Angeles Realtor*, 2: 21 (January 1923).

[40] "The Industrial Land Situation in Los Angeles," *Eberle & Riggleman Economic Service*, III, 7 (February 15, 1926), Part II, pp. 29–32.

The decentralization of commerce and industry followed. In response to the expansion of suburban retail markets and the inaccessibility of central Los Angeles, prominent mercantile concerns relocated old stores and opened new ones along Wilshire, Hollywood, and other fashionable boulevards.[41] Downtown, which now consisted of even fewer shops, hotels, and lofts and more office buildings, governmental structures, and garages, had only about half of the metropolis' commercial and professional enterprise and was only one, and by no means the most stylish, of its business districts. Meanwhile, in conjunction with local realtors, mammoth manufacturing firms established segregated industrial complexes throughout Los Angeles. Steelmakers constructed furnaces at Torrance, oil producers erected refineries at El Segundo, aviation companies built hangars near Santa Monica, and motion picture magnates spread studios over the San Fernando Valley.[42] Hence business decentralization, combined with residential dispersal, created an urban form in greater Los Angeles consistent with its growth and yet unique in the United States in 1930.

It was not stores, factories, or even apartment houses, however, but single-family subdivisions that characterized the Los Angeles landscape. There was, of course, considerable diversity in these developments. They were subdivided between 1900 and 1930 for, among others, retired magnates worth millions, former farmers worth thousands, and ambitious but impecunious newcomers. They were also spread over the countryside, reaching the lowlying plains and the steep hills, the cool, moist coast and warm, dry interior, and varying in accessibility to railways and highways.[43] Despite the differences in chronology, clientele, topography, climate, and location, however, the variations in subdivision design were remarkably slight in greater Los Angeles—a fact indicating that the suburban layout, like residential dispersal and business decentralization, was yet another manifestation of the community's antiurban ethos.

A description of three representative subdivisions reveals the uniformity of suburban layout in the metropolis. Oneonta Park, which

[41] Department of Water and Power, "City of Los Angeles . . . 1934"; California Railroad Commission, *Archives,* Case 1602, Reporter's Transcript, passim; Babcock & Sons, *Regrading the Bunker Hill Area,* plate 6.

[42] Department of Water and Power, "City of Los Angeles . . . 1934"; Los Angeles Chamber of Commerce Minutes, January 10, 1924; N. Alderman, *General Industrial Report of Burbank* (Burbank, 1924), passim; "Industrial Land Situation in Los Angeles," Part II, p. 30.

[43] Kelker, de Leuw & Company, *Rapid Transit Plan for Los Angeles,* plate 6.

was bought shortly after 1900 by the Huntington Land and Improvement Company, consisted of several small contiguous parcels situated in the western San Gabriel Valley ten miles (on the Pacific Electric) from Los Angeles. Huntington Land developed the tract for Los Angeles' middle class, platting the land with perpendicularly intersecting streets sixty to eighty feet wide and dividing the rest into one-quarter to one-half acre suburban lots. It restricted the use of the property, the cost of the buildings, and the setting of the houses. The purchaser of a one-third acre plot was forbidden to erect any but a residential dwelling worth at least $3,500, to face his home anywhere except on a specified street, to place it less than forty feet behind the front line, and to enclose the lawn with a fence or wall higher than four feet.[44]

Owensmouth, which was located in the southwestern San Fernando Valley twenty-five miles from the central business district, was acquired by the Los Angeles Suburban Homes Company around 1910. Like Huntington Land and Improvement, Los Angeles Suburban Homes subdivided its holdings according to the gridiron pattern. But as the San Fernando Valley was less accessible than the San Gabriel Valley, the company laid out lots as large as four acres that could be farmed now and divided later. Appealing to lower middle-class residents and real estate speculators, Los Angeles Suburban Homes did not rigorously restrict its property. It allowed boarding and rooming houses, apartments and hotels, and even garages, prohibited commerce and industry only until 1920, and fixed minimum costs for homes that in no case exceeded $2,000. Finally, the company stipulated that dwellings face the north-south not the east-west streets and stand no less than thirty feet from the front and ten feet from the side lines so as to conform with more exclusive suburban designs.[45]

Huntington Palisades, which was set in the Santa Monica foothills fifteen miles from downtown Los Angeles, was purchased by Robert C. Gillis in the late 1920's. Impressed by the rustic surroundings,

[44] Oneonta Park Account, Huntington Land and Improvement Company Ledger Book 1; Seymour Bisbee's Map of "Oneonta Park and Vicinity South Pasadena, Cal."; Indenture between the Huntington Land and Improvement Company and O. C. Conley, December 13, 1912, all in Huntington Land Company Files.

[45] Map of the Townsite of Owensmouth; "Detailed Outline Reservation and Restriction Governing Sales of Acreage Near the New Town of Owensmouth," February 8, 1912, both in Whitley Papers.

superb views, and towering trees, he decided to transform it into a fashionable upper middle-class community. Unlike most subdividers, he adopted not the gridiron arrangement but a romantic scheme of curved streets and landscaped boulevards which followed the terrain and preserved the vegetation. Gillis also divided the property into lots from about a quarter to more than a full acre and set minimum construction costs from $5,000 for the smaller to $15,000 for the larger parcels. And he prohibited the owners from using lots for other than residential purposes, erecting dwellings of more than two stories, growing hedges to more than five feet, and placing houses without regard for setback lines. Finally, Gillis not only extended these restrictions in perpetuity, but also authorized a property-owners association to enforce them.[46]

That Oneonta Park, Owensmouth, and Huntington Palisades differed somewhat in the arrangement of streets, size of lots, value of buildings, distance of setbacks, and limitation on uses is not surprising. After all, the developers, all of whom realized that the restrictions and layout tended—in their own words—"to guide and automatically regulate the class of citizens," [47] aimed at different markets. What is surprising is that, considering the varied topography, climate, and accessibility of the San Gabriel Valley, San Fernando Valley, and Santa Monica foothills, Oneonta Park, Owensmouth, and Huntington Palisades were so similar. Each was designed for single-family residences, set on sizable lots, fixed in two-tiered blocks, located on improved roads, and isolated from commerce and industry. None permitted any intrusions other than parks, schools, (and sometimes churches) on the domestic environment which, reflecting the suburban vision of the native Americans, everywhere dominated the layout of greater Los Angeles.

[46] Santa Monica Land and Water Corporate Records; Map of "Huntington Palisades 'on Santa Monica Bay' " (July 1927); Williams Engineering Company's Estimate to Complete Improvements at the Huntington Palisades (December 27, 1926); "Tract No. 6753. Restrictions. Huntington Palisades," all in Santa Monica Land and Water Company Files.

[47] Charles H. Cheney to Edgar F. Conant, October 8, 1928, Palos Verdes Homes Association Files. This letter is worth quoting at length. "The type of protective restrictions and the high class scheme of layout which we have provided tends to guide and automatically regulate the class of citizens who are settling here. The restrictions prohibit occupation of land by Negroes or Asiatics. The minimum cost of house restrictions tends to group the people of more or less like income together as far as it is reasonable and advisable to do so."

Perhaps Palos Verdes Estates, a 3,000 acre tract in the hilly south-western corner of Los Angeles County, most clearly illustrated the pattern prevailing by the 1920's. There the developers, led by banker Frank A. Vanderlip, entrusted the subdivision to Frederick Law Olmsted, Jr., and Charles H. Cheney, two of the nation's foremost landscape architects and city planners. Olmsted and Cheney possessed an enviable opportunity—their tract was enormous, their employers wealthy, and their authority considerable—and they exploited it with professional expertise. They separated residential streets from traffic arteries, reserved eight hundred acres for parkland, designed several connecting parkways, created lots for views rather than profits, confined commerce to small centers, and prohibited industry altogether. They thus fashioned the metropolis' finest—but still only another—residential community: a "garden suburb," not, as Cheney admitted, a "garden city," [48] Palos Verdes was the quintessence of Los Angeles.

During the years that the suburban layout epitomized by Palos Verdes Estates emerged, the revival style supplanted the picturesque aesthetic in the domestic architecture of Los Angeles. There, as elsewhere in the nation around 1900, native Americans were so distressed by the discrepancies between the United States of myth and reality that they sought reassurances in the past. Northerners and southerners alike recreated colonial and plantation buildings with as much enthusiasm as they formed genealogical and historical societies. Southern Californians suffered no less from this anxiety and, even worse, had renounced the Puritans and Cavaliers, and had sunk only shallow roots in their adopted region. They tried to resolve this problem by turning to California's geography and history, and, in

[48] Olmsted's description of the layout is revealing for greater Los Angeles as well as for Palos Verdes Estates. "In laying out the local streets . . . the controlling consideration has not been merely to cut up the land into the maximum number of lots of standard sizes with street frontage, but to select all the best sites for houses, having regard first to the views and the excellence of the final result rather than merely to the ease with which ordinary commonplace dwellings could be packed in . . . Accessibility is essential and is provided at Palos Verdes Estates, but if the principal thing a man is asking for is accessibility at a minimum cost for street work and lot improvement he had better pick any one of a hundred thousand lots on the flat plains, all just alike, utterly without views or individuality." Frederick Law Olmsted to Charles H. Cheney, undated, Palos Verdes Homes Association Files. See also, Frederick Law Olmsted, "Palos Verdes Estates," *Landscape Architecture*, 17 (July 1927), passim Map of Palos Verdes Estates and "Tract 6882. Protective Restrictions Palos Verdes Estates, Los Angeles California," both in Palos Verdes Homes Association Files.

effect, embracing Italy and Spain. "No matter how cosmopolitan our population, our environment is definitely racial," they announced. "We are Mediterranean, in climate, in vegetation and sunlight and, deny it who will, in tradition and inheritance." [49]

They proceeded to shape Los Angeles' domestic architecture according to the Mediterranean style. This is not to deny that other fashions were popular. Most subdividers allowed their customers to choose any pattern for their homes, and many builders who found the picturesque too expensive and elaborate imitated the wooden walls, dark colors, steep roofs, and sharp turrets of English Tudor and French Norman houses. Even the demanding Palos Verdes Art Jury, which had to approve the plans for houses built there, accepted certain northern archetypes.[50] It is rather to argue that the Mediterranean style prevailed nonetheless. Some developers discounted lots if the houses were constructed in "Moorish, Mission or Pompeian design," others simply prohibited different types, and many contractors followed plan books published by the Bungalowcraft and other companies that featured Italian and Spanish models. The Palos Verdes Art Jury clearly expressed its preference for houses of southern European inspiration too. Summing up the consequences, a highly-regarded Los Angeles architect declared: "We have arrived at a distinctive architecture which is our own, and which is a real expression of our culture and civilization." [51]

His associates defined it as "California architecture," a style which, they explained, "has been successfully developing in this state, deriving its chief inspiration directly or indirectly from Latin types which developed under similar climatic conditions along the Mediterranean." Its colors were "generally very light in tone"; its materials were

[49] Harwood Hewitt, "A Plea for Distinctive Architecture in Southern California," Allied Architects Association of Los Angeles, *Bulletin*, 1, 5 (March 1, 1925); see also, Los Angeles Chamber of Commerce, *Members Annual [1921]*, pp. 23ff.; Franklin Walker, *A Literary History of Southern California* (Berkeley and Los Angeles, 1950), chap. v.

[50] "Types of Architecture Approved for Palos Verdes Estates," *Bulletin of the Palos Verdes Art Jury* (May 1925), Palos Verdes Homes Association Files; The Bungalowcraft Company, *Homes of the Moment*, 3d ed. (Los Angeles, 1931); G. H. Edgell, *The American Architecture of To-day* (New York, 1928), pp. 87–100.

[51] "California Architecture" (1929), and Palos Verdes Art Jury Minutes, November 21, December 4, 1922, both in Palos Verdes Homes Association Files; Los Angeles Suburban Homes Company Minutes, May 3, 1910. Whitley Papers; The Bungalowcraft Company, *New Spanish Bungalows*, 6th ed. (Los Angeles, 1930), passim.

"plaster, adobe or stucco" or "concrete, brick, stone or artificial stone"; its exteriors were "plaster, adobe or stucco"; and its roofs were "low-pitched [and] usually of tile laid random." [52] Following these guidelines, Los Angeles' architects replaced the verandahs, shingle sidings, protruding bays, and steep tops of the picturesque aesthetic with the patios, massive walls, arched windows, and flat roofs of California architecture. But they were not content to be mere copyists of Italy, Greece or Spain, one architect wrote in 1925. "The test of our architectural abilities is that in drawing upon the rich precedent of the Mediterranean, we should breathe into it such a spirit of originality and fitness for our own needs that we may by degrees evolve an architecture which we shall be proud to call Californian." [53]

By this criterion they failed. A few great mansions, comparable to country villas, achieved the massive simplicity and elegant ornamentation of Mediterranean architecture. But when adapted for suburban lots by uninspired builders, most houses lost all dignity and embellishment. The substitution of open lawns and auto driveways for front walls and central courtyards was particularly incongruous. A few perceived this conflict between aesthetics and culture: "Truly we are a melting pot, not of nationalities, but of architecture," one critic wrote in 1925—"an architectural anachronism, Nordic invasion of the Mediterranean, Attila again in Rome." [54] Nothing proved more poignantly than their architecture that, however similar the climates of southern California and southern Europe, southern Californians

[52] "California Architecture" (1929); Palos Verdes Art Jury Minutes, April 27, 1923, Palos Verdes Homes Association Files; Rex D. Weston, *Weston's Double Bungalows* (Los Angeles, 1924), passim; Edgell, *American Architecture*, pp. 101–109; McWilliams, *Southern California Country*, pp. 354–362.

[53] Donald J. Witmer, "Wherein Styles Differ," Allied Architects Association of Los Angeles, *Bulletin*, 1, 12 (October 21, 1925).

[54] Hewitt, "A Plea for a Distinctive Architecture in Southern California." The protest of Charles Gibbs Adams—"Our Architectural Tragedy," *California Southland*, 103: 28 (July 1928)—is even more graphic: "There are countless Colonial houses all banked with Palms where there should be only boxwood edgings and hollyhocks and Poplar trees. There are fake Italian Villas with the front yards all messed up with miniature Japanese gardens. There are Spanish houses profaned with variegated shrubs, such as Golden Privet, and shiny stylish bushes clipped into formal balls and cones and pyramids, where should be only graceful olives and peppers, figs and oranges, Jasmines and Tuberoses, Century plants and Scarlet Aloes . . . There are Swiss Chalets, fitting only for cool mountain sides, in our lowest hollows with straight cement paths from street to door, and tropical plantings about them, oranges and fan palms in the majority." See also, "Types of Architecture Approved for Palos Verdes Estates"; The Bungalowcraft Company, *New Spanish Homes;* The Bungalowcraft Company, *Homes of the Moment.*

were in heritage and character American not Mediterranean—nothing, except perhaps their indifference to such architects as Charles and Henry Greene, also midwestern immigrants, who expressed through native traditions, indigenous materials, and modern idioms the uniqueness of southern California.[55]

Meanwhile, the utilitarian replaced the picturesque in commercial architecture. In Los Angeles, as in Chicago, burgeoning business generated demand for additional space, while rising land values favored vertical not horizontal construction. Also, such technological innovations as elevators and fireproofing, iron framing and curtain walls enlarged the opportunities available to southern California (as well as midwestern) architects.[56] Following the pattern perfected by Louis Sullivan and others around the turn of the century, they designed buildings ten and twelve rather than four and six stories in the central business district. They supported them with steel skeletons instead of masonry walls, covered them with concrete and glass instead of iron façades, and capped them with flat roofs and simple cornices instead of medieval towers.[57] Although the nationwide classical reaction left a few unimpressive skyscrapers downtown and the regional Mediterranean style inspired some unattractive shops elsewhere, utilitarianism characterized commercial architecture as completely as revivalism distinguished domestic architecture in Los Angeles.

These buildings were an integral part of Los Angeles' landscape. But they were not unfamiliar elsewhere. Spanish bungalows and Italian villas covered cities in Florida and the Southwest, and modern office buildings and department stores stood in Chicago and San Francisco. Residential dispersal and business decentralization, however, were unique to Los Angeles. Nowhere else in the United States did suburbs extend so far into the countryside and downtown decline so drastically as the center of commerce and industry. This process, which reflected the newcomers' preferences, the subdividers' practices, and the businessmen's inclinations, was also self-perpetuating. Dispersal devastated the central business district, and decentralization spurred outlying subdivision. Given additional urbanization, moreover, nothing but the mountains and the sea inhibited the sprawl of

55 Esther McCoy, *Five California Architects* (New York, 1960), passim.
56 Carl Condit, *The Rise of the Skyscraper* (Chicago, 1962), chap. iii.
57 Other than downtown Los Angeles itself, the best sources for commercial architecture are the photograph collections of the Title Insurance and Trust Company and the Security-First National Bank, both in Los Angeles.

the metropolis—a prospect which, whatever the attendant problems, including the failure of the electric railways, the people of Los Angeles saw as their consummate achievement.

This vision was not new in Los Angeles in 1930. Two decades before the people there decided that residential dispersal was imperative. If Los Angeles were to accommodate a large population and yet avoid undue congestion, they reasoned, the metropolis had to spread "until it meet[s] the country, and until beautiful forms of urban life blend almost imperceptibly into beautiful forms of rural life." [58] A decade later they also questioned the value of business centralization. "Is it inevitable or basically sound or desirable that larger and larger crowds be brought into the city's center," they asked; "must all large business, professional and financial operations be conducted in a restricted area[?]" [59] Most answered no. Instead, they envisioned the urban region as "Not another New York, but a new Los Angeles. Not a great homogeneous mass with a pyramiding of population and squalor in a single center, but a federation of communities co-ordinated into a metropolis of sunlight and air." [60] By 1930, however, residential dispersal and business decentralization had transformed Los Angeles into the fragmented—not the co-ordinated—metropolis.

[58] William E. Smythe, "Significance of Southern California," *Out West*, 32: 287ff (April 1910).
[59] Clarence A. Dykstra, "Congestion de Luxe—Do We Want it?" *Pacific Outlook*, 40: 226ff (June 1927).
[60] G. Gordon Whitnall Articles, Los Angeles City Planning Department Scrapbook.

16

Harlem: The Making of a Ghetto— Negro New York, 1890-1930

by GILBERT OSOFSKY

The most profound change that Harlem experienced in the 1920's was its emergence as a slum.

The history of the American city in this century is in no small part the story of the Negro and of his internal migration—from country to city, from South to North. At least three out of four blacks now live in cities, and of these a half live in cities of the North. Today at least ten cities have black populations of more than 250,000. New York has well above 1,000,000, and Chicago is close to that figure. Considerably more than half the population of Washington is black. Washington, Gary, and Cleveland have Negro mayors, and others could elect one soon.

In all the large cities of the North, with the partial exception of the San Francisco Bay area, blacks live in modern ghettos which tend to be more congested, inferior in their institutions and facilities, and generally bearing the symptoms of decay and stagnation. As Kenneth Clark has pointed out, they are not viable communities. The ghetto "cannot support its people; most have to leave it for their daily jobs. Its businesses are geared toward the satisfaction of personal needs and are marginal to the economy of the city as a whole. The ghetto feeds upon itself; it does not produce goods or contribute to the prosperity of the city." *

For the most part, these ghettos have not been the product of a conscious calculated separatism, nor are they merely the latest recurrent chapter in the story of ethnic migration. "Unlike the Irish, Poles, Jews, or Italians," writes Allan Spear, "Negroes banded together not to enjoy a common linguistic, cultural, and religious tradition, but because a

* *Dark Ghetto* (New York, Harper Torchbooks, 1965), p. 27.

systematic pattern of discrimination left them no alternative. Negroes were tied together less by common cultural heritage than by a common set of grievances." †

That the black in America has had a unique historical experience and travail is sharply revealed in Gilbert Osofsky's study of Harlem, once an upper-class community, then a mixed immigrant area, and finally in the twenties and thirties becoming the largest, most concentrated Negro community in the world. Professor Osofsky is able with rich detail to show the endemic deterioration that ate into both the physical assets and the cultural vitality of Harlem. He traces the cycle of decay and how a ghetto turns in upon itself.

Professor Osofsky did his graduate work at Columbia University and wrote his dissertation under Robert Cross. He ranks as one of the outstanding younger scholars of black history and is now a professor of history at the University of Illinois, Circle Campus, in Chicago. He is also the compiler of *The Burden of Race: A Documentary History of Negro-White Relations in America.*

The material in this selection appears in *Harlem: The Making of a Ghetto,* published by Harper and Row, Inc. Copyright in 1963, 1965, and 1966 by Harper and Row, Publishers, Inc., it is reprinted here with their permission. The footnotes, though numerous and in several instances citing sources not accessible to most students, are included to illustrate that black history is by no means untracked land. Much terrain remains unexplored, but guideposts do exist.

> "I sit on my stoop on Seventh
> Avenue and gaze at the sunkissed
> folks strolling up and down and
> think that surely Mississippi is
> here in New York, in Harlem, yes,
> right on Seventh Avenue."
> —*The Messenger*, 1923

> "I have been in places where cattle
> and dogs sleep with masters, but
> never before have I been in such a
> filthy house."
> —Judge William Blau's description
> of a Harlem tenement, 1922

† *Black Chicago, The Making of a Negro Ghetto, 1890–1920* (Chicago, University of Chicago Press, 1967), p. 228.

I

The creation of a Negro community within one large and solid geographic area was unique in city history. New York had never been what realtors call an "open city"—a city in which Negroes lived wherever they chose—but the former Negro sections were traditionally only a few blocks in length, often spread across the island and generally interspersed with residences of white working-class families. Harlem, however, was a Negro world unto itself. A scattered handful of "marooned white families . . . stubbornly remained" in the Negro section, a United States census-taker recorded, but the mid-belly of Harlem was predominantly Negro by 1920.[1]

And the ghetto rapidly expanded. Between the First World War and the Great Depression, Harlem underwent radical changes. When the twenties came to an end Negroes lived as far south as One Hundred and Tenth Street—the northern boundary of Central Park; practically all the older white residents had moved away; the Russian-Jewish and Italian sections of Harlem, founded a short generation earlier, were rapidly being depopulated; and Negro Harlem, within the space of ten years, became the most "incredible slum" in the entire city. In 1920 James Weldon Johnson was able to predict a glowing future for this Negro community: "Have you ever stopped to think what the future Harlem will be?" he wrote. "It will be the greatest Negro city in the world. . . . And what a fine part of New York City [the Negro] has come into possession of!" [2] By the late 1920's and early 1930's, however, Harlem's former "high-class" homes offered, in the words of a housing expert, "the best laboratory for slum clearance . . . in the entire city." "Harlem conditions," a *New York Times* reporter concluded, are "simply deplorable." [3]

II

The Harlem slum of the twenties was the product of a few major urban developments. One of the most important was the deluge of

[1] The Mayor's Commission on Conditions in Harlem, "The Negro in Harlem: A Report on Social and Economic Conditions Responsible for the Outbreak of March 19, 1935" (unpublished manuscript in La Guardia Papers, Municipal Archives), p. 53. This important study, prepared under the direction of E. Franklin Frazier, will hereafter be cited as "The Negro in Harlem."

[2] "The Future Harlem," *The New York Age*, January 10, 1920.

[3] John E. Nail to James Weldon Johnson, March 12, 1934, Johnson Collection, Yale University; "Harlem Conditions Called Deplorable," *The New York Times*, September 6, 1927.

Negro migration to New York City then. The Negro press, now largely dependent on the migrant community for support, changed its former critical attitude of migration to one openly advocating urban settlement. (The exodus was so large, a Negro minister preached, that it must have been "inspired by Almighty God.")[4] If one is looking for a dramatic turning point in the history of the urbanization of the Negro—"a race changing from farm life to city life"—it was certainly the decade of the twenties. Between 1910 and 1920 the Negro population of the city increased 66 per cent (91,709 to 152,467); from 1920 to 1930, it expanded 115 per cent (152,467 to 327,706). In the latter year less than 25 per cent of New York City's Negro population (79,264) was born in New York State. There were more Negroes in the city in 1930 than the combined Negro populations of Birmingham, Memphis and St. Louis. Similar population increases occurred in urban areas throughout the country.[5]

Negro migration in the twenties drew on areas of the South that had previously sent few people to New York City. The seaboard states of the Upper South—especially Virginia and the Carolinas—continued to be the main sources of New York's migrant Negro population, but people from Georgia and Florida and other Deep South states formerly under-represented also came in greater numbers: "Harlem became the symbol of liberty and the Promised Land to Negroes everywhere," the Reverend Dr. Powell wrote. "There was hardly a member of Abyssinian Church who could not count on one or more relatives among the new arrivals." [6] In 1930, some 55,000 foreign-born Negroes added to the growing diversity of the city's Negro population.

The following chart presents an exact description of the geographical origins of Negro migrants to New York City in 1930. I have selected states with 900 or more residents in the city: [7]

[4] "Let Them Come," "The New Exodus," *The New York Age,* March 3, 1923, October 16, 1920, September 14, 1929.

[5] Bureau of the Census, *Fifteenth Census, 1930: Population* (Washington, D.C., 1933), II, 216–218; Walter Laidlaw, *Population of the City of New York, 1890–1930* (New York, 1932), p. 51.

[6] Reverend Dr. Adam Clayton Powell, Sr., *Against the Tide: An Autobiography* (New York, 1938), pp. 70–71.

[7] Bureau of the Census, *Fifteenth Census, 1930:* Population (Washington, D.C., 1933), II, 216–218. Note the difference in Chicago's migrant population. In order of greatest numbers Chicago Negroes came from Mississippi, Tennessee, Georgia, Alabama and Louisiana.

NEGRO IN-MIGRATION, NEW YORK CITY, 1930

Born in:

Virginia	44,471
South Carolina	33,765
North Carolina	26,120
Georgia	19,546
Florida	8,249
Maryland	6,656
Pennsylvania	6,226
New Jersey	5,275
District of Columbia	3,358
Alabama	3,205
Massachusetts	2,329
Louisiana	2,182
Ohio	1,721
Tennessee	1,651
Texas	1,592
Kentucky	1,216
Mississippi	969
Foreign-born	54,754

The rapid settlement of a heterogeneous Negro population coincided with another important population change—the migration of whites from all sections of Manhattan to other boroughs. For the first time since Dutch settlement Manhattan's population *declined* in the 1920's as first- and second-generation immigrants moved to nicer residential areas in the Bronx, Brooklyn and Queens. Many of the homes they left behind had deteriorated significantly. By 1930 a majority of New York City's foreign-born and second-generation residents lived outside Manhattan.[8] As whites moved out of Manhattan, Negroes moved in. The population of that borough declined 18 per cent in the 1920's as its Negro population increased 106 per cent. By 1930 Negroes represented 12 per cent of Manhattan's population—although they composed only 4.7 per cent of the population of the entire city.[9]

Harlem was the New York neighborhood most radically revamped by the population movements of the 1920's, although the Lower East

[8] James Ford, *et al.*, *Slums and Housing: With Special Reference to New York City* (Cambridge, Mass., 1936), II, 311–315.

[9] *Ibid.*, p. 317; Bureau of the Census, *Negroes in the United States, 1920–1932* (Washington, D.C., 1935), p. 55.

Side also changed rapidly. Harlem underwent a revolution—what one contemporary accurately called a "stupendous upheaval." Between 1920 and 1930, 118,792 white people left the neighborhood and 87,417 Negroes arrived.[10] Second-generation Italians and Jews were responding to the same conditions of prosperity that promoted mobility in all the immigrant neighborhoods of Manhattan—they were not *only* moving away because Negroes settled near them. Conditions of life which satisfied immigrant parents were often unacceptable to children: "The tenements which housed their parents," immigration expert Edward Corsi wrote in 1930, "are being left behind by the children. . . ." "East Harlem used to have a great deal larger population," a survey of the Mayor's Committee on City Planning during the Great Depression concluded. "Like others of the older residential districts, it has suffered by the exodus of families to newer surroundings. . . ." [11]

The city's newest migrants moved into the Harlem flats vacated by Italians and Jews. Puerto Ricans came to live in East Harlem, created community organizations, and laid the foundations for "El Barrio" of today. By 1930 some 45,000 Puerto Ricans resided in New York City and most were heavily concentrated in East Harlem.[12] Negroes moved north along St. Nicholas Avenue—"On the Heights," they called it—and south into the heart of "Little Russia," the former Jewish section. "Just Opened for Colored" signs were common in the neighborhood. Mount Olivet Baptist Church occupied, and still occupies, the once exclusive Temple Israel of Harlem. Prince Hall Masons bought a building that "was formerly a home for aged Jews." Graham Court, a magnificent block-length apartment house on One Hundred and Sixteenth Street, with eight separate elevators and apartments of seven to ten rooms, was opened to Negroes in 1928.[13] By 1930, 164,566 Negroes, about 72 per cent of Manhattan's Negro

[10] Winfred B. Nathan, *Health Conditions in North Harlem, 1923–1927* (New York, 1932), pp. 13–14.

[11] *Harlem Magazine,* XIX (June 1930), 8; Mayor's Commission on City Planning, *East Harlem Community Study* (typescript in New York Public Library, 1937), p. 16.

[12] *Slums and Housing,* p. 370; Antonio T. Rivera to La Guardia, June 24, 1935, La Guardia Papers; "Harlem Puerto Ricans Unite to Prove Faith," *The New York Times,* July 2, August 9, 16, 1926; *Opportunity,* IV (October 1926), 330.

[13] *The New York Age,* August 27, 1927, March 31, 1928, January 11, 1930; *The New York Times,* October 19, 1924.

population, lived in Harlem.[14] The Negro ghetto remained and expanded as the other ethnic ghettos disintegrated. The economic and residential mobility permitted white people in the city was, and would continue to be, largely denied Negroes. Most Negroes were "jammed together" in Harlem—even those who could afford to live elsewhere—with little possibility of escape.[15] "One notable difference appears between the immigrant and Negro populations," an important federal study of Negro housing concluded. "In the case of the former, there is the possibility of escape, with improvement in economic status, in the second generation, to more desirable sections of the city. In the case of Negroes, who remain a distinguishable group, the factor of race and certain definite racial attitudes favorable to segregation, interpose difficulties to . . . breaking physical restrictions in residence areas." [16] A rather ponderous paragraph, but a significant truth.

III

The settlement of West Indian Negroes in Harlem in the 1920's added another complicating dimension to the racial problems of this community—one that fostered discord rather than harmony among the city's Negroes. There were ten times as many foreign-born Negroes in New York City as in any other American urban area. In 1930, 54,754 foreign Negroes lived in the city—39,833 of whom resided in Manhattan. Miami, the next largest American city in terms of immigrant Negroes, was settled by only 5,512 people; Boston ranked third with 3,287 West Indians. About 25 per cent of Harlem's population in the twenties was foreign-born. Harlem was America's largest Negro melting pot.[17]

14 *Slums and Housing*, p. 314.
15 The attempt of Negroes to move into Washington Heights, Yonkers and Westchester was opposed in these sections as it had been in Harlem earlier. The Neighborhood Protective Association of Washington Heights urged landlords to sign racially restrictive covenants. Mortgage pressures from financial institutions closed down a Negro housing development in Yonkers. As a result of population pressure, however, another large ghetto was created in the Bedford-Stuyvesant section of Brooklyn in the 1920's. Of the 68,921 Negroes in Brooklyn in 1930, 47,616 lived in what is now called Bedford-Stuyvesant. "Negro Community Near Yonkers Abandoned," *The New York Age*, July 3, 1926, March 24, August 4, 1928, April 19, 26, 1930; *Slums and Housing*, p. 314. For a sketch of Brooklyn's Negro community see Ralph Foster Weld, *Brooklyn Is America* (New York, 1950), pp. 153–173.
16 The President's Conference on Home Building and Home Ownership, *Report of the Committee on Negro Housing* (Washington, D.C., 1931), p. 5.
17 Bureau of the Census, *Fifteenth Census, 1930: Population* (Washington, D.C., 1933), II, 70; Ira De Augustine Reid, *The Negro Immigrant* (New York,

In the era of immigration restriction, West Indian Negroes came to America through what a contemporary called the "side door." The immigration laws of the 1920's seriously restricted the migration of Europeans and totally excluded Orientals but had little effect on peoples of the Caribbean. At first there were no restrictions on West Indian Negroes. After 1924, they could enter the country under quotas set aside for their mother countries. Since these quotas were never filled there was, in reality, a free flow of people from the islands to the United States in the 1920's.[18]

Although American Negroes tended to lump all the migrants together in a uniform image—"There is a general assumption," one migrant wrote, "that there is everything in common among West Indians"—it is important to recognize that Harlem's Negro immigrants represented a diverse group of peoples from dozens of different islands in the Caribbean.[19] Most Negro immigrants felt a strong attachment to their homeland. They demonstrated an "exaggerated" nationalism in America—a buffer against the strangeness of the new culture and the hostility they experienced—which was typical of white immigrant groups. It was common, for example, to find former British subjects at the office of the British consul protesting some difficulty they experienced in America.[20] Nationalistic organizations kept close check on American foreign policy in the Caribbean and often gave banquets for and listened to addresses by West Indian dignitaries. West Indian Negroes from all countries had the lowest rate of naturalization of all immigrant groups. The people white Americans and American Negroes called "West Indians" were really individuals from Jamaica, Trinidad, Barbados, Martinique, St. Vincent, St. Lucia, Dominica, British Guiana, St. Kitts, Nevis, Montserrat, Antigua, Virgin Islands, Bermuda, the Bahamas, and so on. Although the majority spoke English, some considered French their first tongue;

1938), pp. 248–249; Barrington Dunbar, "Factors in the Cultural Background of the American Southern Negro and the British West Indian Negro That Condition Their Adjustment in Harlem" (M.A. thesis, Columbia University, 1935), *foreword*, p. 4.

[18] Reid, *The Negro Immigrant*, pp. 31–35; Reid, "Negro Immigration to the United States," *Social Forces*, XVI (March 1938), 411–417; W. A. Domingo, "Restricted West Indian Immigration and the American Negro," *Opportunity*, II (October 1924), 298–299.

[19] W. A. Domingo, "Gift of the Black Tropics," in Alain Locke, ed., *The New Negro: An Interpretation* (New York, 1925), p. 343.

[20] *The New York Age*, July 9, 1924, February 4, 1928; Harry Robinson, "The Negro Immigrant in New York" (WPA research paper, Schomburg Collection), p. 9.

others Spanish; a few Dutch. The fraternal and benevolent associations they founded were not inclusive organizations for all Negro immigrants, but exclusive ones—*landsmannschaften*—for people from specific islands. Danish settlers kept pictures of the King of Denmark in their homes; former British subjects held coronation pageants and balls ("Boxes, 12s. 6d.—Loges, 8s. 4d.") and flew the Union Jack in Harlem; Frenchmen had annual Bastille Day dances.[21]

Negro immigrants differed from each other in origin, yet in a broader sense they shared general experiences, desires and mores which set them apart *as a group* from their American brethren. Most came from societies in which class distinctions played a more important role in one's life than the color line—although the latter was certainly significant. Unaccustomed to common American racial slurs, they often refused to accept them without protest. The Pullman Company, for example, hesitated to employ West Indian Negroes, it was said, "because of their refusal to accept insults from passengers quietly." [22] Out of this heightened class consciousness came a small group of political and economic radicals in Harlem—"foreign-born agitators," local Negroes called them.[23] Many of Harlem's street-corner orators in the 1920's, though not all, were West Indian migrants. Hubert H. Harrison, a Virgin Islander, was among the most prominent. Harrison was a socialist, an expert in African history, a militant critic of American society and a proud defender of the "Negro's racial heritage." He conducted formal lectures in what he called the "Harlem School of Social Science," and others from street corners—his "outdoor university." A Harlem church, the Hubert H. Harrison Memorial Church, honors his memory. Others presented talks on "Socialism vs. Capitalism," organized tenants' leagues, published Marxist journals and tried to make Harlemites labor-conscious. Richard B. Moore, Frank R. Crosswaith and the Reverend Ethelred Brown—all Negro immigrants—were prominent local candidates for Board of Aldermen, Assembly and Congress on Socialist and Communist tickets—they usually polled an exceedingly small vote. Some

21 Garrie Ward Moore, "A Study of a Group of West Indian Negroes in New York City" (M.A. thesis, Columbia University, 1923), pp. 19–20; Reid, *The Negro Immigrant,* pp. 126–128; *The New York Age,* February 28, 1931, July 29, 1933.

22 "The Negro in New York" (unpublished WPA manuscript, Schomburg Collection), pp. 25–27; Gardner N. Jones, "The Pilgrimage to Freedom" (WPA research paper, Schomburg Collection), p. 25.

23 Reid, *The Negro Immigrant,* p. 159.

organized rent strikes, "rent parades," lobbied for social legislation at City Hall and Albany and distributed radical literature in Harlem. "There is no West Indian slave, no American slave," the short-lived radical magazine *Challenge* commented. "You are all slaves, base, ignoble slaves." [24]

This concern with "class" led to the emergence of a broader tradition in America. What is striking about the Negro immigrant is the way his response to American conditions, such as his exaggerated sense of nationalism, was similar to the typical reactions of most European immigrants. The Negro immigrant "did not suffer from the local anesthesia of custom" [25] and he tried to create a meaningful economic position for himself within American society. Menial labor was, among most first-generation Negro immigrants, considered a sign of· social degradation and looked upon with "disgust." Most were forced to accept such jobs initially, but were strongly motivated by their traditions to improve themselves. As a group, West Indians became noted for their ambition, thrift and business acumen. They were called "pushy," "the Jews of the race," "crafty," "clannish." [26] Negro journalist George S. Schuyler "admired their enterprise in business, their pushfulness." [27] "The West Indians [are] legendary in Harlem for their frugalness and thrift," one student noted. When a West Indian "got ten cents above a beggar," a common local saying ran, "he opened a business." Contemporary surveys of Negro business in Harlem and Columbus Hill demonstrate that a disproportionate number of small stores—the traditional "Race Enterprise"—were owned by Negro immigrants. Dr. P. M. H. Savory, one of the leading spokesmen of New York's foreign-born Negro community from the 1920's to his death in June 1965, owned and published the *Amsterdam News*. Many others achieved economic success within the racial barrier.[28]

[24] *Ibid.*, p. 123; "Communists in Harlem," *The New York Age*, September 21, 1929, October 2, 9, 1926, December 24, 1927, January 21, May 12, December 8, 1928, September 21, 1929.

[25] Domingo, "Gift of the Black Tropics," p. 347.

[26] Robinson, "Negro Immigrant in New York," pp. 21–22; Moore, "West Indian Negroes in New York City," p. 26.

[27] "The Reminiscences of George S. Schuyler" (Oral History Research Office, Columbia University, 1960), p. 73.

[28] Robinson, "Negro Immigrant in New York," p. 9; "The Negro in New York," p. 25; Moore, "West Indian Negroes in New York City," p. 25; Reid, *The Negro Immigrant*, p. 133; *The Messenger*, VII (September 1925), 326, 337–338; *The New York Age*, February 22, 1930; Baltimore *Afro-American*, January 9, 1932.

Another significant distinction between the foreign-born Negro and the American was their attitude toward family life. Slavery initially destroyed the entire concept of family for American Negroes and the slave heritage, bulwarked by economic conditions, continued into the twentieth century to make family instability a common factor in Negro life. This had not been true for most West Indians, and they arrived in America with the orthodox respect for family ties that was traditional of rural people. The West Indian family was patriarchal in structure—contrasted with the typically matriarchal American Negro home. The father, as key worker and wage earner in the islands, ruled the household with a solid hand. It was beneath his dignity to help with domestic chores. (This led American Negroes to brand West Indian men "cruel.")[29] Children were supposed to obey their parents rigidly—American Negroes considered them strait-laced; have long and formal courtships; and receive parental approval before marriage. Illicit sexual relations were considered the worst form of moral evil.[30] These traditions began to change in the second generation, but throughout the 1920's family solidarity was a pervasive force among New York's Negro immigrants.[31]

These differences in style of life were also evident in another important institution—the church. The majority of Harlemites were Baptists and Methodists; the immigrants were predominantly Episcopalian and Catholic.[32] The beautiful St. Martin's Episcopal Church was founded in Harlem in 1928 to minister to the needs of West Indian migrants. Services in immigrant churches were generally staid and quiet; Sunday a day of prayer, rest and visiting—as it had been on the islands. Observers were impressed with the differences between the emotionalism of a typical Harlem religious service and the moderation and restraint shown in churches of the foreign-born. Negro immigrants also objected to the general frivolity and "fast ways" that were part of a typical Sunday in Harlem.[33]

All these factors combined to make Harlem in the 1920's a battleground of intraracial antagonism. American Negro nativism spilled

29 Moore, "West Indian Negroes in New York City," p. 5.
30 Dunbar, "Negro Adjustment in Harlem," pp. 14–25.
31 Reid, *The Negro Immigrant, passim.*
32 *Ibid.,* p. 125; Greater New York Federation of Churches, *Negro Churches in Manhattan* (New York, 1930).
33 Reid, *The Negro Immigrant,* p. 174; Moore, "West Indian Negroes in New York City," pp. 20–25; Dunbar, "Negro Adjustment in Harlem," chap. IV, pp. 22–23.

over to taint Harlemites' reactions to the West Indian. The Negro immigrant was ridiculed; his tropical clothing was mocked; children tossed stones at the people who looked so different; foreigners were taunted with such epithets as "monkey-chaser," "ring-tale," "king Mon," "cockney." "When a monkey-chaser dies/Don't need no undertaker/Just throw him in de Harlem River/He'll float back to Jamaica," was a verse from a Harlem ditty of the twenties. West Indians came to Harlem, ran another common saying, "to teach, open a church, or start trouble." "Bitter resentment grew on both sides." Each group called the other "aggressive." "We have . . . in Harlem," NAACP director Walter White wrote, "this strange mixture of reactions not only to prejudice from without but to equally potent prejudices from within." "If you West Indians don't like how we do things in this country," an American Negro said tersely, "you should go back where you came from. . . ." [34]

The obvious hostility of American Negroes forced Negro immigrants to unite in defense organizations larger than their individual national groups. The West Indian Committee on America, the Foreign-Born Citizens' Alliance and the West Indian Reform Association were founded in the twenties to soften these intraracial tensions and promote "cordial relations between West Indians and colored Americans." Radio programs were devoted to discussions of "Intra-Race Relations in Harlem," and immigrants were urged to become naturalized citizens. American Negroes, in turn, were asked to tone down their "considerable prejudice against West Indians." A semblance of co-operation was achieved as mass meetings were held in Harlem churches. The hatreds of the 1920's did not die, however, until West Indian Negroes stopped migrating to New York. During the Depression more immigrants left New York than entered and intraracial tensions slowly eased. Young Harlemites today, even third-generation descendants of Negro immigrants, are often unaware of these old divisions. The unique type of intraracial hostility so prominent in the twenties has never reappeared. While it lasted, however, it served to

[34] Roi Ottley, *'New World A-Coming': Inside Black America* (New York, 1943), pp. 47–48; Gardner Jones, "The Pilgrimage to Freedom" (WPA research paper, Schomburg Collection), p. 25; Beverly Smith, "Harlem—Negro City," *New York Herald Tribune*, February 14, 1930; Reid, *The Negro Immigrant*, p. 115; *The New York Age*, July 19, 1924, March 17, 1934; Dunbar, "Negro Adjustment in Harlem," chap. III, p. 4; Walter White, "The Paradox of Color," in Alain Locke, ed., *The New Negro: An Interpretation* (New York, 1925), p. 367.

weaken a Negro community in great need of unity. A divided Harlem confronted major social problems that desperately called for the co-operation of all.[35]

IV

The most profound change that Harlem experienced in the 1920's was its emergence as a slum. Largely within the space of a single decade Harlem was transformed from a potentially ideal community to a neighborhood with manifold social and economic problems called "deplorable," "unspeakable," "incredible." "The State would not allow cows to live in some of these apartments used by colored people . . . in Harlem," the chairman of a city housing reform committee said in 1927. The Harlem slum of today was created in the 1920's.[36]

The most important factor which led to the rapid deterioration of Harlem housing was the high cost of living in the community. Rents, traditionally high in Harlem, reached astounding proportions in the 1920's—they skyrocketed in response to the unprecedented demand created by heavy Negro migration and settlement within a restricted geographical area. "Crowded in a black ghetto," a sociologist wrote, "the Negro tenant is forced to pay exorbitant rentals because he cannot escape." In 1919 the average Harlemite paid somewhat above $21 or $22 a month for rent; by 1927 rentals had *doubled* and the "mean average market rent for Negro tenants in a typical block" was $41.77. In 1927 Harlem Negroes paid $8 more than the typical New Yorker for three-room apartments; $10 more for four rooms; and $7 more for five rooms, an Urban League survey noted.[37] Another report concluded that the typical white working-class family in New York City in the late twenties paid $6.67 per room, per month, while Harlem Negroes were charged $9.50.[38]

Realty values which had declined significantly prior to World War I *appreciated* in Harlem in the twenties.[39] Harlem experienced a

35 *The New York Age*, March 3, 24, April 21, 1928; Domingo, "The Gift of the Black Tropics," p. 344–345; Reid, *The Negro Immigrant*, p. 235.

36 "Harlem Slums," *The Crisis*, XLVIII (December 1941), 378–381; *The New York Age*, January 22, 1927.

37 New York Urban League, "Twenty-four Hundred Negro Families in Harlem: An Interpretation of the Living Conditions of Small Wage Earners" (typescript, Schomburg Collection, 1927), pp. 16–18.

38 *Report of the Committee on Negro Housing*, p. 64.

39 "Appreciation" of prices "came [when owners] remained calm. . . ." T. J. Woofter, *et al., Negro Problems in Cities* (New York, 1928), p. 75. *The*

slum boom. "The volume of business done in the section . . . during the last year is . . . unprecedented," *Harlem Magazine* announced in 1920. "Renting conditions have been very satisfactory to the owners and the demand for space . . . is getting keener every year [due] to the steady increase in the negro population," a *New York Times* reporter wrote in 1923. There was, in the language of a Harlem businessman, an "unprecedented demand for Harlem real estate." [40] For landlords—Negro and white (Negro tenants continually complained that Negro landlords fleeced them with equal facility as whites)—Harlem became a profitable slum.[41]

High rents and poor salaries necessarily led to congested and unsanitary conditions. The average Negro Harlemite in the 1920's, as in the 1890's, held some menial or unskilled position which paid low wages—work which was customarily "regarded as Negro jobs." There were generally two types of businesses in New York in terms of Negro hiring policy, E. Franklin Frazier wrote: "Those that employ Negroes in menial positions and those that employ no Negroes at all." Macy's, for example, hired Negroes as elevator operators, escalator attendants and cafeteria workers; Gimbels used none. "We have felt it inadvisable to [hire] colored people," a Metropolitan Life Insurance Company executive explained in 1930, "not because of any prejudice on the part of the company, but because . . . there would be very serious objection on the part of our white employees. . . ." [42] Throughout the city the vast majority of Negro men worked as longshoremen, elevator operators, porters, janitors, teamsters, chauffeurs, waiters and general laborers of all kinds. Negro women continued to work as domestics ("scrub women"), although in the 1920's an increasing number were employed as factory operatives in the garment industry and in laundries. Less than 20 per cent of

New York Times printed dozens of articles on Harlem's new business prosperity.

[40] "Harlem Real Estate Increasing in Value," *Harlem Magazine*, VIII (February 1920), 18b; "Unprecedented Demand for Harlem Real Estate," *ibid.*, X (November 1920), 6; "Revival of Speculative Activity on Harlem's Main Thoroughfare," *The New York Times*, January 18, 1920, July 24, 1921, June 10, 1923, February 13, 1927.

[41] "Of all the gouging landlords in Harlem, the colored landlords and agents are the worst, according to the records of the Seventh District Municipal Court." "Race Landlord Is Hardest on His Tenants," *The New York Age*, November 20, 1920, June 16, September 22, 1923, May 29, 1926.

[42] "The Negro in Harlem," pp. 27–32; *The New York Age*, April 26, 1930.

Harlem's businesses were owned by Negroes.[43] The average Harlem family, according to President Hoover's Conference on Home Building and Home Ownership, earned $1,300 a year in the twenties; the typical white family in the city, $1,570. A variety of social investigations noted that working-class whites expended approximately 20 per cent of their income for rent, considered the proper amount by economists; Harlemites, 33 per cent and more.[44] An Urban League study of 2,160 Harlem families demonstrated that almost half (48 per cent) spent 40 or more per cent of their earnings on rent. A 1928 sample of tenement families found that Harlemites paid 45 per cent of their wages for housing. Similar conclusions were reached in a variety of local community studies.[45] Whatever the exact figure, few Negroes looked to the first of the month with expectancy.

Added to the combination of "high rents and low wages"[46] was the fact that Harlem's apartment houses and brownstones were originally built for people with a radically different family structure from that of the new residents. Seventy-five per cent of Harlem's tenements had been constructed before 1900.[47] The Negro community of the twenties, like all working-class peoples in times of great migration, continued to be most heavily populated by young adults—men and women between the ages of 15 and 44. Family life had not yet begun for many Negro Harlemites—as it had for older Americans and earlier immigrants who lived in the community previously. In 1930, 66.5 per cent of Harlem Negroes were between the ages of 15 and 44, contrasted with 56.5 per cent for the general population of Manhattan and 54.4 per cent for New York City at large. Harlemites who were married had few children. In 1930, 17.5 per cent of Harlem's population was under 14; the corresponding figure for New York City was 24.5 per cent. The number of Harlemites under the age of 15 declined 14 per cent between 1920 and 1930, as whites left

[43] Bureau of the Census, *Fourteenth Census, 1920:* Population (Washington, D.C., 1923), IV, 366–367, 1157–1179; *Fifteenth Census, 1930: Occupations* (Washington, D.C., 1933), 1130–1134; Helen B. Sayre, "Negro Women in Industry," *Opportunity*, II (August 1924), 242–244.

[44] *Report of the Committee on Negro Housing*, p. 64; *Negro Problems in Cities*, p. 122.

[45] "Twenty-four Hundred Negro Families in Harlem," p. 19; Sidney Axelrad, *Tenements and Tenants: A Study of 1104 Tenement Families* (New York, 1932), p. 15; New York Building and Land Utilization Committee, *Harlem Family Income Survey* (New York, 1935), p. 3; James H. Hubert, "Harlem— Its Social Problems," *Hospital Social Service*, XXI (January 1930), 44.

[46] *Report of the Committee on Negro Housing*, p. vii.

[47] William Wilson to La Guardia, October 6, 1944, La Guardia Papers.

the neighborhood. There was a corresponding decrease of 19 per cent for those over 45 years of age.[48]

What all these statistics mean is simply that apartments of five, six, and seven rooms were suitable for older white residents with larger families and larger incomes—they obviously did not meet the needs of the Negro community in the 1920's. "The houses in the section of Harlem inhabited by the Negro were not only built for another race," E. Franklin Frazier noted, "but what is more important, for a group of different economic level, and consisting of families and households of an entirely different composition from those which now occupy these dwellings." "Unfortunately," Eugene Kinckle Jones of the Urban League stated, "the houses built before [the Negroes'] arrival were not designed to meet the needs . . . of Negroes." "The class of houses we are occupying today are not suited to our economic needs," John E. Nail said in 1921. Negro Harlemites desperately needed small apartments at low rentals: "One of the community's greatest needs [is] small apartments for small families with a reasonable rent limit. . . ." [49] Few realtors were philanthropic enough to invest their capital in new construction; older homes, properly subdivided, produced sufficient income. Only a handful of new houses were built in Harlem in the 1920's.[50]

A variety of makeshift solutions were found to make ends meet: "What you gonna do when the rent comes 'round," had been an old Negro song. The most common solution was to rent an apartment larger than one's needs and means and make up the difference by renting rooms to lodgers—"commercializing" one's home. In the twenties, approximately one white Manhattan family in nine (11.2 per cent) took in roomers, contrasted with one in four (26 per cent) for Negroes. Most lodgers were strangers people let into their homes because of economic necessity. It was difficult to separate "the respectable" from "the fast." "The most depraved Negroes lived side

[48] *Health Conditions in North Harlem*, pp. 16–17; *Fifteenth Census, 1930: Population* (Washington, D.C., 1933), II, 733–734; "The Negro in Harlem," p.20.

[49] ". . . The greatest need is the construction of model tenements. These should consist of one, two, three and four room apartments." "Modern Housing Needs," *The New York Age*, February 12, 1921, January 20, 1923, January 26, 1926, January 29, 1927; "The Negro in Harlem," p. 53; Eugene Kinckle Jones, "Negro Migration in New York State," *Opportunity*, IV (January 1926), 9.

[50] Victor R. Daly, "The Housing Crisis in New York City," *The Crisis*, XXXI (December 1920), 61–62.

by side with those who were striving to live respectable lives," a contemporary complained. Urban reformers blamed many of Harlem's social problems on this "lodger evil." [51]

Every conceivable space within a home was utilized to maximum efficiency: "Sometimes even the bathtub is used to sleep on, two individuals taking turns!" Negro educator Roscoe Conkling Bruce wrote. Boardinghouses were established which rented beds by the week, day, night or hour. A large number of brownstones were converted to rooming houses: "Private residences at one time characteristic of this part of the city have been converted into tenements. . . ." One landlord transformed apartments in nine houses into one-room flats, a state commission investigating New York housing reported. Space which formerly grossed $40 a month now brought in $100 to $125. People were said to be living in "coal bins and cellars." In an extreme case, one social investigator discovered seven children sleeping on pallets on the floor of a two-room apartment. More common was the "Repeating" or "Hot Bed System"—as soon as one person awoke and left, his bed was taken over by another.[52]

An additional Harlem method devised to meet the housing crisis of the twenties was the "Rent Party." Tickets of admission were usually printed and sold for a modest price (25c). All who wanted to come were invited to a party. Here is an example: [53]

> If you're looking for a good time,
> don't look no more,
> Just ring my bell and I'll answer
> the door.
> Southern Barbecue
> Given by Charley Johnson and Joe
> Hotboy, and How hot!

Chitterlings, pigs' feet, coleslaw and potato salad were sold. Money was raised in this way to pay the rent: "The rent party," *The New*

[51] National Urban League, *Housing Conditions Among Negroes, New York City* (New York, 1915), *passim; Ford, et al., Slums and Housing,* p. 338.

[52] "Very often it is found that there are two shifts." William Wilson to La Guardia, October 6, 1944, La Guardia Papers; *The New York Age,* March 12, 1921, February 26, 1927; "Along Rainbow Row," *The New York Times,* August 15, 1921, January 27, 1922; "Twenty-four Hundred Negro Families in Harlem," *passim;* Roscoe Conkling Bruce, "The Dunbar Apartment House: An Adventure in Community Building," *The Southern Workman,* LX (October 1931), 418.

[53] *New York Herald Tribune,* February 12, 13, 1930.

York Age editorialized in 1926, "has become a recognized means of meeting the demands of extortionate landlords. . . ." The white world saw rent parties as picturesque affairs—in reality they were a product of economic exploitation and they often degenerated into rowdy, bawdy and violent evenings.[54]

A significant part of the deterioration of the neighborhood was caused by the migrants themselves. Some needed rudimentary training in the simplest processes of good health and sanitation (Booker T. Washington, it will be remembered, preached the "gospel of the toothbrush").[55] E. Franklin Frazier called many Negro Harlemites "ignorant and unsophisticated peasant people without experience [in] urban living. . . ." They often permitted homes and buildings to remain in a state of uncleanliness and disrepair. Landlords complained that apartments were looted and fixtures stolen, that courtyards and hallways were found laden with refuse. Clothes and bedding were hung out of windows; trash sometimes thrown down air shafts; dogs walked on rooftops; profanities shouted across streets; "ragtime" played throughout the night. "Ragtime is a sufficient infliction of itself," one wag complained, "but when it keeps up all night, it becomes unbearable." "Since the so-called 'Negro invasion,' " a colored woman noted, "the streets, the property and the character of everything have undergone a change, and if you are honest, you will frankly acknowledge it has not been for the . . . improvement of the locality. . . . Are we responsible for at least some of the race prejudice which has developed since the entry of Negroes in Harlem?" Negro journals criticized "boisterous" men who laughed "hysterically" and hung around street corners, and those who used "foul language on the streets." An editorial in the *Age,* one of many, attacked "Careless Harlem Tenants": "A great deal might be said about the necessity for training some of the tenants in the matter of common

---

54 "I promoted a weekly party, to get money to pay rent." "Boisterous rent parties, flooded with moonshine, are a quick and sure resource." "The Reminiscences of Benjamin McLaurin" (Oral History Research Office, Columbia University, 1960), p. 155; *The New York Age,* August 11, 1923, June 21, December 11, 1926; Clyde Vernon Kiser, *Sea Island to City* (New York, 1932), pp. 44–45.

55 Booker T. Washington, *Up from Slavery: An Autobiography* (New York 1959), pp. 122–123. Note the following statement of a recent study: "There are many cases in which migratory workers do not understand or properly use ordinary living facilities, such as toilets, showers, bedding, kitchen appliances, and garbage cans. The result has been unnecessary damage to property and needless expense for repairs." 87th Cong., 1st Sess., *Senate Report 1098* (1961), p. 8.

decency," it suggested. The absence of a sense of social and community responsibility, characteristic of urban life, obviously affected Negro Harlemites.[56]

All these factors combined to lead to the rapid decline of Harlem. The higher the rents, sociologists said, the greater the congestion: "Crowding is more prevalent in high-rent cities than in cities in which rent per room is more reasonable." In 1925, Manhattan's population density was 223 people per acre—in the Negro districts it was 336. Philadelphia, the second most congested Negro city in the country, had 111 Negroes to an acre of land; Chicago ranked third with 67. There were two streets in Harlem that were perhaps the most congested blocks in the entire world.[57]

People were packed together to the point of "indecency." [58] Some landlords, after opening houses to Negro tenants, lost interest in caring for their property and permitted it to run down—halls were left dark and dirty, broken pipes were permitted to rot, steam heat was cut off as heating apparatus wore out, dumb-waiters broke down and were boarded up, homes became vermin-infested. Tenants in one rat-infested building started what they called "a crusade against rats." They argued that the rats in their house were "better fed" and "better housed" than the people. Some common tenant complaints in the 1920's read: "No improvement in ten years"; "Rats, rat holes, and roaches"; "Very very cold"; "Not fit to live in"; "Air shaft smells"; "Ceilings in two rooms have fallen"; "My apartment is overrun with rats"; and so on.[59] There were more disputes between tenants and landlords in Harlem's local district court—the Seventh District Court —than in any municipal court in the five boroughs. Traditionally, municipal courts were known as "poor-men's courts"; Harlemites called the Seventh District Court the "rent court." Occasionally, socially conscious judges of this court made personal inspections of

[56] *The New York Age*, August 1, 1912, June 5, 1920, September 16, 1922, July 14, 1928; National Urban League, *Housing Conditions Among Negroes*, pp. 9–10; "The Negro in Harlem," p. 113; Eslanda Goode Robeson, *Paul Robeson: Negro* (London, 1930), p. 46.

[57] Woofter, *et al., Negro Problems in Cities*, pp. 79, 84; "The Negro in Harlem," p. 53; Ernest W. Burgess, "Residential Segregation in American Cities," *The Annals*, CXL (November 1928), 105–115; Ford, *et al., Slums and Housing*, p. 749.

[58] Owen R. Lovejoy, *The Negro Children of New York* (New York, 1932), p. 15.

[59] *The New York Age*, October 28, 1922, January 17, 1925; *Housing Conditions Among Negroes, passim;* "Twenty-four Hundred Negro Families in Harlem," *passim.*

local tenements that were subjects of litigation. Without exception what they saw horrified them: "Conditions in negro tenements in Harlem are deplorable"; "Found few fit for human habitation"; "Negro tenants are being grossly imposed upon by their landlords"; "On the whole I found a need for great reformation"; were some of their comments. One municipal official accurately called the majority of Harlem's houses "diseased properties." [60]

V

And the disease did not confine itself to houses. To touch most areas of Harlem life in the 1920's is to touch tragedy. This was especially true of the health of the community. Theoretically, a section of the city inhabited by relatively young people should have ranked below the general population in mortality and sickness rates. Just the reverse was true. Undertaking was a most profitable Harlem business.[61]

From 1923 to 1927 an Atlanta University professor made an intensive study of Harlem health. His findings were shocking. During these years Harlem's death rate, for all causes, was 42 per cent in excess of that of the entire city. Twice as many Harlem mothers died in childbirth as did mothers in other districts, and almost twice as many Harlem children "passed" as did infants in the rest of New York. Infant mortality in Harlem, 1923–1927, was 111 per thousand live births; for the city, 64.5. Families wept at the processions of "so many little white caskets." Similar statistics are recorded for deaths from tuberculosis (two and a half to three times the city rate), pneumonia, heart disease, cancer and stillbirths.[62] An astounding number of Harlemites had venereal diseases. Negro children com-

[60] "I do not think I need to say that our problem of Harlem is one of the most serious we have to face." Langdon W. Post (Chairman of New York City Housing Authority) to La Guardia, April 30, 1936, La Guardia Papers. "The Negro families of the West Harlem section have undoubtedly the most serious housing problem in the City." Ford, *et al.*, *Slums and Housing*, p. 326. *The New York Times*, September 16, 1920, October 17, 23, 1921, April 22, 1922, January 17, June 13, 1925; *The New York Age*, February 28, August 8, 1925, January 9, 1926; "Preliminary Report on the Subject of Housing (1935)," La Guardia Papers.

[61] "High Cost of Dying." *The New York Age*, February 25, 1928.

[62] *Health Conditions in North Harlem, passim; The Negro Children of New York*, p. 22; "Fighting the Ravages of the White Plague Among New York's Negro Population," *Opportunity*, I (January 1923), 23–24; Dr. Louis R. Wright, "Cancer as It Affects Negroes," *ibid.*, VI (June 1928), 169–170, 187; Louis I. Dublin, "The Effect of Health Education on Negro Mortality," *Proceedings of the National Conference on Social Work, 1924* (Chicago, 1924), 274–279. Hereafter cited as PNCSW.

Health center districts, 1930	Infant mortality per 1,000 live births	TB mortality per 100,000 population	Pulmonary TB new case rate per 100,000 population	Other infectious diseases, rate per 100,000 population	Venereal disease new case rate per 100,000 population	General mortality rate per 1,000 population
Manhattan						
Central Harlem	98	251	487	987	2,826	15.3
Lower East Side	62	116	302	1,160	892	14.0
Kips Bay–Lenox Hill	73	75	184	937	629	12.7
East Harlem	75	137	311	1,326	913	12.0
Lower West Side	83	156	391	1,201	1,318	16.7
Riverside	64	75	196	827	778	12.3
Washington Heights	52	72	203	937	668	10.5
Total	73	122	294	1,049	1,455	13.3

monly suffered from rickets—a disease of malnutrition. More women than ever reported themselves "widows" to census-takers. Negro deaths by violence increased 60 per cent between 1900 and 1925.[63] With the single exception of the Lower West Side Health District, which included the old San Juan Hill neighborhood, Harlem was the most disease-ridden community in Manhattan.[64]

Whatever the causes of Harlem's health problems—and medical investigators continue to search for all the answers—a good deal can be laid at the door of slum environment. Urban reformers consistently showed a high correlation between poverty and congestion on the one hand and disease and death on the other. Mortality rates for infants whose mothers worked away from home, for example—and twice as many Negro women as white women in the city did—was higher than for children whose mothers remained at home; working-class families in old-law tenements (pre-1901) died at a higher-rate than those in newer houses; poverty led to the consumption of the cheapest foods, and this in turn fostered diseases of poor diet; working mothers died more readily in childbirth than unemployed women; and so on.[65] Added to all these considerations, however, was a deep strain of peasant ignorance and superstition embedded in the minds of thousands of migrants—foreign-born as well as native—who settled in Harlem. Quackery abounded in the community in the 1920's.[66]

[63] ". . . Syphilitic infection is one of the most fruitful causes of stillbirths, miscarriages, and early death of infants." New York Association for Improving the Condition of the Poor, *Health Work for Mothers and Children in a Colored Community* (New York, 1924), p. 3; "The Negro's Health Progress During the Last Twenty-five Years," *Weekly Bulletin of the Department of Health*, XV (June 12, 1926), 93–96; *Fifteenth Census, 1930: Population* (Washington, D.C., 1933), II, 959; E. K. Jones, "The Negro's Struggle for Health," *PNCSW, 1923* (Chicago, 1923), 68–72.

[64] Adapted from Godea J. Drolet and Louis Werner, "Vital Statistics in the Development of Neighborhood Health Centers in New York City," *Journal of Preventive Medicine*, VI (January 1932), 69.

[65] In 1920, 30.3 per cent of white women in the city worked, and 57.9 per cent of colored women were employed. *Fourteenth Census, 1920: Population* (Washington, D.C., 1923), IV, 367. Robert Morse Woodbury, *Causal Factors in Infant Mortality* (Washington, D.C., 1925); L. T. Wright, "Factors Controlling Negro Health," *The Crisis*, XLII (September 1935), 264–265, 280, 284; Mildred Jane Watson, "Infant Mortality in New York City, White and Colored, 1929–1936" (M.A. thesis, Columbia University, 1938); Charles Herbert Garvin, "White Plague and Black Folk," *Opportunity*, VIII (August 1930), 232–235.

[66] For "voodoo" and "devil worship" among West Indians see Reid, *The Negro Immigrant*, pp. 48–49, 136–138.

Harlem had the reputation of a "wide-open city." Whatever you wanted, and in whatever quantity, so the impression went, could be bought there. This was certainly true for the variety of "spiritualists," "herb doctors," "African medicine men," "Indian doctors," "dispensers of snake oils," "layers-on-of-hands," "faith healers," "palmists," and phrenologists who performed a twentieth-century brand of necromancy there: "Harlem sick people are flocking to all sorts of Quacksters," an *Age* reporter noted. One man, "Professor Ajapa," sold a "herb juice" guaranteed "to cure consumption, rheumatism, and other troubles that several doctors have failed in." Powders could be purchased to keep one's wife home at night, make women fertile and men sexually appealing. "Black Herman the Magician" and "Sister P. Harreld" held séances and sold "blessed handkerchiefs," "potent powders," love charms, lodestones, amulets and "piles of roots." "Ignorance, cherished superstitions and false knowledge often govern Negroes in illness and hamper recoveries," a colored physician with the Board of Health wrote in 1926. Nine wood lice gathered in a little bag and tied around a baby's neck, some believed, would end teething. An egg fried brown on both sides and placed on a woman's abdomen would hasten labor. If a mother in the course of childbirth kicked a Bible from her bed to the floor, either she or her child would die. People had faith in the medicinal qualities of dried cobwebs, rabbit brains, "dirt-dauber tea," and something called "cockroach rum." In spite of efforts of physicians, health agencies and the Negro press to bring modern-day medical information to the community, quackery "continued to thrive with impunity in Harlem." It aggravated an already tragic situation.[67]

Accompanying the proliferation of healers, and rooted in the same rural consciousness which made quackery possible,[68] was the host of

[67] ". . . Many [are] bringing with them their simple faith in roots, herbs, home remedies, [and are] imposed upon by unscrupulous venders of worthless . . . remedies." Dr. Peter Marshall Murray, "Harlem's Health," *Hospital Social Service*, XXII (October 1930), 309–313; C. V. Roman, "The Negro's Psychology and His Health," *PNCSW, 1924* (Chicago, 1924), 270–274; *Opportunity*, IV (July 1926), 206–207; *The Crisis*, XLII (August 1935), 243; *The New York Age*, September 23, 1922, February 17, July 21, August 11, 25, 1923, January 6, April 5, 1924, February 21, March 14, 1925, January 18, July 23, 1927.

[68] Note the striking similarities between the medical and healing superstitions of urban Negroes in the twentieth century and those of slaves in the early nineteenth century. The following is a description of slave superstition by an ex-slave: "There is much superstition among the slaves. Many of them believe in what they call 'conjuration,' tricking, and witchcraft; and some of

storefront churches founded in Harlem in the twenties. These were places that healed one's soul: "Jesus is the Doctor, Services on Sunday," read a sign which hung over one door. An investigator found 140 Negro churches in a 150-block area of Harlem in 1926. "Harlem is perhaps overchurched," W. E. B. DuBois said modestly. Only about a third—fifty-four—of Harlem's churches were housed in regular church buildings—and these included some of the most magnificent and costly church edifices in New York City. The rest held services in stores and homes and appealed to Harlem's least educated people. "Jack-leg preachers," "cotton-field preachers," as their critics called them, hung out their poorly printed signboards and "preached Jesus" to all who wanted to listen. One self-appointed pastor held meetings in the front room of his home and rented chairs from the local undertaker to seat his small congregation. In Harlem in the twenties one could receive the word of the Lord through such nondenominational sects as: "The Metaphysical Church of the Divine Investigation," "The Temple of the Gospel of the Kingdom," "The Church of the Temple of Love," "Holy Church of the Living God," "Temple of Luxor," "Holy Tabernacle of God," "Royal Fraternity Association," "Knights of the Rose and Cross," "Sons of God," "Sons of Christ," "Sons of Jehovah," "Sanctified Sons of the Holy Ghost," and the "Live-Ever-Die-Never" church. People not only had their worries removed in these places, a Negro clergyman wrote, but "their meager worldly goods as well." [69]

The ministers of these churches preached a fundamentalism which centered around the scheming ways of Satan, who was everywhere, and the terror and joy of divine retribution, with an emphasis on terror. One congregation expelled members who attended the theater or movies. "The devil runs every theatre," its pastor said. "He collects a tax on the souls of men and robs them of their seat in

them pretend to understand the art, and say that by it they can prevent their masters from exercising their will over their slaves. Such are often applied to by others, to give them power to prevent their masters from flogging them. The remedy is most generally some kind of bitter root; they are directed to chew it and spit toward their masters'. . . . At other times they prepare certain kinds of powders, to sprinkle their masters' dwellings." *Narrative of the Life and Adventures of Henry Bibb, An American Slave, Written by Himself* (New York, 1849), pp. 25–31.

[69] Beverly Smith, "Harlem—Negro City," *New York Herald Tribune*, February 11, 1930; Ira De Augustine Reid, "Let Us Prey!" *Opportunity* IV (September 1926), 274–278; Reverend James H. Robinson, *Road Without Turning: An Autobiography* (New York, 1950), 231.

heaven." Services were fervent, loud and boisterous as members felt the spirit of the Lord and shouted and begged for His forgiveness. Tambourines sometimes kept up a rhythmic beat in the background and heightened the emotionalism to a state of frenzy. Neighbors of one storefront church sued the congregation for "conducting a public nuisance." The "weird sounds" which emanated from the building, they complained, seemed like a "jazz orchestra." [70]

> Are you ready-ee? Hah!
> For that great day, hah!
> When the moon shall drape her face in mourning, hah!
> And the sun drip down in blood, hah!
> When the stars, hah!
> Shall burst forth from their diamond sockets, hah!
> And the mountains shall skip like lambs, hah!
> Havoc will be there, my friends, hah!
> With her jaws wide open, hah!
> And the sinner-man, hah!
> And cry, Oh rocks! Hah!
> Hide me! Hah!
> Hide me from the face of an angry God, hah!
> Hide me, Ohhhhh! . . .
> Can't hide, sinner, you can't hide.[71]

Contemporaries were uniformly critical of these evangelists—there were many Harlem "Prophets"—and most of these preachers were probably charlatans in some form. There was at least one exception, however. A new denomination, the Church of Christ, Apostolic Faith, was founded on the streets of Harlem by the Reverend Mr. R. C. Lawson in 1919. The Reverend Mr. Lawson, of New Iberia, Louisiana, "the only real Apostolic–Holy Ghost–Bible Preacher," presented what he called the "Full Gospel" on street corners of Harlem's worst blocks. He decried the lack of emotionalism in the more established urban churches—copying "the white man's style," he said—and offered recent migrants a touch of fire and brimstone and personal Christianity characteristic of religion in the rural South:

---

[70] *The New York Age,* February 19, 1927; *The New York Times,* September 24, 1919.

[71] Zora Neale Hurston, *Dust Tracks on a Road* (Philadelphia, 1942), pp. 279–280.

I have found it, I have found it,
the meaning of life, life in God,
life flowing through me by the
Holy Spirit, life abundant, peace,
joy, life in its fullness.

Lawson started preaching on One Hundred and Thirty-third Street, east of Lenox Avenue. This area "was to Harlem what the Bowery is to the lower East Side," a Negro journalist recorded. From the streets, the Reverend Mr. Lawson moved into a small building and held services for those "fast drifting to a life of eternal darkness" every day and every night of the week. His Refuge Church of Christ became the founding church of the new denomination, and the Reverend Mr. Lawson its first bishop. By 1930 the Apostolic Church had some forty branches throughout the country and ran an orphanage, elementary school and "Bible Supply House"; it continues to prosper today. Annual conventions met in Refuge Church, "the most honored in the sisterhood of the Apostolic Church," and local leaders praised and publicized its good works for Harlem Negroes: "This church has had one of the most remarkable growths of any religious organizations in the country." [72]

Harlem was also a "wide-open city" in terms of vice and gambling.[73] The annual reports of the anti-vice Committee of Fourteen, founded in 1905, showed Harlem as the leading or near-leading prostitution center of Manhattan throughout the twenties. The Committee hired a Negro doctor, Ernest R. Alexander, to do a secret study of Harlem vice in 1928. His report emphasized the "openness of vice conditions in this district." Dr. Alexander personally found sixty-one houses of prostitution in the neighborhood—more than the combined totals of four other investigators hired at the same time to survey other districts. "There is a larger amount and more open immorality in Harlem than this community has known in years," Negro alderman George W. Harris noted in 1922. "It is a house of assignation . . . this black city," Eric D. Walrond wrote bitterly in the Negro journal *The Messenger*.[74]

[72] *The New York Age*, January 15, 1927, February 9, 1929, August 23, 1930, August 8, September 19, 1931, July 23, 1932, August 26, 1933, September 1, 1934.

[73] "A Wide Open Harlem," *ibid.*, September 2, 1922.

[74] Committee of Fourteen, *Annual Reports*, 1914–1930; *The Crisis*, XXXVI (November 1929), 417–418; *The Messenger*, VI (January 1924), 14.

> Her dark brown face
> Is like a withered flower
> On a broken stem.
> Those kind come cheap in Harlem,
> So they say.[75]

The Committee of Fourteen also disclosed that more than 90 per cent of these "daughters of joy" institutions were owned and managed by whites. Other evidence verifies this.[76]

Gambling also prevailed in the neighborhood: "Bootleggers, gamblers, and other panderers to vice have found it profitable to ply their vicious trades in this section." The poorest of the poor sought instant riches through the numbers racket. No sum was too small to bet—starting with pennies. "One can bet with plenty of takers on anything from a horse race to a mule race," the *Age* editorialized. Many Harlemites "would rather gamble than eat," it concluded. People selected numbers to coincide with birthdays, dreams, hymns or chapters and verses of Scripture in expectation that they would coincide with the clearing-house figures of the day. The odds were thousands to one against success, yet the smallest hope for a richer life was better than none and Negroes continued to play "policy" avidly. "The chief pastime of Harlem seems to be playing the numbers," George S. Schuyler wrote in 1925.[77]

"Buffet flats," "hooch joints," "barrel houses," and cabarets supplied Harlemites with illegal liquor, and occasionally other things, in the Prohibition era. Drugstores, cigar stores, sweetshops and delicatessens were used as "fronts" for speakeasies. "Harlem can boast of more drugstores than any similar area in the world," one Negro commented. "A plethora of delicatessen stores may be found in the

[75] Langston Hughes, "Young Prostitute," *The Crisis*, XXVI (August 1923), 162.

[76] "Gambling is popular in Harlem, but the big shots of the racket are white." Fiorello La Guardia, "Harlem: Homelike and Hopeful" (unpublished manuscript, La Guardia Papers), p. 9; "A Summary of Vice Conditions in Harlem," Committee of Fourteen, *Annual Report for 1928* (New York, 1929), 31–34; *The New York Times*, February 13, 1922; *The New York Age*, February 28, 1925, May 18, 1929. Although whites seemed to control most of Harlem vice, Virgin Islander Casper Holstein—well-known as a philanthropist and café owner—was reputed to be a head of the numbers racket.

[77] "Harlem—The Bettor," *The New York Age*, March 7, 1925, November 6, 20, 1926, June 4, 1927, June 23, 1928; *The New York Times*, June 12, 1922, March 11, 1927; "New York: Utopia Deferred," *The Messenger*, VII (October, November 1925), 344–349, 370.

Negro sections of New York, most of which are simply disguised bootlegging stores," a Harlemite concluded in 1924. "And so many confectioners! One never dreamed the Negroes were so much in need of sugar." "Speakeasies downtown are usually carefully camouflaged," a *New York Tribune* reporter noted. "In Harlem they can be spotted a hundred yards off." [78]

Poverty and family instability also led to a high incidence of juvenile delinquency. A community with fewer young teenagers should have shown a proportionally lower juvenile crime rate; as with Negro health, just the reverse was true. "The records of the Children's Court of New York for every year from 1914 to 1927 show a steady increase in the percentage of all crimes committed by Negro boys and girls," Owen R. Lovejoy of the Children's Aid Society reported. In 1914 Negro children represented 2.8 per cent of all cases before the juvenile court of New York City; in 1930 this figure rose to 11.7 per cent.[79]

Working mothers had little time to care for their children. Youngsters "with keys tied around their necks on a ribbon" wandered around the streets until families came home at night. A substantial portion were products of broken homes—families without a male head. One Harlem school principal testified that 699 of his 1,600 pupils came from families whose fathers were not living at home. Nor did the majority of Harlem schoolchildren ever have time to accustom themselves to the regularity of school life; many families were rootless. Three-fourths of all the Negro pupils registered in one Harlem school, for example, transferred to some other before the end of one school year; some schools actually experienced a 100 per cent turnover. Pupils from the South were seriously deficient in educational training: "They are at times 14 to 15 years of age and have not the schooling of boys of eight," a Harlem principal wrote. "We cannot give a boy back seven years of wasted life. . . ." The typical Harlem school of the twenties had double and sometimes triple sessions. The "usual class size" was forty to fifty and conditions were generally "immensely over-crowded": "The school plant as a whole

[78] *The New York Age,* September 16, 1922, April 21, 1923; *New York Herald Tribune,* February 13, 1930; *The Messenger,* VI (August 1924) 247, 262.
[79] Lovejoy, *The Negro Children of New York,* p. 37; *New York Herald Tribune,* February 12, 1930; Joint Committee on Negro Child Study in New York City, *A Study of Delinquent and Neglected Negro Children Before the New York City Children's Court* (New York, 1927).

is old, shabby, and far from modern." In some schools 25 per cent and more of the children were overage or considered retarded.

Negro children in Harlem often led disrupted and harsh lives from the earliest years of their existence: "Testimony has been given before us as to the moral conditions among children, even of tender age," a municipal agency investigating Harlem schools recorded, "which is not to be adequately described by the word 'horrifying.'" These conditions were obviously reflected in high rates of juvenile crime but more subtly, and worst of all, in a loss of respect for oneself and for life in general. Harlem youngsters developed "a sense of subordination, of insecurity, of lack of self-confidence and self-respect, the inability . . . to stand on their own feet and face the world with open eyes and feel that [they have] as good a right as anyone else." [80]

This then was the horror of slum life—the Harlem tragedy of the 1920's. "Court and police precinct records show," a municipal agency maintained, "that in arrests, convictions, misdemeanants, felons, female police problems and juvenile delinquencies, these areas are in the lead. . . ." It was no wonder that narcotics addiction became a serious problem then and that Harlem became "the center of the retail dope traffic of New York"; nor that local violence and hatred for the police were continually reported in the press.[81] The majority of Harlemites even during normal times lived "close to the subsistence level." Many were "under care" of charitable agencies in the period of relatively full employment. Those who needed money quickly and had no other recourse were forced to turn to loan sharks, Negro and white, who charged 30 to 40 per cent interest: Harlem "has been infested by a lot of loan sharks," a municipal magistrate who dealt with such cases stated. In one form or another the sorrow and economic deprivation of the Depression had come to Harlem in the twenties: "The reason why the Depression didn't have the impact on

[80] Jacob Theobald, "Some Facts About P.S. 89, Manhattan," *The New York Age,* January 17, 1920; "Report of Subcommittee on Education," La Guardia Papers; "The Problem of Education and Recreation," *ibid.;* "The Negro in Harlem," p. 73; Lovejoy, *The Negro Children of New York,* p. 22; *The New York Age,* March 12, 1921.

[81] "Results of the Crime and Delinquency Study," La Guardia Papers; *The New York Age,* January 6, February 17, June 23, 1923, June 12, 1926, December 3, 1927, July 28, 1928, January 4, 1930. A white Harlem policeman, at a later date, wrote the following: "Every one of [us] is made to feel like a soldier in an army of occupation. He is engulfed by an atmosphere of antagonism." *The Crisis,* LII (January 1945), 16–17.

the Negroes that it had on the whites," George S. Schuyler said, "was that the Negroes had been in the Depression all the time." [82]

---

[82] Lovejoy, *The Negro Children of New York*, p. 15; "The Negro in Harlem," p. 110; *The New York Age*, February 9, 1929; "The Reminiscences of George S. Schuyler" (Oral History Research Office, Columbia University, 1960), p. 232.

17

The Urban Unease: Community vs. City

by JAMES Q. WILSON

. . . what constitutes the "urban problem" for a large percentage (perhaps a majority) of urban citizens is a sense of the failure of community.

At the end of the Johnson administration there began to be more widely heard new and trenchant criticisms of not only those strategies of social change inherited from the New Deal but also those set in motion by the cluster of legislation enacted in the mid-sixties, one of whose central purposes was to rebuild the American cities. To be sure, there had been some earlier and even influential salvos. In the early days of the Kennedy administration, for example, Jane Jacobs published *The Death and Life of Great American Cities,** which was a wide-ranging attack on the prevailing practices of urban renewal and planning. She viewed them as an aggregate disaster for the "intimate and casual life of cities."

Her catalogue of grievances included:

Low-income projects that become worse centers of delinquency, vandalism and general social hopelessness than the slums they were supposed to replace.
Middle income housing projects which are truly marvels of dullness and regimentation, sealed against any buoyancy or vitality of city life.
Luxury housing projects that mitigate their inanity, or try to, with a vapid vulgarity.
Cultural centers that are unable to support a good bookstore.

* New York, Random House, 1961.

Civic centers that are avoided by everyone but bums. . . .
Commercial centers that are lack-luster imitations of standardized
suburban chain-store shopping.
Promenades that go from no place to nowhere and have no
promenaders.
Freeways that eviscerate great cities.

Today there is a body of critics, eclectic but largely liberal and
Democratic in persuasion, who accept much of this but go beyond
analysis of physical, brick-and-mortar reforms to broader considerations
of social policy. One of the authors of President Johnson's poverty
program, Daniel Patrick Moynihan, saw community action by 1968 as
social scientism run riot with dangerous, if unintended, consequences of
social upheaval and frustration. He also became the most incisive critic
of the welfare system in the nation and raised warnings about "compen-
satory" social policies for only the black which neglected the poor and
uneasy white. A general reaction against overbureaucratization and over-
administration by the federal government began to seize important sectors
of the intellectual community for the first time in several decades.
Though there are a myriad of views on how best to direct reform along
a more decentralized basis, this concept itself has come to have a strong
magnetic attraction for urban thinkers, whether in the field of school
administration, proposals for bloc federal grants to states and cities, or
tax incentives to private industry for ghetto rebuilding and manpower
retraining. Analysts such as Moynihan, Nathan Glazer, and Irving Kristol
see a need for more money, as well as human talent, applied to major
urban needs and also share a strong skepticism about our ability rapidly
to force the rate of change and the dangers of building expectations
too high.

An outstanding exponent and exemplar of the new criticism and of
the new breed of urbanists is James Q. Wilson, professor of government
at Harvard, a native of California, and earlier a student and teacher at
the University of Chicago. A leading force in the work of the Harvard-
MIT Joint Center for Urban Studies, he has before the age of forty pub-
lished bountifully both books and articles. His major writings include
*Negro Politics: A Search for Leadership, The Amateur Democrat, City
Politics* (with Edward C. Banfield), and *Varieties of Police Behavior.*
This essay, reprinted with permission, is from the quarterly *Public Interest,*
Summer, 1968, pp. 25-39, copyright 1968 by National Affairs, Inc.

One of the benefits (if that is the word) of the mounting concern
over "the urban crisis" has been the emergence, for perhaps the first

time since the subject became popular, of a conception of what this crisis really means, from the point of view of the urban citizens. After a decade or more of being told by various leaders that what's wrong with our large cities is inadequate transportation, or declining retail sales, or poor housing, the resident of the big city, black and white alike, is beginning to assert his own definition of that problem—and this definition has very little relationship to the conventional wisdom on the urban crisis.

This common man's view of "the urban problem," as opposed to the elite view, has several interesting properties. Whereas scholars are interested in poverty, this is a national rather than a specifically urban problem; the common man's concern is with what is unique to cities and especially to large cities. Racial discrimination deeply concerns blacks, but only peripherally concerns whites; the problem that is the subject of this article concerns blacks and whites alike, and intensely so. And unlike tax inequities or air pollution, for which government solutions are in principle available, it is far from clear just what, if anything, government can do about the problem that actually concerns the ordinary citizen.

This concern has been indicated in a number of public opinion surveys, but, thus far at least, the larger implications of the findings have been ignored. In a poll of over one thousand Boston home-owners that I recently conducted in conjunction with a colleague, we asked what the respondent thought was the biggest problem facing the city. The "conventional" urban problems—housing, transportation, pollution, urban renewal, and the like—were a major concern of only 18 per cent of those questioned, and these were expressed disproportionately by the wealthier, better-educated respondents. Only 9 per cent mentioned jobs and employment, even though many of those interviewed had incomes at or even below what is often regarded as the poverty level. *The issue which concerned more respondents than any other was variously stated— crime, violence, rebellious youth, racial tension, public immorality, delinquency. However stated, the common theme seemed to be a concern for improper behavior in public places.*

For some white respondents this was no doubt a covert way of indicating anti-Negro feelings. But it was not primarily that, for these same forms of impropriety were mentioned more often than other problems by Negro respondents as well. And among the whites, those who indicated, in answer to another question, that they felt the government ought to do *more* to help Negroes were just as likely to mention impropriety as those who felt the government had already done too much.

Nor is this pattern peculiar to Boston. A survey done for *Fortune* magazine in which over three hundred Negro males were questioned in thirteen major cities showed similar results. In this study, people were not asked what was the biggest problem of their city, but rather what was the biggest problem they faced as individuals. When stated this generally, it was not surprising that the jobs and education were given the highest priority. What is striking is that close behind came the same "urban" problems found in Boston—a concern for crime, violence, the need for more police protection, and the like. Indeed, these issues ranked *ahead* of the expressed desire for a higher income. Surveys reported by the President's Commission on Law Enforcement and Administration of Justice showed crime and violence ranking high as major problems among both Negro and white respondents.

The failure of community

In reading the responses to the Boston survey, I was struck by how various and general were the ways of expressing public concern in this area. "Crime in the streets" was *not* the stock answer, though that came up often enough. Indeed, many of the forms of impropriety mentioned involved little that was criminal in any serious sense— rowdy teenagers, for example, or various indecencies (lurid advertisements in front of neighborhood movies and racy paperbacks in the local drugstore).

What these concerns have in common, and thus what constitutes the "urban problem" for a large percentage (perhaps a majority) of urban citizens, is *a sense of the failure of community.* By "community" I do not mean, as some do, a metaphysical entity or abstract collectivity with which people "need" to affiliate. There may be an "instinct" for "togetherness" arising out of ancient or tribal longings for identification, but different people gratify it in different ways, and for most the gratification has little to do with neighborhood or urban conditions. When I speak of the concern for "community," I refer to a desire for the observance of standards of right and seemly conduct in the public places in which one lives and moves, those standards to be consistent with—and supportive of—the values and life styles of the particular individual. Around one's home, the places where one shops, and the corridors through which one walks there is for each of us a public space wherein our sense of security, self-esteem, and propriety is either reassured or jeopardized by the people and events we encounter. Viewed this way, the concern for community is less the "need" for "belonging" (or in equally vague language, the "need" to overcome feelings of "alienation" or "anomie") than the concerns of any rationally self-interested person with a normal but not compulsive interest in the environment of himself and his family.

A rationally self-interested person would, I argue, take seriously those things which affect him most directly and importantly and over which he feels he can exercise the greatest influence. Next to one's immediate and particular needs for shelter, income, education, and the like, one's social and physical surroundings have perhaps the greatest consequence for oneself and one's family. Furthermore, unlike those city-wide or national forces which influence a person, what happens to him at the neighborhood level is most easily affected by his own actions. The way he behaves will, ideally, alter the behavior of others; the remarks he makes, and the way he presents himself and his home will shape, at least marginally, the common expectations by which the appropriate standards of public conduct in that area are determined. How he dresses, how loudly or politely he speaks, how well he trims his lawn or paints his house, the liberties he permits his children to enjoy—all these not only express what the individual thinks is appropriate conduct, but in some degree influence what his neighbors take to be appropriate conduct.

These relationships at the neighborhood level are to be contrasted with other ways in which a person might perform the duties of an urban citizen. Voting, as a Harvard University colleague delights in pointing out, is strictly speaking an irrational act for anyone who does not derive any personal benefit from it. Lacking any inducement of money or esteem, and ignoring for a moment the sense of duty, there is for most voters no rational reason for casting a ballot. The only way such an act would be reasonable to such a voter is if he can affect (or has a good chance to affect) the outcome of the election —that is, to make or break a tie. Such a possibility is so remote as to be almost nonexistent. Of course, most of us do vote, but primarily out of a sense of duty, or because it is fun or makes us feel good. As a way of influencing those forces which in turn influence us, however, voting is of practically no value.

Similarly with the membership one might have in a civic or voluntary association; unless one happens to command important resources of wealth, power, or status, joining such an organization (provided it is reasonably large) is not likely to affect the ability of that organization to achieve its objectives. And if the organization *does* achieve its objectives (if, for example, it succeeds in getting taxes lowered or an open occupancy law passed or a nuisance abated), nonmembers will benefit equally with members. This problem has been carefully analyzed by Mancur Olson in *The Logic of Collective Action* in a way that calls into serious question the ability of any organization to enlist a mass following when it acts for the common good and gives to its members no individual rewards. Some people will join, but because they will get some personal benefit (the status or influence that goes with being an officer, for example), or out of a sense of duty or, again, because it is "fun." As a way of shaping the urban citizen's environment, however, joining a large civic association is not much more rational than voting.

Controlling the immediate environment

It is primarily at the neighborhood level that meaningful (i.e., potentially rewarding) opportunities for the exercise of urban citizenship exist. And it is the breakdown of neighborhood controls (neighborhood self-government, if you will) that accounts for the principal concerns of urban citizens. When they can neither take for granted nor influence by their actions and those of their neighbors the standards of conduct within their own neighborhood community, they experience what to them are "urban problems"—problems that arise directly out of the unmanageable consequences of living in close proximity.

I suspect that it is this concern for the maintenance of the neighborhood community that explains in part the overwhelming preference Americans have for small cities and towns. According to a Gallup Poll taken in 1963, only 22 per cent of those interviewed wanted to live in cities, 49 per cent preferred small towns, and 28 per cent preferred suburbs. (Only among Negroes, interestingly enough, did a majority prefer large cities—perhaps because the costs of rural or small town life, in terms of poverty and discrimination, are greater for the Negro than the costs, in terms of disorder and insecurity, of big-city life.) Small towns and suburbs, because they are socially more homogeneous than large cities and because local self-government can be used to reinforce informal neighborhood sanctions, apparently make the creation and maintenance of a proper sense of community easier. At any rate, Americans are acting on this preference for small places, whatever its basis. As Daniel Elazar has pointed out, the smaller cities are those which are claiming a growing share of the population; the largest cities are not increasing in size at all and some, indeed, are getting smaller.

A rational concern for community implies a tendency to behave in certain ways which some popular writers have mistakenly thought to be the result of conformity, prejudice, or an excessive concern for appearances. No doubt all of these factors play some role in the behavior of many people and a dominant role in the behavior of a few, but one need not make any such assumptions to explain the nature of most neighborhood conduct. In dealing with one's immediate environment under circumstances that make individual actions efficacious in constraining the actions of others, one will develop a range of sanctions to employ against others and one will, in turn, respond to the sanctions that others use. Such sanctions are typically informal, even casual, and may consist of little more than a gesture, word, or expression. Occasionally direct action is taken—a complaint, or even making a scene, but resort to these measures is rare because they invite counterattacks ("If that's the way he feels about it, I'll just show him!") and because if used frequently they lose their effectiveness. The purpose of the sanctions is to regulate the external consequences of private behavior—to handle, in the language of economists, "third-party effects," "externalities," and "the production of collective goods." I may wish to let my lawn go to pot, but one ugly lawn affects the appearance of the whole neighborhood, just as one sooty incinerator smudges clothes that others have hung out to dry. Rowdy children raise the noise level and tramp down the flowers for everyone, not just for their parents.

Because the sanctions employed are subtle, informal, and delicate, not everyone is equally vulnerable to everyone else's discipline. Furthermore, if there is not a generally shared agreement as to appropriate standards of conduct, these sanctions will be inadequate to correct such deviations as occur. A slight departure from a norm is set right by a casual remark; a commitment to a different norm is very hard to alter, unless of course the deviant party is "eager to fit in," in which case he is not committed to the different norm at all but simply looking for signs as to what the preferred norms may be. Because of these considerations, the members of a community have a general preference for social homogeneity and a suspicion of heterogeneity—a person different in one respect (e.g., income, or race, or speech) may be different in other respects as well (e.g., how much noise or trash he is likely to produce).

Prejudice and diversity

This reasoning sometimes leads to error—people observed to be outwardly different may not in fact behave differently, or such differences in behavior as exist may be irrelevant to the interests of the community. Viewed one way, these errors are exceptions to rule-of-thumb guides or empirical generalizations; viewed another way, they are manifestations of prejudice. And in fact one of the unhappiest complexities of the logic of neighborhood is that it can so often lead one wrongly to impute to another person some behavioral problem on the basis of the latter's membership in a racial or economic group. Even worse, under cover of acting in the interests of the neighborhood, some people may give vent to the most unjustified and neurotic prejudices.

However much we may regret such expressions of prejudice, it does little good to imagine that the occasion for their expression can be wished away. We may even pass laws (as I think we should) making it illegal to use certain outward characteristics (like race) as grounds for excluding people from a neighborhood. But the core problem will remain—owing to the importance of community to most people, and given the process whereby new arrivals are inducted into and constrained by the sanctions of the neighborhood, the suspicion of heterogeneity will remain and will only be overcome when a person proves by his actions that his distinctive characteristic is not a sign of any disposition to violate the community's norms.

Such a view seems to be at odds with the notion that the big city is the center of cosmopolitanism—by which is meant, among other things, diversity. And so it is. A small fraction of the population (in my judgment, a *very* small fraction) may want diversity so much that it will seek out the most cosmopolitan sections of the cities as places to live. Some of these people are intellectuals, others are young, unmarried persons with a taste for excitement before assuming the responsibilities of a family, and still others are "misfits" who have dropped out of society for a variety of reasons. Since one element of this group—the intellectuals—writes the books which define the "urban problem," we are likely to be confused by their preferences and assume that the problem is in part to maintain the heterogeneity and cosmopolitanism of the central city—to attract and hold a neat balance among middle-class families, young culture-lovers, lower-income Negroes, "colorful" Italians, and big business-men. *To assume this is to mistake the preferences of the few for the needs of the many.* And even the few probably exaggerate just how much diversity they wish. Manhattan intellectuals are often as worried about crime in the streets as their cousins in Queens. The desired diversity is "safe" diversity—a harmless variety of specialty stores, esoteric bookshops, "ethnic" restaurants, and highbrow cultural enterprises.

On "middle-class values"

At this point I had better take up explicitly the dark thoughts forming in the minds of some readers that this analysis is little more than an elaborate justification for prejudice, philistinism, conformity, and (worst of all) "middle-class value." The number of satirical books on suburbs seem to suggest that the creation of a sense of community is at best little more than enforcing the lowest common denominator of social behavior by means of *kaffee klatsches* and the exchange of garden tools; at worst, it is the end of privacy and individuality and the beginning of discrimination in its uglier forms.

I have tried to deal with the prejudice argument above, though no doubt inadequately. Prejudice exists; so does the desire for community; both often overlap. There is no "solution" to the problem, though stigmatizing certain kinds of prejudgments (such as those based on race) is helpful. Since (in my opinion) social class is the primary basis (with age and religion not far behind) on which community-maintaining judgments are made, and since social class (again, in my opinion) is a much better predictor of behavior than race, I foresee the time when racial distinctions will be much less salient (though never absent) in handling community problems. Indeed, much of what passes for "race prejudice" today may be little more than class prejudice with race used as a rough indicator of approximate social class.

With respect to the charge of defending "middle-class values," let me stress that the analysis of "neighborhood" offered here makes no assumptions about the substantive values enforced by the communal process. On the contrary, the emphasis is on the process itself; in principle, it could be used to enforce any set of values. To be sure, we most often observe it enforcing the injunctions against noisy children and lawns infested with crabgrass, but I suppose it could also be used to enforce injunctions against turning children into "sissies" and being enslaved by lawn-maintenance chores. In fact, if we turn our attention to the city and end our preoccupation with suburbia, we will find many kinds of neighborhoods with a great variety of substantive values being enforced. Jane Jacobs described how and to what ends informal community controls operate in working-class Italian sections of New York and elsewhere. Middle-class Negro neighborhoods tend also to develop a distinctive code. And Bohemian or "hippie" sections (despite their loud disclaimers of any interest in either restraint or constraint) establish and sustain a characteristic ethos.

People without communities

Viewed historically, the process whereby neighborhoods, in the sense intended in this article, have been formed in the large cities might be thought of as one in which order arose out of chaos to return in time to a new form of disorder.

Immigrants, thrust together in squalid central-city ghettos, gradually worked their way out to establish, first with the aid of streetcar lines and then with the aid of automobiles, more or less homogeneous and ethnically distinct neighborhoods of single-family and two-family houses. In the Boston survey, the *average* respondent had lived in his present neighborhood for *about twenty years*. When asked what his neighborhood had been like when he was growing up, the vast majority of those questioned said that it was "composed of people pretty much like myself"—similar, that is, in income, ethnicity, religion, and so forth. In time, of course, families—especially those of childrearing age—began spilling out over the city limits into the suburbs, and were replaced in the central city by persons lower in income than themselves.

Increasingly, the central city is coming to be made up of persons who face special disabilities in creating and maintaining a sense of community. There are several such groups, each with a particular problem and each with varying degrees of ability to cope with that problem. One is composed of affluent whites without children (young couples, single persons, elderly couples whose children have left home) who either (as with the "young swingers") lack an interest in community or (as with the elderly couples) lack the ability to participate meaningfully in the maintenance of community. But for such persons, there are alternatives to community—principally, the occupancy of a special physical environment that in effect insulates the occupant from such threats as it is the function of community to control. They move into high-rise buildings in which their apartment is connected by an elevator to either a basement garage (where they can step directly into their car) or to a lobby guarded by a doorman and perhaps even a private police force. Thick walls and high fences protect such open spaces as exist from the intrusion of outsiders. The apartments may even be air conditioned, so that the windows need never be opened to admit street noises. Interestingly, a common complaint of such apartment-dwellers is that, in the newer buildings at least, the walls are too thin to ensure privacy—in short, the one failure of the physical substitute for community occasions the major community-oriented complaint.

A second group of noncommunal city residents are the poor whites, often elderly, who financially or for other reasons are unable to leave the old central-city neighborhood when it changes character. For many, that change is the result of the entry of Negroes or Puerto Ricans into the block, and this gives rise to the number of anti-Negro or anti-Puerto Rican remarks which an interviewer encounters. But sometimes the neighborhood is taken over by young college students, or by artists, or by derelicts; then the remarks are anti-youth, anti-student, anti-artist, or anti-drunk. The fact that the change has instituted a new (and to the older resident) less seemly standard of conduct is more important than the attributes of the persons responsible for the change. Elderly persons, because they lack physical vigor and the access to neighbors which having children facilitates, are especially vulnerable to neighborhood changes and find it especially difficult to develop substitutes for community—except, of course, to withdraw behind locked doors and drawn curtains. They cannot afford the high-rise buildings and private security guards that for the wealthier city-dweller are the functional equivalent of communal sanctions.

In the Boston survey, the fear of impropriety and violence was highest for those respondents who were the oldest and the poorest.

Preoccupation with such issues as the major urban problem was greater among women than among men, among those over sixty-five years of age than among those under, among Catholics more than among Jews, and among those earning less than $5,000 a year more than among those earning higher incomes. (Incidentally, these were *not* the same persons most explicitly concerned about and hostile to Negroes—anti-Negro sentiment was more common among middle-aged married couples who had children and modestly good incomes.)

The third group of persons afflicted by the perceived breakdown of community are the Negroes. For them, residential segregation as well as other factors have led to a condition in which there is relatively little spatial differentiation among Negroes of various class levels. Lower-class, working-class, and middle-class Negroes are squeezed into close proximity, one on top of the other, in such a way as to inhibit or prevent the territorial separation necessary for the creation and maintenance of different communal life styles. Segregation in the housing market may be (I suspect it is) much more intense with respect to lower-cost housing than with middle-cost housing, suggesting that middle-class Negroes may find it easier to move into previously all-white neighborhoods. But the constricted supply of low-cost housing means that a successful invasion of a new area by middle-class Negroes often leads to that break being followed rather quickly by working- and lower-class Negroes. As a result, unless middle-class Negroes can leapfrog out to distant white (or new) communities, they will find themselves struggling to assert hegemony over a territory threatened on several sides by Negroes with quite different life styles.

This weakness of community in black areas may be the most serious price we will pay for residential segregation. It is often said that the greatest price is the perpetuation of a divided society, one black and the other white. While there is some merit in this view, it overlooks the fact that most ethnic groups, when reasonably free to choose a place to live, have chosen to live among people similar to themselves. (I am thinking especially of the predominantly Jewish suburbs.) *The real price of segregation, in my opinion, is not that it forces blacks and whites apart but that it forces blacks of different class positions together.*

What city government cannot do

Communal social controls tend to break down either when persons with an interest in, and the competence for, maintaining a community no longer live in the area or when they remain but their neighborhood is not sufficiently distinct, territorially, from areas with different or threatening life styles. In the latter case especially, the collapse of informal social controls leads to demands for the imposition of formal or institutional controls—demands for "more police protection," for more or better public services, and the like. The difficulty, however, is that there is relatively little government can do directly to maintain a neighborhood community. It can, of course, assign more police officers to it, but there are real limits to the value of this response. For one thing, a city only has so many officers and those assigned to one neighborhood must often be taken away from another. And perhaps more important, the police can rarely manage all relevant aspects of conduct in public places whatever may be their success in handling serious crime (such as muggings or the like). Juvenile rowdiness, quarrels among neighbors, landlord-tenant disputes, the unpleasant side effects of a well-patronized tavern—all these are matters which may be annoying enough to warrant police intervention but not to warrant arrests. Managing these kinds of public disorder is a common task for the police, but one that they can rarely manage to everyone's satisfaction—precisely because the disorder arises out of a dispute among residents over what *ought* to be the standard of proper conduct.

In any case, city governments have, over the last few decades, become increasingly remote from neighborhood concerns. Partly this has been the consequence of the growing centralization of local government—mayors are getting stronger at the expense of city councils, city-wide organizations (such as newspapers and civic associations) are getting stronger at the expense of neighborhood-based political parties, and new "superagencies" are being created in city hall to handle such matters as urban renewal, public welfare, and anti-poverty programs. Mayors and citizens alike in many cities have begun to react against this trend and to search for ways of reinvolving government in neighborhood concerns: mayors are setting up "little city halls," going on walking tours of their cities, and meeting with neighborhood and block clubs. But there is a limit to how effective such responses can be, because whatever the institutional structure, the issues that most concern a neighborhood are typically those about which politicians can do relatively little.

For one thing, the issues involve disputes among the residents of a neighborhood, or between the residents of two adjoining neighborhoods, and the mayor takes sides in these matters only at his peril. For another, many of the issues involve no tangible stake—they concern more the *quality* of life and competing standards of propriety and less the dollars-and-cents value of particular services or programs. Officials with experience in organizing little city halls or police-community relations programs often report that a substantial portion (perhaps a majority) of the complaints they receive concern people who "don't keep up their houses," or who "let their children run wild," or who "have noisy parties." Sometimes the city can do something (by, for example, sending around the building inspectors to look over a house that appears to be a firetrap or by having the health department require someone to clean up a lot he has littered), but just as often the city can do little except offer its sympathy.

Poverty and community

Indirectly, and especially over the long run, government can do much more. First and foremost, it can help persons enter into those social classes wherein the creation and maintenance of community is easiest. Lower-class persons are (by definition, I would argue) those who attach little importance to the opinions of others, are preoccupied with the daily struggle for survival and the immediate gratifications that may be attendant on survival, and inclined to uninhibited, expressive conduct. (A lower-*income* person, of course, is not necessarily lower *class;* the former condition reflects how much money he has, while the latter indicates the attitudes he possesses.) Programs designed to increase prosperity and end poverty (defined as having too little money) will enable lower-income persons who do care about the opinions of others to leave areas populated by lower-income persons who don't care (that is, areas populated by lower-class persons).

Whether efforts to eliminate poverty by raising incomes will substantially reduce the size of the lower class is a difficult question. The progress we make will be much slower than is implied by those who are currently demanding an "immediate" and "massive" "commitment" to "end poverty." I favor many of these programs, but I am skeptical that we really know as much about how to end our social problems as those persons who blame our failure simply on a lack of "will" seem to think. I suspect that know-how is in as short supply as will power. But what is clear to me is that *programs that seek to eliminate poverty in the cities will surely fail,* for every improvement in the income and employment situation in the large cities will induce an increased migration of more poor people from rural and small-town areas to those cities. The gains are likely to be wiped out as fast as they are registered. To end urban poverty it is necessary to end rural poverty; thus, programs aimed specifically at the big cities will not succeed, while programs aimed at the nation as a whole may.

The need to consider poverty as a national rather than an urban problem, which has been stated most persuasively by John Kain and others, is directly relevant to the problem of community. *Programs that try to end poverty in the cities, to the extent they succeed, will probably worsen, in the short run, the problems of maintaining a sense of community in those cities—and these communal problems are, for most persons, the fundamental urban problems.* People migrate to the cities now because cities are, on the whole, more prosperous than other places. Increasing the advantage the city now enjoys, without simultaneously improving matters elsewhere, will increase the magnitude of that advantage, increase the flow of poor migrants, and thus make more difficult the creation and maintenance of communal order, especially in those working-class areas most vulnerable to an influx of lower-income newcomers. This will be true whether the migrants are white or black, though it will be especially serious for blacks because of the compression effects of segregation in the housing market.

The differences among people

It is, of course, rather misleading to speak in global terms of "classes" as if all middle-class (or all working-class) persons were alike. Nothing could be further from the truth; indeed, the failure to recognize intraclass differences in life style has been a major defect of those social commentaries on "middle-class values" and "conformity." The book by Herbert J. Gans on Levittown is a refreshing exception to this pattern, in that it calls attention to fundamental cleavages in life style in what to the outside observer appears to be an entirely homogeneous, "middle-class" suburb. Partly the confusion arises out of mistaking economic position with life style—some persons may be economically working-class but expressively middle-class, or vice versa.

To what extent can persons with low incomes display and act upon middle-class values? To what extent is there a substitute for affluence as a resource permitting the creation and maintenance of a strong neighborhood community? Apparently some Italian neighborhoods with relatively low incomes nonetheless develop strong communal controls. The North End of Boston comes to mind. Though economically disadvantaged, and though the conventional signs of "middle-class values" (neat lawns, quiet streets, single-family homes) are almost wholly absent, the regulation of conduct in public places is nonetheless quite strong. The incidence of street crime is low, "outsiders" are carefully watched, and an agreed-on standard of conduct seems to prevail.

Perhaps a strong and stable family structure (as among Italians) permits even persons of limited incomes to maintain a sense of community. If so, taking seriously the reported weakness in the Negro family structure becomes important, not simply because of its connection with employment and other individual problems, but because of its implications for communal order. Indeed, substantial gains in income in areas with weak family and communal systems may produce little or no comparable gain in public order (and I mean here order as judged by the residents of the affected area, not order as judged by some outside observer). What most individuals may want in their public places they may not be able to obtain owing to an inability to take collective action or to make effective their informal sanctions.

"Black Power" and community

It is possible that "Black Power" will contribute to the ability of some neighborhoods to achieve communal order. I say "possible"—it is far from certain, because I am far from certain as to what Black Power implies or as to how dominant an ethos it will become. As I understand it, Black Power is not a set of substantive objectives, much less a clearly worked-out ideology, but rather an attitude, a posture, a communal code that attaches high value to pride, self-respect, and the desire for autonomy. Though it has programmatic implications ("neighborhood self-control," "elect black mayors," and so forth), the attitude is (to me) more significant than the program. Or stated another way, the cultural implications of Black Power may in the long run prove to be more important than its political implications.

In the short run, of course, Black Power—like any movement among persons who are becoming politically self-conscious, whether here or in "developing" nations—will produce its full measure of confusion, disorder, and demagoguery. Indeed, it sometimes appears to be little more than a license to shout slogans, insult "whitey," and make ever more extravagant bids for power and leadership in black organizations. But these may be only the short-term consequences, and I for one am inclined to discount them somewhat. The long-term implications seem to be a growing pride in self and in the community, and these are prerequisites for the creation and maintenance of communal order.

Historians may someday conclude that while Negroes were given emancipation in the nineteenth century, they had to win it in the twentieth. The most important legacy of slavery and segregation was less, perhaps, the inferior economic position that Negroes enjoyed than the inferior cultural position that was inflicted on them. To the extent it is possible for a group to assert communal values even though economically disadvantaged, Negroes were denied that opportunity because the prerequisite of self-improvement—self-respect—was not generally available to them. The present assertion of self-respect is an event of the greatest significance and, in my view, contributes more to explaining the civil disorders and riots of our larger cities than all the theories of "relative deprivation," "economic disadvantage," and the like. The riots, from this perspective, are expressive acts of self-assertion, not instrumental acts designed to achieve particular objectives. And programs of economic improvement and laws to guarantee civil rights, while desirable in themselves, are not likely to end the disorder.

The fact that these forms of self-expression cause such damage to the black areas of a city may in itself contribute to the development of communal order; the people who are paying the price are the Negroes themselves. The destruction they have suffered may lead to an increased sense of stake in the community and a more intense concern about the maintenance of community self-control. Of course, no amount of either self-respect or commitment to community can overcome a serious lack of resources—money, jobs, and business establishments.

No inside without an outside

Because the disorders are partly the result of growing pride and assertiveness does not mean, as some have suggested, that we "let them riot" because it is "therapeutic." For one thing, whites who control the police and military forces have no right to ignore the interests of the nonrioting black majority in favor of the instincts of the rioting black minority. Most Negroes want *more* protection and security, not less, regardless of what certain white radicals might say. Furthermore, the cultural value of Black Power or race pride *depends in part on it being resisted by whites*. The existence of a "white enemy" may be as necessary for the growth of Negro self-respect as the presumed existence of the "capitalist encirclement" was for the growth of socialism in the Soviet Union. As James Stephens once said, there cannot be an inside without an outside.

Nor does Black Power require that control over all political and economic institutions be turned over forthwith to any black organization that happens to demand it. Neighborhoods, black or white, should have control over some functions and not over others, the decision in each case requiring a rather careful analysis of the likely outcomes of alternative distributions of authority. Cultures may be invigorated and even changed by slogans and expressive acts, but constitutions ought to be the result of deliberation and careful choices. The reassertion of neighborhood values, by blacks and whites alike, strikes me as a wholly desirable reaction against the drift to overly bureaucratized central city governments, but there are no simple formulas or rhetorical "principles" on the basis of which some general and all-embracing reallocation of power can take place. Those who find this reservation too timid should bear in mind that functions given to black neighborhoods will also have to be given to white neighborhoods—it is not politically feasible (or perhaps even legally possible) to decentralize power over black communities but centralize it over white ones. Are those radicals eager to have Negro neighborhoods control their own police force equally eager to have adjoining working-class Polish or Italian neighborhoods control theirs?

In any case, no one should be optimistic that progress in creating meaningful communities within central cities will be rapid or easy. The fundamental urban problems, though partly economic and political, are at root questions of values, and these change or assert themselves only slowly, if at all. And whatever gains might accrue from the social functions of Black Power might easily be outweighed by a strong white reaction against it and thus against blacks. The competing demands for territory within our cities is intense and not easily managed, and for some time to come the situation will remain desperately precarious.